Illustrated Dictionary of Real Estate and Appraisal

Henry S. Harrison, MAI, SRPA

Julie S. Harrison

Reston Publishing Company, Inc.
A Prentice-Hall Company
Reston, Virginia

To our parents Nina and Pop-Pop and Minna

Library of Congress Cataloging in Publication Data

Harrison, Henry S.
Illustrated dictionary of real estate and appraisal.

1. Real estate business—Dictionaries. 2. Real property—Dictionaries. I. Harrison, Julie S. II. Title.
HD1365.H37 333.33'03'21 82-394
ISBN 0-8359-3037-8 AACR2

Editorial/production supervision and
interior design by Camelia Townsend

10 9 8 7 6 5 4 3 2 1

PRINTED IN THE UNITED STATES OF AMERICA

Acknowledgments

The research for this book was done by Tom Molloy, who methodically catalogued over 15,000 words and their definitions. Emily Emerson typed much of the manuscript and acted as unofficial initial editor. Pat Torino also helped with the typing.

Many of the custom drawn illustrations and all of the cartoons were prepared by Lorraine Libby. Our friend Bruce Lehman and Lorraine helped with the initial design and prospectus.

We want to thank these contributors for the following illustrations: *Corner Bead,* United States Gypsum Corporation; *Gable Dormer,* Forestry Products Laboratory, U.S. Department of Agriculture; *Plank and Beam Construction,* Canadian Wood Council, Ottawa; *Trimmer Arch,* Brick and Tile Institute of Ontario; *Truss,* Timber Engineering Company; *Wythe,* Forest Products Laboratory, U.S. Department of Agriculture.

We especially appreciate the co-operation we received from the Realtors National Marketing Institute and Llani O'Connor, their Vice President in charge of publishing. All of the material and drawings for the CTS System were initially developed for them and first published in *Houses–The Illustrated Guide to Construction Design and Systems*. We are grateful for their permission to use the material in this dictionary, together with some other miscellaneous illustrations from *Houses*. The other illustrations are from the extensive art library maintained by Reston.

Our love and thanks to Ruth, Eve and Kate who gave up time with us in order to make our work on this dictionary possible.

Preface

Every profession has its own special vocabulary. Physicians and lawyers use words that are often unintelligible to the lay person. This special vocabulary allows them to communicate with each other with more precision. Thus, when one physician says to another that a patient has suffered a myocardial infarct, they are describing just one of many types of heart attacks.

Realtors and appraisers have the same need for special words, such as Land Contract and Functional Obsolescence; and they give common words special meanings such as Price, Cost and Value (each of which to them means something different).

In order to be a part of a profession, it is necessary to know the special vocabulary and special meaning of words people in the profession use to communicate with one another.

By the use of many illustrations and clear definitions, we have tried to make this task as simple as possible.

We designed this book to be useful to new people coming into the real estate profession, especially those who must take a license examination. They will find this book an excellent tool for review.

A

ABANDONMENT The disclaimer, waiver, relinquishment, or surrender of property or rights voluntarily without vesting the interest in any other person.

ABANDONMENT OF HOMESTEAD A recorded document executed by those claiming a homestead giving up said homestead. This is not applicable to all states, and procedure must be according to local statutes. A homestead may also be lost by abandonment when the house is sold or when the homesteader moves on without the intent to return.

ABANDONMENT OF LEASED PREMISES Departure of the lessee from the leased premises before the expiration of the lease and without the lessor's knowledge.

ABATEMENT A reduction, cut, or decrease in taxes approved by the tax authority at the taxpayer's request.

ABATEMENT OF NUISANCE Cessation of a nuisance.

ABILITY TO PAY Concerning taxation, the "ability to pay" principle states that taxes should be progressive instead of regressive. Progressive taxes are those based on the taxpayer's ability to pay, such as an income tax. A regressive tax is based on the principle that all taxpayers are taxed equally, an example would be a sales tax.

ABLE Used in the real estate sense, "able" implies that the customer must have the necessary cash when the title is passed.

ABODE A person's home.

ABROGATE To retract, revoke, annul (a law).

ABSENTEE LANDLORD Someone who leases a property to someone else but does not occupy the premises.

ABLE

Example of the Abstraction Method

Obtaining the value of the land by abstraction from the value of the property:

Total value of property	$90,000
less: estimated value of house	−70,000
less: estimated value of garage	− 5,000
less: estimated value of site improvements	− 1,500
Value of land	$13,500

ABSTRACTION METHOD

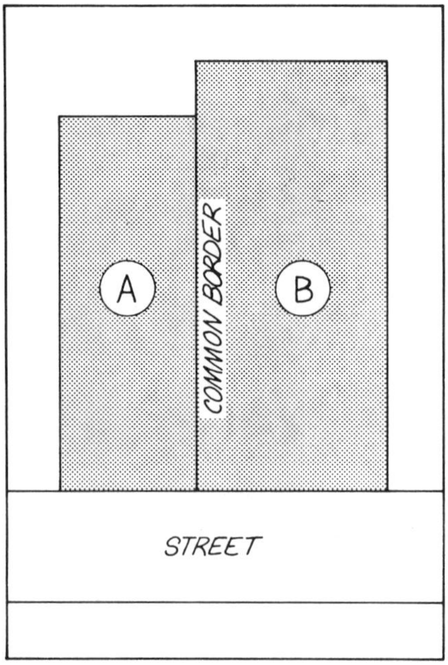

ABUTTING LAND

Types of Accelerated Depreciation

- 200 percent declining balance
- Sum-of-the-years' digits
- 150 percent declining balance
- 125 declining balance
- Straight line method with sixty month useful life.

ACCELERATED DEPRECIATION

ABSENTEE OWNER An owner of property who does not occupy said property. *See* Absentee Landlord.

ABSOLUTE TITLE Title that grants exclusive rights to its owner and gives no one else claim, interest, or rights to the same property.

ABSORPTION FIELD *See* Leaching Field.

ABSORPTION RATE The rate at which a real estate market can absorb properties of a given kind. A given market might absorb 150 new building lots, 200 new homes, 1,300 used homes, and 500 rental apartment units.

ABSORPTION TRENCH *See* Leaching Field.

ABSTRACT A summation. Prior to the development of photostatic copying, abstracts were used to record public transactions because it was too costly to copy and record the whole document.

ABSTRACT OF JUDGMENT A summary of the important parts of a court judgment.

ABSTRACT OF TITLE A summary of all conveyances and deeds upon which title depends. It is a history of the title. It includes conveyance by deed, will, foreclosure, and lawsuits.

ABSTRACTION METHOD An appraisal process where the appraiser selects comparable properties, estimates the value of their improvements, and then subtracts this estimate from the total price to give an estimate of the value of the land.

ABUT To be adjacent to.

ABUTMENT The portion of a wall or column that bears the pressure of an arch or pier, for example, the supports at the ends of a bridge.

ABUTTING LAND Adjacent properties with a common border.

ABUTTING OWNER *See* Abutting Land. Possessor of land that has a common border with a public right of way or with a contiguous property.

ACCELERATED DEPRECIATION A type of depreciation used for income tax purposes. It increases the write-off value of a property faster than normal straight-line depreciation would. A common characteristic of accelerated depreciation is that more depreciation is taken in the early years of ownership and less in the later years. The total depreciation taken over the life of the property can never exceed 100 percent of the cost of the improvements. Common forms of accelerated depreciation are 125 percent declining balance, 150 percent declining balance, 200 percent declining balance, and sum-of-the-years digits.

ACCELERATION CLAUSE A clause in a contract that gives the lender the right to demand total payment when the contract is breached and an installment is not paid.

ACCELERATORS Chemicals (usually calcium chloride) added to cement to speed up hardening in cold weather.

ACCEPTANCE A manifestation of the desire and will to be bound by the terms of an offer.

ACCESS The manner in which a property is reached; the right to enter and leave a property.

ACCESS RIGHT The right of an owner to enter and leave his or her property.

ACCESSIBILITY The way that a property is approached and the amount of difficulty involved in approaching it.

ACCESSION The right of a property owner to all additions made to the property either by nature or by humans.

ACCOMMODATION PARTY A person who signs a document in order to secure credit for another person.

ACCORD AND SATISFACTION A manner of discharging a contract. The "accord" is the consent of the parties, often creditors, to do something besides what is said in the contract. "Satisfaction" evolves when the new tasks are fully performed.

ACCOUNTS PAYABLE Money owning. The term is generally used in business rather than in personal finances.

ACCOUNTS RECEIVABLE Money owed to a business for goods or services. Accounts receivable may be sold or borrowed against. Often, accounts receivable are sold for less than face value (discounted).

ACCREDITED FARM AND LAND MEMBER (AFLM) Designation awarded by the Farm and Land Institute.

ACCREDITED MANAGEMENT ORGANIZATION (AMO) Designation awarded by the Institute of Real Estate Management.

ACCREDITED FARM AND LAND MEMBER (AFLM)

ACCREDITED MANAGEMENT ORGANIZATION (AMO)

ACCREDITED RESIDENT MANAGER

ARM®

ACCREDITED RESIDENT MANAGER (ARM)

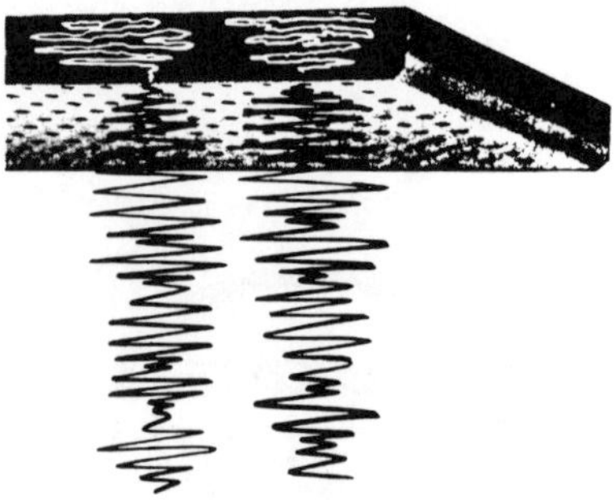

ACCOUSTICAL TILE

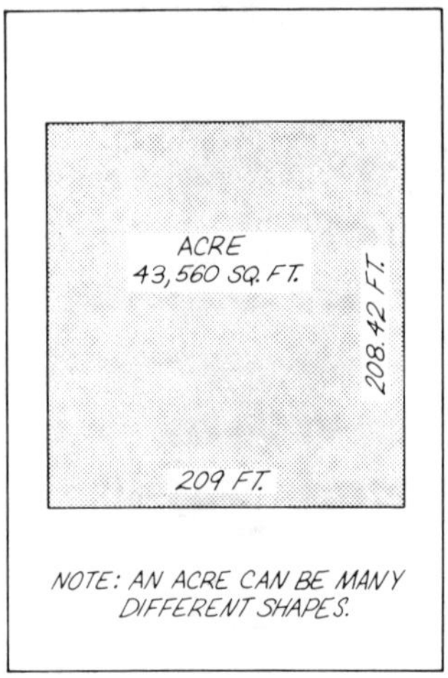

ACRE

ACCREDITED RESIDENT MANAGER (ARM) Designation awarded by the Institute of Real Estate Management.

ACCRETION The small and gradual accumulation of land, such as deposits made by a river or stream, which then becomes the property of the owner of the land on which it has accumulated.

ACCRUAL ACCOUNTING An accounting method under which income and expenses are charged to the periods for which they are applicable, rather than when payment is received or made. The method which requires income and expenses to be based on payment being received or made is called *cash accounting*.

ACCRUE To accumulate. In real estate, depreciation accrues over a period of time as does interest on invested capital.

ACCRUED DEPRECIATION The difference between the cost of replacing a building and its market value as of the same date. Often, it is broken down into the categories of physical deterioration, functional obsolescence, and economic obsolescence.

ACCRUED INTEREST Interest that has been earned but is not payable because the interest-bearing instrument pays interest only at specified periods.

ACKNOWLEDGMENT A written declaration given before an authorized officer.

ACKNOWLEDGMENT OF DEED The process whereby the signer of a deed swears before an authorized officer that the signing of the deed is the free act of the signer.

ACOUSTICAL MATERIAL Materials, such as tile, cork, and fiberglass, that are installed in walls to absorb sound.

ACOUSTICAL TILE *See* Acoustical Material.

ACQUISITION The process of acquiring an interest or ownership in a property.

ACQUISITION APPRAISAL An appraisal made to estimate market value in order to establish correct compensation for the owner of a property that is to be taken for public use by a public authority.

ACRE A unit of land measuring 43,560 square feet, 4,840 square yards, or 160 square rods.

ACREAGE A group of acres used together or collectively, such as residential acreage or farm acreage.

ACREAGE CONTROLS Federal limitations on the number of acres that may be planted in price-supported crops.

ACRE-FOOT (FOOT-ACRE) The volume of water equal to an acre covered to a depth of one foot (43,560 cubic feet of water).

ACRE-INCH The volume of water equal to an acre covered to the depth of one inch (3,630 cubic feet of water).

ACTION TO QUIET TITLE An action by the court to determine ownership of a property. *See also* Cloud on Title.

ACT OF GOD Natural disasters (floods, winds, etc.) that cause damage as opposed to destruction caused by humans.

ACTUAL AGE The actual number of years since a structure was built; the chronological age.

ACTUAL CASH VALUE The market value of a property. It is the cost new, plus appreciation less all forms of depreciation. It is the price a property will bring if offered in a normal market under normal conditions.

ACTUAL EVICTION When a landlord forces a tenant, through physical or legal action, to vacate the leased premises.

ADAMS COLONIAL STYLE A Colonial American house style introduced in New England by Robert Adam, an English architect, in 1759 and promoted by Samuel McIntire and Charles Bulfinch. The Adams Colonial style is characterized by its multi-storied, rectangular shape; large bay windows; and flat roof, topped with a balustrade.

CTS SYSTEM: Colonial American
Adams Colonial
(Adams Co-103)

ADAMS COLONIAL STYLE

ADDENDUM An addition to a letter, contract, or document.

ADDITION A portion of a building added to the original structure after its completion.

ADDITIONAL DEPOSIT A deposit made after the original deposit and after an offer is accepted. This more substantial second deposit is called the *additional deposit*.

ADJACENT A piece of property that is close to or near another property but not actually touching it.

Example of Adjusted Gross Income

Gross potential income	$200,000
less: vacancy and collection loss	− 30,000
Adjusted gross income	$170,000

ADJUSTED GROSS INCOME

ADMINISTRATOR
ADMINISTRATRIX

ADJOINING A piece of property that is contiguous to or touching another property.

ADJUDICATION A decision of a court; judgment.

ADJUSTED BASIS *See* Book Value.

ADJUSTED GROSS INCOME An appraisal term for the estimated income of a property assuming it was fully rented at its current economic rent minus an allowance for vacancies and collection losses.

ADJUSTMENTS **1.** In real estate closing, the changes in the selling price of a property that are made to reflect the apportionment of taxes, utilities, rents, etc. They are usually calculated at the time of the closing (settlement) and reported on a settlement statement. **2.** In appraising, the differences between comparable sales, rentals, listings, etc., and the property being appraised.

AD LITUM (FOR THE SUIT) A guardian representing a minor or incompetent in a lawsuit.

ADMINISTRATOR A person chosen by the court to be the legal representative of a deceased person's estate in cases where the individual dies without a will or without having named an executor for the estate.

ADMINISTRATOR C.T.A. (cum testamento annexo) The administrator of a will when no executor was chosen by the deceased or when the named executor is unwilling or unable to serve.

ADMINISTRATRIX *See* Administrator. Feminine of administrator.

ADMIXTURE Materials added to cement to increase its plasticity and workability and to help it withstand frost and breakage.

ADOBE BRICK A kind of brick made originally by American Indians in the Southwest out of straw and adobe soil baked and hardened in the sun.

ADOBE STYLE *See* Pueblo.

AD VALOREM TAX A tax based on a fixed percentage of a property's value. The value is usually determined by an assessor who is a community official.

ADVANCE A payment made by a lender under the terms of a note. It is commonly used for construction loans. The proceeds of the loan are made to the builder in predetermined steps based on the completion of a project.

ADVANCE FEE A fee that a broker charges a seller in advance to cover part or all of the broker's costs incurred in promoting the property.

ADVERSE POSSESSION A special means of acquiring property established by statute. The statutes usually require that possession is acquired by open, continuous, hostile physical control of the premises by the adverse possessor. Ownership is not acquired unless the current owner has notice of the assertion of ownership.

ADVERTISING REAL ESTATE A sign, newspaper ad, or other media announcement used in order to promote the sale of real estate.

AEOLIAN SOIL Soil composed of material transported and deposited by the wind.

AERATION ZONE The area of the soil from which plants draw their water and which allows excess water to continue to the saturation zone.

AERIAL PHOTO A photograph taken from an airplane.

AESTHETIC That which is beautiful and artistic.

AESTHETIC VALUE The value of a property in relation to its beauty. Attractive design, view, and location may add aesthetic value to a property.

AFFIANT Someone who has made an affidavit.

AFFIDAVIT A voluntary written declaration or statement signed and sworn to before an authorized officer.

AFFIDAVIT OF TITLE An affidavit made by the seller upon the sale of a property to assure the buyer that the seller's title is legitimate. *See* Affidavit.

AFFILIATE BROKER A person employed by a broker, or any other employer in the real estate business, who may engage in any transaction or perform any act normally done by a broker except the completion of the negotiation of any transaction or agreement.

AFFINITY A non-blood relationship.

AFFIRMATION A substitution for an oath when a person objects to making an oath.

AFFIRMATIVE ACTION PROGRAM A government plan to combat the causes and effects of discrimination against minority groups in the areas of employment, training, and hiring. Participants in the program make a special effort to employ, train, and hire people from minority groups.

AERIAL PHOTO

AFFORESTATION The development of a forest where no forest had previously been.

"A" FRAME STYLE A post-World-War-II, American house style in the shape of an "A" characterized by steep, shingled, gable roofs and large front and rear windows. They are very popular in resort areas.

CTS SYSTEM: Post World War II American
"A" Frame
(A Frame-905)

"A" FRAME STYLE

AFTER-TAX CASH FLOW The proceeds owners receive from their income-producing property after all the operating expenses are paid, including the mortgage payments and their estimated income tax on the income from the property.

AFTER-TAX EQUITY YIELD RATE The annual rate of return on an investment after the payment of income taxes by the owner. It is the same as the after-tax internal rate of return.

AFTER-TAX INCOME An accounting term that describes the income left after the payment of income taxes. It is not the same as after-tax equity yield rate.

AFTER-TAX NET CASH PROCEEDS OF RESALE The after-tax proceeds from the sale of a property less commissions paid, taxes paid by the owner, and the payment of all outstanding debts.

AGE (OF STRUCTURE) *See* Actual Age and Effective Age.

AGE-LIFE DEPRECIATION *See* Straight Line Depreciation.

AGE-LIFE METHOD A method of estimating the amount of depreciation a property has suffered. The amount of depreciation is calculated to be the number of years of typical economic life the property is estimated to have divided by the property's estimated effective age.

Example of the Age Life Method of Estimating Depreciation

Formula:

$$\frac{\text{Effective Age}}{\text{Typical Economic Life}} = \frac{\%\text{ Depreciation of}}{\text{reproduction cost}}$$

Example:

Effective age = 25 Years
Typical economic life = 50 Years
$\frac{25}{50} = .50$ or 50% depreciated

Example:

Effective age = 15 Years
Typical economic life = 90 Years
$\frac{15}{90} = .167$ or 16.7% depreciated

AGE-LIFE METHOD

AGENCY A legal relationship between an agent and a principal wherein the agent is contracted to represent the principal in specific dealings with a third party.

AGENCY AGREEMENT (AGENCY LISTING) In some states, this term describes a listing under which a broker's commission is protected against a sale by other agents but not a sale by a principal. It is called a "non-exclusive listing" in some states.

AGENCY BY ESTOPPEL An agency created by operation of law when an agent oversteps his or her authority but the action (or failure to act) by the principal leads one to believe the authority exists. *See* Ostensible Agency.

AGENCY COUPLED WITH INTEREST A contractual relationship with consideration going from agent to principal; the agency is given as return consideration. As an example, a broker agrees to work to obtain property for a builder in return for a listing after the builder has completed the project. The broker would be entitled to be (have an interest in) the listing agency provided the broker did obtain the property for the builder.

AGENT A person who represents another person in legal affairs and business with third parties.

AGENTS IN PRODUCTION *See* Factors in Production.

AGGREGATE Mixture of sand, gravel, or stone that makes up about 75 percent of final composition of concrete.

AGRARIAN Pertaining to land or land division and distribution.

AGREEMENT **1.** A view accepted by, and common to, two or more persons in regard to individual obligations and rights in a given subject. **2.** A properly executed and legally binding contract.

AGREEMENT OF SALE A written agreement between buyer and seller stating the price, terms, and conditions of a real estate sale about which they have agreed.

AGRICULTURAL LIEN A lien taken against crops for payment of money owed for materials to grow the crops.

AGRICULTURAL PROPERTY Property that is zoned for and suitable for the raising of livestock and the production of crops.

AGRICULTURE FOREIGN INVESTMENT DISCLOSURE ACT (AFIDA) A federal law that requires foreign persons and entities who have interests in agricultural land in the United States to report their interest to the Secretary of Agriculture.

A HORIZON Surface soil that is affected by water percolating through it.

AIR CHAMBER Air-filled pipes connected to water pipes to provide a cushion of air to keep the pipes from hammering.

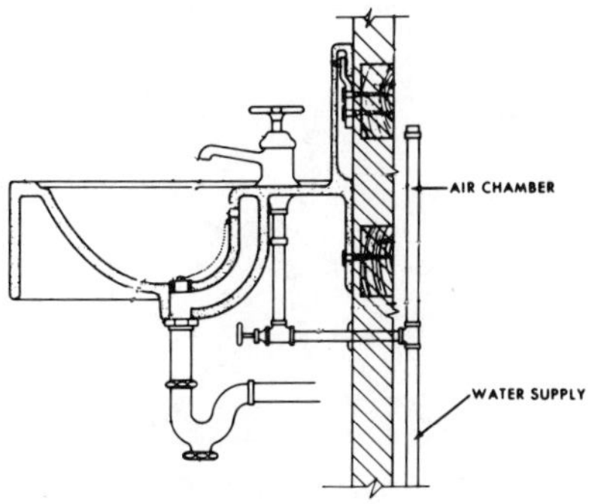

AIR CHAMBER

AIR CONDITIONING A mechanical system designed to control and regulate the temperature, humidity, and cleanliness of the air in a building.

AIR COOLING A cooling system that depends primarily upon moving the air.

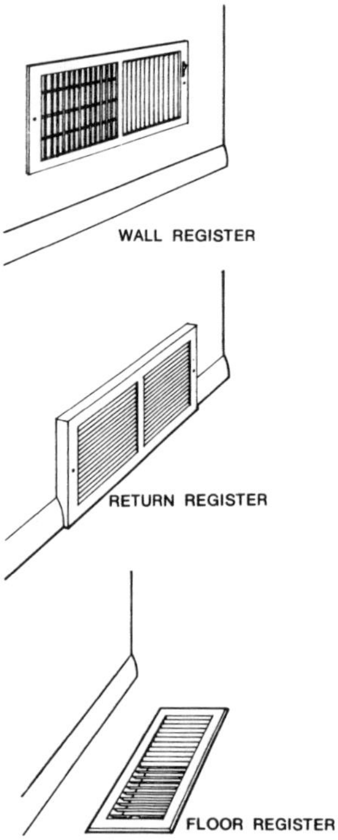

AIR REGISTERS

AIR RIGHTS

AIREA *See* American Institute of Real Estate Appraisers.

AIR-ENTRAINING AGENT An additive that causes air to be incorporated in the form of tiny bubbles in concrete or mortar during the mixing process.

AIR REGISTERS A grill at the end of the ducts in an air heating or cooling system. It often has a damper that can be adjusted to regulate the flow of air.

AIR RIGHTS The rights of an owner to use the air above the property without the rights to use the land below.

ALCOVE A small, recessed area attached to a room or hall.

ALIAS An assumed name.

ALIENATION The voluntary transfer of the owner's interest and property to another person. It may be by sale, gift, or transfer at death by will.

ALIENATION CLAUSE A type of acceleration clause that calls for a debt under a mortgage or deed of trust to be due in its entirety upon transfer of ownership of the secured property. It is also called the *due-on-sale* clause.

ALKALINE SOIL A basic soil that is alkaline.

ALLEGATION An assertion made by a party which the party intends to support with evidence.

ALLEY A narrow passageway. In many cities, it is a narrow street between two regular streets that is intended to permit access to the rear of the buildings that face the regular streets.

ALLEY INFLUENCE The effect an alley has on neighboring properties.

ALL INCLUSIVE DEED OF TRUST *See* Wrap-around Mortgage.

ALLOCATION METHOD *See* Abstraction Method.

ALLODIUM Land held by individuals without obligations of rent or service; a non-feudal system.

ALLOTMENT **1.** A piece of land that has been subdivided. **2.** An allowance made by the U.S.D.A. that designates the amount of crops which may be produced and the amount of land permitted to a specific crop production. **3.** Land given or sold to farmers for cultivation or income supplementation; a practice popular before World War II.

ALLOWANCE FOR VACANCY AND INCOME LOSS A step in the income approach of the appraisal process where an estimate of the loss of income from vacancies and collection losses is deducted from the gross estimated income of the property to give the effective gross income of the property.

ALLUVIAL Pertaining to water sedimentation and deposits. *See also* Alluvion, Alluvium.

ALLUVIAL SOIL Unstable soil formed by alluvial deposits.

ALLUVION The natural increase to a property made by deposits from rivers or streams. The additional land becomes the property of the owner of the land to which it is added.

ALLUVIUM Fine sedimentation, like sand or mud, deposited by flowing water.

ALTERATIONS Changes made in the interior or exterior of a building that do not change the exterior dimensions of the building.

ALTERNATIVE MORTGAGE INSTRUMENT A mortgage instrument that contains non-traditional treatment of an item which traditionally was fixed throughout the life of the mortgage, i.e., amount of principal, interest rate, monthly payments, and repayment terms.

ALUMINUM SIDING A type of siding made out of aluminum for use on the exterior of a building.

AMENDMENT A change or correction in an agreement which does not alter the principal idea.

AMENITY Something other than the construction materials which increases the enjoyment and satisfaction that can be derived from a property. Typical amenities include good design, superior view, and neighbors with good social status.

AMENITY VALUE The extra value that a property has because of one or more of its amenities.

AMERICAN INSTITUTE OF REAL ESTATE APPRAISERS (AIREA) One of the institutes of the NATIONAL ASSOCIATION OF REALTORS.® Its members specialize in the appraisal of real estate.

AMERICAN LAND TITLE ASSOCIATION (ALTA) A group composed of various title insurance companies.

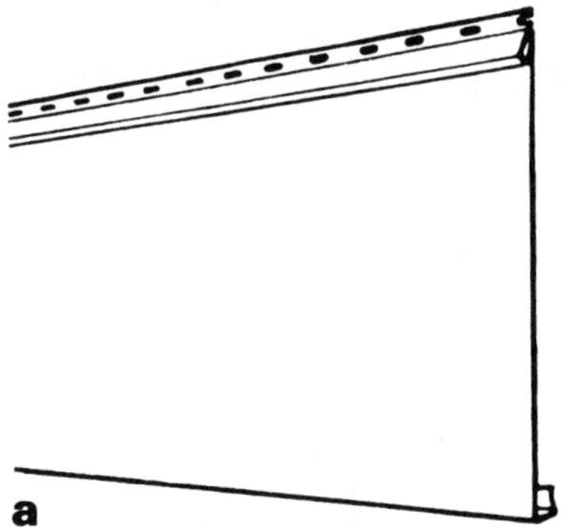

horizontal siding

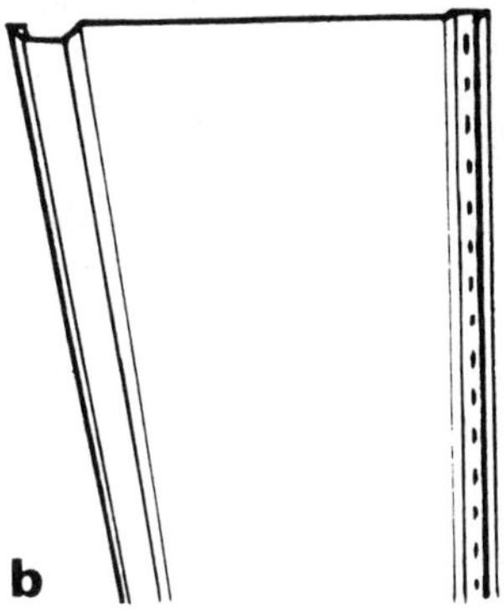

vertical siding

NOTE: Siding is designed so that each successive panel will conceal fasteners and interlock with previous panel.

ALUMINUM SIDING

AMERICAN MANSARD STYLE

AMERICAN MANSARD STYLE

AMERICAN SOCIETY OF APPRAISERS

AMERICAN MANSARD STYLE A nineteenth-century American style of house also known as the second empire style; distinguished by its mansard roof design with protruding dormers. Other distinguishing characteristics are decorative moldings and iron work and French doors and windows. It was originally developed in France by François Mansart in the 1600s and became popular in the U.S. in the reign of Napoleon III (the French Second Empire).

CTS SYSTEM: Nineteenth Century American
American Mansard or
Second Empire Style
(Mansard or 2nd Emp-707)

AMERICAN SOCIETY OF APPRAISERS An organization with members who appraise a wide variety of items. It confers the professional designation of ASA to qualified members.

AMERICAN SOCIETY OF REAL ESTATE COUNSELORS An affiliate of the NATIONAL ASSOCIATION OF REALTORS® for members who specialize in giving competent advice and professional, unbiased counsel on real estate matters.

AMORTIZATION The process of paying a debt through a series of equal payments (including principal and interest) at equal time intervals. Over the payoff period, the amount of each payment that is credited to the loan reduction increases as the amount of interest on the unpaid balance decreases.

AMORTIZATION RATE The ratio of the amortization payment to the total debt to be amortized. *See* Amortization.

AMORTIZE To retire a debt through a series of equal payments at equal intervals. *See also* Amortization.

AMORTIZED MORTGAGE A mortgage to be paid by amortization. *See also* Amortization.

AMOUNT OF ONE PER PERIOD *See* Future Worth of One Per Period.

AMPERE A unit used to measure the flow of electricity through a wire.

ANCESTOR **1.** A person from whom a person is descended; usually refers to people more remote than grandparents. **2.** A relative from whom an estate is inherited.

ANCHOR BOLT A type of bolt that is set in a concrete foundation and which extends through the sill and holds it down.

ANCILLARY BUILDING A building on a property that augments the primary building such as a garage, shed, or barn.

ANNEX To join or add to; usually to a larger, more important thing.

ANNEXATION A permanent addition to a property. Often personal property is annexed when it is attached to the building.

ANNUAL PERCENTAGE RATE (APR) The effective rate of interest on a loan including all the costs and charges. The federal Truth-In-Lending Act requires that it be calculated to the nearest 1/4 percent.

ANNUALS A type of vegetation made up mostly of plants that grow for a single year or season.

ANNUITY A series of fixed payments received at regular intervals. Often, these payments are a result of an accumulation of money over a period of time prior to the start of the annuity payments, or they may be the result of a lump sum being deposited to fund the annuity. When real estate income is of high quality (risk free) and of long duration, it is said to have the qualities of an annuity.

ANNUITY METHOD One of the methods used by real estate appraisers to capitalize an income stream into a value. It is used when the income stream is steady and of long duration.

ANNUM-YEAR Year.

ANODIZE, ANODIZING A process of applying an electrolytic oxide protective coating to aluminum.

ANTICIPATION, PRINCIPLE OF The value of an income property is the present worth of the future income stream plus the present worth of the future sales price.

APARTMENT A unit composed of one or more rooms with at least a bathroom, cooking facilities, and a place to sleep and used as a place to live for an individual or family.

APARTMENT HOUSE A building that generally holds three or more individual residential units that share facilities such as a lobby, elevators, and utilities.

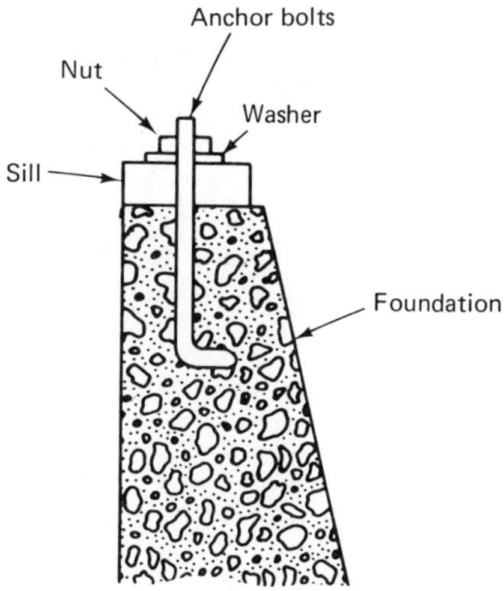

In a Concrete Wall

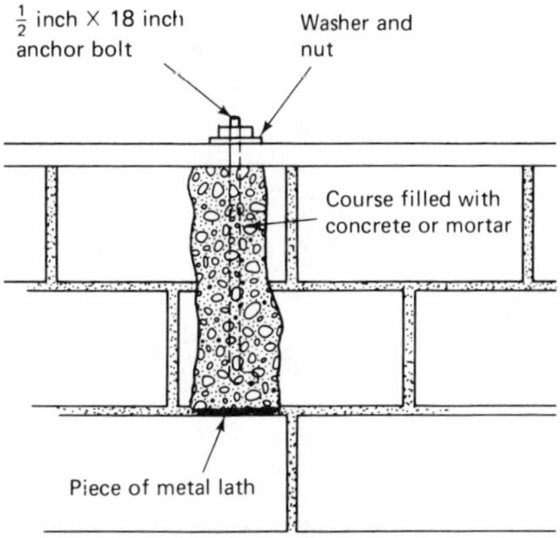

In a Concrete Block Wall

ANCHOR BOLT

APPARENT AUTHORITY The authority a principal allows an agent to exercise even though the principal never granted the authority to the agent.

APPORTIONMENT **1.** Generally, a division of responsibility, liability, or property among several individuals. **2.** At a real estate closing (settlement), the prorating of real estate taxes, insurance, utilities, insurance premiums, and other expenses as of the date of the closing.

Typical Items Prorated at a Real Estate Closing (Settlement)

- Taxes
- Fuel
- Association dues
- Mortgage interest
  (when mortgage is assumed)
- Insurance premiums
  (when insurance is assumed)
- Sewer charges
- Water
- Electricity
- Gas
- Rents from tenants

APPRAISAL A supported estimate of a defined value made by a person knowledgeable about the type of property being appraised.

APPRAISAL BY COMPARISON The process of estimating the value of a property by comparing it to the sales prices of recently sold similar properties.

APPRAISAL DATE The date to which the appraisal evaluation is valid and applicable.

APPRAISAL PROCESS The procedure a professional appraiser uses to estimate the value of a property. It consists of the following series of steps:

Definition of the Problem
Preliminary Survey and Appraisal Plan
Date Collection and Analysis
Application of the Three Approaches
Reconciliation of Value Indications into a Final Estimate of Defined Value
The Appraisal Report

APPRAISAL REPORT A written report of the appraiser's estimation of the value of the property as well as other data concerning said property and evidence to support the evaluation opinion.

APPRAISED VALUE An estimation of the value of a property based on a systematic analysis of facts regarding location, improvements, market conditions, etc., of a property.

APPRAISEMENT *See* Appraisal.

APPRAISER A person who estimates the value of property through experience and analysis of data.

APPRECIATION An increase in property value due to one or more of the following: increase in reproduction cost, elimination of negative factors, greater demand, community growth, and improvement or other factors.

APPROPRIATION **1.** The taking and use of a public property for private and personal use. **2.** The decision of the taxing authority, officially executed, to reach the expense predicted in the budget.

APPURTENANCE Property, articles, interests, and rights that are attached to and are transferred along with the title of a property.

APPURTENANT Accessory to, belonging to.

APPURTENANT EASEMENT *See* Easement.

APRON **1.** The piece of finished wood underneath the window sill. **2.** Any construction resembling a cloth apron, such as the entrance to a loading dock, the part of a driveway connecting to the street, or the part of a wharf between the buildings on it and the water's edge.

AQUATIC RIGHTS Rights to use streams, lakes, rivers, seas, etc., and the soil beneath them.

AQUEDUCT A channel or conduit built to transport water from place to place.

ARABLE Land suited for cultivation.

ARBITRAGE The process of buying and selling the same or similar financial instruments or currencies at the same time in different markets at different prices and making a sure profit based on these differences.

ARBITRATION CLAUSE A special clause put in contracts, such as leases or sales contracts, by which the parties agree not to settle differences by lawsuit. Instead they agree to arbitrate their disagreements and be bound by the decision of the arbitrator.

ARCADE **1.** A series of arches. **2.** An open passageway covered by an arched roof.

ARCH A curved structure of wood, concrete, steel, or stone that supports or covers.

ARCHITECT'S SCALE A measuring device used by architects that divides the inch into four parts and ten parts. It is used to reduce plans to a scale of one foot equals 1/10 inch and one foot equals 1/4 inch.

ARCHITECTURAL STYLES A building's exterior design based on historical styles.

ARCHITECTURE The art and science of designing buildings; also the individual design of a structure.

ARCHITRAVE In Greek architecture, the lowest part of the entablature. In modern use, it is the molding above and on both sides of a door.

ARCH RIB ROOF An arched or crescent-shaped roof used primarily in industrial buildings.

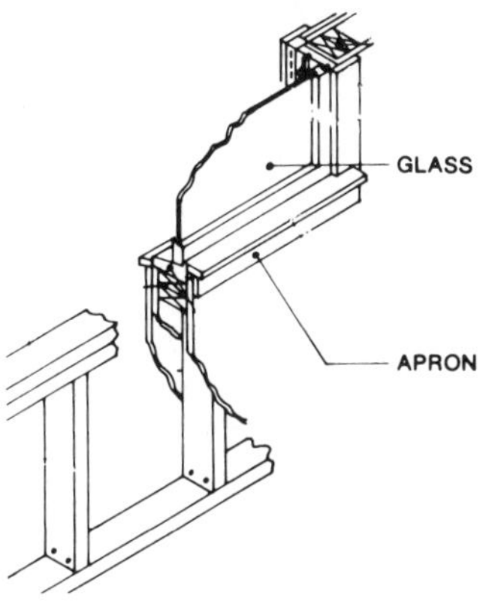

APRON

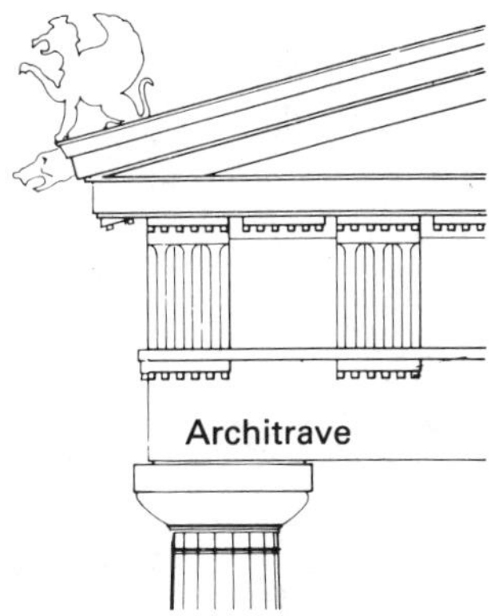

ARQUITRAVE (GREEK)

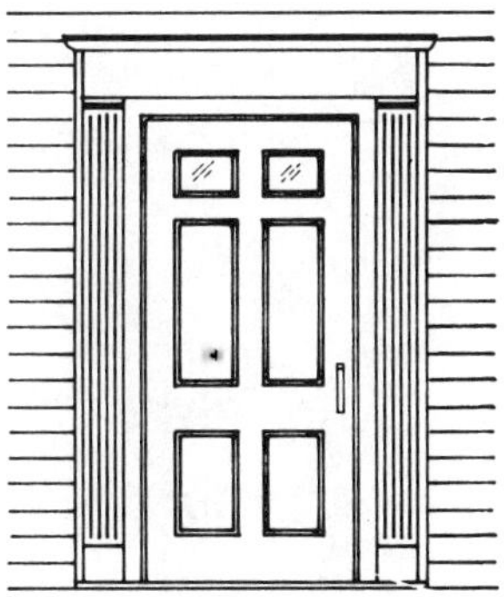

ARQUITRAVE (MODERN)

ARMORED CABLE
(BX CABLE)

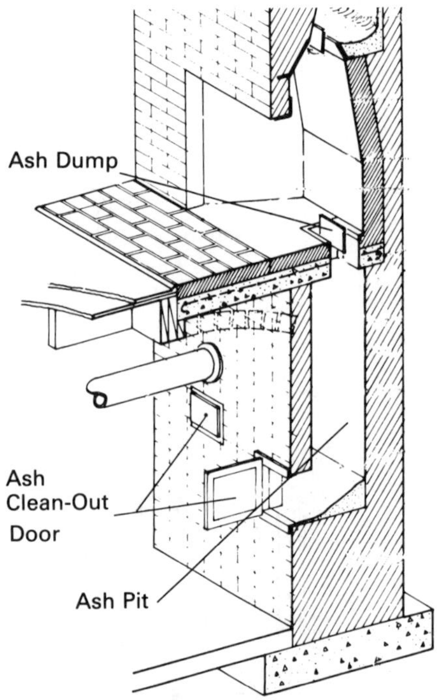

ASH CLEAN-OUT DOOR
ASH DUMP
ASH PIT

AREA **1.** The surface of any unit (building, site) measured in square units. **2.** A term meaning neighborhood or a geographic space. **3.** In residential design, *area* may indicate use, such as work area or play area.

AREAWAY **1.** A word, not frequently used, that means a room or cellar beneath the sidewalk. **2.** A light well, which is an interior portion of a building surrounded by walls in which there are windows without a roof.

ARITHMETIC MEAN The most commonly used average. It is found by dividing the sum of a series of values by the number of values in the group.

ARMORED CABLE (Also known as B.X. cable). A type of house wiring made of insulated wires covered in heavy paper and encased in a wound galvanized steel covering.

ARM'S LENGTH A transaction in which both parties act completely independent from each other and have no connection or relationship to each other.

ARPENT A unit of measure equivalent to about .84625 of an acre; an old French measurement used in the South and parts of Canada.

ARREARS Being behind in the payment of a debt. Some agreements, such as mortgages, call for payments to be made at the end of a period or be in arrears, whereas leases often call for the rent to be paid in advance.

ARTERIAL HIGHWAY A major highway with many branches.

ARTESIAN WELL A well drilled through impermeable strata deep enough to reach water that will rise to the surface by its own internal hydrostatic pressure. It was named after Artois, France, where these wells were first drilled.

ARTICLES OF INCORPORATION A document written when a corporation is formed that states the purpose of the corporation, its powers, and the basic rules for its operation. The exact format is specified by state statutes.

ASBESTOS A non-flammable, heat-resistant fiber used in roofing and insulation.

ASH CLEAN-OUT DOOR In a fireplace, the ash clean-out door is at the base of the ash pit. When it is opened, ash can be swept out and easily removed.

ASH DUMP In a fireplace, a desirable feature is an ash dump, which is a hole in the hearth floor into which ash can be conveniently swept and removed below.

ASHLAR Stone squares of uniform joint thickness used in masonry.

ASH PIT A pit at the base of a chimney for fireplace ashes. *See also* Ash Dump.

"AS IS" CONDITION A clause in a sales contract which states that the buyer agrees to accept the property in the exact condition that it is in and the seller makes no representations as to the condition of the property.

ASKING PRICE The price that the seller is asking for his or her property, not necessarily the price he or she will get.

ASPECT The direction that a building faces. It is described in terms of the points of the compass, such as a northern exposure.

ASPHALT **1.** A thick, sticky substance that occurs both in nature and is mined and is a byproduct of petroleum refining. **2.** A product used for paving consisting of the above combined with aggregate.

ASPHALT FELT UNDERLAYMENT A roofing material that is placed over the roof sheathing and under the outer roof covering.

ASPHALT ROOFING Roofing made out of rolled felt soaked in asphalt and covered with talc or mica.

ASPHALT SHINGLES Shingles cut from coated sheets of asphalt, mica, and felt. *See also* Asphalt Roofing.

ASPHALT SIDING Siding made by a continuous process. Felt rolls are soaked in asphalt, shrunk, and coated.

ASPHALT TILES Tile made from limestone fillers, asbestos fibers, resinous asphaltic binders, and minerals pigment.

ASREC *See* American Society of Real Estate Counselors.

ASSEMBLAGE The act of acquiring two or more abutting properties for single ownership and/or specific use.

ASSEMBLAGE COST The extra cost paid to acquire abutting properties in order to combine them into one larger parcel.

ASSEMBLAGE VALUE The additional value that is developed by combining several abutting properties into one larger property.

ASSESS Used in association with taxes, "assess" means to appraise—to fix a value.

ASSESSED VALUATION A value assigned to a property by the tax assessor to be used as a basis for taxation.

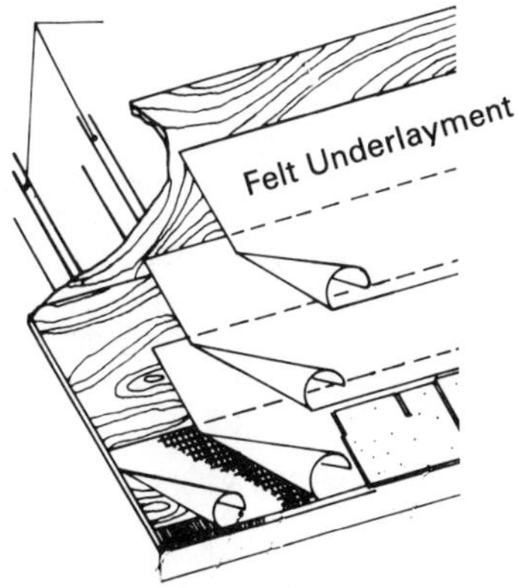

ASPHALT FELT UNDER LAYMENT

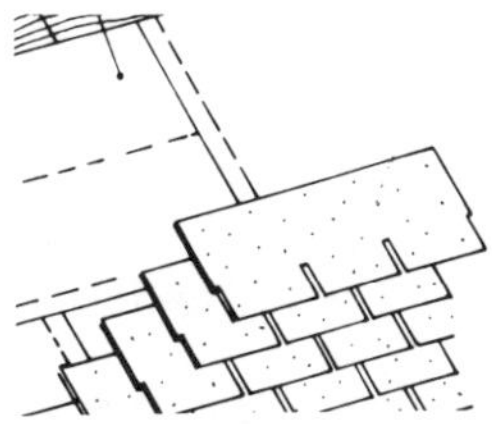

3 tab square butt strip

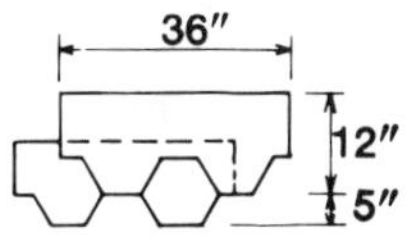

2 tab hexagonal

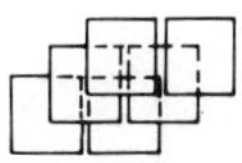

american giant

ASPHALT SHINGLE

Example of an Assessment Ratio Calculations

All the Commercial property in a community

Assessed value	$130,000,000
Market value	$200,000,000

Assessment ratio = .65 = 65%
($130,000,000 ÷ $200,000,000)

A house in the community

Assessed value	$45,000
Market value	$90,000

Assessment ratio = .50 = 50%
($45,000 ÷ $90,000.)

ASSESSMENT RATIO

ASSIGNOR
ASSIGNEE

ASSESSMENT **1.** The evaluation of property for the purpose of taxation. **2.** A special tax levied against a property to pay for a public improvement that benefits the property, such as a sewer, a sidewalk, or street paving.

ASSESSMENT PERIOD The time in which all properties in an assessment district must be reassessed.

ASSESSMENT RATIO The ratio of the market value of property in a community or district to its assessed value. Usually, this is a percentage that is fixed by statute.

ASSESSMENT ROLL An official list of all property by address and owners subject to taxation.

ASSESSOR A public official who estimates property values for ad valorem taxes.

ASSETS Owned property, either financial (such as stocks and bonds) or physical (such as real estate), that has value.

ASSIGN To transfer property from one party (the assignor) to another (the assignee). Typical real estate assignments are sales contracts, leases, mortgages, and options.

ASSIGNEE A person to whom something is transferred.

ASSIGNMENT *See* Assign.

ASSIGNOR A person who makes an assignment.

ASSUMED MORTGAGE An established mortgage that is transferred to a new owner when he or she buys a property and assumes the liability.

ASSUMPTION AGREEMENT An agreement whereby one party agrees to assume the responsibility to make payments that were originally the obligation of another party. The most common real estate contracts that are assumed are mortgages and leases.

ASSUMPTION OF A MORTGAGE The transfer of title of a property whereby the new owner agrees to take over responsibility for paying the existing mortgage.

ATRIUM An area of a structure that has a translucent ceiling to allow sunlight in for the growth of interior plants.

ATTACHED GARAGE A garage directly attached to a house and accessible from the interior of the house.

ATTACHMENT A court order that takes a property into the custody of the court for the purpose of securing it for payment of a court-ordered judgment.

ATTEST To confirm the truth of a document or statement.

ATTESTATION To witness the signing of a document, such as a lease, deed, or sales contract, at the request of the signers of the document.

ATTESTATION CLAUSE A clause at the end of a contract which states that the parties who signed it did in fact do so.

ATTIC Space between the roof and the top floor ceilings usually used for storage.

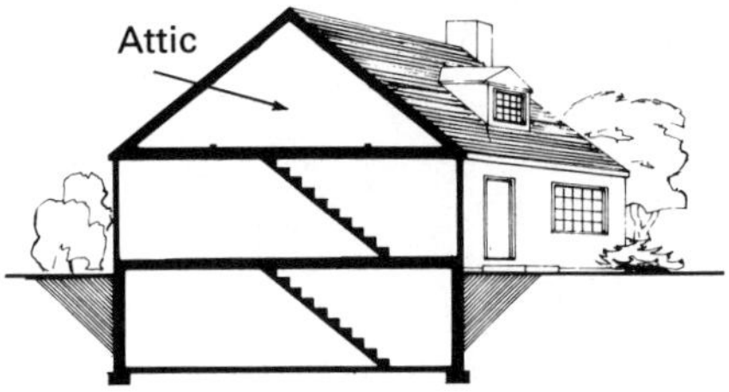

ATTIC

ATTORNEY IN FACT Someone who has been authorized to act for another under a power of attorney.

ATTRACTIVE NUISANCE Something on a property that is dangerous to small children but may attract them, such as a pond or pool.

ATTRACTIVE NUISANCE DOCTRINE A legal doctrine which states that, when a property owner maintains on his or her property a condition which will attract children to the property, the owner is responsible for any injury the children receive while on the property.

AUCTION A public sale where property or merchandise is sold to the highest bidder.

AUTOMATIC DIVERTER CONTROL A control in the shower that switches the water from the showerhead back to the tub after each shower to protect the next user from getting wet or scalded.

AVERAGE A number that sums up and represents a mass of data. The three kinds of averages are: The mean, the median, and the mode.

Example of the Three Types of Averages (Mean, Median, Mode)

$40,000	
41,000	
42,000	
42,500	
43,000)	
43,000)	Mode = $43,000
43,000)	
44,000	Median = $44,000
48,000	
51,000	Mean = $729,500 ÷ 15 =
51,000	$48,633.33
55,500	
60,000	
61,500	
64,000	
$729,500	

AVERAGE

AVERAGE DEVIATION A statistical term for the amount obtained by subtracting the arithmetic mean of all the items in a set of data from each item in the data set and then adding these differences without regard to their plus or minus signs. The sum thus obtained is divided by the number of items in the data set to produce the average deviation.

AVIGATION EASEMENT An aviation easement over a property that permits aircraft to fly over at low heights and prohibits anything being constructed on the property that would interfere with this right.

AVULSION The sudden removal of land from one owner to another when a river or stream changes its course.

AWARD In real estate, the sum paid for a property taken by condemnation.

AWNING A roof-like covering providing protection from the sun or rain for windows, porches, and doorways.

AXIAL GROWTH Urban growth that follows the main transportation routes, making finger-like extensions.

B

BACK BAND CASING A piece of millwork used to cover the gap between wall and window casing or used as a non-functional decorative feature.

BACKFILL The soil or crushed stone that is used to fill in around foundation walls and other areas where excess soil was excavated during the construction process.

BACKFILLING Piling up dirt and stone around the edge of a foundation and basement wall high enough to make a slope for drainage of water away from the foundation.

BACKUP OFFER An offer made in case the first offer to buy a property fails.

BACKWATER Water in rivers or streams that is obstructed and flows back towards its source or is simply stopped.

BACKWATER VALVE A type of valve that automatically prevents sewage in a lateral sewer line from backing up or flowing back to a building.

BALANCE, PRINCIPLE OF An economic principle that applies to real estate which states that, in a free market, the supply and demand for items tend to balance over a period of time. For example, if there is a shortage of housing in an area, new houses will be built to fill the demand.

BALANCE SHEET A part of a bookkeeping system. On a balance sheet are recorded the assets and liabilities of a company, partnership, or individual. When correctly prepared, the total of the assets equals the total of the liabilities (including the net worth or surplus).

BALCONY An open portion of a building that often projects from the outside and is cantilevered or supported by columns.

BALLOON FRAMING A type of framing system where the studs extend unbroken from the sill to the roof. It was

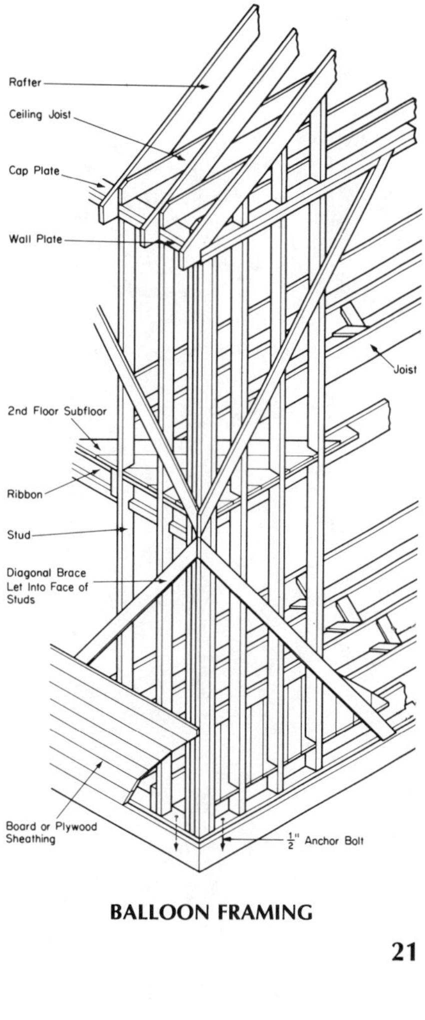

BALLOON FRAMING

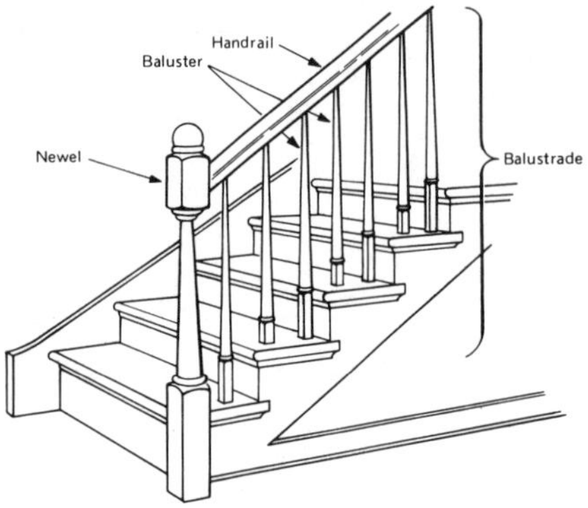

BALUSTER
BALUSTRADE

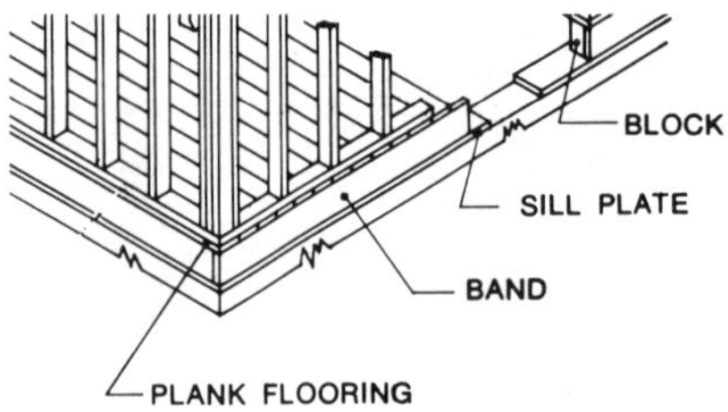

BAND

popular for multi-story brick veneer and masonry veneer structures.

BALLOON MORTGAGE A type of mortgage that is based on a repayment schedule that does not fully pay off the mortgage during its term and therefore a large lump sum payment is required at the end of the mortgage.

BALLOON MORTGAGE PAYMENT The last payment, usually larger than the others, which pays a mortgage in full or is the principal sum in a balloon note.

BALLOON NOTE *See* Balloon Mortgage.

BALTIMORE RULE Also called the Bernard rule, the Baltimore rule is an appraisal technique used to estimate the value of a corner property.

BALUSTER One of a string of small poles used to support the handrail of a stairway.

BALUSTRADE A row of balusters surmounted by a rail or cornice.

BAND A flat, horizontal molding or framing member usually marking a division in a wall.

BAND OF INVESTMENT A technique used by appraisers to develop a capitalization rate to be used in the income approach. It is a weighted average of each portion of the investment and its interest rate.

BANK The elevated portion of land on the side of a stream or river which holds the water in its natural channel. *See also* Commercial Bank and Savings Bank.

BANK DRAFT A draft payable to a third party on demand drawn by one bank upon another bank; often used when a personal check is unsatisfactory.

BANKRUPT *See* Bankruptcy.

BANKRUPTCY The process by which the court, under the Federal Bankruptcy Statutes, removes a debtor's property for distribution among creditors. There are two types of bankruptcy: voluntary (requested by the debtor), or involuntary (requested by the creditors).

BARGAIN AND SALE DEED A type of conveyance deed used to transfer the legal ownership of real property. It usually contains no warranties.

BARGE BOARD A type of molding (often carved or ornamented) that is attached to the projecting edge of a gabled roof.

BARGE COUPLE Either of the pair of outside rafters that support the part of a gabled roof which projects beyond the wall.

BARN A structure for housing farm animals, produce, and equipment.

BARREL A unit of solid or liquid measure that varies from trade to trade. A barrel of oil equals 42 gallons; a barrel of water equals 3-1/2 gallons; a barrel of cement is equivalent to 376 pounds.

BARREN A property where there is no vegetation.

BARTER The exchange of the personal or real property of one person for the personal property, real property, or other things of value of another person, usually without the use of money.

BASAL AREA A forestry term that is a measurement of the area of a cross section of a tree at breast height.

BASE The lowest visible portion of a building. It is different from a foundation because it is visible.

BASEBOARD A piece of interior trim laid around the walls of a room next to the floor. It often consists of three pieces of molding called the base shoe, baseboard, and base molding.

BASEBOARD CONVECTOR A device used to distribute heat into a room.

BASEBOARD HEATING A heating system consisting of heating elements installed in the wall along the baseboard.

BASEBOARD PANELS A heat distribution device used with a hot-water heating system.

BASEBOARD RADIATORS A type of radiator used with a hot-water heating system. Such radiators are long and narrow and fit along the bottom of the wall a few inches off the floor.

BASE FEE A type of ownership often created by a will. It is restricted or limited and may be terminated when specified acts or events occur.

BASE FLASHING A piece of metal or membrane used to seal the joint between a roofing surface and a vertical surface, such as a wall. It is covered with roofing material and sealed with a waterproof compound.

BASE LINE In accordance with the rectangular survey sys-

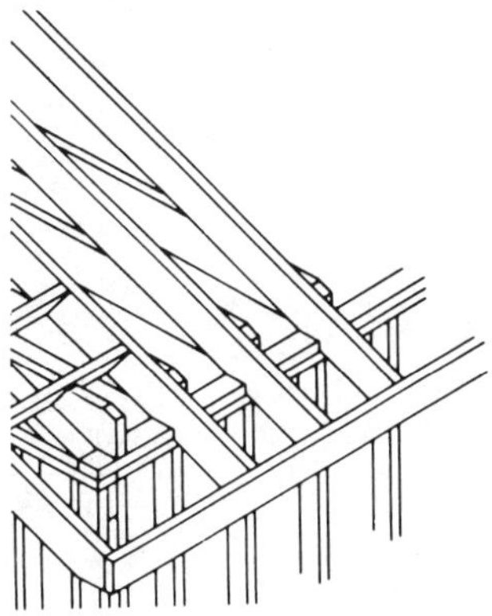

BARGE COUPLE

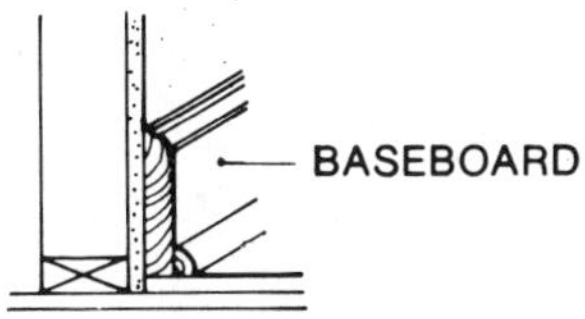

BASEBOARD

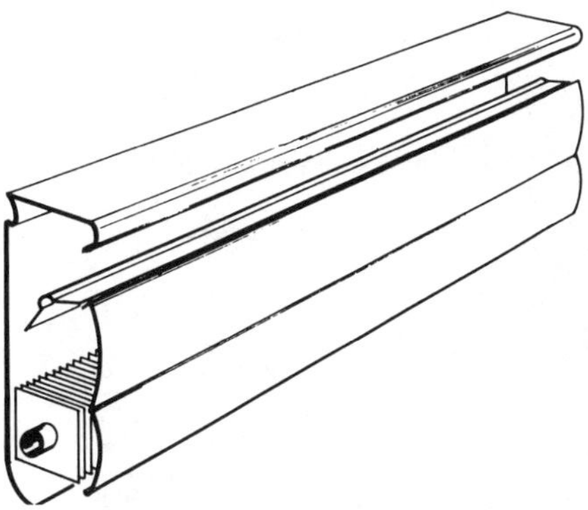

BASEBOARD CONVECTOR

tem, base lines are east-west lines that serve as references for other parallels.

BASE MAP A type of map intended to be used for plotting additional data. It may contain points of reference, such as state, county, or community boundaries or a variety of different physical features.

BASEMENT The lowest story of a building; usually below ground.

BASEMENTLESS SPACE (crawl space) An unfinished accessible space below the first floor that is usually less than a full story in height.

BASE MOLD *See* Base Molding.

BASE MOLDING Ornamental molding used to trim the top of a baseboard.

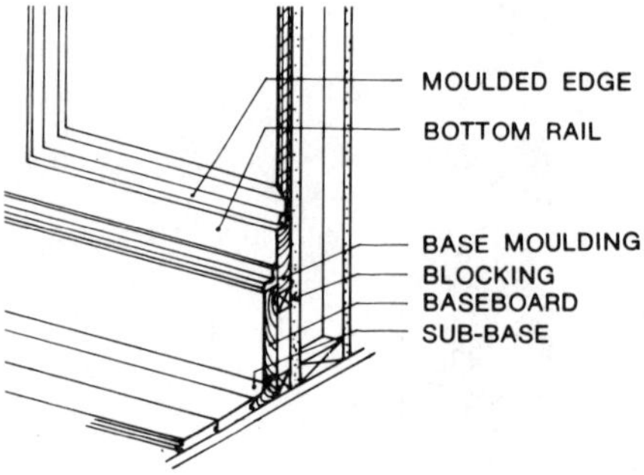

BASE MOLDING

BASE PERIODS A starting period used in making economic and business data indexes. It is not necessarily a normal period.

BASE PLATE A plate, usually made of metal, at the bottom of a column used to distribute the weight more evenly over the supporting footing or surface.

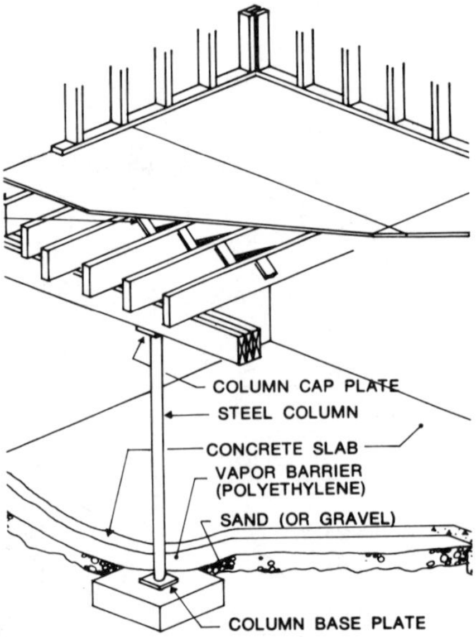

BASE PLATE

BASE PROPERTY The amount of private property that a cattle owner must own under the Taylor Grazing Act before the owner will be issued a permit to allow the cattle to graze on public domain.

BASE RENT A minimum rent a tenant must pay when he or she has a percentage lease that calls for the rent to be a percentage of the sales of a business.

BASE SHOE MOLDING A type of molding installed along the bottom of a baseboard. It is also called *carpeting molding* or *carpet strip*.

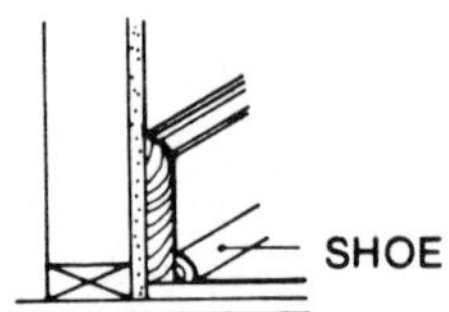

BASE SHOE MOLDING

BASE YEAR A specified year used in a lease with a rent escalation clause. It is the year upon which the escalation provision is based.

BASIC ACTIVITIES Those economic activities in a community that bring in money from outside, such as industry, tourist attractions, and state and federal government operations.

BASIC CAPACITY A measurement of the capacity of a highway. It is the number of automobiles that can pass a specified point in an hour if driving conditions are ideal.

BASIC CROPS Farm crops that are considered basic necessities by the government, such as corn, wheat, cotton, and similar crops. To ensure their continued high level of production, the government supports their prices.

BASIC EMPLOYMENT, URBAN GROWTH EMPLOYMENT Employment in those economic activities in a community that bring in money from outside the community.

BASIC INCOME Income brought into a community by its basic economic activities.

BASIC RATE A term used in mortgage equity capitalization. It is referred to as (r) to distinguish it from the overall rate (R). It does not include any provision for depreciation or appreciation.

BASIS The original cost of a property plus the value of any improvements made by the seller and minus the depreciation taken by the seller. It is the amount that is subtracted from a sales price to determine how much of the sale is subject to capital gains tax.

BASIS FOR DEPRECIATION *See* Basis.

BASKET STRAINER A cover installed on the top of a leader to prevent leaves, twigs, and other debris from clogging the system.

BATHROOM A room that provides facilities for taking a bath or a shower. It often also has a toilet and a washbasin.

BATHTUB A fixture in the bathroom used for sit-down bathing. The average tub is five feet long and 14–15 inches deep.

BATT INSULATION A strip of insulation that fits closely between the studs of a wall.

BATTEN A narrow board used to cover the space between siding boards or sheathing; also a special type of board used for flooring.

BATTER The slope of a bank, wall, pier, etc., which does not rise straight up but rather slopes at an angle.

BATTLEMENT A style of exterior wall copied from castles, towers, and fortresses. It has notches along the top historically used by soldiers to shoot through.

BATTURE LAND The portion of land between the water's edge and the riverbank which is covered with water when the water level is normal.

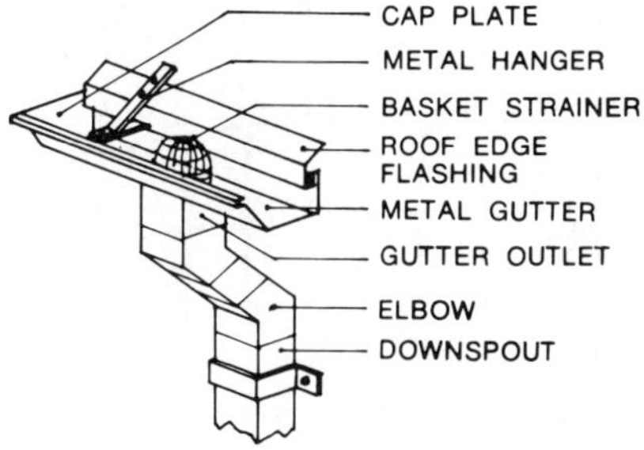

BASKET STRAINER

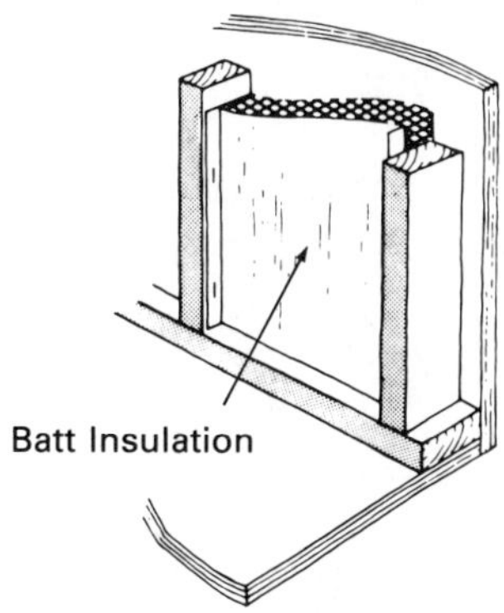

BATT INSULATION

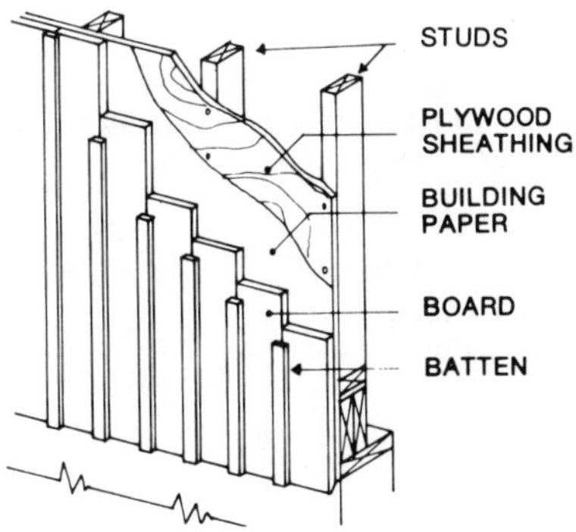

BATTEN

BAY WINDOW

Example of How Value Is Estimated Using the Before and After Method

Estimated value of the property before the taking	$110,000
Estimated value of the remaining property after the taking	– 75,000
Estimated value of the parcel taken	$ 35,000

BEFORE AND AFTER METHOD

BAY An open area between two walls or columns which creates a room-like space.

BAY WINDOW A window projecting outward from the wall of a house and supported by an extension of the foundation.

BEACH The part of the shore that ordinarily falls between high and low water marks.

BEADED JOINTS A type of masonry joint that has a bead cut into it; primarily used for decorative purposes.

BEAM A horizontal or vertical load-bearing structure made of wood, steel, concrete, or other strong material.

BEAM POCKET The space in a wall where the beam rests in place.

BEARING **1.** That portion of a structure, such as a beam or truss, which rests upon its support. **2.** A direction from an object to a point on the compass.

BEARING BEAM A large piece of wood, steel, stone, or other material used to support a structure. It usually runs from foundation wall to foundation wall and is supported with poles, columns, or pillars.

BEARING VALUE The ability of the soil to support the weight of a structure.

BEARING WALL A wall that supports the ceiling, floor, or roof.

BED MOLD A type of molding used as an ornamental strip usually under a projection such as the juncture of the frieze and cornice soffit.

BEDROCK A solid rock layer, usually found a few feet beneath the topsoil, that makes an excellent foundation support.

BEDROOM A room used for sleeping.

BEDROOM COMMUNITY A community near a large city in which many people who work in the city live.

BEFORE AND AFTER METHOD An appraisal technique used to estimate the value of property taken by condemnation. The value of the parcel taken is calculated by estimating the value of the whole parcel prior to the taking and then estimating the value of the remaining parcel after the taking. The difference between these values is the value of the parcel that was taken.

BEFORE-TAX CASH FLOW The cash that is available to the

owners of a property after all the expenses, including the mortgage, have been paid but before any income tax liability. *See also* Cash Throw-off.

BELTWAY A highway with limited access that surrounds a city and has entrances and exits only at selected principal streets.

BELVEDERE A glass-enclosed, small room on the roof of a house used as a lookout, and often reached through a trap door. *See also* Gazebo and Cupola.

BELVEDERE

BENCH MARK A permanent mark upon which local surveys are based. It is used in topographic surveys and tidal observations.

BENEFICIAL An owner who has equitable title only to a property without holding legal ownership.

BENEFICIARY **1.** The recipient of the proceeds of an insurance policy. **2.** One who receives benefits from the gifts or acts of another, as from a will or trust.

BENEFIT OF THE BARGAIN A rule of damages which states that a defrauded buyer is entitled to the difference between the actual value and the price paid.

BENEFITS The increase in value of a property that results when only part of the property is taken by eminent domain. The increase in value is caused by the general improvements that are made as a result of the project that caused the taking.

BENT A framework that runs transverse to the length of a structure. It is used for supporting horizontal or vertical loads.

BEQUEATH Originally, to leave personal property by will. The word has been expanded by the courts to mean the leaving of both personal and real property by will.

BEQUEST Property which is given in accordance with a will.

BERM A mound of earth or pavement used to control the flow of surface water.

BERNARD RULE *See* Baltimore Rule.

BETTERMENT An improvement that is not simply a restoration or repair and which increases property value, such as the paving of an adjoining road or improved drainage facilities.

BEVELED SIDING

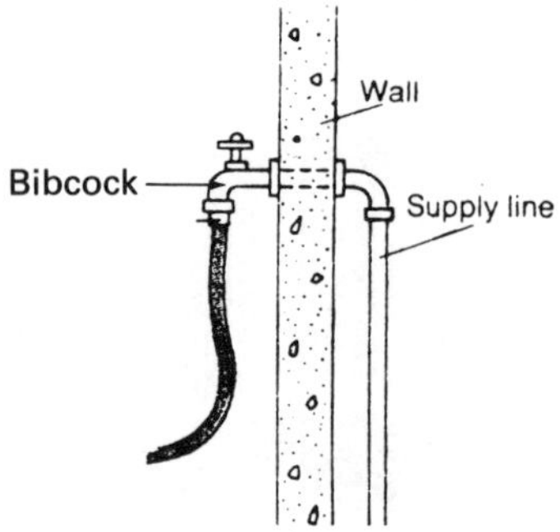

BIBCOCK

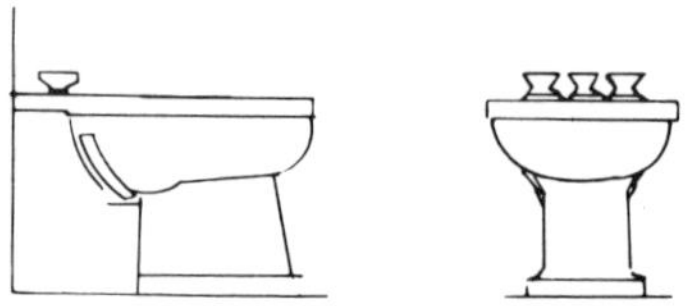

BIDET

BILLBOARD

BEVELED SIDING A type of house siding that is thicker on one edge than on the other when installed.

BIBCOCK A water faucet on the outside of the house with a screw nose to which a hose can be connected.

BID **1.** An offer of what one is willing to pay for something or an offer of what fee one will accept for performing a certain task. **2.** In some states, a bid is an offer to buy a property.

BIDET A bathroom fixture used to wash the perineal area after using the toilet.

BILATERAL CONTRACT A contract wherein there is a mutual promise for the performance of certain acts; each party is both a promisor and a promisee.

BILLBOARD A structure made to hold advertising and annexed to a piece of land. It is usually located so that it is visible from a highway, railroad track, sports arena, or other place where many people will see it.

BILL OF LADING An agreement between a customer (shipper) and the moving company (carrier). It details what their responsibilities and limits of liability are.

BILL OF SALE A written contract or instrument that transfers personal property from one person to another.

BINDER A preliminary agreement and down payment certifying the good faith of a purchaser.

BIRD DOGGING A real estate slang term for a person who seeks out listings and customers and turns them over to more experienced people who, in turn, share their commission with the person who secured the listing or sales lead.

BIRTH RATE The number of births per 1,000 persons in a certain area during a given time period, usually a year.

BLACK ACRE A name invented by legal writers to describe a property with no further description.

BLACKTOP (BITUMINOUS CONCRETE) A paving material made of asphalt or coal.

BLANKET DEED OF TRUST A deed of trust that covers more than one property.

BLANKET MORTGAGE One mortgage on two or more pieces of real property pledged as security for a debt.

BLANKETS, BATS A type of insulation, usually 2 to 3½ inches thick and 15 to 23 inches wide, that comes in long rolls. Often, it is nailed between the studs of an exterior wall. It is usually made of mineral wool, wood fiber, glass fiber, cotton, eel grass, or cattle hair.

BLIGHT In real estate, the decay of physical appearance and condition of property within a neighborhood.

BLIGHTED AREA A rundown area where real estate value has noticeably depreciated.

BLIND ADVERTISING The placement of an advertisment which does not state that the party advertising is a real estate broker. (The ad only supplies an address or phone number.) Such an ad may lead the public to believe that the advertiser is a private owner. This practice is prohibited in many states.

BLIND CORNER A corner where a driver's view is obstructed by shrubs or trees so that the driver cannot see to make a turn into traffic.

BLIND NAILING A type of nailing done in such a way that nails are hammered deep into the surface and covered with putty so they cannot be seen.

BLOCK The area enclosed by four streets.

BLOCKBUSTING An illegal practice of persuading homeowners to sell their property because of the fear that people of a different race or religion will move in and lower property values. The property is bought cheaply and then resold at a higher price.

BLUE LAWS Laws which originated in colonial times in New England that govern personal and religious conduct, especially the conducting of business on Sunday.

BLUEPRINT A plan of a building printed in white on a blue background that is detailed enough to allow workers to build from it.

BLUE SKY LAWS State statutes designed to reduce fraud and misrepresentation in the sale of securities and real estate.

BOARD **1.** A piece of lumber less than two inches thick and eight to twelve inches wide. **2.** A group of people who have the authority to practice control and management of a private corporation or public function.

BOARD AND BATTEN *See* Board and Batten Siding.

BOARD AND BATTEN SIDING A type of house siding that consists of wide boards butted together with a narrow board nailed over the joint.

BLIND CORNER

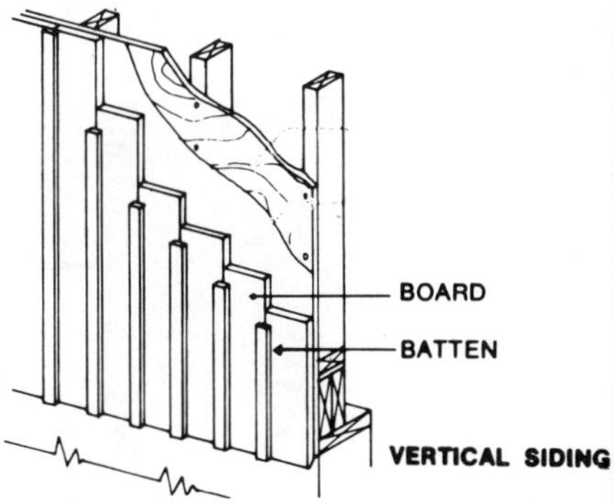

BOARD AND BATTEN SIDING

BOARD FOOT

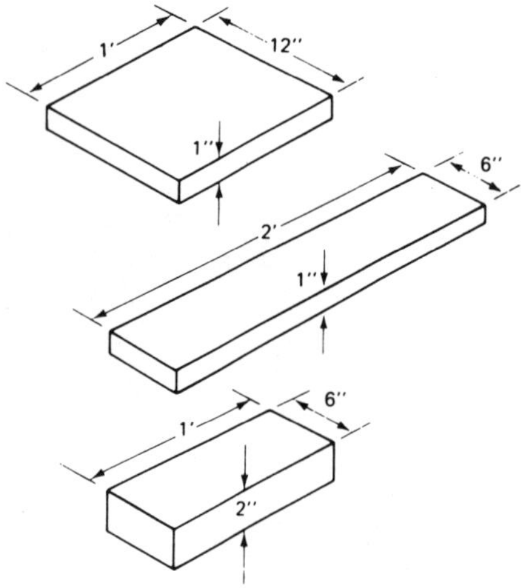

BOARD FOOT

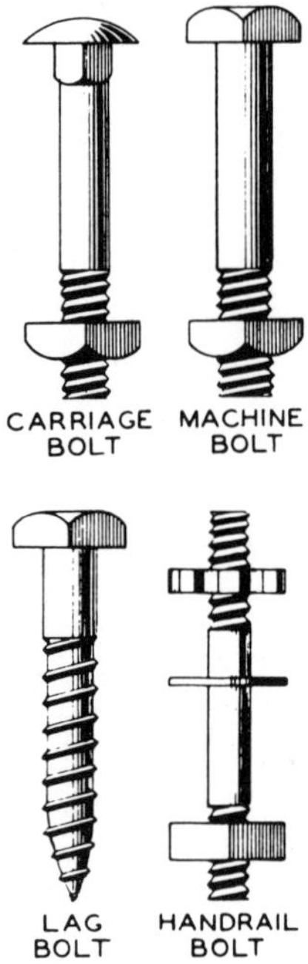

BOLT

BOARD FOOT A measurement of lumber. One board foot is twelve inches by twelve inches by one inch or 144 cubic inches.

BOARDING HOUSE A once popular kind of housing where one received meals for a price included in the rent of a room.

BOARD MEASURE A way of measuring cut lumber in units of board feet. *See* Board Foot.

BOARD OF EQUALIZATION A state or county board established for the purpose of adjusting inequitable tax assessments. The board compares assessments within its territory and equalizes them in order to spread the burden of taxation as evenly and fairly as possible over all the property within the territory.

BOG SOIL A type of spongy, wet ground made of decaying matter found in subhumid and humid climates.

BOILER The part of a hot water or steam furnace that holds the water being heated by the ignited fuel.

BOILER PLATE The formal language used for deeds, documents, and contracts where specifics are written in the appropriate place each time.

BOILER PLATING *See* Boiler Plate.

BOLSTER **1.** A short timber or metal horizontal support used to compensate for undersized beams or girders. **2.** A piece of wood used to cap a post, pillar, or column and spread the bearing load being supported.

BOLT A metallic screw pin or fastening having a head and an external thread.

BONA FIDE Good faith; no intent to defraud.

BONA FIDE PURCHASER A buyer who purchases without the knowledge of adverse claims against the property. A bona fide purchaser is protected against claims of third parties unless they are recorded prior to the sale being closed.

BOND **1.** A formal written promise by a borrower to pay a lender specified payments at future specified times. It is very similar to a note and is used as a substitute for a note based on local laws and customs. **2.** A form of security provided by an individual or a bonding company which guarantees that specified payments will be made or specified work will be performed.

BOND BEAM A continuous beam of concrete or reinforced brick that adds lateral stability to masonry walls.

BOND FOR DEED *See* Land Contract and Conditional Sales Contract.

BONUS CLAUSE *See* No Bonus Clause.

BOOK COST *See* Book Value. The original cost of a property as shown in the accounting records of a company.

BOOK DEPRECIATION The sum reserved on the books for future retirement or replacement of an asset.

BOOK VALUE The value of a property as written in personal, corporate, or partnership financial books. It is equal to the cost less depreciation plus additions to value.

BOOM 1. A crane or lift arm. **2.** Rapid expansion and growth in facilities, activities, and market value.

BOOT Money or other property given in addition to (along with) a property to be exchanged in order to equalize the value of the items traded.

BORING TEST Holes drilled in the ground to obtain samples for a soil study.

BORROW Sand, soil, or gravel brought in from outside to use for grading of backfilling (fill).

BORROW BANK The source of borrow. *See* Borrow.

BORROW PIT The hole left behind after borrow is removed. It is sometimes turned into a lake.

BORROWED LIGHT A glazed frame in an interior partition that lets light fall from one interior space to another.

BREATHER ROOF A type of storage tank roof that can fluctuate with the level of liquid or gas in the tank.

BREEZEWAY A covered passageway between the house and garage.

BRICK A building unit of clay or shale shaped into rectangles and then fired in a kiln.

BRICK CAVITY WALL A wall with a space between the inner and outer layers of brick.

BRICKLAYING The process of laying bricks and mortar to make them into a part of a building, such as a wall or floor.

BRICK MASONRY BOND An arrangement of bricks on a wall where some are laid parallel to the wall and some are perpendicular in order to give the wall additional strength. Some standard arrangements are common

Example of a Book Value Calculation

Original cost	$300,000
Cost of additions and improvements	+305,000
Total cost	$605,000
Depreciation	−205,000
Book value	$400,000

BOOK VALUE

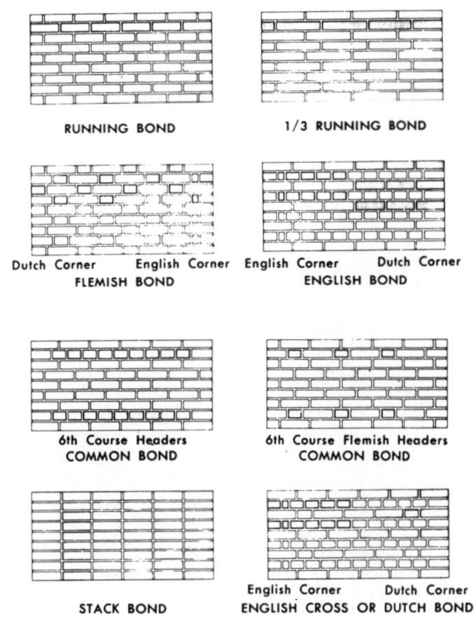

BRICK MASONRY BOND

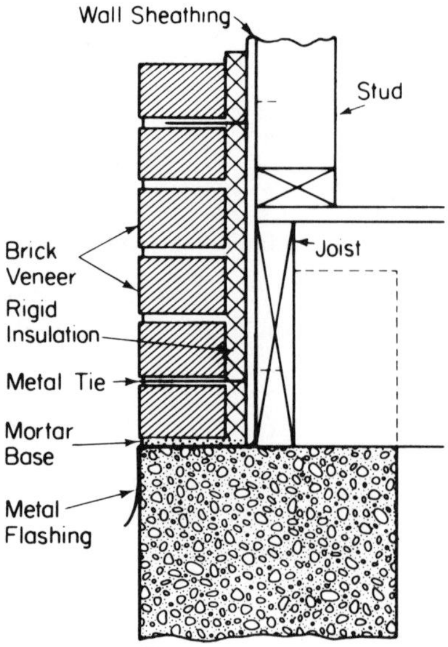

BRICK VENEER

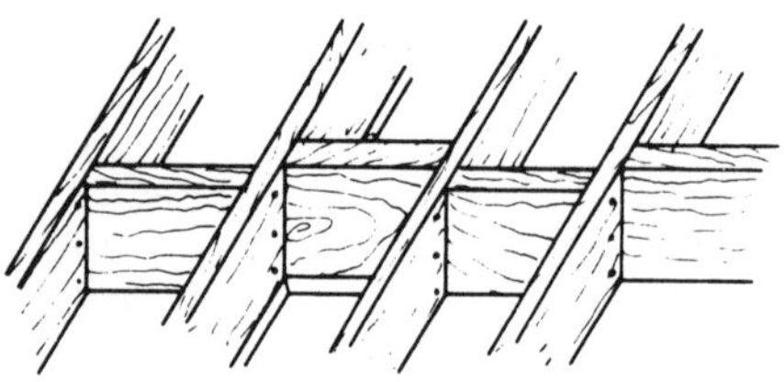

(a) Solid bridging

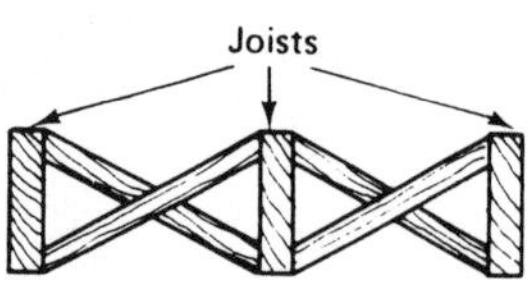

(b) 1 X 3 cross bridging

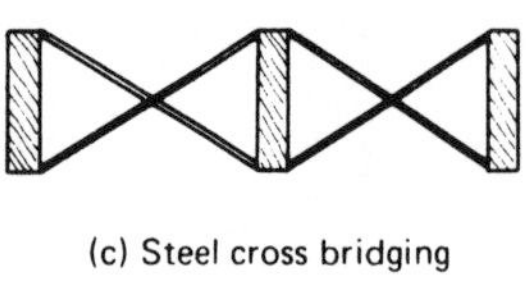

(c) Steel cross bridging

BRIDGING

bond, English bond, English cross, Flemish bond, and Flemish cross.

BRICK ROW HOUSE A house style that became popular in the 1800s. Each house shares one or more walls with its neighboring houses. Often such houses cover an entire block. They were constructed of brick that was sometimes decorated with brown stone. *See* Brownstone.

BRICK VENEER A decorative (non-supportive) layer of brick attached as the facing of a wall but not structurally bonded to it.

BRICK VENEER ON CONCRETE BLOCK WALL A type of wall construction consisting of one layer of concrete block and one layer of brick (which is usually on the outside). *See also* Brick Veneer.

BRICK VENEER ON FRAME WALL A popular wall type used for houses. It consists of a frame wall covered on the outside with a single layer of face brick. *See also* Brick Veneer.

BRICK VENEER WALL *See* Brick Veneer.

BRIDGE A structure that extends over a river or a waterway or across any two points at a height above ground level to provide easy passage for travelers.

BRIDGE FINANCING A type of short-term financing used to bridge the time gap between the end of one loan and the beginning of another loan. It is also used as an acquisition loan when a property will be improved and a larger permanent mortgage will be available when the improvements are completed.

BRIDGING A small piece of wood or strips of metal nailed between joists or studs to give them lateral rigidity.

BRIDLE PATH (ROAD) A road or trail especially designed for horseback riding.

BRITISH THERMAL UNIT (BTU) *See* BTU.

BROAD-LEAVED TREES A type of vegetation that includes all deciduous (leaf-dropping) trees.

BROKER A general term used for people who act as intermediaries to bring buyers and sellers together. Brokers market a wide variety of things including real estate, securities, commodities, boats, and jewelry.

BROKER, REAL ESTATE A person licensed to deal in real estate and receive a commission for bringing buyers and sellers, tenants and owners, etc., together.

BROKERAGE The business of a broker.

BROODER HOUSE A house especially designed and heated for the raising of young fowl.

BROOM CLEAN An expression which means that the floors of a building are clean and swept and ready for a buyer or tenant.

BROWN COAT The second of three coats of plaster that make up a plaster wall. It is the roughly finished plaster beneath the outer finished coat.

BROWNSTONE A nineteenth-century American house style, also known as a brick row house or Eastern Townhouse, that became popular in the late 1800s in New York and other large Eastern cities. Brownstone row houses generally cover an entire city block and have four or five stories with a stoop leading to the first floor. Each house shares side walls with its neighboring houses. Brownstones are characterized by their chocolate sandstone (brownstone) facing and flat roofs.

CTS SYSTEM: Nineteen Century American
Brownstone or
Brick Row House or
Eastern Townhouse
(Brown S or Br Row or E Town-713)

BROWNSTONE

BRUSHED PLYWOOD Plywood with a special finish that is produced by drawing rotating wire brushes over its surface.

BTU (BRITISH THERMAL UNIT) A measurement of heating and cooling capacity. It is the amount of heat required to raise the temperature of one pound of water one degree Fahrenheit.

BUCK A wood or metal frame set into a masonry wall in which the finished frame is placed.

BUCKED Cut into logs.

BUFFER STRIP A piece of land, often landscaped, that separates two different areas, such as a residential and an industrial area.

BUFFER STRIP

BUILDER Someone who works to improve land by building on it. A person or organization that contracts for and supervises the construction of buildings.

BUILDERS' HARDWARE Hardware used in the construction of a building that is both functional and decorative; for example, locks, hinges, and catches.

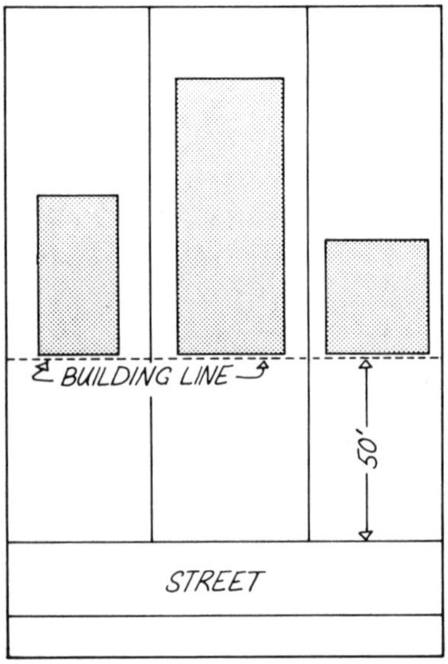

BUILDING LINE

Example of the Building Residual Technique

Income	
Gross potential income	$ 85,000
less: vacancy and collection loss	−3,000
Adjusted gross income	$ 83,000
Expenses	
Fixed expenses	−23,000
Variable expenses	−26,000
Reserves for replacement	− 4,000
Total expenses and reserves	−$ 53,000
Net operating income	$ 30,000
Estimated value of site $25,000	
Income allocated to site ($25,000 @ 12% interest)	−3,000
Income from building	$ 27,000
Capitalized at .16	÷16
(12% interest and 4% recapture)	
Value of building ($27,000÷.16)	$168,750
Value of site	+$ 25,000
Total value of the property	$193,750

BUILDING RESIDUAL TECHNIQUE

BUILDING A structure created to provide shelter for people, animals, or goods.

BUILDING AND LOAN ASSOCIATION *See* Savings and Loan Association.

BUILDING BRICK *See* Common Brick.

BUILDING CAPITALIZATION RATE In appraising, a capitalization rate used in the income approach to convert that portion of the income attributable to improvements into the value of the improvements. It consists of the interest rate plus a rate that reflects the projected rate of capital recapture.

BUILDING CODES The set of government regulations that specify minimum construction standards. Often there are separate codes for the electrical and plumbing systems.

BUILDING CONTRACT A contract that defines the terms for the construction of buildings or other property improvements. Many standard contracts have been prepared by the American Institute of Architects.

BUILDING FELT A type of heavy paper used in the construction process.

BUILDING LINE A line set a specified distance from the street edge by local ordinance. There can be no construction beyond this line because it is undesirable to have buildings too close to the street for safety and for aesthetic reasons.

BUILDING LOAN AGREEMENT A document, usually more detailed than the mortgage, that spells out the conditions which must exist for a lender to make a series of construction loan payments to a developer.

BUILDING PAPER A heavy, waterproofed paper used for insulation in the construction of a roof or wall.

BUILDING PERMIT Authorization given by local governments for building construction, alterations, or remodeling.

BUILDING RESIDUAL TECHNIQUE A technique used by appraisers as part of the income approach. The income of the property is first allocated to the land, and whatever is left over is attributed to the improvements and capitalized into an improvement value.

BUILDING RESTRICTIONS Limitations made by legislation on the use of property and on what may be constructed on it.

BUILDING SERVICE SYSTEMS The systems that provide water, heat, light, ventilation, electricity, etc., for a building.

BUILD TO SUIT An arrangement where a landlord builds or alters a property to the specifications of the tenant and recovers the cost of the improvements as part of the rent.

BUILT-INS Appliances, such as dishwashers and stoves, that are built into a house and are not movable.

BUILT-IN-PLACE STAIR A type of stair made by cutting the carriages and nailing the top to the upper floor and the bottom to the lower floor.

BUILT-UP METHOD A technique used by appraisers to construct a capitalization rate for use in the income approach. The appraisers start with a pure interest rate and add to it to reflect the estimated amount of risk, management, and lack of liquidity for the property they are appraising.

BUILT-UP ROOFING A roof made of layers of felt paper and asphalt and coated with fine gravel.

BULKHEAD **1.** A retaining wall along a waterfront. **2.** A structure covering a stairway yet providing adequate head room.

BULKHEAD LINE A line off the shore in a body of water established by the Army Corps of Engineers beyond which nothing may be built.

BULK SALE A sale transferring all or nearly all of the inventory of a business from one owner to another.

BULK SALES ACT Laws that prevent merchants from secretly selling all their goods without paying their creditors. The laws mandate certain notice before the event of the bulk sale and can void improper sales.

BULK ZONING A type of zoning that restricts the number of buildings which can be built within a given area. It controls the density of land use in the area.

BUMPER STRIPS Wood placed at the end of a loading dock to provide protection from the bumping of trucks.

BUNDLE OF RIGHTS THEORY A concept of property ownership that comes from English common law. It states that ownership of property consists of a bundle of rights that are divided into two groups. The rights of the government include the right to regulate the use of property for the good of all the people by using po-

Example of the Built-Up Method of Capitalization Rate Construction

Pure interest rate	.12
Risk	.04
Management (Money)	.01
Lack of liquidity	.03
Total capitalization rate	.20

BUILT-UP METHOD

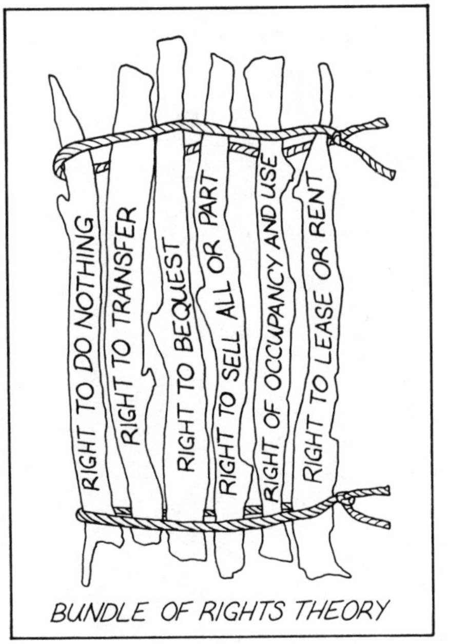

BUNDLE OF RIGHTS THEORY

lice power. The government also has the right to tax, the right to take property for the use of the public, and the right to receive property free if the chain of title ends (escheat). The private owner has the right to use his or her property, sell it, inherit it, give it away, or do none of these things.

BUNGALOW An early twentieth-century American house style popular in the shore communities of both the east and west coasts. The bungalow is a small, one-story house that usually has porch and is characterized by its wood siding and shingled roof.

CTS SYSTEM: Early Twentieth Century American Bungalow.
(Bungalow-802)

BUNGALOW

BUNGALOW SIDING A type of clapboard siding that has a width of at least eight inches.

BURGLAR ALARM SYSTEM A system to protect a house or commercial property from being robbed. It usually consists of a variety of sensing devices that are connected to warning systems either on or off the premises. An intruder sets off the sensing devices which, in turn, trigger the warning system.

BUS A heavy-duty, rigid rod, tube, or bar that conducts electricity. It is often used in heavy-duty commercial and industrial electrical situations.

BUS DUCT A conduit that protects and encloses a bus.

BUSINESS A commercial, industrial, service, or professional activity in which people engage for the purpose of making money.

BUSINESS CYCLE An economic cycle flowing from prosperity to decline to recovery to prosperity.

BUSINESS OPPORTUNITY A business that is being offered for sale.

BUSINESS RISK The internal and external risks of running a business.

BUSINESS TAX A special tax that is levied against business activities.

BUTT **1.** A short section of roofing material. **2.** A door hinge.

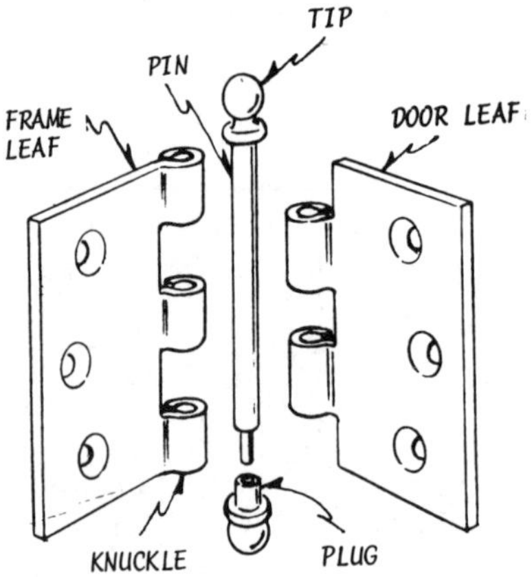

BUTT

BUTTE A steep, flat-topped hill.

BUTTERFLY ROOF A roof with two sides that rise from the center to the eaves and have a valley so that they resemble a butterfly.

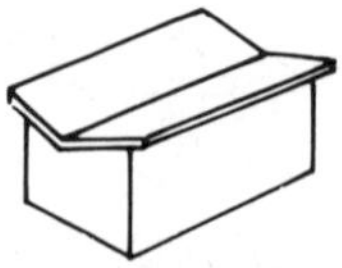

BUTTERFLY ROOF

BUTT JOINT The meeting of two members which creates a right-angled joint.

BUTT LOG The log right above the tree stump.

BUTTRESS An external support for a wall. A projecting buttress that supports by lateral pressure is called a *flying buttress.*

BUYER'S MARKET A market condition wherein there are few buyers and many available properties so that prices tend to be low and conditions favor the buyer.

BUY-SELL AGREEMENT An agreement among the owners of a business that allows owners who wish to remain in the business to buy the interests of owners who wish to be bought out. Often the agreement contains agreed-upon prices for the buy out and includes provisions that the estates of deceased owners must sell at an agreed-upon price to surviving owners.

B.X. CABLE Prefabricated electrical cable consisting of rubber-insulated wires surrounded in a steel strip and used mostly for wiring houses.

BY-LAWS Rules and regulations of a project, association, or corporation.

BYPASS *See* Beltway.

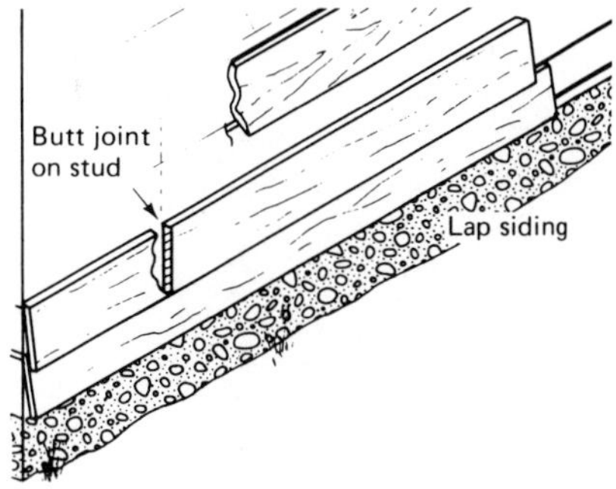

BUTT JOINT

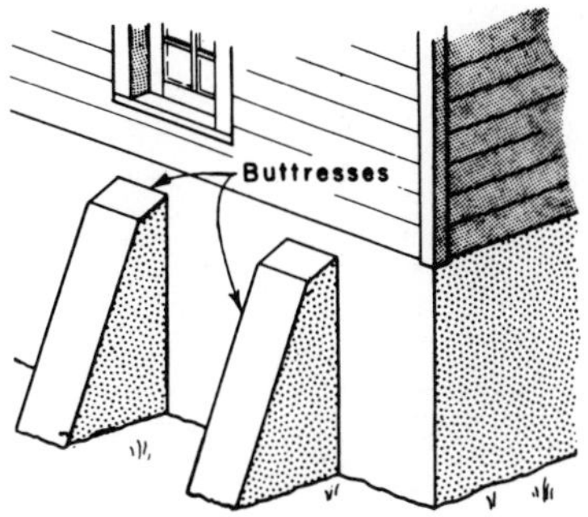

BUTTRESS

C

CABINET **1.** An enclosure with hinged, sliding, or folding doors, shelves, and drawers used for storage. **2.** A box for the housing of electrical devices. **3.** A private room or study.

CABINET SPACE The space within cabinets available for storage.

CABINET WORK Interior carpentry work of fine quality.

CADASTRAL PROGRAM A part of the assessment process that consists of making a complete inventory of all the property within a specified area.

CAE (CERTIFIED ASSESSMENT EVALUATOR) A designation awarded by the International Association of Assessing Officers to members who have required experience and have taken prescribed courses and examinations.

CERTIFIED ASSESSMENT EVALUATOR

CAISSON A large, strong, watertight chamber in which men work underwater or in an open excavation where loose soil or sand could cave in on the workers. Often caissons are filled with concrete after being used, and they become permanent supports.

CAISSON FOUNDATION A foundation made by driving a tube into the ground down to bearing soil and then filling it with concrete.

CAISSON PILE *See* Caisson Foundation.

CALCAREOUS SOIL Soil that contains a significant amount of limestone (carbonate of calcium).

CALIFORNIA BUNGALOW STYLE An early twentieth-century American house style. It is usually a one-story, compact house made of wood and often has traces of South Seas, Spanish, and Japanese influences.

CTS SYSTEM: Early Twentieth Century American
California Bungalow
(Cal Bung-805)

CALIFORNIA BUNGALOW STYLE

CALIFORNIA RANCH STYLE

CALIFORNIA RANCH STYLE

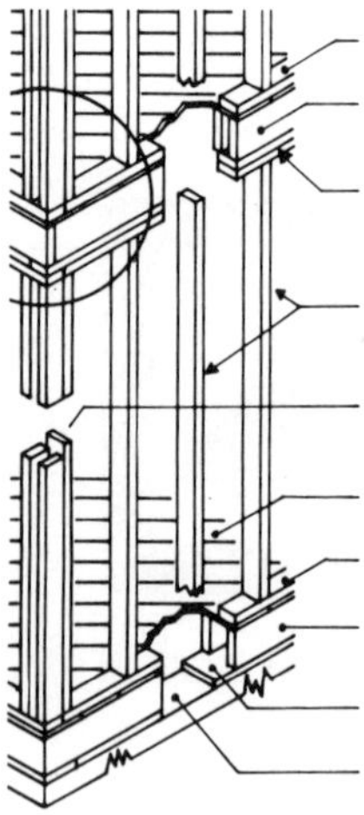

CAP

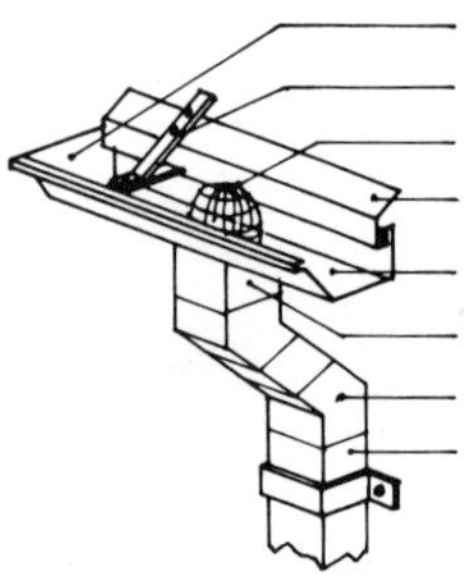

CAP PLATE

CALIFORNIA RANCH STYLE A post-World-War-II American house style. It is usually a one-story, ground-hugging house with a low, pitched roof. It often has a large double-hung, sliding door and picture windows leading onto patios.

CTS SYSTEM: Early Twentieth Century American
California Ranch
(C Ranch-901)

CAL-VET LOANS Real estate loans available to armed forces veterans from California at low interest rates.

CAMBER A slight, convex arching that is intentionally built into a beam, truss, girder, flooring, etc., to prevent it from sagging when under a load.

CAMINO A Spanish word meaning highway.

CAMPANILE A free-standing bell tower.

CANAL **1.** A groove or channel in Greek or Roman architecture such as those found on Ionic capitals. **2.** A man-made waterway connecting two bodies of water. **3.** A trench used to carry irrigation water.

CANALIS *See* Canal.

CANCELLATION CLAUSE A clause in a contract or lease specifying the conditions under which the contract or lease may be cancelled by either party.

CANDLE **1.** A solid, often cylindrical mass of wax, tallow, or other substance in which a wick is embedded. It is burned to produce light. **2.** A measure of light.

CANDLE POWER *See* Candle.

CANTILEVER A beam, truss, girder, bracket, or other structural member that is supported at only one end and which projects beyond the wall, column, or other building part that supports it.

CANTILEVER BEAM *See* Cantilever.

CANTILEVER CONSTRUCTION *See* Cantilever.

CANT STRIP A piece of wood that is placed at the intersection of a wall and roof and provides a gradual transition for the roofing material applied over it.

CAP **1.** The top piece of such structural members as columns, cornices, lintels, doors, and walls. **2.** A fitting used to seal the end of a pipe.

CAPACITY **1.** The volume of material a container will hold. **2.** The number of livestock that can be supported on a piece of land. **3.** The amount of traffic a road will carry. **4.** The ability, in a legal sense, to carry out one's own affairs, based on the person's age and mental state.

CAPE ANN COLONIAL STYLE An American house style. It is usually a small, symmetrical, one and one-half story, compact house distinguished by its gambrel roof. A variation of the Cape Cod style, it started in the Cape Ann area of Massachusetts.

CTS SYSTEM: Colonial American
Cape Ann Colonial
(Cape Ann-105)

CAPE ANN COLONIAL STYLE

CAPE COD COLONIAL STYLE An American house style first built on Cape Cod, Massachusetts. It is a small, symmetrical one and one-half story compact house with a steep gable roof covered with shingles and is the earliest dwelling type built by the colonists that is still popular today.

CTS SYSTEM: Colonial American
Cape Cod Colonial
(Cape Cod-104)

CAPE COD COLONIAL STYLE

CAPITA An expression commonly used to mean people. Literally it means heads. *See also* Per Capita.

CAPITAL **1.** A community that is the seat of government. **2.** Wealth that is accumulated for the purpose of future use. **3.** The top of a pillar or column in Greek and Roman architecture. **4.** An upper case letter.

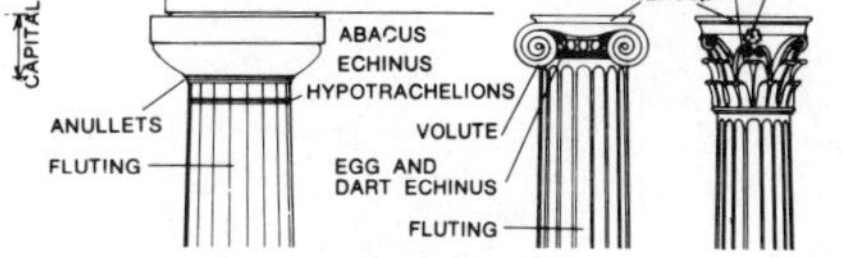

CAPITAL

CAPITAL ASSETS Permanent assets (buildings, land, equipment, machinery) used for the manufacture of income.

CAPITAL EXPENDITURES Money spent on additions, betterments, or improvements such as buildings, land, or equipment.

CAPITAL EXPENSE The yearly sum necessary to pay return and provide for the ultimate return of the investment.

CAPITAL GAINS Gains realized from the sale of capital assets. Generally, the difference between cost and selling price, less certain deductible expenses. Usually for income tax purposes. A profit from sale of a capital asset. Capital gains are taxed at a lower rate than ordinary income.

CAPITAL GAINS TAX A tax applied to gain or profit realized on the sale or exchange of a capital asset.

CAPITAL GOOD A man-made good used in the manufacture of wealth.

CAPITAL GRANT A cash subsidy given by the government towards the cost of a local project.

CAPITALISM An economic system founded on the principles of private ownership and personal rights.

CAPITALIZATION In real estate, it is the procedure of reflecting future income into the present value of a property—changing income into value. It is a process commonly found in the income approach in an appraisal.

CAPITALIZATION APPROACH *See* Income Approach.

CAPITALIZATION IN PERPETUITY The process of capitalizing an income stream that is expected to go on for a very long period of time with change. A capitalization rate based on this assumption will provide for a return on the investment but no return of the investment.

CAPITALIZATION RATE A rate that reflects the relationship between the value of a property and its net operating income (NOI).

Example of the Direct Method of Capitalization Rate Construction

Net operating income (N.O.I.)	$ 37,000
Value of property	$295,000
Capitalization rate ($37,000 ÷ $295,000)	.085

CAPITALIZATION RATE

CAPITALIZE The process of converting a future income stream into a present value.

CAPITALIZED VALUE The indicated value of the property after use of the capitalization process in the income approach of an appraisal.

CAPITAL LOSS A loss from the sale of a capital asset. *See also* Capital Gains.

CAPITAL RECAPTURE *See* Capital Recovery.

CAPITAL RECOVERY (RECAPTURE) The return to an investor in real estate of the capital invested in the property over a period of time. It is intended to reimburse the investor for that portion of the investment that will be lost during the holding period because of the depreciation of the improvements and/or the decrease in value of the site and site improvements.

CAPITAL RECOVERY (RECAPTURE) METHOD A method used by investors to recover the capital they expect to be lost during the period they own a real estate investment.

CAPITAL RECOVERY (RECAPTURE) PAYMENTS Annual payments needed to give an investor in real estate a return of his or her contemplated lost capital investment. *See* Capital Recovery (Recapture).

CAPITAL RECOVERY (RECAPTURE) PERIOD A period of time forecasted to be the holding period of a real estate investment during which an investor should plan to recover his or her capital invested in the project. *See* Capital Recovery (Recapture).

CAPITAL RECOVERY (RECAPTURE) RATE The amount of money required annually to reimburse the investor for that portion of the investment that will be lost during the life of the investment. It is expressed as a ratio of the value of the whole real estate investment. *See* Capital Recovery (Recapture).

CAPITAL REQUIREMENTS The total money necessary for running a business.

CAPITAL STOCK Shares of a corporation issued to investors who, in turn, invest capital into the corporation. The total number of shares a corporation may issue is fixed by its articles of incorporation. A corporation does not have to issue all of its authorized capital stock. The percentage of ownership of a corporation is determined by what percentage of the issued capital stock one owns.

CAPITAL SURPLUS An accounting term that includes paid-in surpluses, donated surpluses, and surpluses caused by the revaluation of the corporation's assets. It does not include earned surplus.

CAP PLATE A piece of wood that covers the tops of a series of vertical structures.

CAPRICIOUS VALUE An appraised value based on emotion and not on fair market value.

CARAVAN A viewing conducted of newly listed properties by sales personnel of a real estate company. The sales personnel travel from listing to listing together in order to gain knowledge about the listings their company has for sale.

CAR FLOAT BRIDGE A vertically mobile bridge used to move railroad cars from land to a barge.

CARPENTER GOTHIC STYLE A nineteenth-century American house style also known as Stick Style that originated in the 1800s as a fad manifesting the public's fascination with the ornate parts that could be cheaply produced with the new automatic bandsaw. It is a loosely defined style characterized by complex silhou-

CARPENTER GOTHIC STYLE

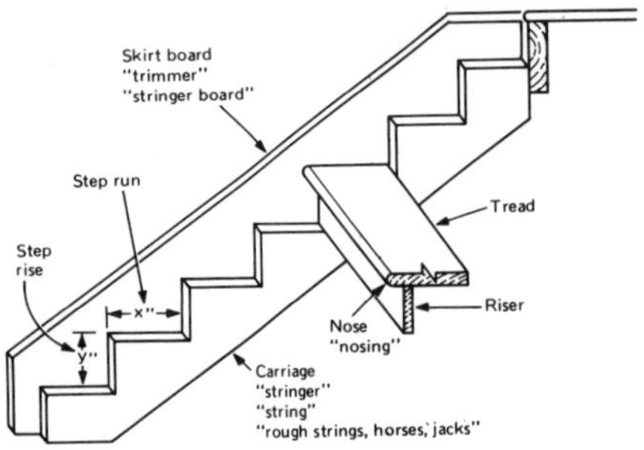

CARRIAGE

CARVED DROP

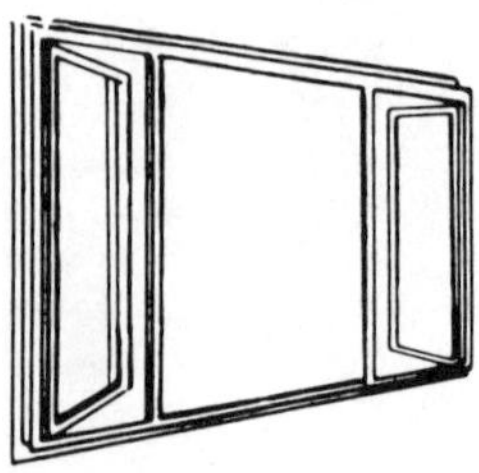

CASEMENT WINDOW

ettes; exposed framing members; high, steep roofs; diagonal braces; lots of gingerbread trim; and ornate windows and doors.

CTS SYSTEM: Nineteenth Century American
Stick Style or Carpenter Gothic
(Stick or C Goth-708)

CARPETING A floor covering made of woven material that can be installed over either the subflooring or finished flooring. Carpets were woven in Babylon over 5,000 years ago. Carpeting is chosen as a floor covering because it is comfortable, decorative, and muffles sound.

CARPORT An open-sided, roofed shelter often made by extending the house roof to one side.

CARRIAGE An important component of a staircase; an inclined beam that supports the steps. *See also* Stringer.

CARRYING CAPACITY A farming term that signifies the maximum number of animals that can graze on a piece of land without setting a downward trend in forage production, soil, and quality of animal.

CARRYING CHARGES Expenses for maintaining a property that is meant to produce income but is not yet doing so. An example would be taxes on an idle property.

CARTOUCHE A scrolled tablet used for ornamental purposes. It may also contain an inscription.

CARVED DROP An ornamentation on the underside of the front overhang of a Garrison colonial house. Originally, it was the bottom end of the vertical timbers. Today, it is usually a foot high and is shaped like an inverted pineapple or acorn.

CASE **1.** The external covering of a building. **2.** A court action.

CASEMENT WINDOW A type of window hinged to open at one of its vertical edges.

CASH Ready money; legal currency such as dollars in the United States.

CASH ASSETS Money that is immediately available to meet the requirements of operating a business on a day-to-day basis.

CASH CROP Crops grown for direct sale instead of for use on the farm.

CASH EQUIVALENT A price expressed in terms of all cash as opposed to a price that is expressed in terms of cash and securities, notes, mortgages, other property, or any other thing that cannot readily be converted into cash at face value.

CASH FLOW The net income an investor will hold after deducting operating expenses and loan payments from his or her gross income.

CASH FLOW DIVIDEND *See* Equity Dividend.

CASHIER'S CHECK A check that a bank draws upon itself; a promissory note by the bank since the bank is both the drawer and drawee. It is preferred to a personal check. A cashier's check can be used without waiting for the check to clear.

CASH ON CASH The ratio of cash throw-off to the original cash invested in a real estate investment. *See also* Cash Throw-Off.

CASH OUT When used in a listing or offering, it indicates that the buyer wants to receive all cash.

CASH RENT **1.** The amount of rent paid in cash to the landlord. It does not include the value of any services performed by the tenant for the landlord as partial consideration of being allowed to occupy the property. **2.** A farming term for a fixed amount of rent for a farm.

CASH SALE A sale made for all cash without any financing.

CASH THROW-OFF The amount of income received by the owner of a property after all expenses are paid, including payment of the mortgage. *See also* Before-Tax Cash Flow.

CASING A piece of trim material around the top and sides of doors and windows. Some common types are back band, butt, clamshell, colonial, corner block, and mitered.

CASTING A process of pouring metal or plaster into a mold to produce a shaped form.

CAST IRON An iron alloy with high compressive strength.

CAST IRON BOILER A type of boiler made with portions of cast iron.

CAST STONE Artificial stone; a mixture of stone chips embedded in mortar, cement, or plaster.

CATENA A type of soil.

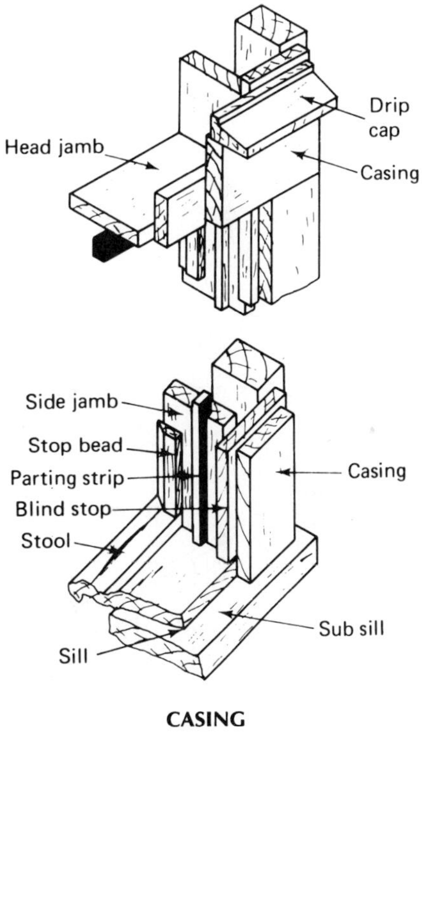

CASING

CATSLIDE *See* Saltbox.

CATTLE GUARD A grill or grating placed in the ground over which cattle will not cross. It is used instead of a gate at the opening of a fence.

CATTLE SQUEEZE A device put into a corral chute to immobilize an animal so it can be branded or dehorned.

CATWALK A narrow, elevated walkway that provides access to an area (such as a bridge) where repairs may be necessary.

CAULKING A compound used to seal cracks and fill joints.

CAUSEWAY A raised, paved road that traverses low land.

CAVEAT A formal notice given by an interested party to the court not to perform certain acts until said party has been notified and heard in the matter.

CAVEAT EMPTOR A legal phrase meaning, in Latin, "Let the buyer beware." The maxim indicates that the buyer takes on the risk as to the quality and condition of the contracted property unless there is a warranty either expressed or implied.

CAVITY WALL A wall, usually of brick or stone, which has an inner and outer layer separated by an air space. The air space furnishes insulation.

CBD See Central Business District.

CCIM *See* Certified Commercial-Investment Member.

CEDAR CLOSET A closet made of cedar, which protects clothes from moths and gives them a cedar scent.

CEILING INSULATION Insulation installed in the ceiling, often under the flooring of the attic. The most common types are batts and loose fill.

CEILING JOISTS

CEILING JOISTS Small beams that carry the ceiling.

CEILING OUTLET Outlet on the ceiling that provides power for the fixtures which are mounted on it.

CEILING TRIM *See* Cornice.

CELLAR The portion of a building that is below the ground and usually used for storage.

CELLULAR CONCRETE A light-weight concrete that has a homogeneous cell structure.

CELLULAR STEEL DECK A floor system composed of two pieces of sheet metal shaped and welded to form cells.

CEMENT A material or mixture of materials which, when mixed with water, form a plastic and cohesive substance that dries and hardens in place.

CEMENT BLOCK *See* Concrete Block.

CEMENT SYMBOL An architectural symbol for cement.

CEMETERY An area of land designated for the burial of deceased persons.

CENTER-TO-CENTER *See* On Center.

CENTRAL AIR CONDITIONING A system in which air is cooled and treated in a central area and piped or blown into other spaces through ducts.

CENTRAL ASSESSMENT An assessment of a property, such as a utility or railroad, that has single ownership but is situated in one or more assessment districts.

CENTRAL BUSINESS DISTRICT The downtown area of a city. The major business, shopping, governmental, and service areas.

CENTRAL CITY **1.** The downtown area of a city. **2.** A city which is geographically central to many other cities and therefore provides certain market and service functions.

CENTRAL HEATING SYSTEMS A system where air is heated in one location outside the area served and piped through ducts into areas where it is needed.

CERAMIC TILE A flat, fired clay tile that comes in a variety of types, such as glazed, unglazed, non-vitrified, and vitreous. When attached to walls, floors, and countertops, it may form a decorative, hard, durable surface.

CERTIFICATE **1.** The portion of an appraisal that contains the limiting conditions, the appraiser's conclusion, and his or her signature signifying that the report is, to the best of his or her knowledge, correct and true. **2.** A written instrument that gives assurances of the existence of some fact(s).

CERTIFICATE OF COMPLETION A document required for FHA-insured loans that is signed by homeowners affirming their satisfaction with the labor and materials that went into their home and authorizing the lender to pay the builder.

CERTIFICATE OF DEPOSIT An amount of money left in a savings institution for a specific length of time that exchanges early withdrawal privileges for higher interest.

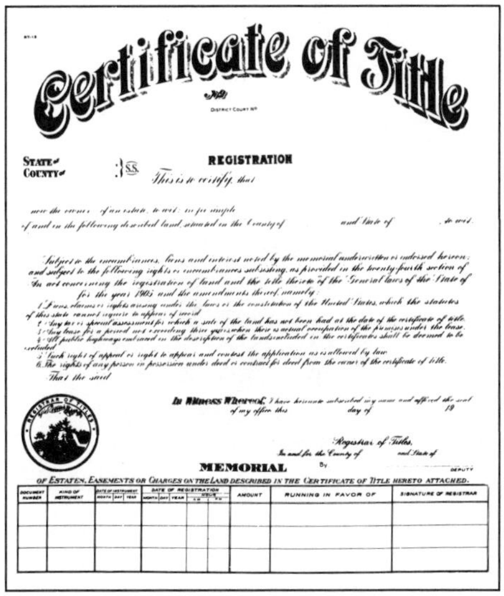

CERTIFICATE

CERTIFICATE OF ELIGIBILITY A certificate given by the Veteran's Administration (VA) to a veteran which states that the applicant is eligible for a VA-insured loan.

CERTIFICATE OF ESTOPPEL A certificate that states some facts, such as a mortgage balance or an amount of rent past due, and which prevents the party who issues the certificate from claiming later that the facts are different from those set forth in the certificate.

CERTIFICATE OF NO DEFENSE An instrument executed by the mortgagor, upon the sale of the mortgage to a third party, as to the validity of the mortgage debt. Many mortgages contain a provision that requires the mortgagor to execute a certificate of no defense upon request from the mortgagee. *See* Estoppel Certificate.

CERTIFICATE OF OCCUPANCY A document issued to a builder by a local building department which certifies that a building is free of building code violations and fit for occupancy.

CERTIFICATE OF REASONABLE VALUE (CRV) A document issued by the Veteran's Administration that states a property's current market value, based on a VA-approved appraisal.

CERTIFICATE OF TITLE A signed document made by a title examiner that is usually presented to the buyer along with the deed. It certifies that the seller of a property has good title.

CERTIFICATION OF VALUE A written instrument that states the appraiser's opinion of the value of a property. It also states that the appraiser has no interest in the property.

CERTIFIED CHECK A check that the bank has certified as good. The bank will set aside sufficient funds to cover the check and will not pay other checks if such payment would cause the certified check to bounce.

CERTIFIED COMMERCIAL-INVESTMENT MEMBER (CCIM) A designation awarded by the Realtors National Marketing Institute of the NATIONAL ASSOCIATION OF REALTORS® to realtors who have achieved superior levels of knowledge, competence, and high standing of character in their field and community.

CERTIFIED PERSONALITY EVALUATOR (CPE) A professional designation given by the International Association of Assessing Officers to members who demonstrate their ability to assess personal property such as automobiles, furniture, fixtures, and equipment.

CCIM

CERTIFIED COMMERCIAL INVESTMENT MEMBER

INTERNATIONAL ASSOCIATION OF ASSESSING OFFICERS · CPE

CERTIFIED PERSONALITY EVALUATOR

CERTIFIED PROPERTY MANAGER (CPM) A designation conferred by the Institute of Real Property Management of the NATIONAL ASSOCIATION OF REALTORS® upon one who has completed certain required courses and has been active in property management.

CERTIFIED RESIDENTIAL BROKER (CRB) A designation granted by the Realtors National Marketing Institute to those individuals who have proven competence in the management of a real estate brokerage operation.

CERTIFIED RESIDENTIAL SPECIALIST (CRS) A designation awarded by the Realtors National Marketing Institute of the NATIONAL ASSOCIATION OF REALTORS® to realtors who have demonstrated expertise, superior knowledge, and ethical practice in their field and community.

CESSPOOL Part of a waste disposal system that functions similarly to a septic tank; a covered cistern of stone, brick, or concrete block. The liquid seeps out through the walls directly into the surrounding earth.

CHAIN *See* Chain Measures.

CHAIN MEASURES A surveyor's standard measuring distance. Ten square chains of land equal one acre.

CHAIN OF TITLE The list of conveyances, in chronological order, from the original owner to the present one.

CHAINS AND LINKS In real estate, a surveying measurement wherein one link equals 7.92 inches; 10 square chains equal one acre. There are 100 links to a chain.

CHAIN STORE A retail store that is one of many stores under central management and which resembles the other stores in design, policy, and service.

CHAIN, SURVEYOR'S *See* Chain Measures.

CHAIR RAIL A type of molding installed around a room at chairback height to protect the walls from damage.

CHANGE *See* Change, Principle of.

CHANGE OF NAME The changing of documents to reflect a person's change of name.

CHANGE, PRINCIPLE OF A real estate principle which contends that economic and social forces continually cause changes. Appraisers must be acutely aware of these changes. An appraiser always sees the market in transition, where the future, not the past, is more important.

CHANNEL **1.** A duct. **2.** In carpentry or masonry, a

CERTIFIED PROPERTY MANAGER

CERTIFIED RESIDENTIAL BROKER

CERTIFIED RESIDENTIAL SPECIALIST

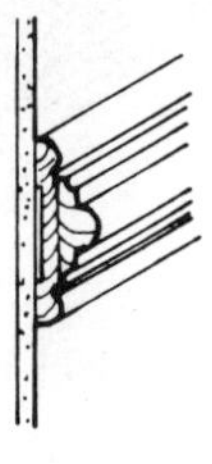

CHAIR RAIL

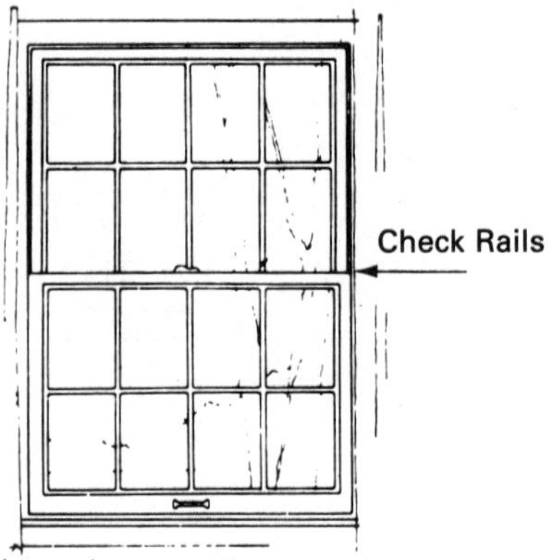

CHECK RAIL

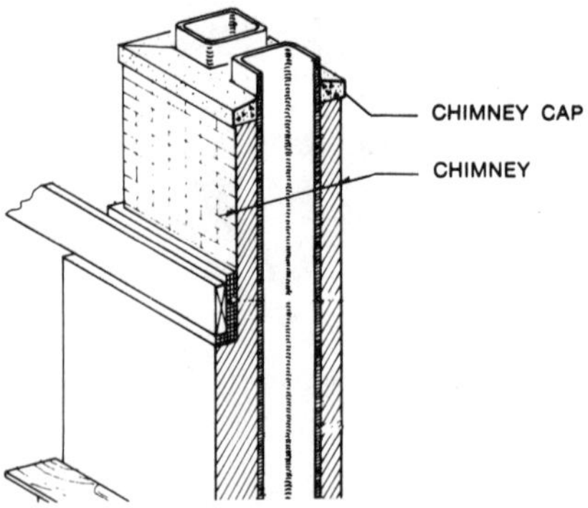

CHIMNEY
CHIMNEY CAP

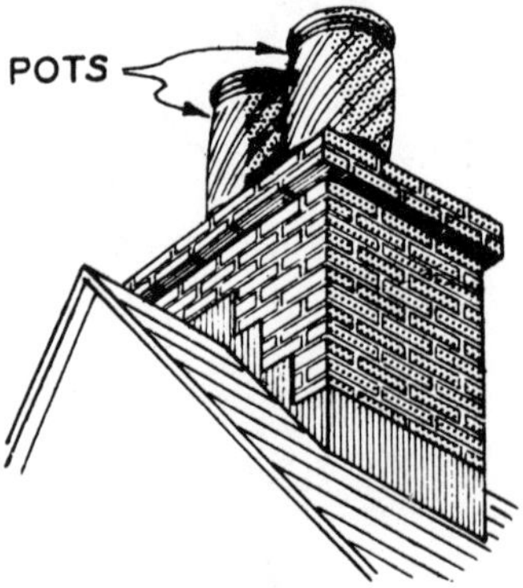

CHIMNEY POT

groove or gutter. **3.** The deepest portion of a body of water that provides the best passageway for ships.

CHAPEL A place of worship that is not necessarily part of a church, such as a hospital chapel.

CHARLESTON COLONIAL STYLE *See* English Colonial.

CHATTEL Tangible personal property other than real estate, such as furniture, artwork, and silverware.

CHATTEL INTEREST A right to real estate, other than ownership, such as a loan or leasehold.

CHATTEL MORTGAGE A security device whereby a security interest is taken by the mortgagee in the personal property of the mortgagor.

CHATTEL,PERSONAL A movable item of property.

CHATTEL, REAL An estate or interest connected or concerned with real estate.

CHECK RAIL A horizontal member of a double-hung window that forms the bottom of the upper portion and the top of the lower piece.

CHECK VALVE An automatic valve that keeps material flowing in one direction and prevents back up.

CHIMNEY A vertical structure, usually brick, that carries smoke and other products of combustion from the fireplace into the air above a building.

CHIMNEY BACK The back wall of a fireplace.

CHIMNEY CAP The sloped metal, concrete, or stone "cap" that crowns a chimney.

CHIMNEY FLASHING Impervious material placed over a chimney to furnish drainage and prevent water penetration.

CHIMNEY FOUNDATION Concrete footings that support the chimney and keep it from settling faster than the rest of the house.

CHIMNEY POT An extension at the top of the chimney made of tile or sheet metal and used to improve the draft.

CHURCH A public place of worship. *See also* Temple and Synagogue.

CINDER BLOCK A lightweight building block made of cinders and concrete.

CIRCLEHEAD WINDOW A window, usually above a door, that has no movable parts and is semi-circular in shape.

CIRCUIT BREAKER A permanent safety device used as a substitute for a fuse. It automatically turns off an electric circuit when it is overloaded.

CIRCULATION PATTERN Pedestrian and automotive traffic pattern.

CIRCULATORS In a hot-water system, circulators are devices that pump water through finger-size tubes into radiators and baseboards.

CIRCUMFERENTIAL HIGHWAY *See* Beltway.

CISTERN A tank used for the storage of rainwater.

CITY A large, incorporated town. More technically, it is a municipal corporation that votes by representation instead of directly.

CLAIMANT Someone who asserts a title or right.

CLAPBOARD A long board used as siding, thicker on one side than the other. It is installed so that the thick side overlaps the thin side.

CLARIFIER An underground filter system used for the removal of dangerous wastes from the water before it enters sewers or septic tanks.

CLASS Used in the CTS system to denote the number of families the unit being described will accommodate and whether the units are detached or have a party wall.

CLASSIC COLONIAL STYLE An American house style based on classic Greek architecture and introduced in 1772 by Thomas Jefferson. Classic colonials are two- to three-story, large houses with a columned exterior characterized by pilasters and a variety of roof shapes on the same house.

CTS SYSTEM: Colonial American
Classic Colonial
(Classic-111)

CLASSIFIED PROPERTY TAX An *ad valorem* property tax where the tax rate is different for different classes of property, i.e., residential, commercial, or industrial.

CLASS OF CONSTRUCTION A system of classifying struc-

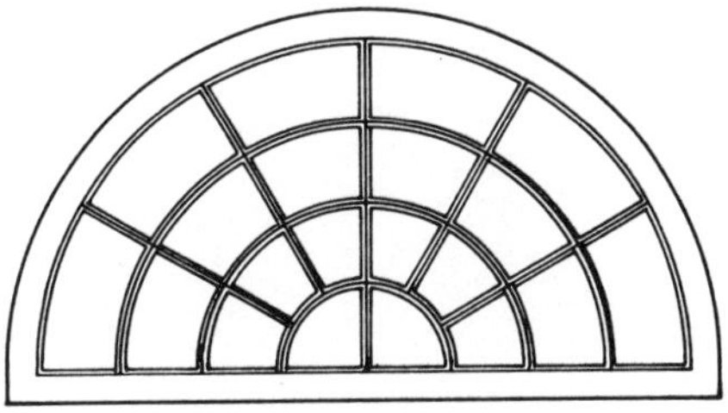

CIRCLE HEAD WINDOW

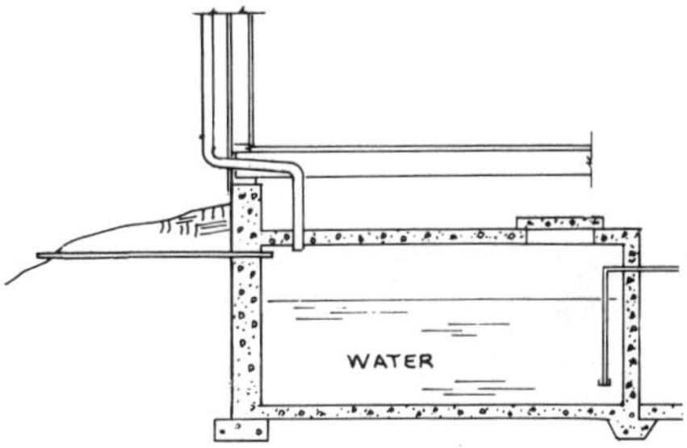

CISTERN

CLASSIC COLONIAL STYLE

tures according to the degree of fire resistance of materials from which they are constructed.

CLAY A type of fine-grained soil composed mostly of hydrous aluminum silicates. It is plastic when wet but rigid when dried.

CLAY AND BRICK TILES Masonry units composed of shales, surface clays, and fire clays. Bricks are solid throughout; tiles have a hollow interior.

CLAYPAN A type of soil that is very dense and heavy and is found just under the upper portion of the soil.

CLEAN-OUT DOOR *See* Ash Clean-out Door.

CLEAN ROOM A room that has a controlled atmosphere.

CLEARANCE The elimination of buildings for an urban renewal project. It is accompanied by the relocation of families and then redevelopment.

CLEAR HEADWAY The distance from the lowest overhead framing member to the floor.

CLEAR LUMBER Lumber free of knots and other defects.

CLEAR SPAN A large, open area that does not have posts or columns in it to support the roof.

CLEAR TITLE An unencumbered title.

CLERESTORY A wall or portion of a wall to which the roof attaches at a higher level than the other walls or portions of walls of a building. Often, there is a window at the top of the clerestory wall.

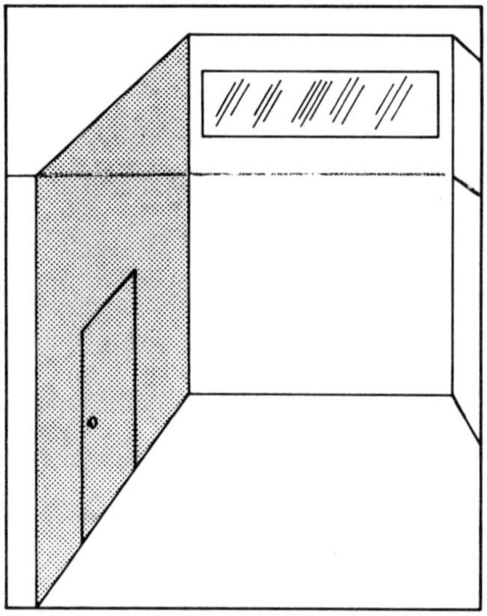

CLERESTORY

CLERESTORY WINDOW *See* Clerestory.

CLIENT Traditionally, one who employs an attorney. It is now used to refer to the customers of real estate agents, insurance agents, stockbrokers, etc.

CLOSING In real estate, the date when the seller gives the title to the buyer in exchange for the agreed-upon purchase price. In many parts of the country, it is called a settlement. At a closing, the deed is delivered to the buyer, and the seller's money is distributed.

CLOSING COSTS The costs involved with the sale of real estate, such as appraisal fees, attorney's fees, and recording fees.

CLOSING STATEMENT A document prepared as part of a real estate closing. It shows the price being paid for the property, all of the adjustments, the closing costs, the financing, any other charges or credits due the buyer or seller, and the net proceeds to be received by the seller.

CLOSING TITLE *See* Closing.

CLOTHES DRYER An automatic mechanism that dries clothes with a stream of hot air and tumbling action.

CLOUD ON TITLE A claim or encumbrance on a property that can injure the owner's title if not removed by a quitclaim deed or court action.

CLOVERLEAF A highway intersection designed to eradicate traffic conflicts. Seen from above, the intersection looks like a cloverleaf.

CLUSTER HOUSING A housing system wherein houses are placed close together to create a big common area.

CO-ADMINISTRATOR A person who holds the responsibility of administrator with one or more other persons.

COARSE-TEXTURED SOIL A type of soil mainly composed of grains larger than .25 mm.

COAST Land bordering on the ocean.

COASTAL COMMISSION An ordinance to limit coastal construction. Construction within the designated coastal areas is controlled by the commission.

COAT A layer of paint or plaster.

CODE A group of laws that govern a specific subject, such as the building code.

CODE OF ETHICS A system of rules, regulations, and standards for ethical conduct. The NATIONAL ASSOCIATION OF REALTORS® has its own code of ethics; other boards and commissions incorporate this code or employ their own. Codes of ethics differ from laws in that members of the organization with the code of ethics voluntarily agree to abide by the code. Enforcement is done by members of the organization. Codes of ethics usually require a higher standard of conduct than government laws and regulations.

CO-EXECUTOR One who shares the duties of executor with one or more other executors.

COIGNES Stone used as the corner of a masonry wall.

COINSURANCE A provision in a standard fire policy which requires that a property be insured to a specified percentage of its value. When the insured fails to com-

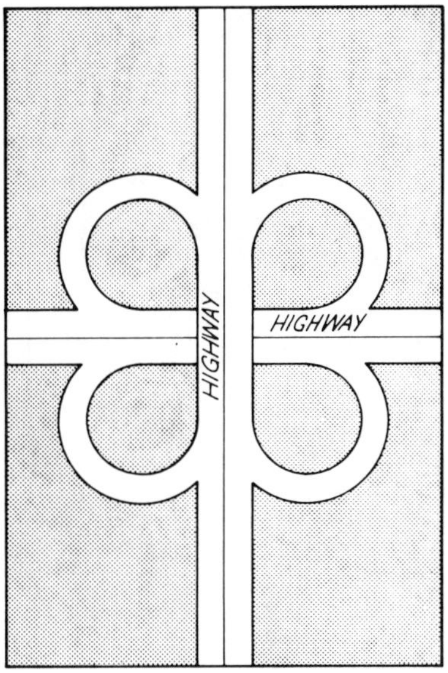

CLOVERLEAF

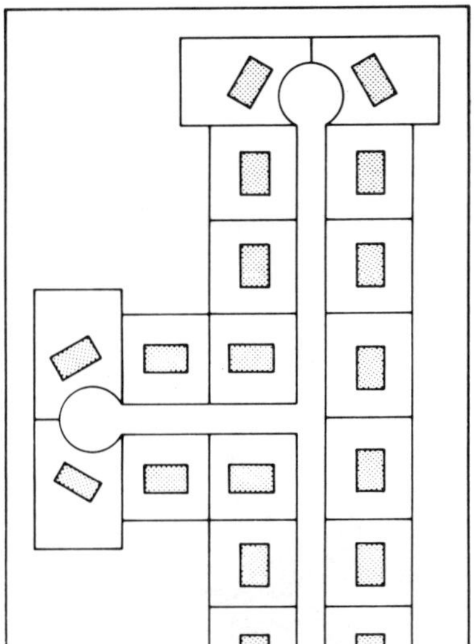

CLUSTER HOUSING

COLD WALL EFFECT

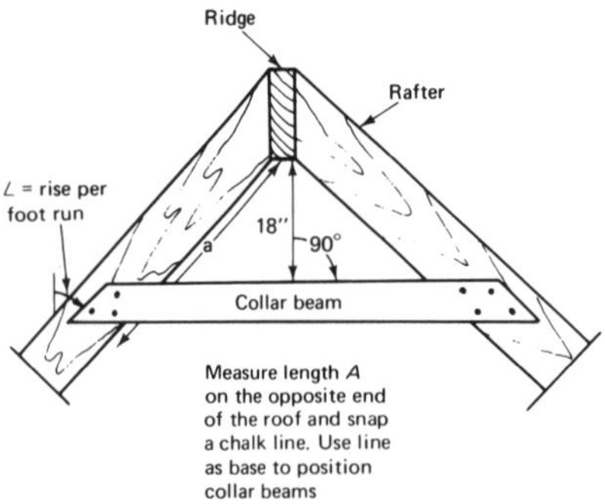

COLLAR BEAM

COLONNADE

ply with this policy provision, the amount paid on claims is reduced.

COLD CANVAS Door-to-door solicitation made without any previous contact.

COLD STORAGE The holding of perishables in an artificially cooled area.

"COLD WALL" EFFECT The chilled feeling that results when body heat is drawn towards a wall, ceiling, or floor where the temperature is cooler than room temperature.

COLD WATER PIPE A pipe that carries cold water.

COLLAR BEAM A beam that unites and stiffens two opposite roof rafters.

COLLAR TIE *See* Tie beam.

COLLATERAL Auxiliary, additional. Something valuable that serves as additional security for a loan.

COLLATERAL ASSIGNMENT The assignment of property for the purpose of providing a third party with additional security. A common form is the assignment of a lease to a mortgagee by a property owner giving the mortgagee first claim on the rents in the event the owner fails to make the mortgage payments. Stock certificates, bank books, certificates of deposit, and insurance policies are other items often assigned to provide additional security in a real estate transaction.

COLLATERAL SECURITY Security that is given to a lender in addition to the primary security offered for the loan. Securities are often given as collateral security for a mortgage loan when the lender feels that the property being mortgaged is not sufficient.

COLLUVIAL SOIL A type of soil that has been deposited on the bottom of a steep hill.

COLONIAL ARCHITECTURE A broad group of building styles used in the United States during the eighteenth and nineteenth centuries.

COLONNADE A line of columns at regular intervals usually used to support an architrave.

COLOR OF TITLE A document that appears to convey good title to real estate but does not really do so. A common example is a deed signed by a party who does not own the property.

COLUMN A long, slender structure that serves as support or decoration.

COLUMN BASE PLATE The small plate at the bottom of a column that helps to distribute the column load to the supporting structures below.

COLUMN CAP PLATE The plate at the top of a column that helps to support a load.

COLUMN FOOTING The base, usually made of reinforced concrete, that supports a load-bearing column.

COLUMN LOTS Small areas meant for the location of load-bearing columns.

COLUMN STEEL Steel placed inside columns for support and reinforcement.

COMBED PLYWOOD A grooved plywood.

COMBINATION DOOR An outer doorframe having an inside removable section for year-round utility. A screen panel is inserted in warm weather and a glass panel in winter.

COMBINATION SEWER A system that handles storm water and sanitary sewage together. See Sewers.

COMBINATION WINDOWS A window that can hold interchangeable panels of screen or glass.

COMMERCIAL BANKS Banks whose primary function is to serve business by providing checking accounts and short-term loans. Their primary source of deposits is demand deposits made in checking accounts. In real estate, they are the major source of construction loans. When they make permanent mortgages, they tend to do so on commercial and investment property owned by customers of the bank.

COMMERCIAL PAPER Bills and notes used instead of money.

COMMERCIAL PROPERTIES Properties intended for business use, such as retail and wholesale stores, offices, restaurants, and hotels.

COMMINGLE In real estate, the mixing of a client's funds into a broker's personal account. Such practice may cause the broker to lose his or her license, although commingling is not always an intentional misappropriation of funds.

COMMISSION The sum, usually a percentage of the sell-

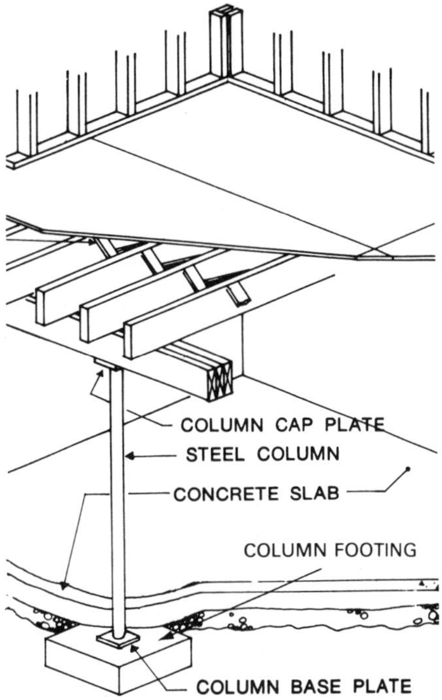

COLUMN
COLUMN BASE PLATE
COLUMN CAP PLATE
COLUMN FOOTING

ing or rental price, paid to the real estate broker for his or her services. Usually, commissions are paid only when the transaction is successfully completed.

COMMITMENT An agreement by a lending institution to give a mortgage on a property either when it is purchased or when it is constructed.

COMMON AREA The area owned by an association of owners of a condominium or planned unit development.

COMMON BRICK A brick not specially treated for texture or color, so each brick is a different color. It is used for general building purposes.

COMMON LAW **1.** A system of law developed in England. **2.** Laws within a system that have universal and general application. **3.** Laws resulting from usage and court judgment.

COMMON-LAW MORTGAGE A mortgage made in accordance with common law.

COMMON PROPERTY Public land in which all people hold equal rights. It is also a legal term indicating an incorporeal hereditament—an inherited right of one person to use the land of another.

COMMON STOCK Capital shares in a corporation that have claim on the net income of the corporation.

COMMON WALL *See* Party Wall.

COMMUNITY ASSOCIATIONS INSTITUTE (CAI) A national association of homeowners' associations.

COMMUNITY PROPERTY A type of ownership that exists in about 10 states, where each spouse is an equal and concurrent co-owner of the property acquired during the period of time they are married to each other. Community property laws differ from state to state.

COMMUNITY SHOPPING CENTER A medium-sized shopping area that may have a small department store and other small shops. A community shopping area is bigger than a neighborhood center but smaller than a regional one.

COMMUTATION CLAUSE A change or substitution. It is usually the substitution of one form of payment for another.

COMMUTATION OF TAXES A reduction or elimination of the requirement to pay taxes on a property because of some special status of the owner or because of hardship.

COMPACTION The process of compacting extra soil used as fill in a lot so that it can properly bear the weight of the building.

COMPARABLES An appraisal term for properties that are similar in value to a particular property and are used to indicate fair market value for that property.

COMPARATIVE ANALYSIS Another name for the market data approach in appraising. *See* Market Data Approach.

COMPARATIVE METHOD A technique used by appraisers to compare one property with another. Often the comparison is done on the basis of a common unit such as square feet or cubic feet.

COMPARATIVE UNIT METHOD *See* Comparative Method.

COMPARISON METHOD Another name for the market data approach in appraising. *See* Market Data Approach.

COMPENSABLE DAMAGES Certain types of damages caused by the taking of property. Generally, the only damage that is compensable is the reduction in value of the property. Sentimental value, inconvenience, and loss of business not related to the real estate are not compensable damages.

COMPENSATING BALANCE A requirement made by banks, as a condition to making a loan, that the borrower leave an agreed-upon amount of money in the bank. This money is usually left in the borrower's checking account.

COMPENSATION A sum of money paid to make amends for an injury. In condemnation, it is the amount paid when a property is taken without the owner's consent.

COMPETENT Legally qualified and fit.

COMPETITION, PRINCIPLE OF A principle which states that, when a situation in a free market produces excess or high profits, competition will soon develop for those profits. For example, if a drugstore is making high profits in a community, another drugstore will soon open if a suitable location is available.

COMPONENT An individual element of construction.

COMPONENT CONSTRUCTION Modular construction. *See also* Prefabrication.

COMPONENT DEPRECIATION A method of estimating the depreciation of an improvement. The improvement is broken down into its component parts, and a rate of depreciation is estimated for each part.

COMPONENT PANEL A wall that is prefabricated and ready for installation.

COMPOSITE RATE A rate used in appraising in the income approach. It is an overall rate. It is called "R" in the Ellwood capitalization formula.

COMPOSITION SHINGLES Shingles covered with a mixture of gravel or stones.

COMPOSITION SIDING A type of siding material that is prefabricated, often in imitation brick.

COMPOUND AMOUNT OF AN ANNUITY The total amount of money at the end of a given period, including investment and reinvestment of the annuity payments.

COMPOUND AMOUNT OF AN INVESTED SUM The total amount of money at the end of a given period, including the reinvestment of all interest plus the original amount invested.

COMPOUND AMOUNT OF ONE PER PERIOD *See* Amount of One Per Period.

COMPOUND DISCOUNT A method of discounting money. It is the opposite of compound interest.

COMPOUND INTEREST A method of paying interest where the interest earned during a period of time is added to the principal sum at the end of the period. During the next period, the interest earned is on both the original principal sum and the accumulated interest. This process continues over a series of equal time periods for a specified length of time. It is the type of interest usually paid on savings accounts.

COMPOUND SLOPE A slope composed of two or more separate slopes with different grade angles.

COMPREHENSIVE COMMUNITY PLAN *See* Master Plan.

COMPRESSION STRENGTH TEST A test to measure the strength of concrete.

COMPUTER-ASSISTED MASS APPRAISAL PROGRAM The use of computer technology to find the answer to an appraisal problem.

COMPUTER LISTING A type of multiple listing system used by Realtors where a telephone call to the computer will tell the caller of available listings, which are coded by area, number of bedrooms, etc.

CONCEALED HEATING *See* Panel Heating.

CONCESSION A franchise to use an area or building for business. It is granted by the government or a private group.

CONCLUSION OF VALUE *See* Certification of Value.

CONCRETE A mixture of cement, water, admixtures, and aggregates. Solid concrete will stay solid forever. It is an important building material because it is strong, durable, watertight, and workable in its plastic state.

CONCRETE BLOCK Masonry units—solid or hollow—made out of concrete composed of Portland cement, aggregates, admixtures, and water.

CONCRETE BLOCK WALL A type of masonry wall consisting of concrete blocks and a plaster coating.

CONCRETE PIERS Concrete supports for a floor-framing system.

CONCRETE SLAB *See* Slab-on-Ground.

CONCRETE TESTS Tests to measure the strength and consistency of concrete.

CONCRETE TILT-UP A method of constructing walls by pouring concrete into forms flat on the ground, allowing it to harden, and then raising the forms with a crane or tackle to a vertical position.

CONDEMNATION The power of government to take private property by due process of law for public use or benefit. The government does not need the owner's consent. The owner is entitled to receive just compensation. *See* Eminent Domain.

CONDEMNATION VALUE The value of property taken by condemnation that must be paid to the owner whose property was condemned.

CONDEMNEE The owner of property taken by condemnation (eminent domain).

CONDEMNER The party taking property by condemnation (eminent domain).

CONDENSATION The formation of water from warm air being cooled.

CONDENSATION DUCT A duct that drains away water (resulting from condensation) from an air-conditioning unit.

CONDITION In real estate, a provision in a contract or

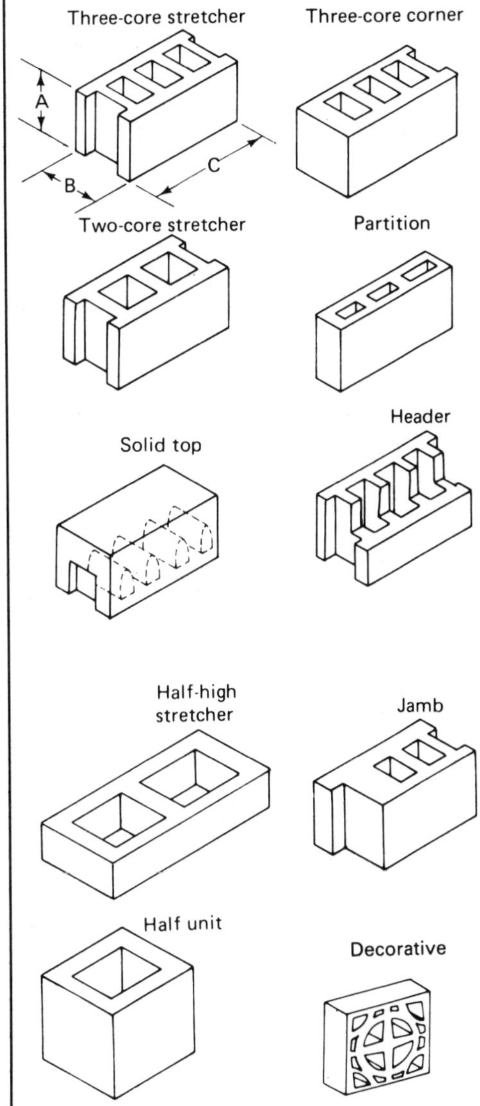

CONCRETE BLOCKS

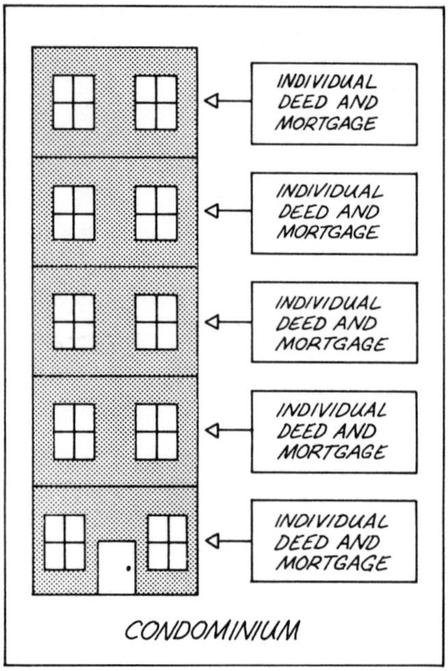

CONDOMINIUM

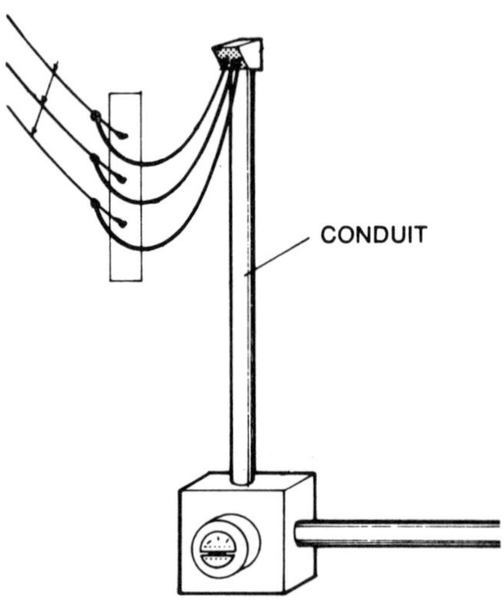

CONDUIT

deed that limits the deed or contract based on a future event that may occur.

CONDITIONAL COMMITMENT A commitment made by a lending institution to give a mortgage on a property provided specified conditions are met, such as the completion of construction or remodeling or the renting of an agreed-upon percentage of the space.

CONDITIONAL FEE *See* Fee Simple, Conditional.

CONDITIONAL SALE *See* Bond for Deed. A sale where complete title passes some time in the future when specified conditions, usually the making of a series of payments in a timely manner, are met.

CONDITIONAL SALES CONTRACT *See* Land Contract.

CONDOMINIUM A form of ownership in which each owner owns the fee to the individual unit, and a percentage of the fee to the common areas.

CONDOMINIUM CONVERSION The changing of rental units to condominium, individually owned units.

CONDOMINIUM MAP (PLAN) A recorded map showing the condominium units and common area. The map includes both horizontal and vertical measurements of the units.

CONDOMINIUM OWNER'S ASSOCIATION *See* Homeowner's Association.

CONDUCTOR In electricity, a wire or path through which electric current flows.

CONDUIT **1.** An artificial or natural channel for the conveyance of water. **2.** Figuratively, something that is a channel for knowledge. **3.** A metal pipe through which electric wire runs.

CONDUIT, ELECTRICAL A metal pipe through which electric wiring is installed. It is the best and safest method of electric wiring.

CONFIRMATION A contract, memorandum, or deliberate act which validates a previous agreement that might otherwise have been void.

CONFISCATION The seizure of property by the government from a private owner without paying the owner just compensation.

CONFORMITY, PRINCIPLE OF An appraisal principle which holds that uniformity of properties in a neighborhood produces maximum value. This principle seems to be less applicable now than it was in the past.

CONGRUOUS A property that conforms to other properties in the same neighborhood.

CONIFER A type of evergreen, cone-bearing tree, such as a pine, spruce, hemlock, or fir.

CONIFEROUS TREE *See* Conifer.

CONNECTION A piece that joins or links.

CONSENT JUDGMENT An agreement between a plaintiff and a defendant who are engaged in a lawsuit to have a judgment entered and recorded. Although the court does no actual finding for one party or the other, the judgment, once approved by the court, is binding on both parties.

CONSEQUENTIAL DAMAGES Damages caused to a property by the taking of a nearby property of another owner. They may also be caused by the construction of improvements on nearby properties. The right to receive compensation for this type of damage varies from state to state. *See* Severance Damage.

CONSERVATION **1.** In real estate, the protection and preservation of good neighborhoods. **2.** The preservation and protection of natural resources so they will not be destroyed.

CONSERVATOR A court-appointed guardian.

CONSIDERATION **1.** An inducement to enter a contract; money, commodity exchange, etc. **2.** In real estate, the actual selling price of a property.

CONSIGNEE The person a shipper delivers the goods to at the final destination.

CONSISTENT USE THEORY An appraisal theory which maintains that, when a property is evaluated, the land and the improvements must be evaluated on the assumption that they are both being used for the same purpose.

CONSOLIDATION The coming together, either through merger or partial ownership, of two or more corporations.

CONSTANT A factor or percentage that expresses the relationship between the principal amount of a mortgage and the payments. *See* Mortgage Constant.

CONIFER

CONSTANT PAYMENT MORTGAGE A type of mortgage by which the borrower pays a fixed amount each month, with part to be applied to repayment of principal and part to payment of interest.

CONSTRUCTION COST The total cost of constructing a building including the price of land, labor, materials, and profit.

CONSTRUCTION LOAN A short-term loan used to finance improvements to real estate. It often has a long-term commitment for more permanent financing.

CONSTRUCTION LOAN AGREEMENT *See* Building Loan Agreement.

CONSTRUCTION LOAN MORTGAGE A short-term mortgage often made by a commercial bank to a developer to provide funds during the construction of a real estate project. When the project is completed, the construction mortgage is paid off and replaced with a permanent mortgage.

CONSTRUCTIVE EVICTION **1.** Any act where the landlord interferes with the tenant's use of the leased premises. **2.** Incapability of the purchaser to obtain possession because premises are unfit or hazardous.

CONSTRUCTIVE MORTGAGE *See* Equitable Mortgage.

CONSTRUCTIVE NOTICE Notice made public through recording or newspaper; a legal notification that may not actually notify involved parties.

CONSULTANT Someone who is given a fee in exchange for his or her advice, regardless of the outcome.

CONSUMER GOODS Goods bought primarily for noncommercial use; personal or household goods.

CONTEMPORARY ARCHITECTURE A general term encompassing any number of modern building designs that do not conform to the traditional styles of the past.

CONTEMPORARY STYLE

CONTEMPORARY STYLE A post-World-War-II American house style started by the revolutionary work of Frank Lloyd Wright, Hobson Richardson, and the German architects of the Bauhaus. The modern house tries to integrate indoor and outdoor space. It is characterized by its use of modern building materials, extensive use of glass, and lack of ornamentation.

CTS SYSTEM: Post World War II American
Functional Modern or Contemporary
(Fun Mod or Contemp-903)

CONTIGUOUS A property that is touching, bordering, or very near to another property.

CONTINGENCIES Possible occurrences that are conditioned on the precipitation of a future event. A purchase agreement might be contingent upon a termite inspection or the acquisition of adequate funds.

CONTINGENT COMMISSIONS A commission to be paid to a broker or salesperson only in the event of a future occurrence, such as the actual sale or leasing of a property.

CONTINUOUS HEADER The horizontal member of a frame made of joined timbers to form a continuous, rigid framework.

CONTOUR FURROWS Lateral furrows plowed at close intervals on a hill to control water flow distribution and erosion.

CONTOUR LEVELING Land leveling that forms terraced platforms.

CONTOUR LINE A line on a map that connects points of equal elevation or outlines a water body.

CONTOUR MAP A topographical map that uses lines to connect points of equal elevation and outline their shape.

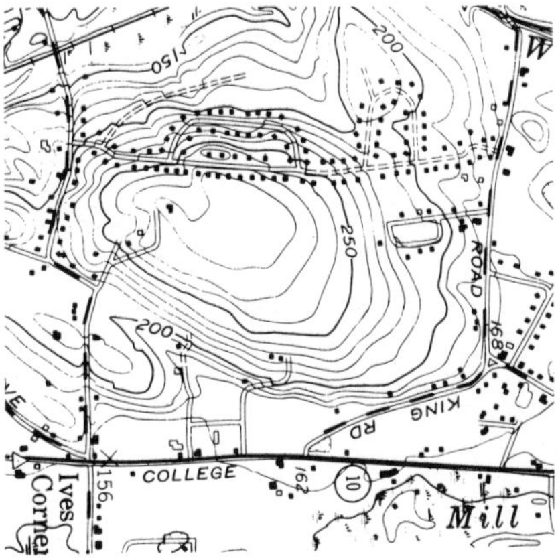

CONTOUR MAP

CONTRACT A written or oral agreement between two or more parties to perform or not perform specified obligations. A contract to be valid and binding must: (1) be entered into by competent parties, (2) be bound by a consideration, (3) possess mutuality, (4) represent an actual meeting of minds, and (5) cover a legal and moral act.

CONTRACT FOR DEED *See* Bond for Deed and Land Contract.

CONTRACT OF SALE In some areas of the country, this is synonymous with *land contract.* In other areas, it is synonymous with *purchase agreement.*

CONTRACTOR *See* General Contractor and Subcontractor.

CONTRACTOR'S OVERHEAD *See* Overhead.

CONTRACTOR'S PROFIT *See* Profit.

CONTRACT RENT The actual rent paid for the use of a property. It is not necessarily the market or economic rent.

CONTRACT SALE *See* Land Contract.

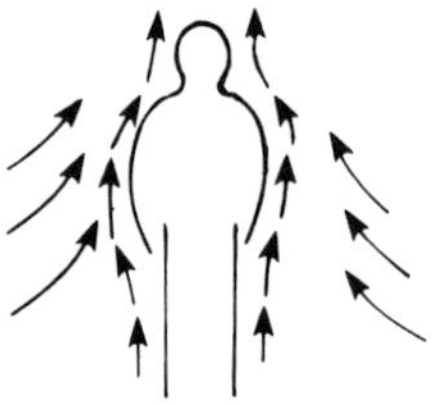

CONVECTION

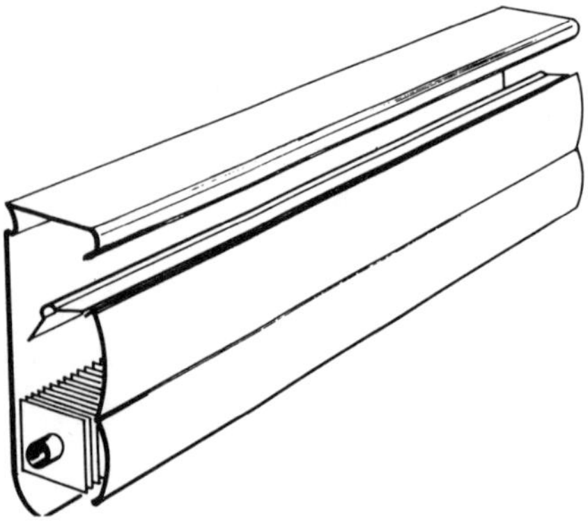

CONVECTOR RADIATOR

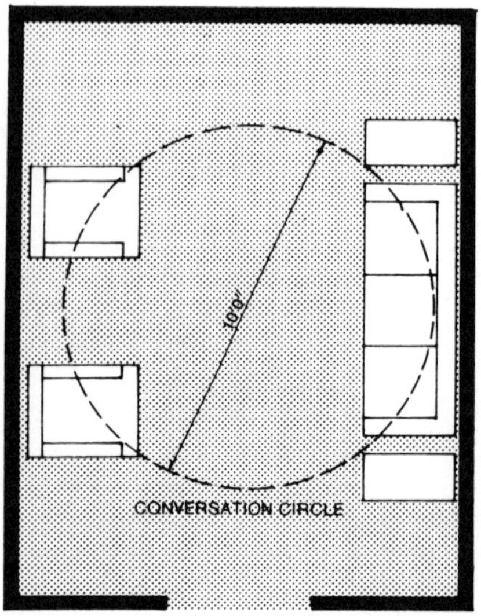

CONVERSATION CIRCLE

CONTRIBUTION, PRINCIPLE OF An economic principle that applies to real estate and is used by real estate appraisers. It states that each portion of a property contributes to the property's ability to produce income.

CONTRIBUTORY VALUE OF IMPROVEMENTS A term used in farm appraising to express the amount of value the buildings add to the value of the property.

CONTROL DATA An appraisal technique that uses the transactions of a group of studied real properties to adjust the difference between comparable sales or rentals and the property being appraised.

CONTROLLED ACCESS HIGHWAY *See* Limited Access Highway.

CONTROLS The restrictions imposed by the government to limit the use, density, etc., of properties within a renewal project.

CONVECTION The transfer of heat by the heating of the air, which moves throughout the area to be heated either naturally or blown by fans.

CONVECTOR RADIATOR A type of heat distribution system consisting of pipes with many fins attached at short intervals. Hot water or steam flows through the pipes, heating the fins, which in turn heat the surrounding air.

CONVENIENCE OUTLETS Electrical outlets which have two receptacles that accept three-pronged plugs.

CONVENTIONAL HOME A home that is constructed at the site. It is the opposite of a factory-built house, mobile home, or manufactured house.

CONVENTIONAL LOAN *See* Conventional Mortgage.

CONVENTIONAL MORTGAGE A mortgage that is made by a lender, such as a savings and loan association, bank, insurance company, pension fund, etc., who is not insured by a government agency (e.g., Federal Housing Administration, Veteran's Administration).

CONVERSATION CIRCLE A circle that is ideally about ten feet in diameter in which furniture can be arranged for easy sit-down communication. Circles for standing conversation need only be six feet in diameter.

CONVERSION Changing the use or ownership of a property from its existing use or ownership type to another. The most common ownership conversions are from fee simple to condominium or cooperative ownership.

CONVEYANCE A written instrument that transfers an interest in real estate from one party to another.

CONVEYANCE TAX *See* Transfer Tax.

CONVEYANCING *See* Conveyance.

COOLING TOWER A water tower in which water is cooled by evaporation. It is part of an air-conditioning system.

COOP A structure to house chickens, pigeons, and other birds.

COOPERATING BROKER The broker who sells or leases a property that was listed by another broker and shares the commission with the listing broker.

COOPERATIVE A form of ownership in which each owner shares in a corporation that owns an entire property and has the exclusive right to occupy part of the property. The corporation is run by directors, who are elected by the corporation stockholders.

COOPERATIVE APARTMENT An apartment in cooperative ownership. *See* Cooperative.

COOPERATIVE HOUSING A type of housing project where the occupants are shareholders in a special corporation that is created to own the project. This type of project is often financed by mortgages insured by the FHA according to Section 213 of Title II of the National Housing Act.

COOPERATIVE OWNERSHIP *See* Cooperative.

COOPERATIVE SALE *See* Cooperating Broker.

COPING A protective top of a wall, chimney, pilaster, or parapet usually sloped to allow the run-off of water.

CORBEL A piece of wood or masonry projecting from a wall used to support some part of the house above it.

CORD A unit of measurement of logs. It is 128 cubic feet, which is a pile of logs 4 feet high, 4 feet wide, and 8 feet long.

CORED BRICK A brick that has up to and over 20 holes and still is classified as solid.

CORK TILE A type of tile made from cork. Cork tile is attractive, resilient, and makes a quiet floor covering. However, cork has low resistance to stains, burns, and indentations.

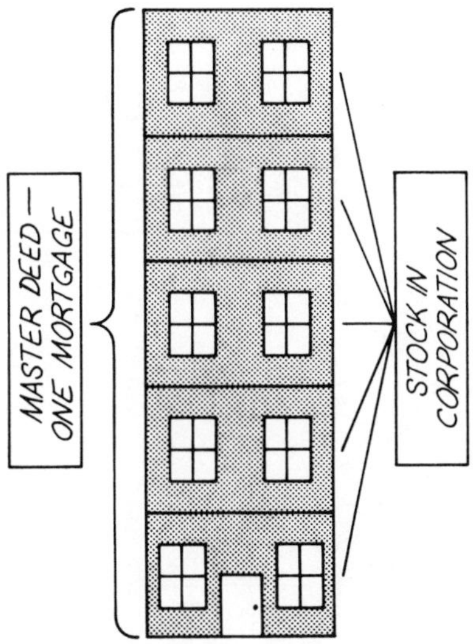

COOPERATIVE

CORN CRIB

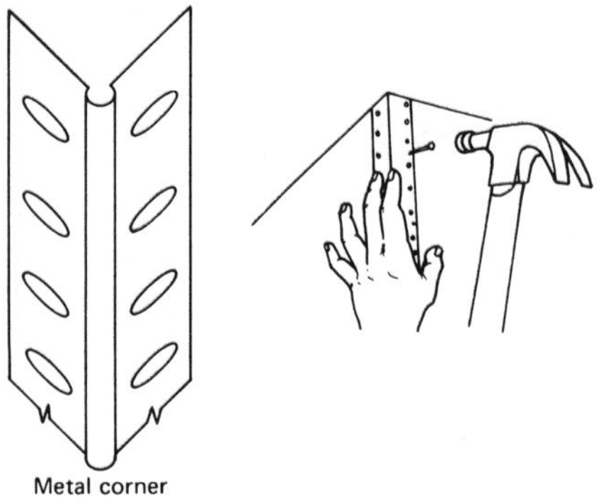

CORNER BEAD

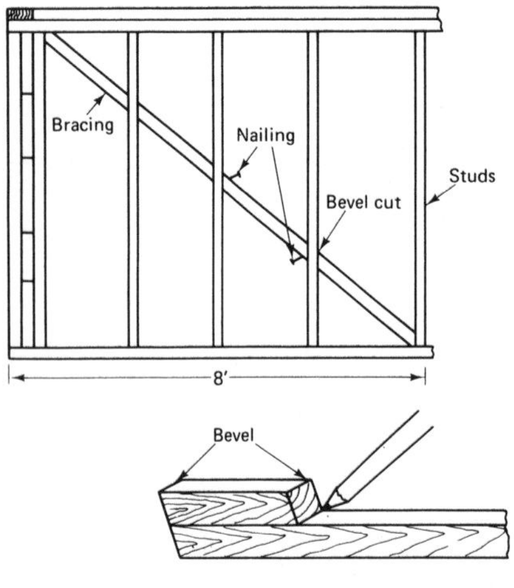

CORNER BRACES

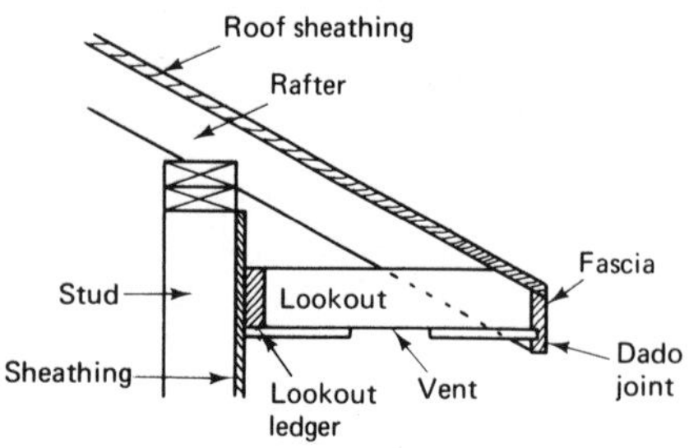

CORNICE

CORN CRIB A building made to store unshelled, undried corn.

CORNER **1.** A location where two or more streets meet. **2.** The acute angle formed by the intersection of walls on a building.

CORNER BEAD A strip of iron with metal lath that is placed in corners before plastering to provide reinforcement.

CORNER BOARDS The boards (trim) covering the external corners of a frame building.

CORNER BRACES Braces nailed diagonally to the studs as reinforcement at corners.

CORNER INFLUENCE An appraisal theory that attributes some portion of the value of a property to the fact that it is a corner location.

CORNER INFLUENCE TABLE A table of factors that supposedly apply to all areas of the country. This table attempts to reflect the additional value accorded to a lot with a corner location. However, experience has shown that, in many areas, corner locations add little or no extra value to a property and may even decrease the value.

CORNER LOT A lot located at the intersection of two or more streets. *See also* Corner and Corner Influence.

CORNICE A molded projection at the top of an interior or exterior wall. The enclosure at the roof eaves or at the rake (side edge) of the roof.

CORPORATION A special entity created by law that is treated as an individual unit with its own rights and liabilities. It is usually owned by stockholders. Its functions and duration of existence are limited by its charter or set forth in its certificate of incorporation.

CORRAL A fenced-in space for horses and cattle.

CORRECTION DEED A deed that rectifies a mistake in a previous deed.

CORRECTION LINE *See* Standard Parallels.

CORRELATION An appraisal term. *See* Reconciliation.

CORRIDOR A long passageway that furnishes access to several rooms.

CORRUGATED SIDING Siding composed of sheet metal or asbestos cement composition board.

CO-SIGNATORY An individual who signs a note or mortgage along with the person who borrows the money and thereby guarantees that the debt will be paid.

COST In appraising, it is the expenditure made to produce the improvements. In general use, it is often synonymous with *price* and *value*. *See also* Reproduction Cost and Replacement Cost.

COST APPROACH TO VALUE One of the three traditional approaches to value used by real estate appraisers. It is based on the theory that the value of a property is the sum of the value of the land plus the reproduction cost of all the improvements, less depreciation from all causes.

COST-BENEFIT RATIO The ratio of the return from an improvement to the cost of the improvement.

COST-BENEFIT STUDY A study made of a proposed development or of an addition or alteration to determine whether the benefits received are sufficient to warrant the cost of the project.

COST ESTIMATING The process of breaking a building down into its components, estimating the value of each component, and adding the results together to obtain an estimated cost of the building.

COST OF LIVING ESCALATION *See* Escalation Clause.

COST OF LIVING INDEX A government estimation of the living cost per average person per month.

COST OF OCCUPANCY *See* Occupancy, Cost of.

COST-PLUS CONTRACT A contract which specifies that the amount to be paid for services received is the provider's actual cost plus an agreed-upon profit.

CO-TENANCY A form of common ownership or possession. It is often a tenancy in common or joint tenancy.

COTSWOLD COTTAGE An English house style first built in the Cotswold Hills of England around 1066. This romantic design became very popular in the United States in the 1920s and 1930s. The Cotswold is the smallest of the English styles. Ground-hugging and asymmetrical, the Cotswold is also characterized by a prominent brick or stone chimney, steep gabled roof, casement windows, and walls built of brick, stone, and timber.

CTS SYSTEM: English
Cotswold Cottage
(Cotscot-201)

Steps of the Cost Approach

1. Estimate the value of the site (land) in its highest and best use as if vacant.
2. Estimate the reproduction cost or replacement cost new of all the improvements (excluding any that were included as part of the site value).
3. Estimate accrued depreciation from all causes.
4. Deduct the total of accrued depreciation (Step 3) from the cost new of the improvements (Step 2) to arrive at a depreciated value of the improvements recognized as the market value.
5. Add the site (land) value (Step 2) to the depreciated value of the improvements (Step 4) to arrive at a market value of the property indicated by the cost approach.

COST APPROACH

COTSWOLD COTTAGE

COTTAGE A small house usually used for vacations. It is often located near a body of water.

COULOMB A measure of electricity equal to a one-second electrical charge in a current having a constant flow of one ampere.

COUNSELING *See* Counselor.

COUNSELOR **1.** A lawyer. **2.** A real estate professional who specializes in giving real estate advice for a fee.

COUNSELOR OF REAL ESTATE (CRE) Designation awarded by the American Society of Real Estate Counselors of the NATIONAL ASSOCIATION OF REALTORS.®

COUNSELOR OF REAL ESTATE
AMERICAN SOCIETY OF REAL ESTATE COUNSELORS

COUNTERFLASHING A piece of sheet metal used to cover flashing to keep water from entering the joints. *See also* Flashing.

COUNTER OFFER A new offer made to counter and cancel an original offer. In real estate, it is often done by the seller, who changes the offer made by the buyer, initials the changes, and sends the altered contract back to the buyer. If the buyer agrees to the changes and initials the contract, he or she has accepted the counter offer.

COUNT PLOTS Sample plots in which trees are recorded by type to find an average tree's truck area per unit of area.

COUNTY A civil division created within a state for political and judicial purposes.

COUNTY HIGHWAY A road that falls under the control of a county and is not a federal or state road.

COUNTY ROAD *See* County Highway.

COURSE **1.** The path of a river or stream. **2.** The direction of a line in relation to true north. **3.** A continuous horizontal layer of tile, brick, shingles, etc.

COURT **1.** An uncovered area, entirely or partially surrounded by walls. **2.** A blind alley. **3.** A courtroom.

COVE **1.** A concave corner or molding. **2.** A small bay.

COVE LIGHTING Lighting that is behind a concave molding near the ceiling.

COVE MOLDING A small, concave, faced molding used to cover a narrow gap or angle.

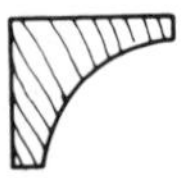

Cove

Cove

COVE MOLDING

COVENANT Popularly, the word *covenant* is synonymous with contract. More specifically, it is a written agreement executed by sealing and delivering. *See also* Restrictive Covenant.

COVENANT OF QUIET ENJOYMENT A special clause in a deed or an agreement whereby the grantor guarantees that the grantee will have the right to a property free from the interference of other parties who may claim an interest in the property.

COVENANTS OF TITLE Guarantees of seisin, quiet enjoyment, and against encumbrances made by a grantor when property is conveyed by a warranty deed.

COVENANTS RUNNING WITH THE LAND *See* Running With The Land.

COVER CROP A crop planted to control wind and water erosion. The crop is later plowed under.

COVERT Undiscovered or hidden (defects).

CRAWL SPACE In basementless houses, the open space between the underside of the floor joists and the ground.

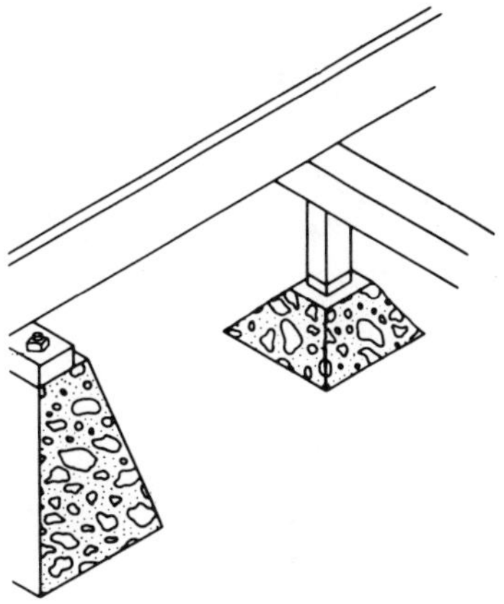

CRAWL SPACE

CREDIT **1.** The ability of a businessperson to borrow money or obtain goods on time. **2.** An accounting term correlative to debt; money receivable.

CREDIT REPORT A record, prepared by a credit reporting organization, of a loan applicant's past capability to pay installment loan payments and other debts.

CREDIT UNION A cooperative organization of workers created for the purpose of lending money to members. Loans made by the credit union are repaid from regular deductions made from the members' pay. Pay is deducted from all members on a regular basis and held in interest-bearing savings accounts like a bank.

CREEK A stream that empties into a bay or river.

CREOLE A house style also known as Louisiana or New Orleans that originated near New Orleans and has French, Spanish, and West Indian influences. The Creole house is distinguished by a balcony with extensive, lacy ironwork. It is a two-to-three-story, symmetrical house. Many were built in the 1700s and 1800s.

CREOLE

CTS SYSTEM: French
Creole or Louisiana or New Orleans
(Creole or Louisia or New Or-304)

CRICKET

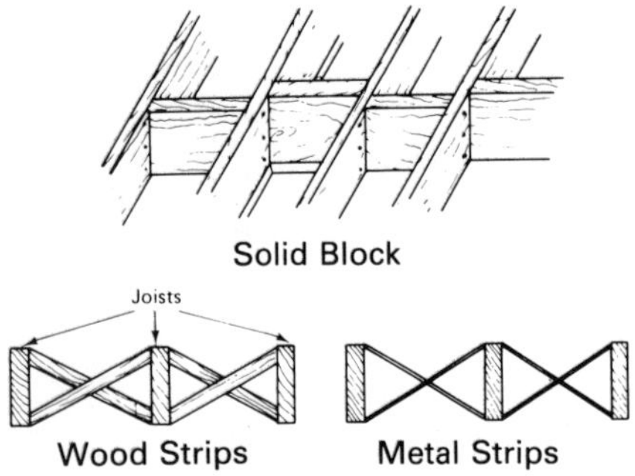

CROSS BRIDGING

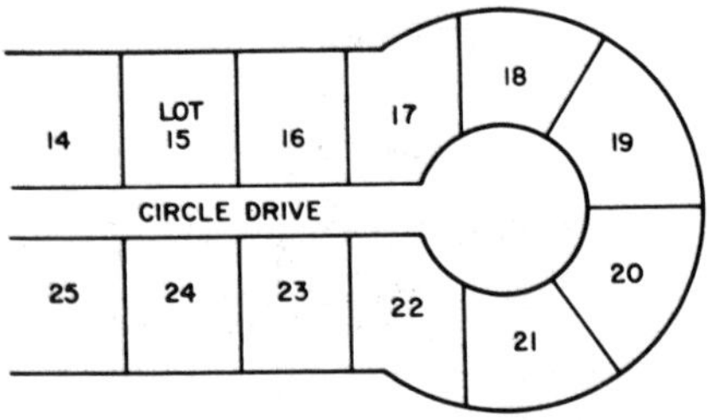

CUL-DE-SAC

CRICKET A small, convex roof projecting from a larger roof. It is used to divert water.

CROP The harvest of a single type of plant during one growing season, for example, the oat crop.

CROSS-BRIDGING Diagonal bracing between joists that gives support and stops the joists from shifting laterally. Cross-bridging is usually made of strips or blocks of wood or metal strips.

CROSS TIE A lightweight brace used between rafters on opposite roof slopes.

CROWN MOLDING A molding that forms the crown on a cornice.

CRUISE A survey made to find and evaluate the standing timber in a given area.

CTS (CLASS, TYPE, STYLE) SYSTEM A uniform method for describing houses developed for the Realtors National Marketing Institute of the NATIONAL ASSOCIATION OF REALTORS® by Henry S. Harrison.

CUBIC CONTENT The number of cubic feet in a building.

CUBIC FOOT COST Cost per cubic foot for construction.

CUBIC FOOT METHOD *See* Comparative Method.

CUL-DE-SAC A deadend street that is at the end to allow cars to make a U turn. *See also* Deadend Street.

CULTURAL FEATURES Man-made changes to land.

CULVERT A structure, such as a drainage ditch, that facilitates drainage.

CUPOLA *See* Belvedere.

CURABLE DEPRECIATION A curable deficiency. The criterion that classifies the deficiency as curable is not whether it is physically possible to cure the deficiency but rather whether it is economically feasible to do so.

CURABLE FUNCTIONAL OBSOLESCENCE Impairments or defects in a property that detract from its value which are economically feasible to correct.

CURB The raised rim of concrete, stone, or wood that edges a sidewalk, street, floor, or well opening.

CURB CUT The portion of a curb that goes down to street level to make the apron of a driveway.

CURB LINE The line that separates the road from the sidewalk.

CURRENT ASSETS An accounting term meaning cash or those things that can be readily converted to cash, such as short-term accounts receivable.

CURRENT LIABILITIES Short-term debts, usually due in a year.

CURTAIN WALL A wall that encloses but does not support.

CURTESY The right that a husband has to his deceased wife's estate under common law.

CURTILAGE The grounds and secondary buildings adjacent to a house, such as a yard or grade.

CURVILINEAR Bounded by curved lines.

CUSTOM BUILDER A builder who constructs for a specific owner to suit the owner's needs instead of building first and then seeking a purchaser.

CUSTOM-BUILT HOUSE A house that is built to the owner's specifications and purchased before construction begins.

CUTS The excavation of land into terraces.

D

DADO **1.** To reinforce by placing in a groove. **2.** To make a groove.

DAM A structure that restricts or prevents water flow.

DAMAGES Payment to a person who suffers a loss or injury. In real estate, it is the sum paid for a portion of property taken in condemnation.

DAMPER A metal plate in a flue that can be adjusted to regulate the draft. It is also a device to control vibrations.

DAMPPROOFING *See* Waterproofing.

DARK STORE CLAUSE A special clause found in shopping center leases that requires the tenant to keep his or her store open for business during specified hours.

DATA PLANT Records and information on real properties kept by appraisers, lenders, etc.

DATE OF APPRAISAL The date to which an appraisal is applicable. It may or may not be the date when a property is inspected for appraisal purposes.

DEAD END STREET A street that is closed at one end and does not have an enlarged space for U turns as a cul-de-sac does.

DEAD LOAD The permanent weight that structural parts of a building must support, such as the weight of the roof and upper floor of the bearing walls. *See also* Load, Live Load, and Total Load.

DEAD RENT A fixed annual rent paid for the use of a mine or quarry, exclusive of royalties.

DEAD STORAGE Storage of cars and other items that are not in active use.

DEALER A person who buys and sells real estate as a business.

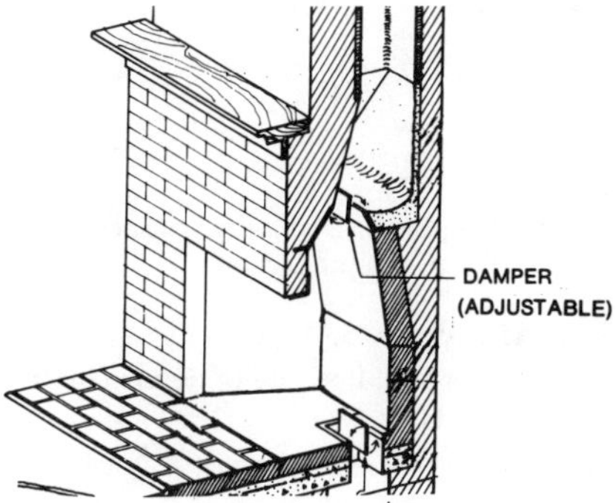

DAMPER

Examples of Declining Balance Depreciation

Building cost new $300,000

Estimated straight line rate of depreciation 5% (20 year life)

Annual dollars of depreciation $15,000

Same building using 125% declining balance:

Depreciation		
	1st Year=	$18,750
	2nd "	17,578
	3rd "	16,749
	4th "	15,449
	5th "	14,484
	10th "	10,489
	20th "	5,501

Same building using 150% declining balance:

Depreciation		
	1st Year	$22,500
	2nd "	20,813
	3rd "	19,252
	4th "	17,807
	5th "	16,472
	10th "	11,154
	20th "	5,115

Same building using 200% declining method:

Depreciation		
	1st Year	$30,000
	2nd "	27,000
	3rd "	24,300
	4th "	21,870
	5th "	19,683
	10th "	11,623
	20th "	4,052

DECLINING BALANCE METHOD

DEBT Money owed that must be repaid, such as a loan.

DEBTOR'S POSITION Also called equity; the part of the market price that exceeds the amount of the mortgage.

DEBT SERVICE **1.** Annual sum to be paid by the mortgagor. **2.** The mortgages or trust deeds on a property.

DECAY-RESISTANT WOOD Wood, such as cedar, redwood, black locust, and walnut, that naturally resists decay.

DECENTRALIZATION Dispersion of people and business from a city or central area to the suburbs.

DECIBEL A unit of measurement for noise.

DECIDUOUS TREES Trees that do not keep their leaves all year long.

DECK Any flat, open surface.

DECKING Light-gauge sheets that are used in the construction of a floor or roof.

DECK PAINT A durable exterior paint.

DECLARATION OF CONDOMINIUM A document required by state statute to be filed as part of the process of establishing a condominium form of ownership for a property. It usually contains a description of the property, a description of the common elements, and designations of the individually owned units.

DECLARATION OF HOMESTEAD *See* Homestead.

DECLINING (DECREASING) ANNUITY An annuity that reduces in benefits over the course of time.

DECLINING BALANCE DEPRECIATION *See* Declining Balance Method.

DECLINING BALANCE METHOD A method of reporting depreciation for income tax purposes that allocates more depreciation to the early years of ownership and less to the later years. A percentage is selected (125, 150, or 200) depending upon the class of property and the current income tax regulations. This percentage is applied to the undepreciated cost of the improvements rather than to the total cost of the improvements (as is allowed by the straight line method).

DECORATE To ornament or increase the beauty of something in a superficial manner.

DEDICATED Property that has been voluntarily donated for public use.

DEDICATION The voluntary donation of a private property for public use.

DEED A legal, written instrument that conveys title to a described real property.

DEED DESCRIPTION A portion of a deed that describes the property being conveyed.

DEED IN FEE A conveyance by fee simple that is good and sufficient and free of all encumbrances.

DEED OF RELEASE An instrument given by a mortgagee whereby the mortgaged property is absolved from the lien of the mortgage. It is usually given when the mortgage is paid off to clear the title.

DEED OF TRUST *See* Trust Deed.

DEED, QUITCLAIM *See* Quitclaim Deed.

DEED RESTRICTIONS Limitations on the use of property that are written in a deed. These restrictions apply even after the property is sold. They may be for a specified period of time or forever. Restrictions that are illegal, such as restrictions against race or religion, are not valid.

DEED, WARRANTY *See* Warranty Deed.

DEFACTO CONTRACT A contract that is created between two parties because of a series of events that actually take place rather than as a result of a written document.

DEFAULT Failure to fulfill a legal obligation.

DEFAULT JUDGMENT A judgment made against a party who does not appear in court at the appropriate time.

DEFEASANCE A condition attached to a deed which, when performed, defeats it.

DEFEASIBLE TITLE Title with a defeasance. *See also* Defeasance.

DEFECTIVE TITLE A title that would be injured should an outstanding claim be verified as valid.

DEFENDANT The person sued in a lawsuit.

DEFERRED LIABILITY A liability that will be created in the future if a specified event takes place. For example, a percentage of the selling price of a property over a specified amount may be due the previous owner according to the provisions of a contract between the current owner and the former owner.

DEFERRED MAINTENANCE Repairs that need to be done

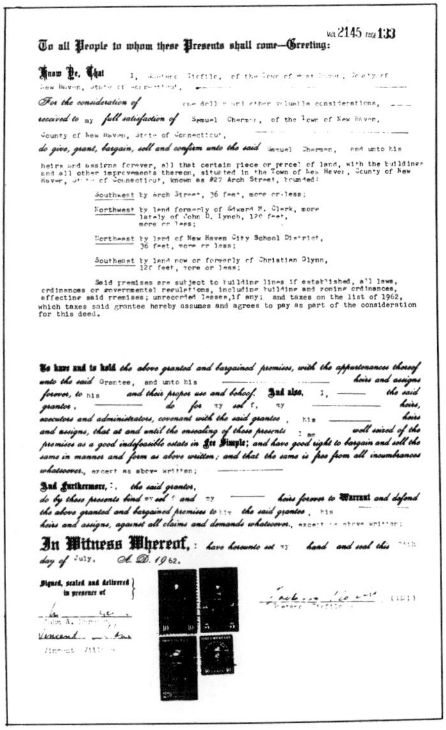

VOL 2145 PAGE 133

To all People to whom these Presents shall come—Greeting:

Know Ye, That I, [illegible] of the Town of [illegible], County of New Haven, State of Connecticut,

For the consideration of one dollar and other valuable considerations, received to my full satisfaction of Samuel Cherman, of the Town of New Haven, County of New Haven, State of Connecticut,

do give, grant, bargain, sell and confirm unto the said Samuel Cherman, and unto his heirs and assigns forever, all that certain piece or parcel of land, with the buildings and all other improvements thereon, situated in the Town of New Haven, County of New Haven, State of Connecticut, known as #27 Arch Street, bounded:

Southwest by Arch Street, 36 feet, more or less;

Northwest by land formerly of Edward M. Clerk, more lately of John D. Lynch, 120 feet, more or less;

Northeast by land of New Haven City School District, 36 feet, more or less;

Southeast by land now or formerly of Christian Glynn, 120 feet, more or less;

Said premises are subject to building lines if established, all laws, ordinances or governmental regulations, including building and zoning ordinances, affecting said premises; unrecorded leases, if any; and taxes on the list of 1962, which taxes said grantee hereby assumes and agrees to pay as part of the consideration for this deed.

To have and to hold the above granted and bargained premises, with the appurtenances thereof unto the said Grantee, and unto his heirs and assigns forever, to his and their proper use and behoof. And also, I, the said grantor, do for my self, my heirs, executors and administrators, covenant with the said grantee, his heirs and assigns, that at and until the ensealing of these presents I am well seized of the premises as a good indefeasible estate in Fee Simple; and have good right to bargain and sell the same in manner and form as above written; and that the same is free from all incumbrances whatsoever, except as above written;

And Furthermore, I, the said grantor, do by these presents bind my self and my heirs forever to Warrant and defend the above granted and bargained premises to him the said grantee, his heirs and assigns, against all claims and demands whatsoever, except as above written;

In Witness Whereof, I have hereunto set my hand and seal this [illegible] day of July, A. D. 1962.

Signed, sealed and delivered in presence of

DEED

Example of Degree Day Calculations for a Month

Day	*Ave Temp*	*Degree Days*
1	40	25
2	36	29
3	30	35
4	50	15
5	45	20
6	30	35
7	18	47
8	19	46
9	12	53
10	15	50
11	18	47
12	32	33
13	40	25
14	50	15
15	55	10
16	58	7
17	56	9
18	60	5
19	40	25
20	32	33
21	28	37
22	17	48
23	10	55
24	9	56
25	−2	67
26	1	64
27	−1	66
28	10	55
29	18	47
30	29	36
Total degree days in the month		1095

DEGREE DAY

to rehabilitate a property but which have not yet been done.

DEFERRED PAYMENTS Payments to commence at a future time.

DEFICIENCY The part of a mortgage debt that is not recovered by the sale of the mortgaged property.

DEFICIENCY JUDGMENT The judgment for the portion of a debt a borrower is responsible for if a foreclosure sale does not recover all the money due for the foreclosure mortgage.

DEFICIT A falling short in necessary funds.

DEFINITIVE LOAN A loan that is secured by a long-term lease. This loan is commonly used in renewal projects which have the participation of the federal government.

DEFLATION A lessening in money supply; a price drop; the opposite of inflation.

DEGREE DAY A system used to estimate fuel consumption. It is based on the number of days the temperature is below 65° Fahrenheit. If the average temperature is 40° for a day, then 25° days are accummulated.

DELIVERY The transfer of a deed from buyer to seller so that the seller cannot recall his or her deed.

DEMAND **1.** The quantity of goods or services that will be bought at a specific price at a specific time. **2.** A note from a lender stating the amount owed to pay off a trust deed or mortgage.

DEMAND MORTGAGE A note that is repayable on the demand of the holder.

DEMINIMIS PUD A term used by the Federal Home Loan Mortgage Corporation to describe a PUD in which the common property has a relatively insignificant influence upon the enjoyment of the premises or has little or no effect upon the value of the property. *See also* Planned Unit Development.

DEMISE A transfer of estate or interest to another for years, life, or at will.

DEMOGRAPHIC Relating to a population structure.

DEMOGRAPHIC CHARACTERISTICS Economic, social, and political characteristics of a population of people.

DEN A "family" room where one can work, study, or play.

DENSITY **1.** The number of houses, people, etc., per square mile. **2.** Thickness.

DENSITY ZONING A zoning system under which occupancy is restricted by the number of families per plot rather than the number of families per building.

DENTIL Alternate square blocks and blank spaces on a cornice that give the appearance of teeth.

DEPLETION A decrease in the value of an asset due to exhaustion of resources, such as the taking of oil from a well.

DEPLETION RATE The percentage of a wasting asset that is used up (mined, cut, or drilled, etc.) yearly. For income tax purposes, it is a deduction similar to depreciation.

DEPOSIT **1.** Also called earnest money. A deposit is given by the potential purchaser along with an offer to buy. **2.** A natural collection of oil, gold, silver, etc.

DEPOSIT EARNEST MONEY *See* Deposit (1).

DEPOSIT RECEIPT A simple form of contract used to make an offer to buy real estate in some areas. In addition to being a receipt for the deposit, it also states the amount being offered and other conditions of the offer.

DEPOT **1.** A bus or railroad station. **2.** A storage area for goods.

DEPRECIABLE LIFE The duration of time over which an asset may be depreciated. The longer the period of time, the lower the rate of depreciation is.

DEPRECIABLE PROPERTY A real property which has a determinable lifespan that can be measured for depreciation.

DEPRECIATED COST Cost new of a property less accrued depreciation from all causes.

DEPRECIATION The difference between the reproduction cost of improvements and their value. It is the loss in value suffered by improvements to property and personal property caused by physical deterioration, functional obsolescence, and economic obsolescense. Income tax regulations specify a variety of ways to estimate depreciation. Appraisers tend to use still different methods when they use the cost approach.

DEPRECIATION ACCRUED The amount of depreciation in a specific property at a specific date.

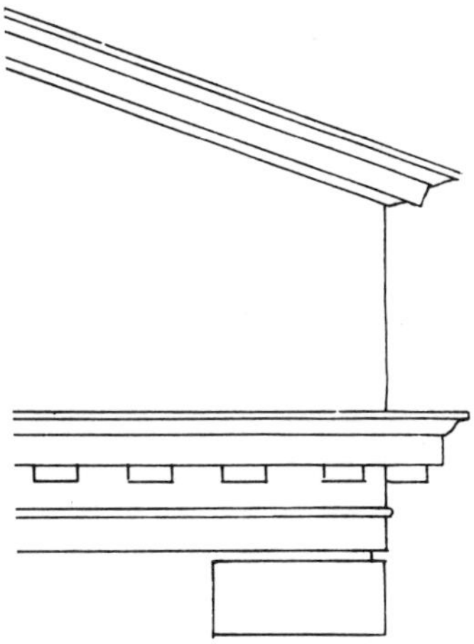

DENTILS

Provisions Typically Found in a Deposit Receipt

- Amount of down payment
- Subject to first loan (mortgage or deed of trust)
  - of a specified amount
  - at a specified interest rate
  - for a specified term with specified points and fees
- Subject to seller financing (loan, second mortgage or deed of trust)
  - of a specified amount
  - at a specified interest rate
  - for a specified term (or upon sale of the property)
- Requirement that seller deliver leases and rental agreements
- Subject to a pest control inspection report
- Personal property included
- When seller takes possession

DEPOSIT RECEIPT

Example of the Sum of the Years Digits Method of Depreciation

Property with a 10 Year Life

Building cost new	$425,000
Estimated straight line rate of depreciation	10%
Annual dollars of straight line depreciation	$ 42,500

Same building using the sum of the years digits method of depreciation:

Formula for 1st Year

$\frac{10}{10+9+8+7+6+5+4+3+2+1} = \frac{10}{55} = .182 =$

$18.2\% \times 425{,}000 = \$77{,}350$ depreciation

Formula for 2nd Year

$\frac{9}{55} = .164 = 16.4\%$

$16.4\% \times 425{,}000 = \$69{,}700$

Formula for 3rd Year

$\frac{8}{55} = .145 = 14.5\%$

$\$425{,}000 \times 14.5\% = \$61{,}625$ depreciation

Formula for 4th Year

$\frac{7}{55} = .127 = 12.7\%$

$\$425{,}000 \times 12.7\% = \$53{,}975$ depreciation

Formula for 5th Year

$\frac{6}{55} = .11 = 11\%$

$\$425{,}000 \times 11\% = \$46{,}750$ depreciation

Formula for 6th Year

$\frac{5}{55} = .091 = 9.1\%$

$\$425{,}000 \times 9.1\% = \$38{,}675$ depreciation

Formula for 7th Year

$\frac{4}{55} = .073 = 7.3\%$

$\$425{,}000 \times 7.3\% = \$31{,}025$ depreciation

Formula for 8th Year

$\frac{3}{55} = .055 = 5.5\%$

$\$425{,}000 \times 5.5\% = \$19{,}125$ depreciation

Formula for 9th Year

$\frac{2}{55} = .037 = 3.7\%$

$\$425{,}000 \times 3.7\% = \$15{,}725$ depreciation

Formula for 10th Year

$\frac{1}{55} = .018 = 1.8\%$

$\$425{,}000 \times 1.8\% = \$7{,}650$ depreciation

DEPRECIATION ALLOWANCE The sum to be claimed or permitted for depreciation.

DEPRECIATION BASE The value of an asset that is to be depreciated. It is usually the original cost of the improvements plus the cost of all of the additions. It may also be the acquisition cost of used improvements to the current owner.

DEPRECIATION, DECLINING BALANCE *See* Declining Balance Method.

DEPRECIATION METHODS The various methods of depreciation that are specified in the Internal Revenue Code for income tax purposes. For real estate, there are currently two methods: straight line and accelerated. Both systems are based on the estimated useful life of the items being depreciated.

DEPRECIATION RATE The rate or percentage at which a property depreciates (is used up).

DEPRECIATION, STRAIGHT LINE This method of depreciation is based on estimating the useful life of the asset being depreciated and determining the rate of depreciation by dividing the amount of depreciation to be taken into equal parts to be taken over the estimated useful life.

DEPRECIATION, SUM OF THE YEAR'S DIGITS An accelerated depreciation method allowed by the Internal Revenue Service Code for income tax purposes. It is calculated by making a fraction whose numerator is year's digits in inverse order and whose denominator is the sum of the years. For example, if a property has an estimated useful life of 7 years, the denominator is the sum of 1+2+3+4+5+6+7 or 28. The numerator will be 7 for the first year, 6 for the second year, etc. In the first year, the fraction would be 7/28 or 25 percent depreciation. For the second year, the fraction would be 6/28 or 21.4 percent depreciation.

DEPRESSION The low point of a business and economic cycle where unemployment skyrockets and production, prices, and demand are low.

DEPTH FACTOR The decrease in the value of a lot as the depth decreases. It is usually a modification of the 4-3-2-1 rule wherein the first quarter of the depth of a lot is worth 40 percent of the total, the second quarter 30 percent, the third 20 percent, and the last 10 percent.

DEPTH INFLUENCE The effect that a deviation from the standard lot depth has on a property value.

DEPTH TABLE A statistical table which uses the theory that added depth increases the value of land by a standard amount that can be expressed as a standard factor per foot of extra depth.

DESCENT To pass real estate title by succession or to pass title without a will.

DESCRIPTION *See* Legal Description.

DESIGN A plan of a building showing all facets of the building's appearance and purpose.

DESIST AND REFRAIN ORDER In certain states, an order by the real estate commissioner to stop a procedure that is in breach of the real estate law.

DETACHED GARAGE A garage that is not directly attached to a house.

DETERIORATION A gradual worsening in the condition of a property through wear and tear, the elements, and disintegration. It is a cause of depreciation.

DETERMINABLE FEE A fee is an estate that can last forever. A determinable fee may possibly end upon the happening of a certain event.

DEVELOPER Someone who readies raw land for construction and then either sells it to a builder or acts as a builder and proceeds to construct improvements on the property.

DEVELOPMENT A preplanned construction project where the buildings are usually related in some way.

DEVELOPMENT COST *See* Off-site Improvements.

DEVELOPMENT LOAN A loan to buy land or make site improvements. It is usually a short-term loan that is replaced by construction financing and eventually by a permanent mortgage.

DEVELOPMENT METHOD An appraisal technique for estimating the value of land. The value of the completely developed site is estimated first. Next, all the costs of development are estimated and subtracted from the value of the completed development. The result is the value of the land.

DEVEST (DIVEST) To take a right, estate, or interest away from somebody.

DEVISE
DEVISEE
DEVISOR

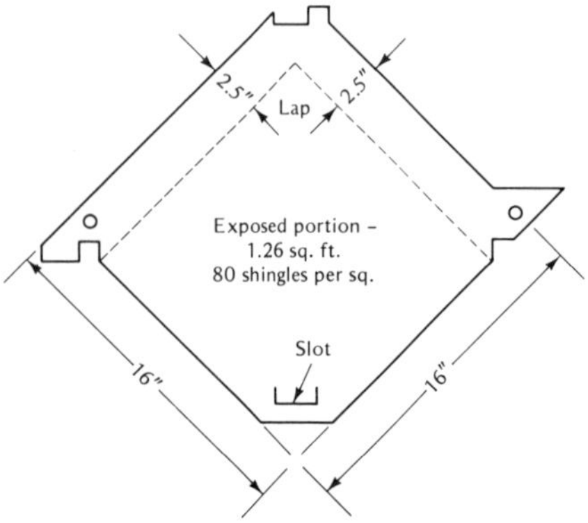

DIAMOND SHINGLES

DEVISE Real property given by last will and testament.

DEVISEE Someone to whom land is left in a will.

DEVISOR Someone who leaves real estate by will.

DIAMOND SHINGLES A type of shingle designed especially to reduce the required amount of overlap, thereby saving materials.

DIKE **1.** A water channel. **2.** A levee.

DILUVIUM A deposit of soil created by a flood or glacier.

DIMENSION LUMBER Lumber cut to a specified size and stocked by lumberyards for the building industry. Sizes range from 2 to 5 inches thick and 5 to 12 inches wide.

DIMENSION SHINGLES Uniformly sized shingles.

DIMINISHED ASSETS *See* Wasting Assets.

DIMINISHED UTILITY *See* Accrued Depreciation.

DIMMER SWITCHES Switches used to vary light intensity.

DINING ROOM A room, separate from the kitchen, used primarily for the serving of meals.

DIRECT CAPITALIZATION An appraisal technique whereby a capitalization rate is developed by abstracting it from the market. Sales are analyzed, and the sale price is divided into the net operating income (NOI) to produce a capitalization rate. This rate can then be divided into the NOI of properties being appraised to give an indication of their value via the income approach.

DIRECT COSTS One of the classes of costs of a real estate development or project. It consists of the cost of labor and material. The cost of acquiring the site is also considered a direct cost.

DIRECTIONAL GROWTH The direction in which an urban area is predicted to expand.

DIRECT LABOR Labor costs related to a specific building project. This is not to be confused with indirect labor—overhead and management.

DIRECT REDUCTION MORTGAGE A mortgage that is to be paid by amortization. It consists of periodic, usually monthly, payments in fixed amounts plus interest on the unpaid balance.

DIRECT SALES COMPARISON APPROACH *See* Market Data Approach.

DIRECT STEAM SYSTEM A radiator system where the radiators are heated by steam or vapor piped from a steam boiler.

DIRT TANK A small water supply built with an earth-filled dam that collects natural run-off to furnish livestock with water.

DISCLAIMER **1.** A denial and renunciation of an interest or estate. **2.** A written statement that tries to deny liability should certain information prove false.

DISCOUNT **1.** To sell something at a reduced price. **2.** To reduce the proceeds of a loan to a borrower and thereby increase the effective interest yield to the lender. **3.** The process whereby a lender sells a mortgage at less than its face value in the secondary mortgage market in order to increase the yield.

DISCOUNTED CASH FLOW An appraisal technique that analyzes an income property by discounting the future cash flow using a rate of return the appraiser estimates is required to attract an investor to the type of investment being appraised.

DISCOUNTED RATE OF RETURN A rate of return (annual) that is required to attract investment capital to a particular investment. It varies with the risks, lack of liquidity, and amount of management required by the investment.

DISCOUNT HOUSE A store that sells merchandise at a price lower than regular retail stores.

DISCOUNTING **1.** Selling a mortgage or note to a third party at less than its face value. **2.** Giving a borrower less than the face value of the note or mortgage.

DISCOUNT POINT A one-percent discount.

DISCOUNT RATE The relationship between dollars loaned by a lender and dollars that the borrower repays. It is calculated by dividing the difference between the amount borrowed and the amount to be back by the amount to be paid back.

DISHWASHER An electric household appliance that washes dishes.

DISINTERMEDIATION When investors remove their money

Examples of How a Discount Rate is Calculated

Example 1

Loan Amount	\$10,000.
Amount Received by Borrower	\$ 9,500.
Discount	\$ 500.
Amount to Be Paid Back	\$10,000.

Discount Rate:

$$\frac{\$500.}{\$10{,}000.} = 5\%$$

Example 2

Loan Amount	\$30,000.
Amount Received by Borrower	\$24,000.
Discount	\$ 6,000.
Amount to Be Paid Back	\$30,000.

Discount Rate:

$$\frac{\$6{,}000.}{\$30{,}000.} = 20\%$$

DISCOUNT RATE

from thrift institutions to reinvest where the rates of return are thought to be higher.

DISPERSION **1.** The spread of building and other improvements from a central point on the property. **2.** A statistical term expressing the degree of scatter of data, usually around the median or mean.

DISPOSABLE INCOME Household money left after taxes; spendable income.

DISPOSAL FIELD A drainage area made of clay tiles and gravel used to filter and disperse waste from septic tanks.

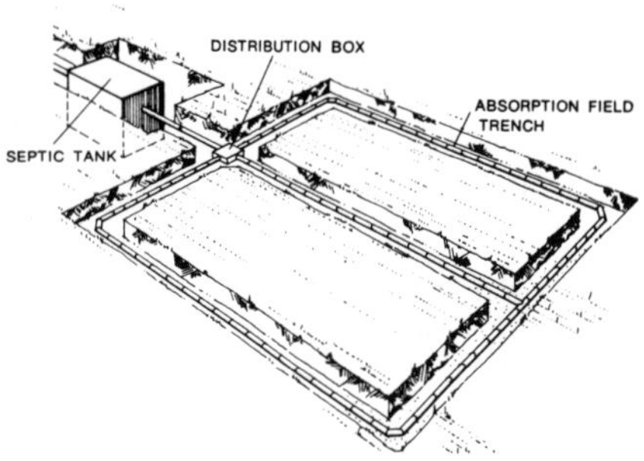

DISPOSAL FIELD

DISPOSITION A relinquishment or alienation of property.

DISPOSSESS To take away someone's real estate possessions.

DISSEISIN The incorrect and wrongful dispossession of someone who actually has rightful possession of a property.

DISSOLUTION Termination of a contract, bond, or business association.

DISTRAIN The collection of rent, on the premises, by the landlord.

DISTRESS PROPERTY **1.** Property that is producing income insufficient to pay the expenses of ownership. **2.** Property in the process of being constructed, where the cost of construction exceeds the projections to such an extent that there are insufficient funds available to complete the project.

DISTRESS SALE When a seller sells a property under great pressure to sell. Usually, the property is bought for less than market value.

DISTRIBUTED LOAD A load that is evenly distributed and measured in tons (or pounds) per square foot.

DISTRIBUTION METHOD A method used by appraisers to estimate the value of a property. Some system is used to divide the total price of the property between the land and the improvements. If the value of the land is to be abstracted, the value of the improvements is estimated and subtracted from the whole value to give the land value.

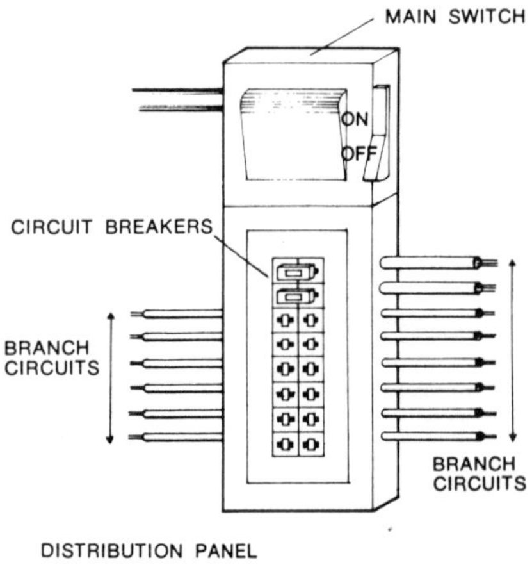

DISTRIBUTION PANEL BOX

DISTRIBUTION PANEL BOX In an electrical system, a metal box containing the fuses (fuse box) or circuit breakers. It is used to divide a supply line into branch circuits. In a septic system, it is an underground box that divides the waste flowing from the septic tank and distributes it to the laterals leading to the disposal field. *See also* Fuse Box.

DISTRIBUTION TILE The concrete or clay tile used for drainage in a disposal field.

DITCH A natural or man-made drain or excavation.

DIVERSIFIED FARMING Farming where income is derived from several sources.

DIVERTER A device that keeps water from roofs from flowing onto uncovered steps or platforms.

DIVIDED INTEREST An interest in some part of a whole property.

DIVIDED RATE *See* Split Rate.

DIVIDEND **1.** A word synonymous in appraising with *net operating income*. *See* Net Operating Income. **2.** Money divided among shareholders.

DIVIDEND YIELD The ratio of cash flow to cash invested expressed in a percentage.

DIVISION WALL **1.** A wall that is shared by two buildings but which does not belong to either. **2.** A load-bearing interior wall.

DOCK **1.** A loading platform for ships, railroad cars, or trucks. **2.** A landing pier for boats and ships. **3.** The portion of a courtroom where a prisoner is held.

DOCUMENT *See* Instrument.

DOME A roof in the shape of an upside-down bowl.

DOMESTIC HOT WATER SYSTEM A mechanical system designed to produce hot water for household purposes.

DOMICILE **1.** A legal term meaning someone's permanent home where, if he or she leaves it, he or she intends to return. **2.** The country where a corporation is chartered.

DOMINANT TENEMENT A parcel of land that benefits from an easement over another property.

DOOR A sliding or hinged structure, usually constructed of wood, glass, or metal, that serves as an entrance or exit or covering to a cupboard.

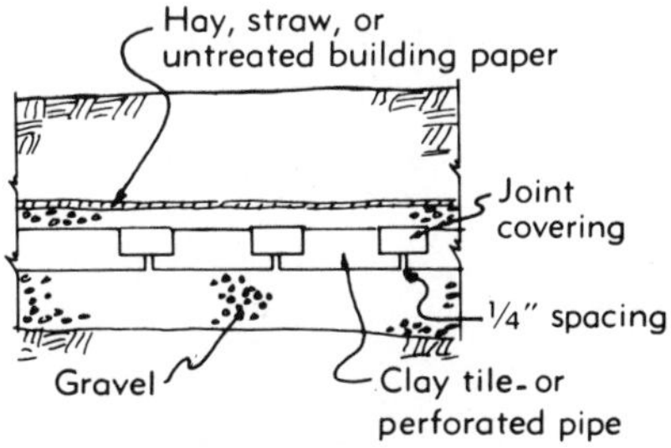

DISTRIBUTION TILE

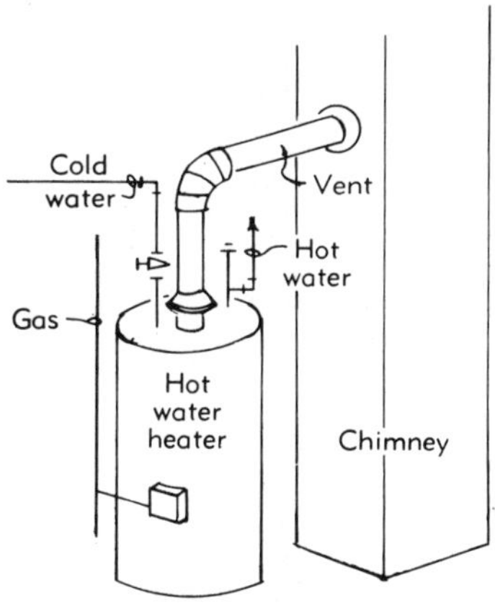

DOMESTIC HOT WATER SYSTEM

DOOR

Example of the Double Declining Balance Method of Depreciation

$\frac{100\%}{15 \text{ years}} =$ 06.66% per year, straight line

.0666% × 2 = 13.33% double declining method applied on to undepreciated balance

Value of building new = $300,000

1st Year

$300,000 × .1333 = $40,000 depreciation
$300,000 − $40,000 = $260,000 balance

2nd Year

$260,000 × .1333 = $34,667 depreciation
$225,333 − $34,667 = $190,666 balance

Year	*Depreciation*	*Balance*
3	$25,416	$166,250
4	22,161	144,089
5	19,211	124,878
6	16,646	108,232
7	14,431	93,801
8	12,506	81,295
10	10,836	70,459
11	9,392	61,067
12	8,142	52,925
13	7,056	45,869
14	6,117	39,752
15	5,300	34,452

DOUBLE-DECLINING BALANCE METHOD OF DEPRECIATION

DOUBLE-HUNG WINDOW

DOORBELL A mechanical or electrical device used to permit guests to make their presence known by activating an audible signal.

DOOR BUCK A wood or metal subframe set in a wall. The finished door frame is attached to it. *See also* Door Jamb.

DOOR JAMB The vertical pieces surrounding a door opening.

DOOR SCHEDULES Plans, usually on blueprints, that list all the door requirements of a building.

DOOR SILL The framing member at the bottom of a door opening that serves as a threshold.

DOOR STOP A device attached to the wall or floor to prevent a door from opening too far and damaging the wall.

DORMER A projection built out from the slope of a roof. It is used to house windows on the upper floor and to provide additional headroom. Common types are the gable dormer and the shed dormer.

DORMER WINDOW A vertical window in small gable that projects from a sloping roof.

DOUBLE COURSES A double layer of shingles or similar material.

DOUBLE-DECLINING BALANCE METHOD OF DEPRECIATION A form of accelerated depreciation also known as the 200 percent declining balance method. The rate is equal to double the straight line depreciation, but unlike straight line depreciation, it is not applied to the original cost or acquisition cost. It is applied to the declining balance (i.e., cost less accumulated depreciation for prior tax years).

DOUBLE FLOOR A wooden floor and subfloor.

DOUBLE FRAMING A way of increasing strength by doubling the usual number of framing members.

DOUBLE GLAZING *See* Thermal Window.

DOUBLE-HUNG WINDOW A window with two sashes that move up and down independently in tracks.

DOUBLE-PITCH ROOF A roof that comes to a peak at the center and slopes away in two successive planes.

DOUBLE-STRENGTH GLASS A thickness of glass between

.118 inches and .113 inches that is fit for most regular window glass use.

DOUBLE TAXATION A situation where income tax is first paid by a corporation. Then, when the remaining income is distributed to the stockholders (usually by dividends), the individuals receiving the income are taxed again at their own personal income tax rate.

DOUBLING UP When two or more families occupy one housing unit.

DOVETAIL A projecting end of a piece that has a fan or dovetailed shape.

DOWEL A pin of wood or metal used to hold or strengthen two pieces of wood where they join.

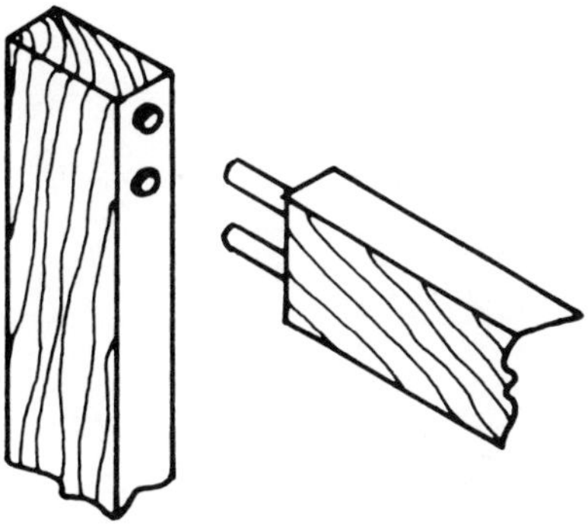

DOWEL

DOWER The legal rights that a widow has to her husband's estate.

DOWN PAYMENT A portion of the sales price to be paid by the purchaser from his or her own funds and not from any financing he or she may have received.

DOWNSPOUT A pipe used for carrying rainwater from the roof of a house to the ground or into a dry well or sewer connection.

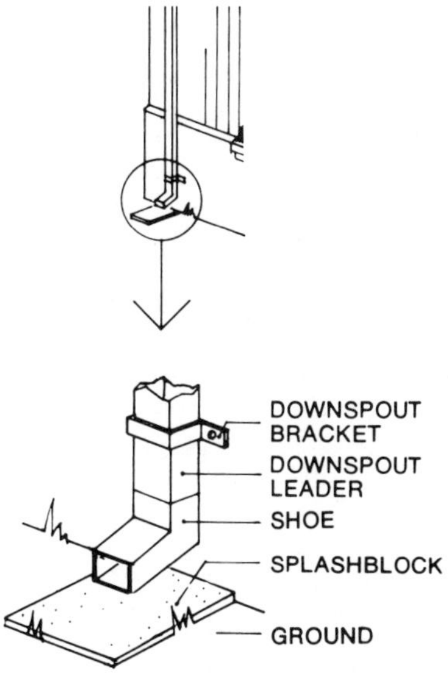

DOWNSPOUT

DOWNTOWN The central business area in a small city or town. In a bigger city, it is a business area separate from midtown or uptown.

DOWNZONING A change in zoning made by local government that lowers the classification an area previously held, such as decreasing the allowable density to fewer housing units or fewer stores and shops.

DRAFT CURTAINS A non-combustible partition hung tightly against a roof to help prevent the spread of fire by directing heat and smoke toward vents.

DRAGNET CLAUSE A mortgage clause which makes the real estate a security for any debt that the mortgagor might already have or will make in the future with the mortgagee.

DRAINAGE A system that removes surface water through tiles and pipes.

DRAINAGE DISTRICT A geographic area where the local government controls the construction and operation of the drainage systems.

DRAINAGE DITCH *See* Ditch.

DRAINAGE EASEMENT *See* Drainage Right of Way.

DRAINAGE RIGHT OF WAY The right of an owner to let surface water flow over one or more adjacent owners' properties.

DRAIN FIELD *See* Absorption Field.

DRAINS A pipe, channel, or conduit that carries away waste or water.

DRAIN TILE Hollow tile used to drain water-saturated soil or disperse liquid into the ground, as in an absorption field.

DREDGE **1.** A machine that removes soil and rock from under water. **2.** To excavate by using a dredge.

DRESS To complete or decorate.

DRESSED AND MATCHED Lumber which has been planed until it is smooth and cut so that the tongue of one piece fits into the groove of another.

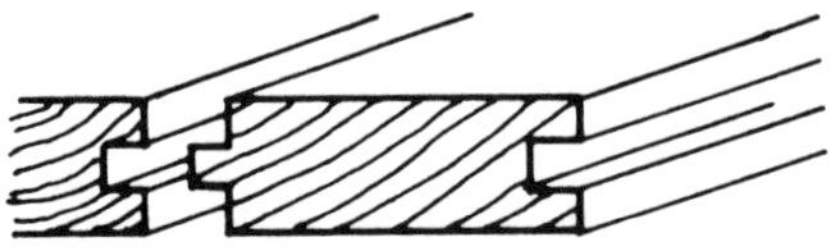

DRESSED AND MATCHED

DRESSED LUMBER Lumber that has been machined and surfaced at the lumber mill.

DRESSING ROOM A small room off a bedroom that is used especially for dressing.

DRILL TRACK A section of railroad track that connects the main track with a spur track that leads onto private property. Spur tracks are usually privately owned and are individually used. The drill track is often owned by the railroad or by a group of spur track owners.

DRIP A piece of molding placed at the edge of a door or window to divert water away from the opening so it will fall free to the ground.

DRIP CAP A projection from the vertical face of an exterior wall used to make rainwater drip from the outer edge of the wall rather than run down the wall face.

DRIVEWAY A small, private roadway that serves as an access from a public street to a garage, carport, etc.

DROP PANEL The thickened part of a concrete slab that surrounds a column or bracket.

DROPS *See* Carved Drop.

DROP SIDING A type of tongue-and-grooved exterior board siding.

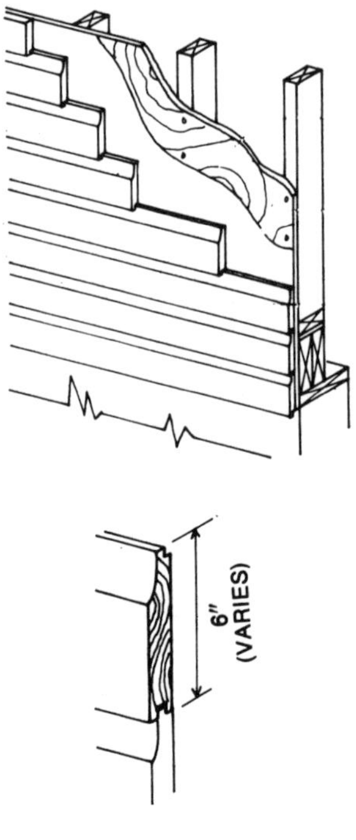

DROP SIDING

DROUGHT Lack of water over an extended period of time that causes crop or other damage.

DRYER A device used to dehydrate farm crops before storage.

DRY FARMING A special kind of farming used in dry areas where no irrigation is available. A fine surface mulch is maintained, which protects the natural moisture of the soil from evaporation.

DRY ROT Decay of seasoned wood; caused by fungus.

DRYWALL **1.** A masonry wall put up without mortar. **2.** An interior wall finished with something other than plaster. It is commonly used to refer to a gypsum board wall.

DRYWALL CONSTRUCTION Interior wall construction that uses wallboard, plywood, and other sheet materials instead of wet plaster.

DRY WELL A hole in the ground lined with stone used to disburse waste or rainwater into the ground.

DUAL AGENCY A situation where the broker or salesperson represents both parties to a transaction and receives compensation from both parties. In some states, it is illegal. It is usually a bad practice even when permitted by law or by the NAR code of ethics.

DUCTS In construction, these are pipes of metal, plastic, or other material used for distributing or collecting air.

DUE-ON-SALE CLAUSE *See* Alienation Clause.

DUPLEX A building having two dwelling units either side by side, with a common wall and roof, or one above the other. Usually, there is a separate entrance for each family.

DUPLEX OUTLET An electrical outlet that can receive two plugs. It is the most common type of outlet used.

DUPLEX RECEPTACLE *See* Duplex Outlet.

DURABLE CAPITAL GOODS Long-lasting goods that can be used again and again, like office machinery. They should be distinguished from raw materials.

DURABLE GOODS Durable consumer goods, such as a stove or refrigerator, to be distinguished from perishable items, such as milk or paper towels.

DURESS Unlawful pressure to coerce someone to do something against his or her will.

DUTCH COLONIAL STYLE A colonial American house style that originated in Pennsylvania and not in Hol-

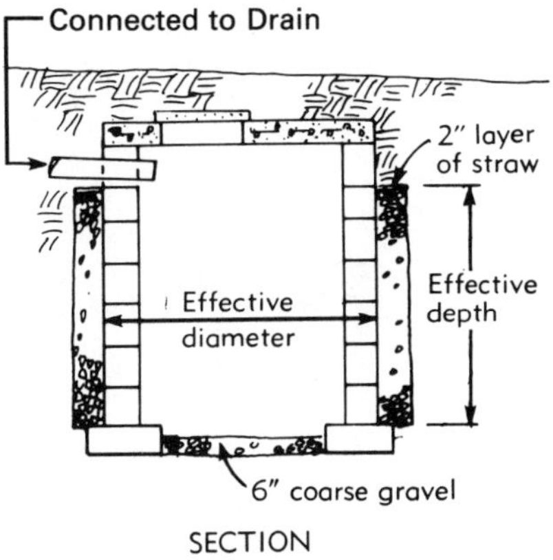

DRY WELL

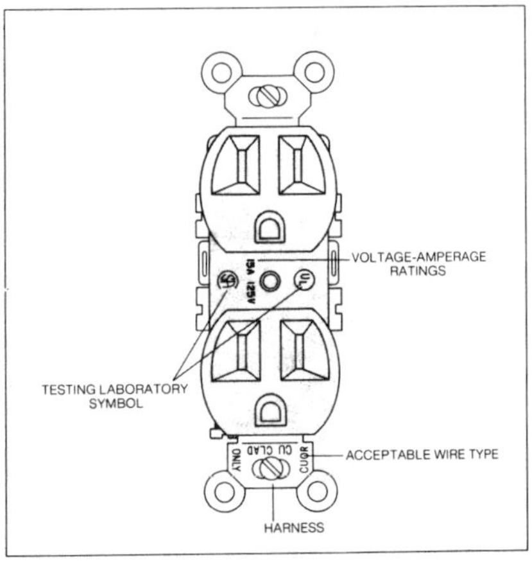

DUPLEX OUTLET

DUTCH COLONIAL STYLE

land as popularly believed. Built by Dutch settlers, the Dutch Colonial is a two- to-two-and-one-half-story house characterized by a gambrel roof, an off-center chimney, and eaves that flare outward.

CTS SYSTEM: Colonial American
Dutch Colonial
(Dutch Co-108)

DUTCH DOOR

DUTCH DOOR A door that is divided horizontally in the middle so the halves may be opened and closed independently or together.

DUTCHMAN A small wedge or piece used to stop up an opening or cover a defect.

DWELLING A building designed or used as living quarters for one or more families.

DWELLING, DETACHED A living unit that is completely surrounded by open space.

DWELLING, DUPLEX *See* Duplex

DWELLING, END-ROW *See* Dwelling, Semi-detached.

DWELLING, ROW A living unit, the walls on two opposite sides of which are party or common walls. Configurations, such as quadruplexes and triplexes, containing living units with two party or common walls not necessarily opposite to each other may be considered row or end-row houses. (See Party Wall)

DWELLING, SEMI-DETACHED A living unit of which one side wall is a party or common wall.

DWELLING UNIT (DWELLING HOUSE) The area (apartment or building) occupied by a person as a place of residence.

E

EARLY GEORGIAN STYLE An architectural style, also called Williamsburg Georgian, based on the styles developed in England during the reign of the four Georges. The houses built in Williamsburg were representative of the Georgian Houses built in America throughout the early 1700s. These two- to-three-story, rectangular houses have simple exterior lines and are characterized by two large chimneys, sliding double-hung windows, and simple front entrances.

CTS SYSTEM: English
Williamsburg Georgian or
Early Georgian
(Williams or E Georg-204)

EARLY GEORGIAN STYLE

EARLY GOTHIC REVIVAL STYLE A house style characterized by pointed arches and doors and windows in the same shape. Gothic houses are asymmetrical and are usually made in one color and of one material (most commonly wood). The house has a "fragile" appearance because of the use of tracery, pinnacles, and molding. In Europe, Gothic architecture was widely used from the twelfth to the fifteenth centuries. It was copied in the U.S. in the 1700s and 1800s.

CTS SYSTEM: Nineteenth Century American
Early Gothic Revival
(E Goth-701)

EARLY GOTHIC REVIVAL STYLE

EARNEST MONEY Money paid in advance to demonstrate good faith when an offer to buy is submitted to a property owner by a prospective purchaser.

EARNINGS Money earned from labor or personal services rather than money received as return on capital.

EARTHQUAKES A series of tremors and waves in the earth's crust.

EASEMENT A liberty, privilege, or right that one has to use land for a specific purpose distinct from ownership of the soil, such as the right to cross X to get to Y.

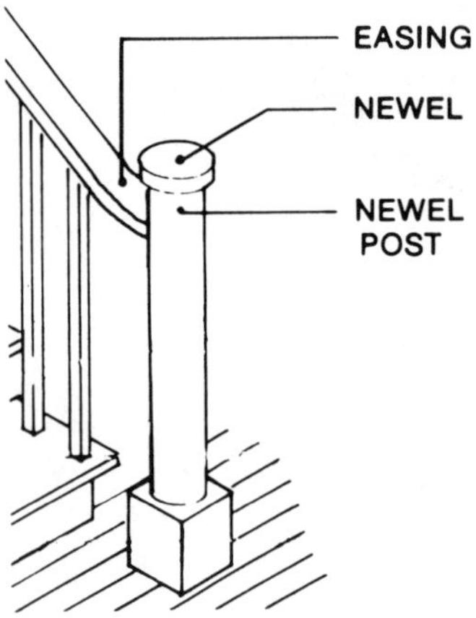

EASING

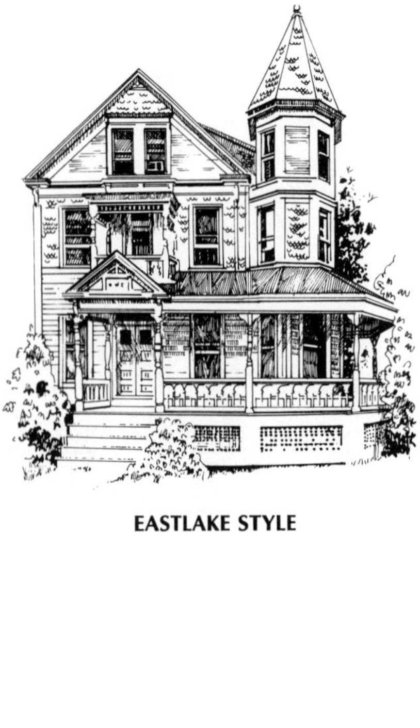

EASTLAKE STYLE

EASING The part of a handrail that curves parallel to the floor.

EASTERN TOWNHOUSE *See* Brownstone.

EASTLAKE STYLE A nineteenth-century American house (and furniture) style that became popular in the late 1800s when a book, *Hints On Household Taste,* by English architect Charles Lock Eastlake, was published in the United States. The designs in the book became the basis of Eastlake style furniture and houses. The Eastlake house is very similar to a Queen Anne but is characterized by three-dimensional ornamentation, with some of the decorating resembling furniture legs and knobs. Eastlake houses have rectangular shapes, open front porches, towers, and gable roofs.

CTS SYSTEM: Nineteenth Century American
Eastlake
(East L-709)

EAVE FLASHING Metal strips attached to eaves and gutters to prevent water absorption and provide drainage.

EAVES The lowest projecting part of the roof.

EAVESTROUGH, GUTTER A channel of wood or metal on or at the edge of the roof to carry off water from rain and melting snow.

EAVE VENT A vent located under the eaves of a house.

ECOLOGY The science of the relationship between living things and their environment.

ECONOMIC APPROACH *See* Income Approach.

ECONOMIC BASE The major economic activities of a community that provide its support by bringing in funds from outside the community.

ECONOMIC BASE ANALYSIS A technique for the analysis of the major economic supports of a community. It is used as a means of predicting income and population or other variables that affect real estate value.

ECONOMIC FEASIBILITY A study of the projected income and expenses of a project to determine whether the project warrants the proposed cost to develop it.

ECONOMIC LIFE The length of time improvements can be profitably utilized. It is the length of time the improvements contribute value to the property. When the improvements no longer contribute any value, they have reached the end of their economic life.

ECONOMIC OBSOLESCENCE A decrease in desirability or value resulting from economic forces off the property, such as a change in zoning, in traffic patterns, or in supply/demand relationships. Loss in value from economic obsolescence is to be distinguished from functional obsolescence and physical deterioration, which are caused by things on the property.

ECONOMIC RENT The rent that a property would command on the market at any given time, if it were vacant and available for lease, even though actual rent may be different.

EFFECTIVE AGE The age an improvement appears to be, as compared to other improvements in the market, considering its condition and design. The effective age is often different from the actual age.

EFFECTIVE DEMAND The desire to purchase combined with the ability to pay.

EFFECTIVE GROSS INCOME The total estimated potential income produced by a property including rents and all miscellaneous income less an allowance for the income that will not be collected because of vacancies and collection losses.

EFFECTIVE GROSS REVENUE *See* Effective Gross Income.

EFFECTIVE RATE The actual rate of interest paid on a loan or mortgage.

EFFECTIVE RATE OF CAPITAL RECOVERY (EFFECTIVE CAPITAL RECOVERY RATE) The difference between the overall rate and the discount rate. The capital recovery rate weighted by the percentage of investment in the improvements.

EFFECTIVE TAX RATE The taxes on a property expressed as a ratio between the market value of the property and the annual taxes. This is used as a method of comparing the taxes on properties located in different communities with different assessment percentages and different tax rates.

EFFICIENCY (APARTMENT) An apartment that has one room divided into areas for a kitchen, bedroom, etc.

EFFICIENCY RATE In appraising, the ratio of rentable square feet of office space to gross square footage.

EFFLORESCENCE White salts that form on the surface of brick or stone walls and can be washed off.

Examples of Effective Tax Rate Calculations

Formula:

$$\frac{\text{Actual annual taxes}}{\text{Value of property}} = \text{Effective tax rate}$$

$$\frac{\$3{,}300 \text{ Tax}}{\$65{,}000 \text{ Value}} = .051 \text{ Tax rate}$$

$$\frac{\$33{,}000 \text{ Tax}}{\$1{,}200{,}000 \text{ Value}} = .0275 \text{ Tax rate}$$

$$\frac{\$1{,}735 \text{ Tax}}{\$89{,}000 \text{ Value}} = .0195 \text{ Tax rate}$$

EFFECTIVE TAX RATE

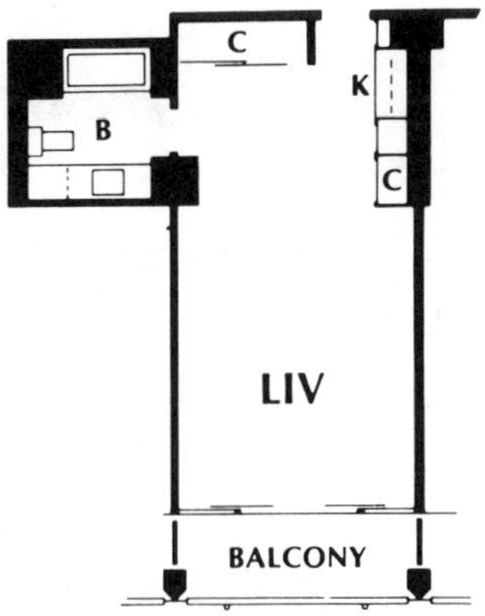

EFFICIENCY (APARTMENT)

EGYPTIAN REVIVAL STYLE

Symbols for Electrical Outlets

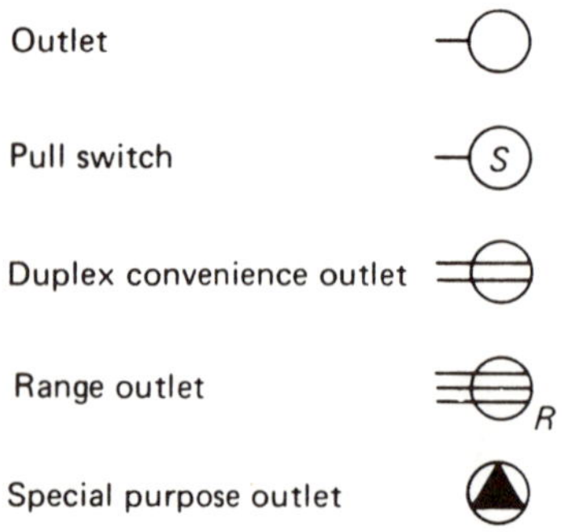

ELECTRICAL OUTLET

EFFLUENT Liquid sewage after some stage of treatment.

EGRESS An exit; an outlet.

EGYPTIAN REVIVAL STYLE A nineteenth-century American architectural style based on Egyptian architecture. The Egyptian Revival style house is box-like with Egyptian columns in the front. This style was never very popular in the United States. The best examples of Egyptian architecture are found in cemetery gates.

CTS SYSTEM: Nineteenth Century American
Egyptian Revival
(Egypt-702)

EJECTMENT A legal action permitted in some states to regain possession of a property from tenants, former owners, trespassers, squatters, and others who occupy the property unlawfully. *See* Eviction.

ELECTRIC AIR CLEANER An electronic device that charges dust particles with electricity and removes them by attracting the particles to metal collecting rods. This method can remove as much as 90 percent of the dust particles in the air.

ELECTRICAL OUTLET A point in an electrical system at which current is available to power equipment or lighting.

ELECTRIC HEAT A heating system run by converting electricity into heat. The heat may be transferred directly by radiation or it may be used to heat air which, in turn, moves to the area by a process called *convection*. Some heating systems use a combination of both methods of heat transfer.

ELECTRIC SYSTEM One of the major mechanical systems of most buildings. Electricity from a power source is brought into the building usually through a meter and main switch to a distribution panel. Here it is divided into branch circuits, each with a protection device (fuse or circuit breaker), and carried by wire to outlets. From the outlets, the electricity is conducted to the lighting fixtures and electrical equipment.

ELEEMOSYNARY CORPORATION *See* Non-profit Corporation.

ELEVATION **1.** Height above sea level or height measured from any point. **2.** An illustration showing the vertical exterior design of a building. **3.** A geometrical projection of a vertical plane perpendicular to a horizontal plane.

ELEVATOR **1.** A raising and lowering mechanism equipped with a car or platform that moves in tracks up and down between the floors of a building and is used to transport passengers and freight. **2.** A farm storage building in which commodities, such as wheat, are housed.

ELIZABETHAN STYLE An architectural style that originated in England during the prosperous reign of Queen Elizabeth I (1558–1603). The Elizabethan style is a two- to two-and-one-half-story house, and it often has the second story overhanging the first. This characteristic protrusion originated in London, where extra space could be obtained in this way. The house is characterized by stone and stucco walls, half timbers, massive sculptured chimneys, high-peaked roofs, large fireplaces, and small leaded windows.

CTS SYSTEM English
Elizabethan or Half Timber
(Eliz or Halftim-202)

ELIZABETHAN STYLE

ELLWOOD A capitalization process used to convert the projected income stream of a property into a value. Originated by L. W. Ellwood, it has become a classic appraisal theory.

Ellwood Mortgage Equity Formula

R = Overall rate
Y = Equity yield rate
M = Ratio of mortgage to value
C = Mortgage coefficient
DEP = Depreciation in property value for the projection period
APP = Appreciation in property value for the projection period
SFF = Sinking-fund factor at Y rate for the ownership projection period

$$R = Y - MC \frac{+dep}{-app} (SFF)$$

ELLWOOD

ELLWOOD PREMISE L. W. Ellwood's extension of the basic mortgage-equity analysis which involved additional assumptions.

ELUVIATION The movement of soil caused by water in the soil.

EMINENT DOMAIN The right of the government to acquire private property for public use by condemnation with just compensation.

ENCLOSURE Land enclosed within a visible boundary, such as a fence, used to protect a property from encroachment by animals.

ENCROACHMENT An intrusion of one person's property upon the property of another. It may be a wall, a fence, or a cornice or casement window that extends upon adjoining property.

ENCUMBRANCE Any claim, charge, or lien attached to a real property that does not prevent conveyance of the fee by the property owner. Some examples are mortgages, tax liens, easements, and restrictions. Most encumbrances reduce the value of the property.

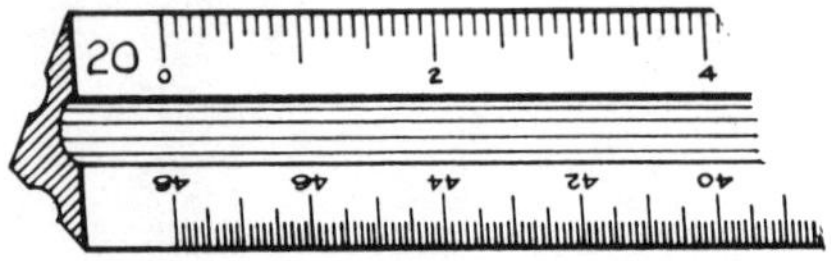

1 INCH = 10 FEET

1″ = ⊢—— 10′ ——⊣

1 INCH = 1 FOOT

1″ = ⊢—— 1′ ——⊣

ENGINEER'S SCALE

ENGLISH COLONIAL STYLE

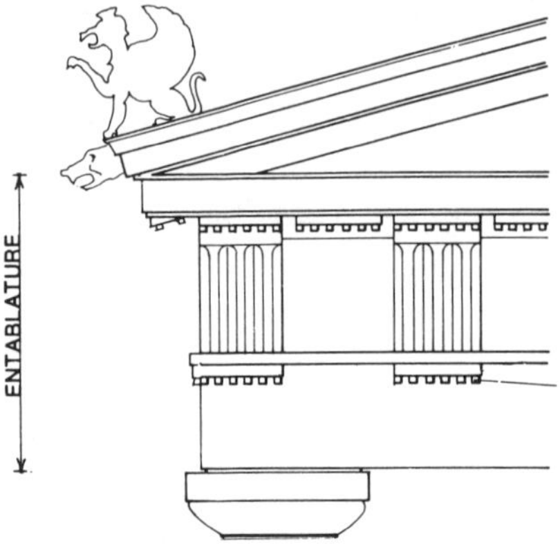

ENTABLATURE

ENDORSEMENT A method of transferring the ownership of a check, note, or other negotiable instrument by writing one's name on the back of the document.

ENGINEERING BREAKDOWN METHOD A method of figuring accrued depreciation by making separate estimates for individual components and totaling their sum.

ENGINEER'S SCALE A scale used by engineers which reduces the foot into units of 10ths, 20ths, up to 60ths.

ENGLISH ARCHITECTURE Some common English styles found in the United States are:

Cotswold Cottage	Williamsburg
Elizabethan	Early Georgian
Half Timber	Regency
Tudor	Georgian

ENGLISH BASEMENT The floor of an apartment building or row house that is about half below ground level. It often has windows and is used as a dwelling unit.

ENGLISH COLONIAL STYLE A colonial American architectural style that evolved from the Cape Cod. The English Colonial is a two-and-one-half-story, rectangular, box-like house. Its protruding front wing distinguishes it from a New England Colonial. Other distinguishing characteristics are gable roofs, cornices, double-hung windows, use of clapboard, and a central entrance in the front wing. The front wing has stone columns on the four corners. Bedrooms are on the second floor.

CTS SYSTEM: Colonial American
Front Gable New England Colonial or
Charleston Colonial or English Colonial
(F Gab-NE or Charles or Eng Col-114)

ENGLISH COTSWOLD ARCHITECTURE *See* Cotswold Cottage.

ENGLISH HALF-TIMBERED (ELIZABETHAN) ARCHITECTURE *See* Elizabethan.

ENGLISH TILE A type of clay roofing tile having interlocking sides.

ENGLISH TUDOR ARCHITECTURE *See* Tudor.

ENSILAGE Green fodder kept in a silo.

ENTABLATURE In Greek architecture, that part of the building which rests horizontally upon the columns. Its major parts are the cornice, frieze, and architrave.

ENTRANCE The point of entry (such as a door) into a building or enclosed area.

ENVIRONMENT The physical, social, political, etc., characteristics of a property's surroundings.

ENVIRONMENTAL DEFICIENCY Conditions in a property's surroundings that decrease value, such as high crime rate, overcrowding, and poorly designed streets.

ENVIRONMENTAL IMPACT STUDY A report made by an independent company of the probable effect of a development on the environment. The report is made according to federal, state, and local guidelines.

ENVIRONMENTAL OBSOLESCENCE *See* Economic Obsolescence.

ENVIRONMENTAL PROTECTION AGENCY A federal agency that deals with the protection of land, water, and air.

EQUALIZATION *See* Board of Equalization.

EQUIPMENT Fixed assets other than real estate, such as office or automotive equipment, which are separate from other assets under the category of fixtures because of their physical attachment to a realty.

EQUITABLE CONVERSION A procedure that occurs when a buyer and seller sign a contract for the property. The purchaser's interest is treated as a real property interest, even though the seller has legal title. The seller's interest is regarded as a security interest.

EQUITABLE LIEN A lien that is created even without a proper contract. It is based on the principles of fairness and justice as interpreted by the courts. Such a lien may be created when a mortgage is defective or when a seller accepts a deposit and then refuses to sell the property.

EQUITABLE MORTGAGE **1.** A mortgage that is enforceable in a court of equity but is not legally a mortgage. **2.** A deed given as security of debt is regarded as a mortgage.

EQUITABLE OWNERSHIP *See* Equitable Conversion.

EQUITABLE TITLE A person's right to obtain absolute ownership to a property that has legal title in someone else's name.

EQUITY **1.** Justice. **2.** The market value of a property less the amount of existing mortgages, etc.

EQUITY BUILD-UP The increase in equity that an investor receives when the property is financed with a mortgage that amortizes over a period of time. As time proceeds,

Example of Equity Build-Up

Purchase price:	$300,000
Cash:	$ 50,000
Mortgage:	$250,000
(12% for 20 yrs. – monthly payments)	

1. Assuming the value at the end of 10 years is the same as the purchase price:
   (If the property was purchased for cash the rate of return would have been 0%)

Value at end of 10 yrs.	= $300,000
Mortgage balance at end of 10 years	$191,865
Equity at end of 10 years ($300,000 – $191,865)	$108,135
Increase in equity ($108,135 – $50,000)	$58,135
Percentage increase ($58,135 ÷ $50,000)	116%

2. Assuming the value at the end of 10 years is double the purchase price:

Value at end of 10 years	= $600,000
(If property was purchased for cash the rate of return would have been 100%)	
Mortgage balance at end of 10 years	$191,865
Equity at end of 10 years ($600,000 – $191,865)	$308,135
Increase in equity ($308,135 – $50,000)	$258,135
Percentage increase ($258,135 ÷ $50,000)	516%

EQUITY BUILD-UP

the amount of the investor's equity increases, and the amount of the mortgage decreases. It is used as part of the Ellwood mortgage equity formulation.

EQUITY CONSTANT *See* Equity Dividend Rate.

EQUITY DIVIDEND The cash throw off of a property. It consists of all the income minus all the expenses and a deduction for the annual debt service. In mortgage capitalization formulas (Ellwood method), it is designated by the symbol d_e.

EQUITY DIVIDEND RATE The ratio of the original investment in cash to before-tax cash flow. It is the cash received on the cash invested in a property.

EQUITY INTEREST *See* Equity.

EQUITY KICKER A percentage of ownership given to a mortgage lender in order to induce the lender to give a mortgage. The mortgage lender shares an interest in the property (in addition to the interest as mortgagee).

EQUITY OF REDEMPTION A mortgagor's (borrower's) right to redeem property during the foreclosure period.

EQUITY PARTICIPATION The right of a mortgage lender to receive a portion of the equity in a property as a result of giving a mortgage and other assistance to the project. The mortgage lender in fact becomes a partner of the property owner. This partnership is outside the terms of the mortgage and extends beyond the length of the mortgage.

EQUITY PURCHASER Someone who purchases an equity in a property without necessarily assuming all of the indebtedness.

EQUITY RATIO The ratio of down payment to total price. It is the part of an investment that is free of debt.

EQUITY YIELD The return on the equity from all sources. It includes the annual equity dividend and any excess or deficit over the original equity investment at the termination of the investment.

EQUITY YIELD RATE The effective rate of return on an equity capital investment including the annual dividends and the effect of any gain or loss as a result of the sale of the investment. It is also called the internal rate of return (IRR).

EROSION The wearing away of rock and earth caused by running water, glaciers, and winds.

ESCALATION CLAUSE A clause in a lease that adjusts the rent during the term of the lease to reflect changing conditions. Some escalation clauses adjust for the cost of living by tying the amount of rent to an index such as the U.S Department of Labor cost of living index. It is also common to adjust the rent to reflect the amount of business the tenant is doing on the premises.

ESCALATOR CLAUSE *See* Escalation Clause.

ESCHEAT One of the powers of government with reference to property ownership. The ownership of property reverts to the State when it is abandoned or when an owner dies without any heirs. It has its roots in English common law. Now many state statutes re-enforce it in detail.

ESCROW The process of depositing money with a third party. In a real estate sale, the deposit is held by the broker or other designated escrow agent until specific conditions set forth in the sales contract take place. Sometimes there is a separate escrow agreement that sets forth the conditions of the escrow.

Steps of a Typical Escrow Closing

- Buyer gives a deposit and obtains a deposit receipt
- Seller accepts the offer and turns the documents over to an escrow agent
- Buyer turns balance of down payment over to the escrow agent
- Lender turns mortgage proceeds over to escrow agent
- Escrow agent has buyer sign mortgage note and deed
- Escrow agent has seller sign deed and/or bill of sale
- Escrow agent obtains title search and title insurance
- Escrow agent prepares closing statements
- Escrow agent sends deed and closing statement to buyer
- Escrow agent sends mortgage note and deed to lender(s)
- Escrow agent arranges to record all appropriate documents

ESCROW

ESCROW ACCOUNT **1.** A special bank account established by an agent in which funds being held in escrow are deposited. In many states, every licensed broker is required to have an escrow account. **2.** An account established by mortgage lenders in which is deposited a portion of the mortgage payment that is set aside to pay taxes, insurance, and other expenses as required by the terms of the mortgage.

ESTATE **1.** An interest in property. The nature of the estate depends upon the quantity, degree, nature, and extent of the interest in the property. There are a variety of different kinds of estates in real property, such as fee simple, life estate, leasehold estate, and joint tenancy. **2.** The property left by a decedent. **3.** The property of an incompetent, a bankrupt, or a ward of the court.

ESTATE IN REVERSION An estate that takes effect some time in the future when another estate ends. For example, when a life estate is granted to someone, the estate that starts at the end of that person's life is an estate in reversion.

ESTATE OF INHERITANCE An unusual estate where the

holder has the right to use the property during his or her lifetime. The holder may also sell the estate during his or her lifetime or will it to heirs. However, if the holder fails to either sell or will it during his or her lifetime, the estate passes to those who survive according to an established order of descent.

ESTIMATE An appraisal term for an opinion that is based on the analysis of adequate data about a property by a person competent to make the analysis as a result of experience and education.

ESTIMATED SELLING PRICE (ESP) A statistical term used to express the projection made by regression analysis.

ESTOPPEL A legal doctrine which states that a person is forbidden to contradict or deny his or her own previous statement, act, or deed when an innocent third party has relied on the statement, act, or deed. For example, if a lender gives the wrong mortgage balance to a purchaser of a property when the purchaser is going to assume the mortgage (and the purchaser relies on this figure), the lender will have to abide by the figure given in error.

EVICTION A court action for the physical removal of a person, usually a tenant, from a real property.

EVICTION NOTICE A notice given to a tenant to vacate the premises due to non-payment of rent or other breach of the lease agreement.

EVIDENCE OF TITLE A document showing ownership of property.

EXCAVATION **1.** A hole dug to provide safe and adequate support for footings and foundations. **2.** The process of digging up and removing dirt and rocks from land.

EXCESS CONDEMNATION When more property than necessary is taken by right of eminent domain, the excess property is sold at auction after the completion of the project.

EXCESS INCOME *See* Excess Rent.

EXCESS RENT Rent that exceeds the fair market rent. It is usually paid because of a lease.

EXCESS VALUE A value greater than market value that is created when a property is leased to a good tenant at a rental that exceeds the fair market rent of the property. *See also* Excess Rent.

EXCHANGE The act of trading an equity in a piece of property for equity in another piece of property. This reciprocal transfer has certain tax advantages over a sale.

EXCHANGE AGREEMENT Instrument used in exchange. *See also* Exchange.

EXCLUSIVE AGENCY A contract that gives an agent exclusive right to sell a property. The owner usually reserves the right to sell the property without having to pay a commission. The term is also applied to a property with such a contract.

EXCLUSIVE AGENCY AGREEMENT *See* Agency Agreement.

EXCLUSIVE AGENCY LISTING A contract which states that the agent will receive a commission if a property is sold as a result of his or her efforts but not as the result of the efforts of the principal.

EXCLUSIVE LISTING A written contract between a property owner and a real estate broker wherein the owner promises the broker a fee or commission if the property is sold during a stated period. There are two basic types of exclusive listing: exclusive agency listing and exclusive right to sell.

Summary of the Differences Between the Types of Exclusive Listing Contracts

Exclusive agency
1. Agent has the exclusive right to sell the property.
2. Owner may sell the property without having to pay the agent a commission.

Exclusive right to sell
1. Same as Exclusive Agency
2. If owner sells the property the agent is paid a commission.

EXCLUSIVE AGENCY
EXCLUSIVE LISTING
EXCLUSIVE RIGHT TO SELL

EXCLUSIVE RIGHT TO SELL A listing agreement between the owner of a property and a real estate broker giving the broker the exclusive right to sell the property and receive the agreed-upon commission when the property is sold, regardless of who is responsible for producing the buyer.

EXECUTE To make a document valid, i.e., make it into a contract, by having all of the parties sign it. A deed is executed when it is signed, sealed, and delivered.

EXECUTION OF JUDGMENT A court order allowing an official of the court to put into effect a judgment of the court.

EXECUTOR A person who is appointed as the one to carry out requests in a will.

EXECUTOR'S DEED A court-approved deed where the grantor is the executor.

EXEMPTION *See* Tax Exemption.

EXISTING MORTGAGE The mortgage belonging to the seller of a property which is assumed by the buyer.

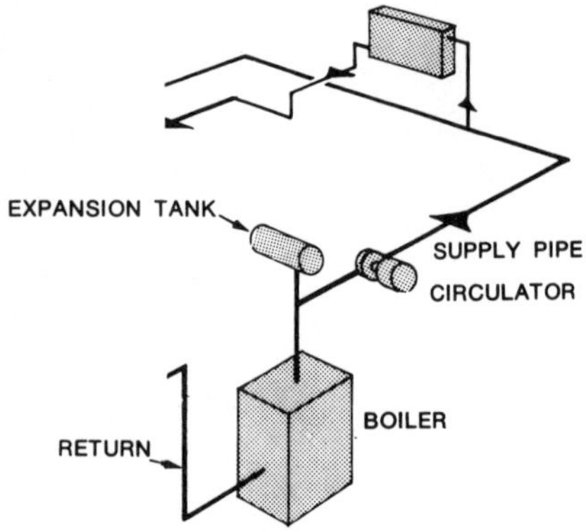

EXPANSION TANK

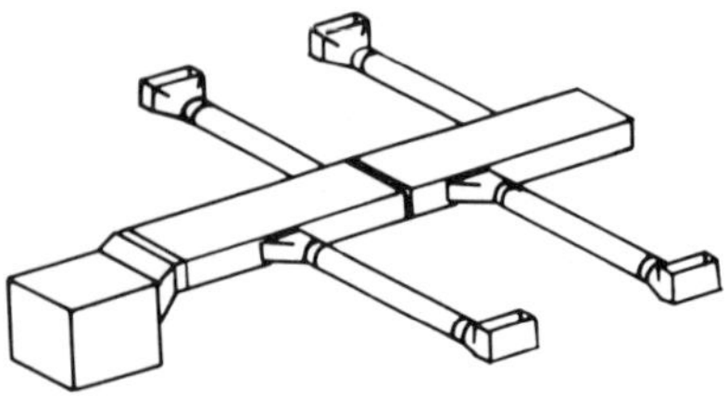

EXTENDED PLENUM SYSTEM

EXIT That portion of a means of egress which provides a way of travel to the exterior.

EXPANSIBLE HOUSE A house especially built for expansion or additions.

EXPANSION JOINT A joint or gap between adjacent parts of a building, units of concrete, or any structure that allows for expansion as a result of temperature changes.

EXPANSION TANK An air-filled tank in a hot-water heating system which provides space for the increased volume of water that results from heating the water.

EXPENSE RATIO The ratio of expenses to gross income. In appraising, it is the ratio of stabilized expenses to projected effective gross income.

EXPENSES *See* Operating Expenses.

EXPERT A person who has special knowledge and skills in a field because of education and experience.

EXPERT TESTIMONY Testimony made by someone acknowledged as a specialist in a particular field on a particular subject.

EXPERT WITNESS A person acknowledged to have special training, knowledge, and experience in testifying on a particular subject.

EXPOSURE **1.** The extent to which a property for sale, lease, etc. is exposed to prospective purchasers through the media and multiple listing service groups. **2.** The direction in which a building or property faces.

EXPRESSWAY A highway with control of access that does not have tolls. Major streets cross it at different grade levels.

EXPROPRIATION **1.** The act of taking private property for public use. **2.** The term is also used to describe the situation where a foreign government takes property of nationals of other countries with adequate compensation.

EXTENDED PLENUM SYSTEM A system of ducts in a hot-air heating system. A main duct runs lengthwise through the middle of the building, and smaller ducts extend from the main plenum throughout the building.

EXTENSION AGREEMENT A document that extends the term of a mortgage.

EXTERIOR The outside surface of any structure.

EXTERIOR FINISH The outside coating or covering of a building, such as wood, stucco, and brick.

EXTERIOR STAIRS Stairs constructed outdoors when the topography of a lot is so steep that walks cannot be built within the maximum grades permitted.

EXTERIOR TYPE PLYWOOD A type of softwood plywood used wherever the wood will get wet. It can be used for fences, sheathing, siding, etc.

EXTERIOR WALL Any outer vertical surface that encloses the entire structure. For appraisal purposes, the dimensions of this wall are used to figure the gross area of the enclosure.

F

FACADE *See* Face.

FACE **1.** The facade or front of a structure. **2.** A structure's position, such as an "ocean face." **3.** The outer surface of a structure or object.

FACE BRICK A high-quality, treated brick used for exterior finishes.

FACIA (FASCIA) A piece of horizontal trim running along the perimeter of a flat roof. In Greek architecture, it is the horizontal band in the architrave.

FACTORS OF PRODUCTION An old economic theory which states that the four factors of production are labor, coordination (management), capital, and land. It goes on to state that labor has the first claim on any income that is produced and that capital has the last claim after all the other factors are satisfied.

FAIR CASH VALUE *See* Market Value.

FAIR CREDIT REPORTING ACT A federal law designed to protect the consumer. Its two most important aspects are that it requires that, when loans are made, the effective or true interest be disclosed to the borrower, and that, when credit reports are used, the consumer be advised of that fact and of who made the report. If the report is derogatory, the consumer must be given the derogatory information and the opportunity to correct it if it is in error.

FAIR HOUSING *See* Federal Fair Housing Law.

FAIR MARKET VALUE *See* Market Value.

FAIR RENTAL *See* Economic Rent.

FAIR VALUE **1.** *See* Market Value. **2.** The establishment of a reasonable value by a court or board for the setting of public utility rates.

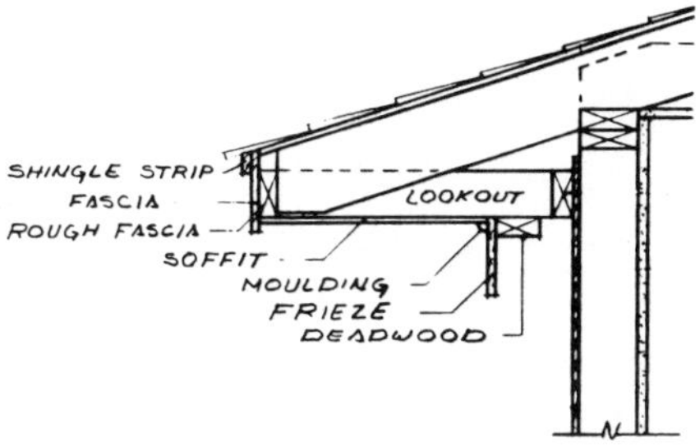

FACIA (MODERN)

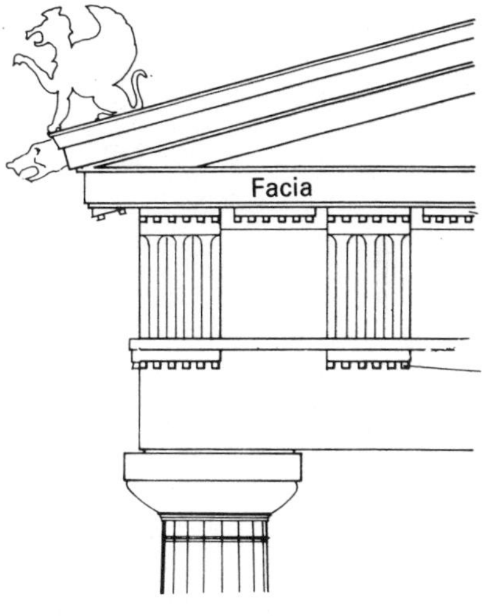

FACIA (GREEK)

FAIRWAY **1.** The navigable portion of a bay or river through which vessels travel. **2.** The part of a golf course between the tees and the greens.

FALSE ADVERTISING In real estate, advertising that misrepresents the property, terms, or price. A broker may have his or her license revoked for this offense.

FAMILY ENTRANCE An entrance that is used by a family and not guests. It ideally leads from the garage or carport into the kitchen or circulation area directly connecting to the kitchen.

FAMILY ROOM A room that a family uses for play, study, hobbies, and recreation. Ideally, it is built near the kitchen and is visible from it.

FANLIGHT *See* Circlehead Window.

FANNIE MAE *See* Federal National Mortgage Association.

FAN WINDOW *See* Circlehead Window.

FARM **1.** Land used to grow crops. **2.** Land used for raising dairy products or certain fish or animals. **3.** The physical area in which a real estate brokerage concentrates its business efforts. The brokerage tries to become well known in this area so sellers and buyers will seek them out when they need the services of a real estate broker or salesperson.

FARM AND LAND INSTITUTE (FLI) An institute of the NATIONAL ASSOCIATION OF REALTORS® that specializes in the development of courses, publications, and programs for members who specialize in land.

FARM BROKER A broker who specializes in the sale of farm and ranch properties.

FARMER'S HOME ADMINISTRATION (FmHA) A government agency that is part of the U.S. Department of Agriculture. Its main function is to make farm loans and provide rural housing.

FARM LAND Land used for agricultural production. It is usually the land that makes up a farm, including tillable and untillable land.

FASCIA PLATE *See Facia.*

FAST FOOD RESTAURANT A restaurant that offers fast, over-the-counter service at relatively low prices. Often it has a limited menu and specializes in a particular type of food.

FAUCET, SPIGOT, TAP, OR COCK A device at the end of a pipe to control the flow of water.

FEASIBILITY *See* Feasibility Study.

FEASIBILITY STUDY (SURVEY) The analysis of a project before construction. It involves examining the cost-benefit ratio to estimate the probable financial success of the project.

FEDERAL BOARD *See* Interstate Highway System

FEDERAL CRIME INSURANCE PROGRAM A program whereby the federal government provides crime insurance to the public at a reasonable cost. Coverage cannot be denied because of the location of the property. However, there is a requirement that the property be made secure.

FEDERAL DEPOSIT INSURANCE CORPORATION (FDIC) The federal agency that insures against loss of deposits in commercial and savings banks up to a maximum amount (currently $100,000).

FEDERAL FAIR HOUSING LAW Title VIII of the Civil Rights Act, called the Federal Fair Housing Law, forbids discrimination on the basis of race, color, sex, religion, or national origin in the sale of most residential property and vacant land intended for housing purposes. The laws do not apply to commercial or industrial properties, which are covered under other laws.

FEDERAL HOME LOAN BANK (FHLB) Banks created under the Federal Home Loan Bank of 1932 lend only to member financial institutions in order to keep a permanent supply of money available for home financing. Insurance companies, savings and loans, and other similar companies may become members and borrow from one of the many regional banks.

FEDERAL HOME LOAN BANK BOARD (FHLBB) The administrative board that charters federal savings and loan associations and has regulatory authority over members of the Federal Home Loan Bank System.

FEDERAL HOME LOAN BANK SYSTEM (FHLBS) It now consists of a number of federal agencies and federally sponsored organizations. The principal agency in the group is the Federal Home Loan Bank Board.

FEDERAL HOME LOAN MORTGAGE CORPORATION (FHLMC) This federal agency created in 1970 is commonly known as "Freddie Mac." Its primary purpose is to buy conventional mortgages from savings and loan associations, thus giving them the liquidity they need to remain active in the mortgage lending field even when money is tight. It also buys some FHA- and VA-

EQUAL HOUSING OPPORTUNITY

FEDERAL FAIR HOUSING LAW

insured loans. It raises money by selling mortgage-backed securities and certificates. The agency has been a leader in the establishment of standard forms for use throughout the industry.

FEDERAL HOUSING ADMINISTRATION (FHA) A federal agency that is now a division of the Department of Housing and Urban Development. Its major activity is to promote good housing by insuring residential mortgage loans. The FHA has made a major contribution to improving housing throughout the country by the establishment of minimum property standards. The agency is involved in a wide variety of programs to improve housing.

FEDERAL HOUSING ADMINISTRATION-MINIMUM PROPERTY STANDARDS (FHA-MPS) Minimum requirements for various types of housing published by the FHA. All new buildings that are insured by the FHA must be constructed to meet these minimum standards.

FEDERAL HOUSING ADMINISTRATION MINIMUM PROPERTY STANDARDS FOR ONE AND TWO LIVING UNITS A unified set of technical and environmental standards developed by the Department of Housing and Urban Development to encourage improvement in housing and residential land development standards and conditions. They are constantly being revised and updated. They are generally referred to as "MPS."

FEDERAL LAND BANK A bank run by the Farm Credit Administration that supplies long-term, first mortgage loans to farmers and, under certain limitations, to livestock corporations.

FEDERAL NATIONAL MORTGAGE ASSOCIATION (FNMA) Popularly known as "Fannie Mae." It was created as a federal agency to buy and sell FHA- and VA-guaranteed mortgage loans. It is now a privately owned corporation set up to make a profit for its stockholders. Its primary function is to borrow money from the capital markets and then use this money to buy mortgages. It also sells mortgages when there is easy money available. The goal of FNMA is to buy mortgages when money is tight and interest rates are high and to sell mortgages when money is available and interest rates are lower and thus make a profit.

FEDERAL REVENUE STAMPS

FEDERAL REVENUE STAMPS Also called IRS Stamps. A transfer of tax of $.55 per $500 that was based on the sale price of real estate (less remaining loans) was involved. The tax ended as a federal tax and was taken up by most states with slight changes in some areas.

FEDERAL SAVINGS AND LOAN ASSOCIATION A type of thrift institution that is federally chartered. It may be owned by stockholders or by its depositors. Individual savings and loan associations operate similarly to banks. They accept time deposits in a variety of forms on which they pay interest. They loan money for mortgages on houses and for home improvement. They are members of a Federal Home Loan Bank and are regulated by the Federal Home Loan Bank Board. Deposits are insured by the Federal Savings and Loan Insurance Corporation (FSLIC).

FEDERAL SAVINGS AND LOAN INSURANCE CORPORATION (FSLIC) A federal agency that insures savers' accounts at savings and loan associations. This insurance is mandatory for all federal savings and loan associations and is optional for state-chartered savings and loan associations. The FSLIC may make loans to savings and loan associations that are in financial trouble and take a variety of other steps to help troubled institutions.

FEDERAL STYLE A colonial American house style that was prevalent throughout Eastern cities in the 1700s. The Federal is a multi-story, symmetrical, box-shaped house with a flat roof. Its distinguishing characteristics are: clapboard or brick exterior walls, beautiful ornamentation, a balustrade, windows with small glass panes, and one or more chimneys protruding through the roof.

CTS SYSTEM: Colonial American
Federal
(Federal-101)

FEDERAL STYLE

FEDERAL TAX LIEN A lien placed on a property because the owner has failed to pay some kind of federal tax, such as a federal estate tax, income tax, or payroll tax.

FEE **1.** A charge made for a professional service. It is based primarily on the time spent by the professional, the skill and training of the professional, and the difficulty of the assignment. It is due when the services are rendered and is not contingent upon a sale, rental, or other event being made as is a commission. **2.** An ownership in land that can be inherited. It is the best title and most complete form of ownership. It is also known as fee simple or fee absolute.

FEE SIMPLE The best and most complete title an owner can have to a piece of real estate.

FEE SIMPLE ABSOLUTE Unconditional ownership and control. It is the best form of ownership.

FEE SIMPLE CONDITIONAL A fee that rests on a certain condition. A common condition used to be that the person who inherited the title had to have a son. If he or she didn't the title reverted to the estate of the donor.

FEE SIMPLE DEFEASIBLE An ownership that will terminate if some condition is no longer met. A common example is the continued use of the property for a specified purpose.

FEE TAIL An estate of inheritance limited to some specified class of heirs of the person to whom it is granted. Estates in fee tail have been abolished in most states.

FELT PAPER A type of highly absorbent, porous building paper.

FENCE A barrier made of wood, brick, or wire used to enclose a lot, yard, or field.

FENESTRATION The overall manner or plan of placing doors or windows in a structure.

FHA *See* Federal Housing Administration.

FHLMC *See* Federal Home Loan Mortgage Corporation.

FIBERBOARD A type of building board used for insulation and made of fibrous material, such as wood, cane, or vegetable fibers.

FIBERGLASS Filaments of glass that are made into continuous, thread-like filaments. Fiberglass is used for textiles, glass fabrics, and electrical insulation or made into wool-like material used for insulation.

FICTITIOUS *See* Fictitious Instrument.

FICTITIOUS INSTRUMENT A method that shortens the process of recording deeds and mortgages. It entails filing a document pertaining to no particular property. It is referred to in mortgages and deeds that convey or encumber specific properties.

FICTITIOUS MORTGAGE *See* Fictitious Instrument.

FICTITIOUS NAME A company name in an unincorporated business. Also called a **dba** (doing business as).

FIDELITY BOND Also known as a security bond, it is the guarantee from a bonding company that employees or others entrusted with money or other valuable assets will carry out their duties honestly.

FIDUCIARY A person who acts in a relationship of trust or confidence with respect to another person.

FIDUCIARY RELATIONSHIP A relationship where a person is put in a position of trust. The relationship is often such that the trusted person has special information and obligations which, if misused, would cause harm to the person who entrusted the information or relied upon the faithful performance of the duties.

FIELD TILE A porous tile laid under and around a foundation or slab to drain away underground water.

FILL **1.** To furnish an area with additional material to equalize or raise topography to a desired level. **2.** The materials used for fill, such as dirt and gravel.

FILLED LAND Land not suitable for building because of its typography, wetness, or poor bearing quality that is improved by dumping dirt, rock, gravel, or other solid material on it.

FILTERING The process by which the creation of new housing for middle- and upper-income families creates housing for lower-income families, who move into the used houses when the middle- and upper-income people move out.

FILTERING DOWN *See* Filtering.

FINAL RECONCILIATION An appraisal term for the process of choosing the most appropriate data and selecting from among alternative conclusions developed in the approaches to value to estimate a final value for the property being appraised.

FINAL VALUE ESTIMATE An opinion made by an appraiser after all of the steps of the appraisal process and after the final reconciliation as to what the appraiser feels the value of a property is.

FINANCIAL INSTITUTIONS A broad term used to describe intermediary organizations that obtain their capital primarily from deposits of various types and, in turn, lend this money in order to earn a return and pay interest on the deposits (or perform services such as checking accounts). The five largest classes of financial institutions (based on their assets in the United States) in order of size are: commercial banks, savings and loan

FINIAL

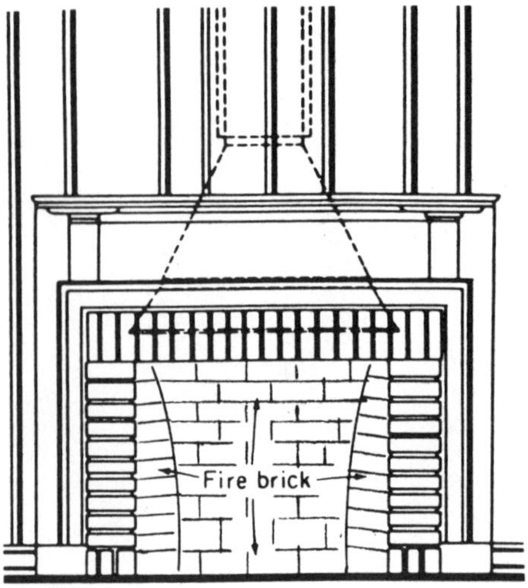

FIREBRICK

associations, life insurance companies, private pension funds, and mutual savings banks.

FINANCIAL STATEMENT A statement listing the assets and liabilities of a person or company.

FINANCING STATEMENT A recorded document filed with the registrar of deeds or secretary of state which indicates that personal property is encumbered with a debt.

FINDER'S FEE A fee paid to someone who brings two parties together to make a deal to purchase property or to enter into some type of non-real-estate enterprise or other type of transaction that is profitable to the parties involved.

FINE SANDY LOAM A type of soil that has a fine texture and contains large quantities of sand with enough silt and clay to make it coherent.

FINE TEXTURED SOIL A type of soil that has a high percentage of fine particles (.003 mm in diameter or less). This type of soil is often called *clay*.

FINIAL The decorative top of a cupola or gable that usually forms the base of a flagpole or weather vane.

FINISH COAT The last layer or final layer of plaster that furnishes either a decorative surface or a base for decoration.

FINISH FLOOR The floor applied over the subfloor. It is the final covering of the subflooring, usually hardwood, tile, cork, linoleum, or tile, that provides the completed floor surface.

FINISH HARDWARE See Builders' Hardware.

FINISHING COSTS The interest and other charges related to borrowing money to build or buy real estate.

FINISH RATING The time it takes for the stud, joist, or core to reach an average temperature of 250°F or an individual temperature of 325° as measured on the plane of the stud, joist, or core nearest the fire in accordance with the ASTM E119 test.

FIREBACK *See* Chimney Back.

FIREBRICK A brick of fire clay that is made to withstand the effects of high heat used in fireplaces and heating chambers of furnaces.

FIRE CLAYS A type of clay found deep within the earth and which is mined out. Fire clay has good resistance to heat.

FIRE DOORS AND WALLS Doors and walls especially constructed with fire-resistant materials. They are installed to prevent the spread of fire.

FIRE INSURANCE Insurance against loss or damage by fire to specific property. It is usually written together with extended coverage insurance. Often, it is grouped with a variety of other coverages into a package policy.

FIREPLACE A rectangular, arched, or square opening at the base of a chimney that is lined with masonry in which an open fire can be built.

FIREPROOF CONSTRUCTION Construction designed to withstand fire without impairment of its structural integrity. All load-bearing members are build out of noncombustible material, and all structural members are fireproofed.

FIREPROOFING Non-combustible material applied to structural elements that provides increased fire resistance but usually has no structural function.

FIRE-RESISTANT CONSTRUCTION Construction that can withstand ordinary fire conditions for at least one hour without serious damage to the structure.

FIRE-RESISTIVE *See* Fire-Resistant Construction.

FIRE-RETARDANT MATERIAL Material that inhibits combustion.

FIRE SPRINKLER SYSTEM *See* Sprinkler System.

FIRE STOP A method of preventing smoke and fire from spreading through a structure by filling concealed air spaces with fire-resistant materials or structural members.

FIRE STOPPING Material used to block the air spaces in walls to prevent the spread of fire through these air passages.

FIRE WALL A wall built between buildings or built to divide parts of a building to prevent the spread of fire.

FIRM COMMITMENT A promise by a lending institution to make a mortgage on a property when specified conditions are met. The conditions might be the purchase by an approved buyer, the construction and renting of a new project, or the improvement of an existing project.

FIRST LIEN A term used by the Federal Home Loan Mortgage Corporation to describe a lien meeting the requirements of any investment statute or regulation issued thereunder by any governmental agency under state or federal law authorized to supervise and exam-

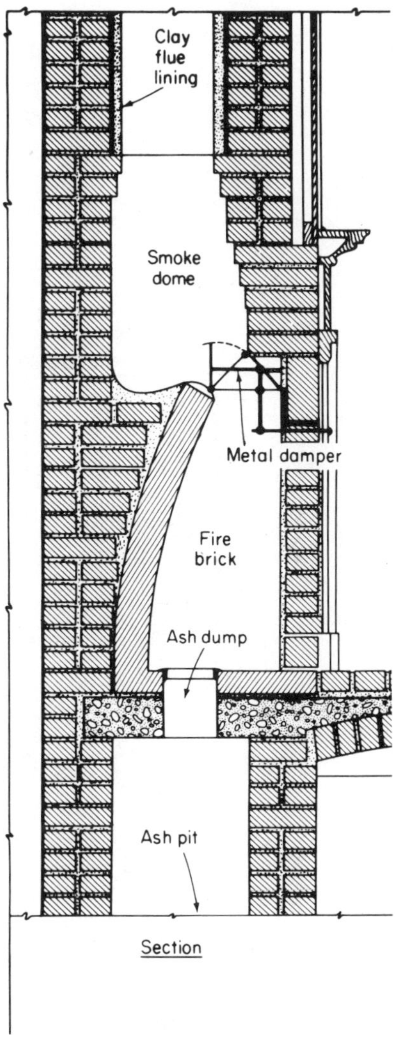

FIREPLACE

ine the operations, activities, or investments of lenders relating "first mortgages," "unencumbered property," "first liens," or words of similar import."[1]

FIRST MORTGAGE A mortgage that has priority over all other voluntary liens on that property.

FIRST REFUSAL RIGHT A right usually granted by an owner to a lessee that gives the lessee the first chance to purchase the property if the owner decides to sell.

FIRST USER The first person to use a piece of real estate after improvements are constructed.

FISCAL YEAR An accounting year, which may be the calendar year or any other 12-month period.

FIXED ASSETS Permanent assets not readily converted into cash that are necessary for the operation of a business, such as buildings and heavy machinery.

FIXED EXPENSES (CHARGES) Expenses associated with real estate that tend to remain the same regardless of the occupancy of the property, such as taxes and fire insurance.

FIXED WINDOW A window that has no movable parts and does not open, such as a picture window, a fixed bay window, or a fixed bow window.

FIXED WINDOW

FIXITY OF LOCATION A unique characteristic of real estate. Because it cannot be moved, it is subject to the influence of its surroundings, and it cannot escape from such influences.

FIXTURE Personal property that loses its identity as such by its association with real property and becomes accessory to the real estate and part and parcel of it, such as toilets, light fixtures, and furnaces.

FLAGSTONE A decorative flat stone used as a stepping stone or in walkways and terraces. It is processed in a range of colors.

FLANGE A projecting border, collar, edge, rib, rim, etc.

FLASHING A piece of material, usually metal or composition, used to protect, cover, or deflect water in places where two materials join or form angles, such as roof valleys and chimney protrusions.

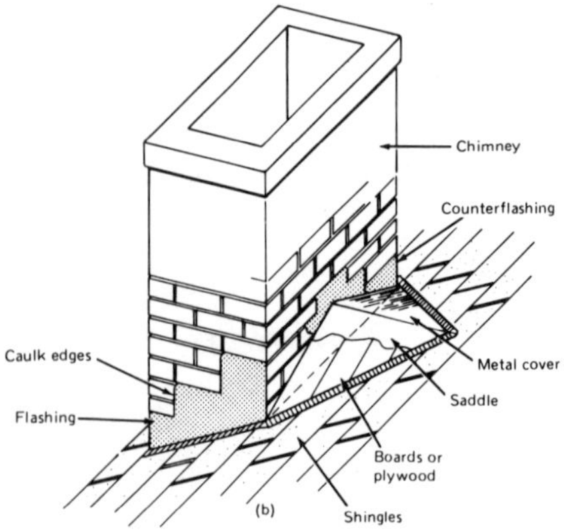

FLASHING

FLAT A suite of rooms, usually all on one floor, that together make up a single living unit. *See also* Apartment.

---

[1] *Seller's Guide*. Federal Home Loan Mortgage Corporation. Washington, 1980.

FLAT COAT A coat of paint used as a base for the top coat; an intermediate coat applied to a finished structure.

FLAT LEAST *See* Straight Lease.

FLAT ROOF A roof having a slope just sufficient to provide water drainage and a pitch not over 1 to 20. *See* Roof Pitch.

FLEMISH BOND A type of bond used in brick work consisting of headers and stretchers laid alternately.

FLEXIBLE CONDUIT An electric conduit made of flexible material.

FLEXIBLE INTEREST RATE *See* Variable Interest Rate.

FLEXIBLE PAYMENT LOAN A note secured by a mortgage where amortization of principal is not required during an initial period; however, the required payments during such period must be sufficient to pay interest. Such note must require repayment in monthly installments in accordance with a payment schedule stated in the note, and the required payments after the initial period must be sufficient to retire the entire obligation, both interest and principal, within the remainder of the mortgage term.[1]

FLIGHT PATTERN The area used by aircraft approaching and departing from an airport.

FLITCH BEAM A beam made up of two or more structural timbers that are bolted together with a metal plate sandwiched between for additional strength.

FLOAT A tool used to smooth cement and plaster by hand. It can also be used to make textured surfaces.

FLOAT FINISH A concrete or mortar surface created by finishing with a float.

FLOATING FOUNDATION A type of foundation that is quite rigid and does not float. It consists of concrete slabs covering an entire foundation area. Such foundations often contain reinforcing bars.

FLOATING RATE *See* Variable Interest Rate.

FLOATING ZONE A special provision of some zoning regulations that permits planned development of a portion of the land within a designated area for a use not permitted in the balance of the area. This use is permitted only when a development plan that is considered to be

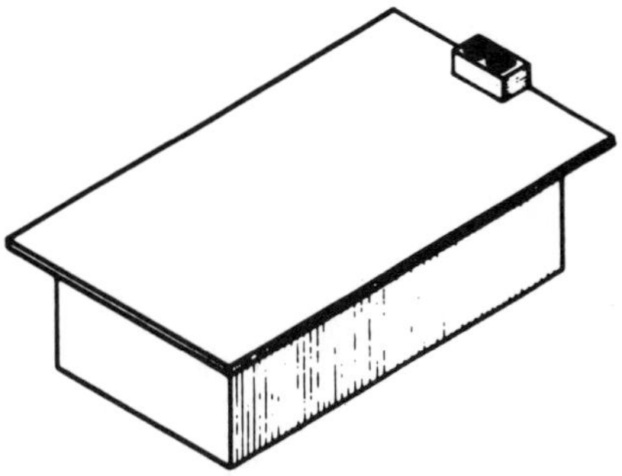

FLAT ROOF

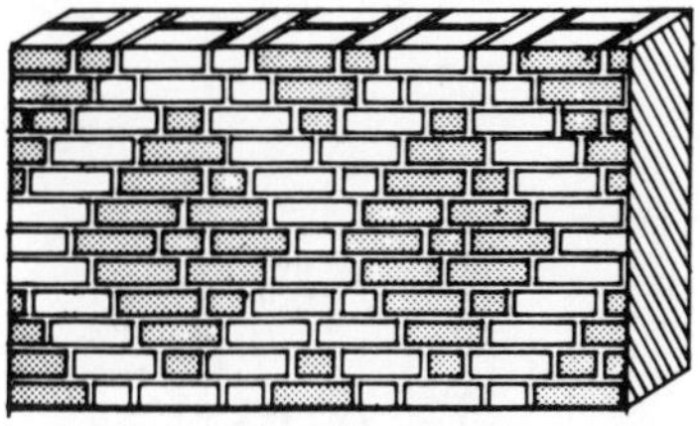

FLEMISH BOND

[1] *Seller's Guide,* The Mortgage Corporation, Washington, 1980.

in the best interests of the entire community is submitted to the zoning authority.

FLOODING As defined in a typical flood insurance policy, it is a general and temporary condition of partial or complete inundation of normally dry land areas.

FLOOD INSURANCE A special insurance policy that provides insurance protection for losses caused by flooding. It is usually written by the federal government through the National Flood Insurance Program.

FLOODLIGHTS A type of light designed to illuminate a large area or to illuminate one object more than its surroundings.

FLOOD PLAIN The flat surfaces on the banks of rivers and streams that are subject to flooding.

FLOOR **1.** The lowest horizontal level of a room or building on which one stands and walks. **2.** The different horizontal levels of a building.

FLOOR AREA The area within the outside walls of a building as measured from the inside surface of the exterior walls.

FLOOR-AREA RATIO The ratio of the total floor area of a building to the area of the plot on which it stands.

FLOOR BEAMS Beams that support the floor of a building or the deck of a bridge.

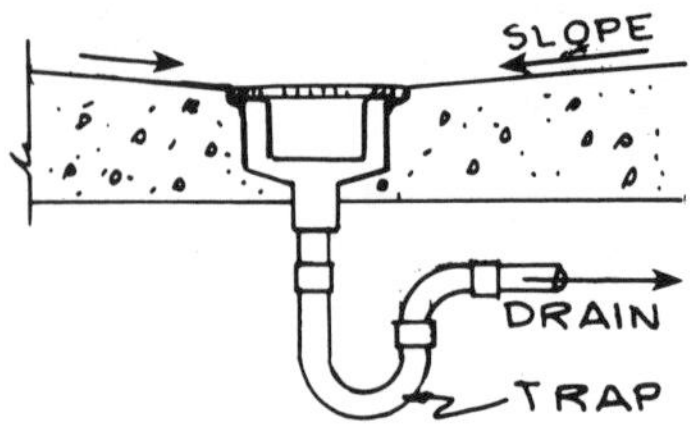

FLOOR DRAINS

FLOOR DRAINS Drains placed in the floor of a building to furnish an opening to drain water into a waste disposal system.

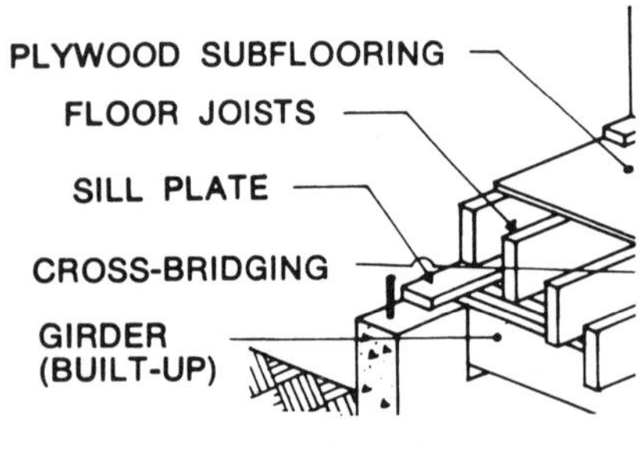

FLOOR FRAMING

FLOOR FRAMING The framing that supplies support for the floor. It consists of floor joists, cross and solid bridges, and other members.

FLOOR FURNACE A type of hot-air heating unit that is installed directly under the floor with its grilled upper surface flush with the finished floor.

FLOOR HANGER A stirrup; an iron brace used to support a floor joist.

FLOORING Material used in laying a floor.

FLOOR INSULATION Insulation installed under the floor.

FLOOR JOISTS A joist (horizontal framing lumber) to support flooring to which it is attached.

FLOOR LOAD The live load support capacity of a floor is

measured in pounds per square foot that the floor may safely support if the load is uniformly distributed.

FLOOR LOAN Part of a type of mortgage loan written for new construction where part of the money is advanced during the construction phase of the development. The balance is due when the project is rented to a specified percentage of the available space. The portion that is advanced during the construction phase is the floor plan.

FLOOR OUTLET An electrical outlet recessed in the floor.

FLOOR PLAN The part of a set of architectural drawings that shows the layout of a horizontal section of the building. There is usually a drawing for each floor of the building.

FLOOR TIME A set time during the working day when a salesperson is responsible for walk-ins or telephone calls concerning property listed in the broker's office.

FLOOR-TO-CEILING LOAN *See* Floor Loan.

FLOWAGE EASEMENT An easement that provides the right to let water flow over the land and even to flood the land under prescribed circumstances. It restrains the owner of the property from preventing the water from flowing over the land.

FLOW LINE A line that shows the low point of a drainage channel.

FLOW TIDE High tide.

FLUE An enclosed passageway in a chimney or any duct or pipe through which smoke, hot air, and gases pass upward.

FLUE GASES Smoke and hot air found in flues.

FLUE LINING The tile, pipe, or brick inside a chimney.

FLUME **1.** A natural channel through which a river or stream flows. **2.** An artificial channel used to carry running water on which logs are floating.

FLUORESCENT LIGHTING Lighting created by light fixtures that hold fluorescent tubes.

FLUORESCENT TUBE A type of lightbulb. It is a glass tube capped by two bases, which are fitted with pins to carry electricity to cathodes. Inside the tube are inert argon or argon-neon gases and minute droplets of mercury. The interior of the tube is coated with a fluores-

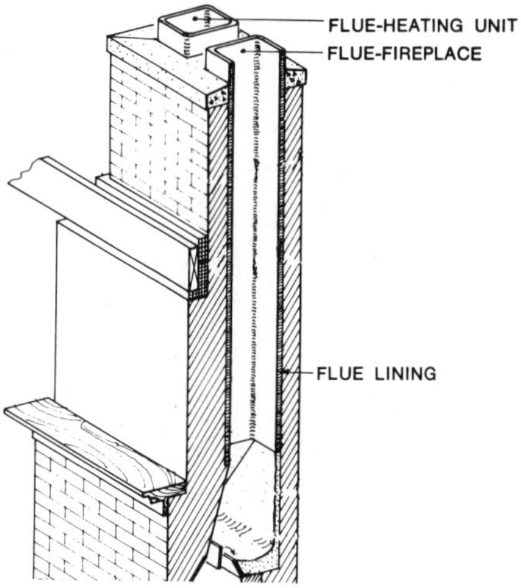

FLUE

FLUSH AND RODDED JOINT

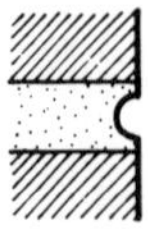

FLUSH AND RODDED JOINT

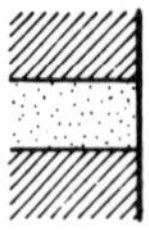

FLUSH OR RAIN CUT JOINT

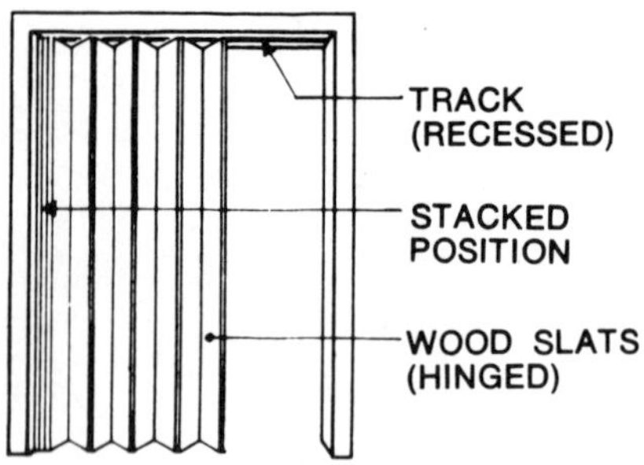

FOLDING DOOR

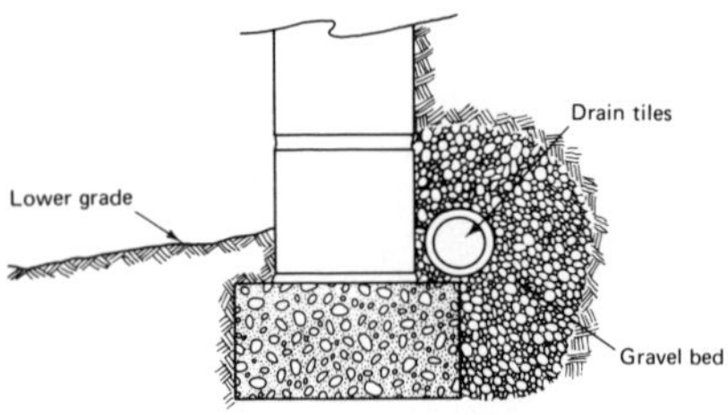

FOOTINGS

cent powder, which glows when an electron vaporizes the atoms of mercury and creates ultraviolet rays.

FLUSH AND RODDED JOINT A type of troweled brick joint.

FLUSH DOOR A door without panels that has two flat surfaces. Often, it has a hollow core.

FLUSH OR RAIN CUT JOINT A type of troweled joint that is finished flush with the surface.

FLUSH SIDING A siding of tongue and groove boards laid flush on the sidewalls.

FNMA (FANNIE MAE) *See* Federal National Mortgage Association.

FOLDING DOOR A door with panels that bend back on each other when opened.

FOOTINGS A concrete support under a foundation, chimney, or column that usually rests on solid ground and is wider than the structure being supported.

FORCED-AIR FURNACE A furnace that uses a fan to force the warm air through the ducts instead of relying on gravity to circulate the air.

FORCED SALE A sale that is made under compulsion, such as to satisfy a debt.

FORCED SALE VALUE The price that is realized at the forced sale.

FORCED VALUE *See* Forced Sale Value.

FORCED WARM AIR SYSTEMS Heating systems that rely on fans and blowers rather than gravity to circulate warm air.

FORCE MAJEURE (FRENCH) Things beyond the control of the parties involved, such as acts of God and acts of man (riots, strikes, arson, etc.).

FORECASTING To predict future happenings and conditions.

FORECLOSURE The legal proceedings by which a mortgagee, after default by the mortgagor, makes the mortgagor sell the property in order to recover the loan.

FORECLOSURE SALE When a property is sold upon court order to satisfy a debt.

FOREIGN CORPORATION A corporation incorporated in another state or country.

FORESHORE The land between the high and low water marks.

FORFEITURE When personal property is taken by the government because an individual has violated the law. In the United States, private property can only be taken by eminent domain, with just compensation, or for non-payment of taxes.

FORGERY **1.** A false signature or counterfeited document. **2.** The legal offense of using false signatures and documents with intent to deceive.

FORMICA A trade name for plastic material often used for countertops and paneling.

FORMS **1.** Temporary restraints used to control the shape of concrete, or the like, until it hardens. **2.** Instruments and documents printed in quantity with blank spaces left to be filled in with specific facts.

FOUNDATION Construction, usually below or partly below grade, that provides support for exterior walls or other structural parts of a building.

FOUNDATION WALL *See* Foundation.

FOURPLEX A class of house having four separate units connected by party walls.

FOUR-THREE-TWO-ONE RULE *See* Depth Factor.

FOYER **1.** The lobby in a theater or hotel. **2.** The small open area encountered upon entering a house.

FRACTIONAL INTEREST *See* Divided Interest.

FRACTIONAL PROPERTY A portion of a property regarded as separate from the whole property for insurance or appraisal purposes.

FRAME (WOOD) CONSTRUCTION A type of construction in which walls, partitions, and other structural members are made of wood or are dependent upon a wooden frame for support.

FRAMING A part of the building process that consists of putting together the lumber "skeleton" of the building.

FRAMING ANCHORS *See* Anchor Bolt.

FRANCHISE **1.** Specific privileges conferred by government grant, such as permission to form a corporation. **2.** A right sold by a business to operate a branch of the business using a common name and common operating techniques. **3.** The exclusive right

FORESHORE

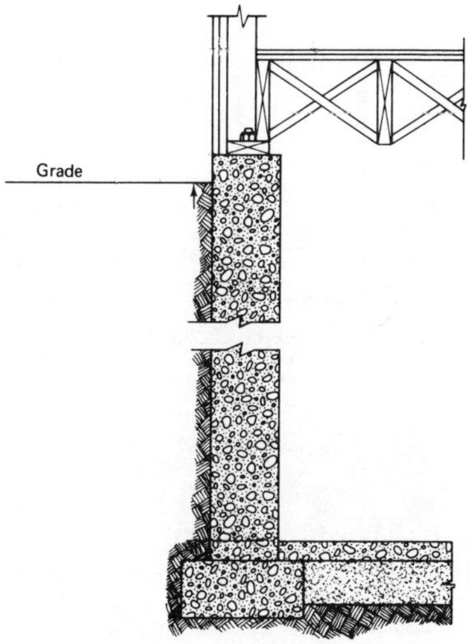

FOUNDATION

FRANKLIN STOVE

FRENCH DOORS

FRENCH FARM HOUSE STYLE

to sell a product or perform a service in a specified territory.

FRANKLIN STOVE A stove invented by Benjamin Franklin. It has cast-iron sides that radiate heat throughout a room.

FRAUD Intentional deception to gain an unfair advantage over another person because he or she relies on deceptive statements or acts.

FREE AND CLEAR Real property that has no liens against it.

FREE-BORD The area outside a fence that is included with the land inside the fence when a claim is made based on land that is fenced in.

FREEHOLD An estate held for at least the life of the owner in real property. It may be held in fee simple, conditional fee, or fee tail.

FREE-STANDING BUILDING A building that holds one business rather than a string of stores with a common roof and side walls.

FREE SWITCHING A railroad term for a rail tariff that includes switching cars to and from sidings without an extra charge to the shipper. This free service extends beyond the railroad that files the tariff because of reciprocal arrangements.

FREE SWITCHING LIMITS A railroad term for the area within which the railroad will perform switching operations.

FREEWAY A highway that charges no tolls and has all crossroads at a different grade level.

FRENCH DOORS OR WINDOWS A pair of doors that have glass panes throughout and are hinged at the jamb. They serve as both doors and windows. They look and act like doors because they extend to ground level.

FRENCH FARM HOUSE STYLE A house style based on the farm houses found in the various, widespread provinces of France. It was popular in the U.S. in the early 1900s as a design for large homes for the rich. The style varies widely as it does in France. A high, hip roof; many different materials; and many stories are common features. Half timbers are common, as are dormers that break the cornice line.

CTS SYSTEM: French
French Farm House
(Fr Farm-301)

FRENCH NORMANDY STYLE A French house style that originated in Normandy, France, where the house and barn are one building. The distinguishing turret, now usually a staircase, was originally used for grain storage or ensilage. The French Normandy has one and one-half to two and one-half stories, large chimneys, and an asymmetrical shape. Half timber, brick, stone, and stucco can be used in the exterior walls.

CTS SYSTEM: French
French Normandy
(Fr Norm-303)

FRENCH PROVINCIAL STYLE A French house style that originated in France during the reign of Louis XIV (1643–1715). The French Provincial is a perfectly balanced, one and one-half to two and one-half story house. It has a high, steep roof and curved-head upper windows that break through the cornice. French Provincials are usually built of brick and have French windows or shutters on the first floor.

CTS SYSTEM: French
French Provincial
(Fr Prov-302)

FREON A gas used as a refrigerant in air conditioners and refrigerators to produce cold air.

FRESCO A painting method where paint is applied to wet plaster on a wall. The paint dries and becomes part of the wall.

FRIEZE **1.** A horizontal trim immediately below the cornice soffit. **2.** In Greek architecture, the part above the architrave and below the cornice.

FRONT **1.** The primary face of a building; the facade. **2.** The portion of a property bordering a river, ocean, street, etc.

FRONTAGE The length of the boundary line that touches the street.

FRONTAGE ROAD A street that runs parallel to a limited access highway. Its purpose is to service abutting properties without direct access to the highway and to gather and control traffic entering and exiting from the highway. They are also called service roads.

FRONT ELEVATION The front view of a building. It is an orthographic drawing (one without perspective) of the building that is part of a complete set of plans.

FRENCH NORMANDY STYLE

FRENCH PROVINCIAL STYLE

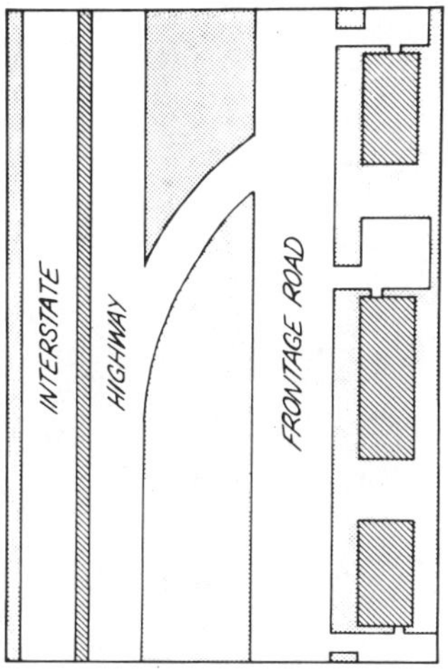

FRONTAGE ROAD

FRONT FOOT A measure of one foot wide along a property frontage.

FRONT FOOTAGE The portion of a property fronting on a major street or walkway.

FRONT FOOT VALUE The value of a piece of property expressed in terms of front foot units.

FRONT GABLE NEW ENGLAND COLONIAL STYLE *See* English Colonial Style.

FRONT MONEY **1.** The initial cash needed by an owner or developer to start a project. **2.** Money a developer must expend prior to knowing for sure that the project will go forward and that financing will be available.

FROSTLINE The depth to which frost will enter the soil. It is necessary that building footing extend below this level.

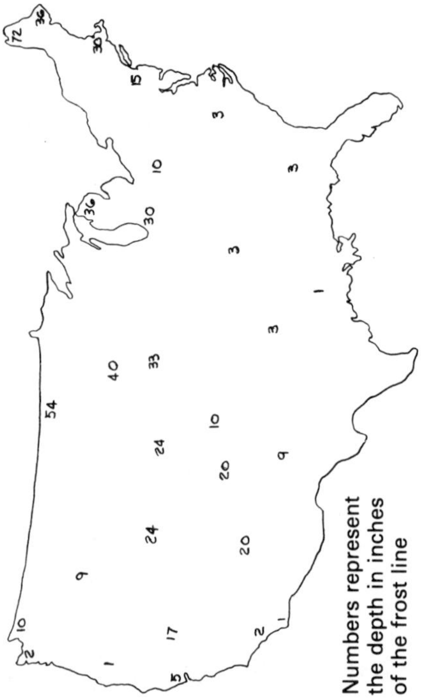

FROSTLINE

FRUCTUS NATURALES Things created by nature, like trees (if not planted by man) or minerals in the earth.

FUEL Anything that is consumed to produce energy. Common fuels used to supply energy to real estate are electricity, gas (both natural and man made), oil, wood, and coal.

FULL DISCLOSURE **1.** As used in real estate, it refers to the broker's, builder's, and owner's obligation to tell a buyer all of the known pertinent facts about the property being sold or rented. **2.** The obligation of a broker to inform all parties if a commission is being received from both the buyer and the seller.

FUNCTIONAL Something is functional if it successfully performs its intended use or purpose.

FUNCTIONAL CURABLE OBSOLESCENCE *See* Curable Functional Obsolescence.

FUNCTIONAL INCURABLE OBSOLESCENCE *See* Incurable Functional Obsolescence.

FUNCTIONAL MODERN STYLE *See* Contemporary.

FUNCTIONAL OBSOLESCENCE Impairment or defects in functional capacity or efficiency. It is all the items, including the design, quality of construction, condition, etc., on a property that detract from the property value.

FUNCTIONAL UTILITY The total of a property's attractiveness and usefulness.

FUNCTION OF THE APPRAISAL The reason that the appraisal is being made (for a mortgage, estate valuation, estimated selling price for seller, etc.).

FURNACE A heating device. An enclosure in which fuel, such as gas, coal, oil, or wood, is burned to produce energy.

FURNITURE AND FIXTURES An accounting term which refers to the movable property of a business that is not classified as stock or inventory or leasehold improvements. Often, it includes as fixtures some items which are technically not classified as such in the state where they exist.

FURRING Thin strips of wood used to level a wall and provide air space between the wall and the plaster, wallboard, or other wall surface.

FURRING STRIP *See* Furring.

FUSE An electrical safety device that protects the wiring from overheating and becoming a fire hazard. When too much electricity is being drawn through the wiring, the fuse melts, stopping the flow of electricity.

FUSEBOX A box which holds the main wiring and fuses that control the electrical circuits of a structure.

FUSUMA Japanese sliding panels.

FUTURE ADVANCE CLAUSE A clause in a mortage that lets the borrower receive additional loans without having to prepare a new mortgage. It is contained in an open end mortgage.

FUTURE DEPRECIATION An estimate of the additional loss of value that a property will suffer in the future.

FUTURE INTEREST An interest that a party has in a property that will not become effective until some time in the future.

FUTURE WORTH OF ONE A compound interest factor that, when multipled by a sum of money, shows how much that sum of money will grow to over a specified period of time at a given rate of interest.

FUTURE WORTH OF ONE PER PERIOD A factor that is multiplied by the amount of a series of level payments to determine what they will be worth in the future, including the compound interest they will earn.

FUTURE WORTH OF ONE PER PERIOD

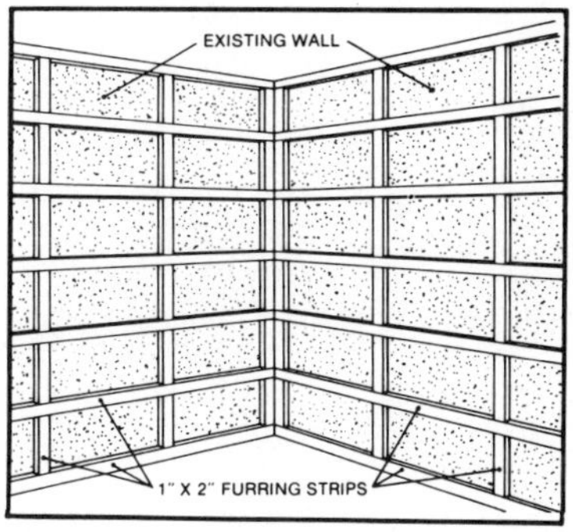

FURRING

Formula For the Factor Used to Calculate the Future Worth of One

S^n = The factor used to calculate the amount to which an investment will grow in a given number of time periods including the accumulation of interest.
n = Number of periods
i = Interest per period
$S^n = (1 + i)^n$

Example
Amount invested = \$2,347.
n = 12 year term of investment
i = 14% annual rate of interest
$S^n = (1 + .14)^{12}$
$= (1.14)^{12}$
$= 4.817905$
$\$2,347 \times 4.817905 = \$11,307.62$

FUTURE WORTH OF ONE

Formula for the Factor Used to Calculate the Future Worth of One Per Period

S_n = Factor used to calculate the future worth of one per period to which an investment will grow in a given period including the accumulation of interest.
n = Number of periods
i = Interest per period

$$S_n = \frac{S^n - 1}{i}$$

FUTURE WORTH OF ONE PER PERIOD

G

GABLE The vertical, triangular portion of a building formed by the inclining edges of a pitched roof.

GABLE DORMER A dormer with a two-plane gable roof. It is sometimes called a *doghouse* dormer.

GABLE ROOF A triangular gable formed by the ends of a ridged roof.

GABLE VENT A triangular vent beneath the joining of two roof eaves.

GAIN *See* Profit.

GALLERY **1.** A long, covered walkway used as a corridor inside or outside of a building or between buildings. **2.** The highest theater balcony. **3.** A building used for the display of art exhibits.

GALLONS PER MINUTE A measurement of the rate of the flow of a liquid, such as water from a well.

GAMBREL ROOF A two-pitched roof style that has its slope broken by an obtuse angle so that the lower slope is steeper than the upper slope.

GAP COMMITMENT A commitment received from a lender to loan the difference between the floor amount of a construction loan and the full amount. The commitment is issued to enable a contractor or developer to borrow the full amount of a take out commitment, rather than only the floor amount. The commitment is usually for a second mortgage. *See* Floor Loan and Take Out Loan.

GAP LOAN A special type of loan made to developers when their project fails to meet the conditions of their original mortgage commitment soon enough to satisfy the developer's cash needs, and some of the committed money is withheld by the original lender. The gap loan is usually made by another lender at higher inter-

GABLE DORMER

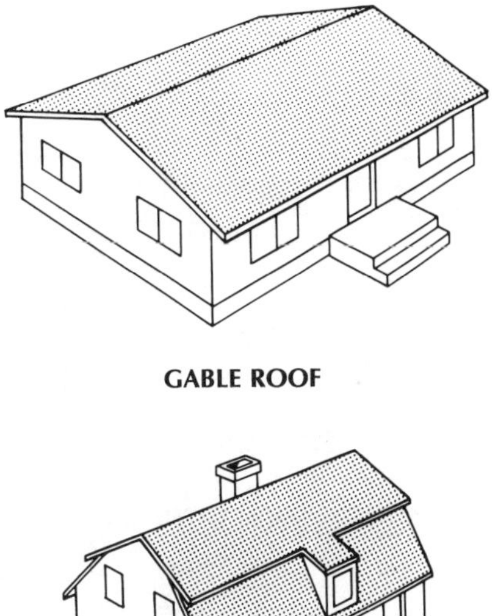

GABLE ROOF

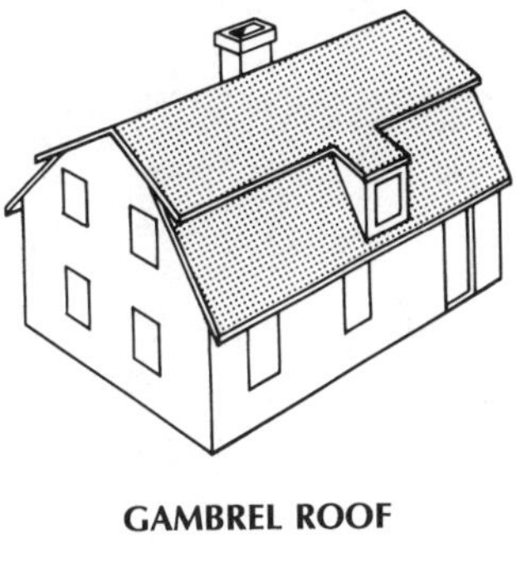

GAMBREL ROOF

est rates (because of the added risk) to provide the developer with needed funds in place of the withheld portion of the original loan.

GARAGE **1.** A building or portion of a building where motor vehicles are kept. **2.** A place for the repair and maintenance of motor vehicles.

GARBAGE DISPOSAL An electrical appliance made of a small tank with metal grinders, usually installed in a sink, that grinds food into small enough particles to be washed into the sewer system by running water.

GARDEN A small piece of land that is used for the cultivation of flowers, fruit, or vegetables that are usually for the owner's personal use.

GARDEN APARTMENT Apartments that originally were two- to three-story walk-up structures surrounded by flowers, a lawn, and plants, creating a garden-like atmosphere. Now it is an apartment project consisting of a group of buildings usually without elevators and rarely over three stories high. Often, they are built in the suburbs where land is not as expensive as in the urban centers.

GARNISHMENT A legal proceeding under which a person's money or property is taken for payment of a debt. For example, a percentage (set by statutes) of a salary is taken as payment.

GARRET *See* Attic.

GARRISON COLONIAL STYLE An American colonial house style. Although thought to have been patterned after frontier block houses, this style is probably an outgrowth of the overhang style of the Elizabethan Town House. The Garrison Colonial is a two-and-one-half story, symmetrical house with a second-story overhang in the front, traditionally ornamented with four pineapple- or acorn-shaped carved drops. Other distinguishing characteristics are a steep gable roof, an exterior chimney at one end, and dormers that often break through the cornice line.

CTS SYSTEM: Colonial American
Garrison Colonial
(Garr Co-106)

GARRISON COLONIAL STYLE

GAS LINE A pipe used to carry natural or man-made gas over long distances.

GAS STATION *See* Service Station.

GAS VENT A chimney designed and approved for use by gas-burning appliances only.

GAZEBO An open structure in which one can sit and enjoy the view. *See also* Belvedere.

GENERAL BENEFITS In condemnations, benefits to the surrounding property and community caused by the project being developed that was the cause of the taking.

GENERAL CONTRACTOR A person who contracts for the construction of an entire project and then hires subcontractors, coordinates all work, and is responsible for paying the subcontractors (plumbing contractors, electrical contractors, etc.).

GENERAL INDEX (GI) In some communities, the books used to find liens against individuals that may affect real property but which are not recorded against the property, such as liens against a buyer. General indexes can usually be found in courthouses or town halls.

GENERAL LIEN **1.** A lien that attaches to all property of the debtor rather than to specific property only. **2.** The right of a creditor to hold personal property of a debtor for payment of a debt not associated with the property being sold.

GENERAL MORTGAGE BOND A written instrument representing an obligation secured by a mortgage but preceded by senior issues (prior mortgages).

GENERAL OVERHEAD COSTS *See* Indirect Construction Costs.

GENERAL PARTNER A member in a partnership who shares in the profits and losses and has authority to bind the partnership.

GENERAL PARTNERSHIP A partnership made up of only general partners, without limited partners. General partners are responsible for the management of their partnerships and are personally liable for the debts and obligations of the partnership.

GENERAL PLAN RESTRICTIONS Restrictions imposed on an entire subdivision.

GENERAL WARRANTY The covenant in a deed whereby the grantor agrees to personally defend the title against any claim against it.

GENERATOR A machine that converts mechanical power into electrical power.

GAZEBO

GEOCODE A code number containing information about geographic locations.

GEODETIC SYSTEM The United States Coast and Geodetic Survey System. A system that consists of a network of surveyor's marks (bench marks) located by latitude and longitude. Originally used to identify federal land, the system has since been extended throughout the nation.

GEOGRAPHICAL SEQUENCE A method of filing appraisal data. Property record cards are filed by location—first by lot number, then by blocks, and finally by subdivision.

GEORGIAN STYLE

GEORGIAN STYLE An English house style that became popular in England during the reign of the four King Georges. This style was built in large numbers in the United States in the 1700s and 1800s. The Georgian is a large, formal, two-to-three-story house. It is characterized by classic lines and ornamentation. Traditionally built of brick, the Georgian has a gable or hip roof with slate shingles or copper roofing. The front entrance has Greek columns. Two large chimneys rise high above the roof at each end. Many have Palladian windows.

CTS SYSTEM: English
Georgian
(George-206)

GEORGIAN COLONIAL ARCHITECTURE *See* Georgian.

GERMANTOWN HOOD

GERMANTOWN HOOD A style of entry hood, unsupported by columns, that is found in Pennsylvania Dutch houses.

GERRYMANDER To divide an area into districts, going against apparent natural divisions, for some unlawful purpose; for example, the division of a voting district to give power to a certain political group.

GIFT A voluntary transfer of property without valuable consideration.

GIFT CAUSA MORTIS A gift conditioned upon the death of the donor which the donor may revoke before his or her death.

GIFT DEED A deed that is given without the grantor receiving any consideration.

GIFT TAX A special state or federal tax on transfers of property that are made without significant consideration.

GI LOAN A mortgage loan made by a lender for which veterans are eligible and which is partially guaranteed by the Veterans Administration, subject to VA regulations.

GINGERBREAD WORK A term used to describe extensive wooden ornamentation on a house.

GIRDER A large, horizontal beam often carrying other beams and joists, on which the floor is laid.

GIRT A horizontal member in braced framing that runs between columns, studs, and posts.

GLA *See* Gross Living Area.

GLASS A hard, transparent, or translucent substance made by melting a silica (such as sand), a flux, and a stabilizer. Molten glass can be blown, drawn, rolled, pressed, or cast. Glass comes in a large variety of colors (achieved by adding metallic oxide), sizes, and shapes.

GLASS BLOCK A hollow block made of glass and used as decoration in non-load-bearing walls.

GLASS FIBER INSULATION Insulation made out of glass fibers. It may be loose, blankets or bats, or foil backed.

GLASS-WOOL INSULATION Insulation made from glass wool (spun glass fibers that resemble wool) that has been covered with water-resistant or asphalt-treated paper.

GLAZE **1.** To finish with a glossy surface. **2.** To install glass in windows, doors, etc.

GLAZED BRICK Brick that has a ceramic glaze finish.

GLAZED TILE A ceramic tile to which a ceramic glaze is applied so that it fuses into a glass-like coating on the tile during the burning procedure.

GLAZING The act or art of installing and securing glass or glass-like (plastic) materials in prepared openings of installations (such as doors, windows,) and enclosures. Openings in which glass or glass-like materials have been installed are defined as having been glazed.

GLAZING MATERIAL, SAFETY Rubber welt, flexible adhesive, and other special-purpose materials and devices used in installing or securing safety glazing panels in prepared openings (such as doors or windows) and enclosures.

GINGERBREAD WORK

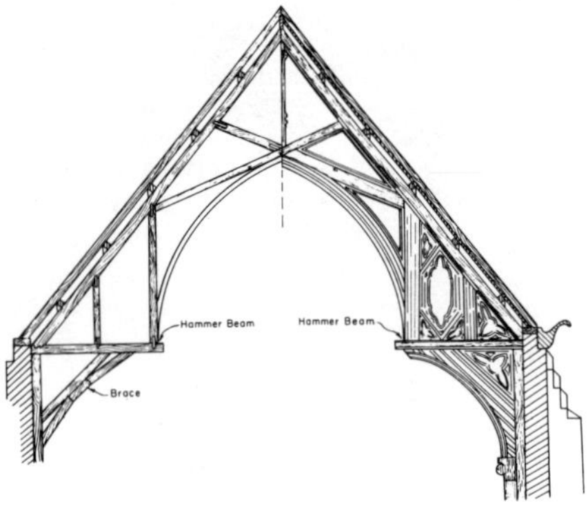

GOTHIC ARCH

GOTHIC ARCH WINDOW

GLAZING PANEL Glass or glass-like (plastic) material that is transparent or translucent, in the form of a pane or sheet, which is installed in prepared openings (such as doors or windows) and enclosures.

GLAZING PANEL, SAFETY A glazing panel constructed, treated, or combined with other materials to minimize the likelihood of accidental cutting and piercing injuries resulting from human contact and breakage of the safety glazing panel. Specifically defined wire glass, tempered glass, laminated glass, rigid plastics, and other materials that meet the test requirements of ANI Z97–1 are classified as safety glazing panels.

GLUE LAMINATED BEAMS Beams made of layers of wood, none greater than two inches thick, glued together and used to support roof rafters.

GNMA (GINNIE MAE) Government National Mortgage Association (GNMA) is a federal agency that is a part of the FHA. It specializes in the purchase of FHA-insured mortgages in the secondary mortgage market that were made at below market interest rates or that have higher than normal risk. Such mortgages could not be profitably purchased by the private sector.

GOING CONCERN VALUE The special value that a property or business has while it is in operation. The value will cease to exist when the business operation is not functioning.

GOOD FAITH Something done with good intentions (bona fide).

GOOD TITLE A title free from encumbrances, as shown by a recorded abstract of title.

GOODWILL An intangible asset based on good business reputation rather than on some physical asset.

GOODWILL VALUE An intangible value of a business resulting from its reputation in the business community and the status of its customer relations, as opposed to the value of the plant or stock.

GORE A small parcel of land, triangular in shape.

GOTHIC ARCH A pointed arch.

GOTHIC ARCH WINDOW A window in the Gothic shape with a pointed arch at the top.

GOVERNMENT LOTS Irregularly shaped pieces of land, usually along a river or lake, that could not practically be divided into sections and quarters under government survey.

GOVERNMENT NATIONAL MORTGAGE ASSOCIATION *See* GNMA.

GOVERNMENT SURVEY The system of land division and description used in parts of the the United States wherein land is divided into townships six miles square containing six sections of 640 acres.

GRACE PERIOD A period of time past the due date for an obligation during which payment may be made without being considered delinquent.

GRADE BEAM A reinforced concrete beam spanning piers and in contact with the earth. It is used for supporting wall or column construction.

GRADED LEASE *See* Step-Up Lease.

GRADE SEPARATION A structure used to enable traffic on one road to cross traffic on another road without interference.

GRADED TAX A tax designed to promote local development by imposing a progressively heavier tax rate on land and a decreasing tax burden on improvements.

GRADIENT The slope or rate of increase or decrease in elevation of a surface, road, or pipe expressed in inches of rise or fall per horizontal linear foot or as a percentage.

GRADING Plowing and raking a lot to give it a desired contour and drainage.

GRADUATED LEASE A lease that provides for a certain rent for an initial period, followed by an increase or decrease in rent over stated periods.

GRADUATE REALTORS INSTITUTE (GRI) Designation awarded by the individual state boards of Realtors. The program is supervised by the Realtors National Marketing Institute of the NATIONAL ASSOCIATION OF REALTORS®

GRAIN **1.** The arrangement of fibers in wood, leather, etc. **2.** Seeds from cereal plants. **3.** A small particle, such as a grain of sand. **4.** A unit of weight equal to 1/7000 of a pound.

GRAIN ELEVATOR **1.** A structure designed for the process-

GRADUATE REALTORS INSTITUTE

ing and storage of grain. **2.** A piece of modern farm equipment used for loading and unloading grain from trucks to storage bins.

GRANDFATHER CLAUSE A clause in a law that permits people or businesses established prior to the law to continue their operations without complying with the provisions of the law. For example, real estate brokers in business prior to some real estate license laws could obtain a license without taking tests or meeting new educational requirements.

GRANTEE
GRANTOR

GRAND LIST The term used for the tax roll or assessment list in New England communities.

GRANT A transfer of title to real property by a written instrument. A private grant is the transfer of real property from one person to another. A public grant is the transfer of real property from the government to a person.

GRANT DEED A deed used in some areas where specific covenants are created by statute and do not have to be spelled out in the deed. The covenants are automatically included in the deed by the use of the word *grant*. Often the grantor warrants that he or she has not previously conveyed the property to someone else and that he or she will convey any future interest received in the property.

GRANTEE A person who receives a transfer of real property by deed.

GRANTING CLAUSE A required clause in the deed where the seller agrees to transfer the property involved.

GRANTOR A person who transfers real property by deed.

GRANTOR-GRANTEE INDEX The record of the passing of title to all the properties in a community as kept by the recorder's office. Property is checked by tracing the names of the sellers and buyers (chain of title).

GRAVEL Loose rock found naturally or formed by rock that is crushed. Gravel will pass a 76.1 mm sieve and be retained on a 4.76 mm sieve.

GRAVEL PIT An excavation from which gravel is removed. *See also* Borrow Pit.

GRAVEL STOP A projecting collar, rib, etc. (usually a metal strip) used to keep gravel or loose surfacing from washing off a roof.

GRAVEL STOP FLASHING Metal or wood barriers installed

on built-up roofs that stop the gravel from spilling off the roof over the edge or onto another roof plane.

GRAVEYARD *See* Cemetery.

GRAVITY FURNACE A hot-air furnace that relies on gravity instead of a fan to circulate different weights of hot and cold air. It works on the principle that hot air rises and cold air settles toward the ground.

GRAZING CAPACITY *See* Capacity.

GREAT PONDS Natural ponds that have a surface area greater than 10 acres. The state has rights to such ponds. This law may vary from state to state.

GREEK ARCHITECTURE AND TERMINOLOGY A group of special terms used to describe traditional Greek ornamentations used on many buildings in the United States. For example, Greek-style columns may be Doric, Ionic, or Corinthian.

GREEK REVIVAL STYLE A colonial American house style that looks like a traditional Greek temple and is very similar to the Classic Colonial style. The Greek Revival style is a two- or three-story, symmetrical house complete with columns, architraves, friezes, and cornices—just like the classical Greek temples.

CTS SYSTEM: Colonial American
Greek Revival
(Greek-112)

GREEK REVIVAL STYLE

GREEK TILE A type of interlocking roof tile.

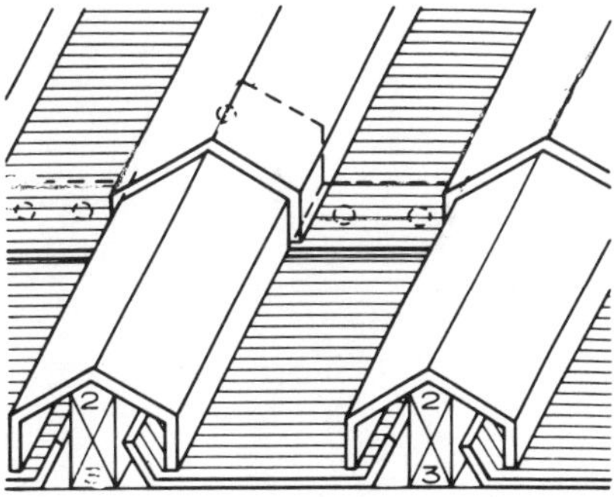

GREEK TILE

GREEN LUMBER Unseasoned lumber that has a higher moisture content than seasoned lumber.

GRID **1.** A network of cross bars equally spaced, with parallel lines intersecting at right angles. **2.** A chart that rates risk. It is used by insurance and lending companies.

GRIDIRON PATTERN The rectangular street pattern of cities that resembles a gridiron.

GROIN (GROYNE) **1.** The edge formed by the intersection where arched ceilings or roofs meet each other. **2.** A structure usually made of pilings and used as a breakwater or to resist shifting coastal sands.

GROSS Total with no deductions, such as gross sales and gross income.

GROSS ACRE An acre (43,560 sq. ft.).

GROSS AREA A way of measuring the size of a building based on its outside dimensions. It includes all of the building area, regardless of how it is finished or how it is used.

GROSS EARNINGS The total revenue from operating sources before deducting expenses incurred from gaining such revenues.

GROSS EFFECTIVE INCOME *See* Adjusted Gross Income.

GROSS INCOME Total income before the deduction of any expenses.

GROSS INCOME MULTIPLIER A figure which, when multiplied by a property's annual gross income, will produce an estimate of the value of that property. The figure is obtained by taking a sample of similar properties and dividing each property's selling price by its annual gross income (rent and other income). The results are reconciled into a single multiplier or range of multipliers.

GROSS LEASE A lease under which the lessor pays all or most of the expenses of the property, such as taxes, insurance, maintenance, and some of the utilities.

GROSS LIVING AREA A system of measuring the size of a house that is widely used by appraisers. It calls for measuring around the outside of the house above the foundation. If there are multiple stories, each story is included. Areas that are classified as garages, porches, basements, or attics are excluded from the calculations.

GROSS NATIONAL PRODUCT (GNP) The total value of all goods and services produced by a country's economy in any given time period.

GROSS PROFITS Profits before deductions. The total profits of a property or business computed before the deduction of expenses (except the cost of goods).

GROSS RENT MULTIPLIER A figure which, when multiplied by the monthly gross income, will produce an estimate of the value of that property (usually a residence). The figure is obtained by taking a sample of similar properties and dividing each property's selling price by its monthly gross income based on the property being unfurnished and without utilities being supplied. The results are reconciled into a single multiplier or range of multipliers.

GROSS RENT MULTIPLIER APPROACH A version of the income approach used by appraisers mostly for estimating the value of residences. The estimated monthly rent of the property (without furniture or utilities) is multiplied by the gross rent multiplier to produce a value or range of values.

GROSS REVENUE Total revenue before deducting expenses resulting from gaining such revenue.

GROSS SALES Total sales before the deduction of returns, allowances, etc.

GROUND FLOOR The floor in a building that is nearest the ground.

GROUND LEASE A lease for land only, exclusive of any buildings that may be on it.

GROUND LEVEL Something at the same level as the ground.

GROUND RENT Rent paid for the use of vacant land. If the property is improved, it is the portion of the total rent that is attributable to the land.

GROUNDS **1.** A large area surrounding a building that goes with the property and is under the same ownership as the building. **2.** Strips of wood attached to a wall to which trimming is attached.

GROUNDWATER An area of contained underground or perched water whose upper level provides a subsurface water table.

GROUNDWATER DRAIN A drain designed and constructed to convey groundwater away from a saturated zone of earth.

GROUT Masonry mortar of pouring consistency such as that used to fill voids and joints of masonry units.

GROVE A planting of fruit or nut-bearing trees, usually citrus trees.

GUARANTEED MORTGAGE *See* Insured Mortgage.

GUARANTEE (OF SALE) The written commitment by a broker that, within a certain period of time, the broker will, in absence of a sale, purchase a given piece of property for a specified sum.

GUARANTOR A person who makes a guaranty that some act will be performed or a payment will be made.

GUARANTY A contract, either written or verbal, in which the guarantor promises that someone else will perform an act or pay a debt.

GUEST ENTRANCE

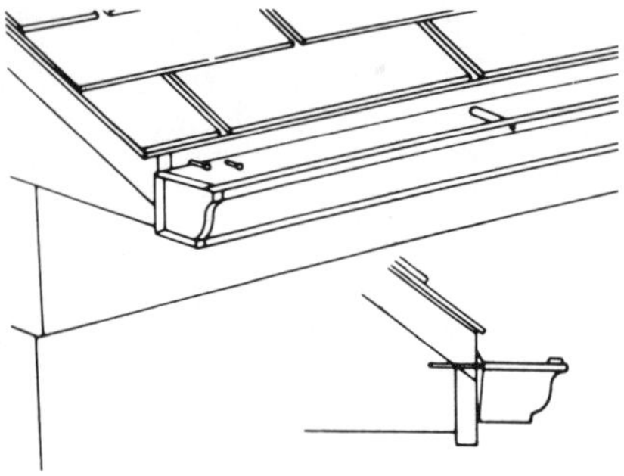

GUTTER

GUEST ENTRANCE An entrance used by guests. It is usually a front hall next to the living room. Family members may enter in the rear or through the kitchen.

GUIDE MERIDIAN A line, used in a rectangular survey, that runs due north and south as a correction line to compensate for the narrowing of the earth.

GUTTER **1.** A shallow channel of metal or wood placed directly below the eaves of a building to direct rainwater into a downspout. **2.** The channel formed by the meeting of a street and a curb.

GYPSUM A soft mineral (hydrated calcium sulphate) used to make gypsum plaster or used as a retarder in Portland cement.

GYPSUM BLOCK A building block made of gypsum and used in non-load-bearing walls and partitions.

GYPSUM PLASTER A coarse plaster used as a basecoat.

GYPSUM SHEATHING BOARDS *See* Gypsum Wallboard.

GYPSUM WALLBOARD A sheet composed of a mixture of gypsum and fiber and used as a building material. It is covered on all sides with paper. The most common size it comes in is four feet by eight feet. Sheetrock is a popular brand of gypsum wallboard.

H

HABENDUM One of the standard clauses in a deed that defines the extent of the ownership of the grantee.

HABITABLE ROOM A room designed and used for living, sleeping, eating, cooking, or a combination thereof. Bathrooms, toilet compartments, closets, halls, storage spaces, laundry and utility rooms, basement recreation rooms, and similar areas are not considered habitable rooms.

HABITANCY A place where a person lives and returns to after being absent for periods of time.

HACIENDA Spanish word for a large estate. It is still used in regions that were once under Spanish influence.

HACK STAND An area where taxicabs line up to solicit passengers.

HALF SECTION One half of a section of land that has been divided in half either north and south or east and west.

HALF TIMBER A piece of timber measuring not less than 5 inches by 10 inches.

HALF-TIMBERING Historically, a sixteenth and seventeenth century method of construction that left the strong timber frames exposed, and the spaces between were filled with plaster or brick. Today, timbers are often applied on walls for decorative purposes only.

HALF TIMBERING

HALL **1.** A term synonymous with hallway; a corridor between rooms. **2.** Traditionally, a room or building used as a meeting place.

HAMLET A small village or town.

HANDICAPPED A person with physical impairment(s) that: (1) Is (are) expected to be of long and indefinite

HANDICAPPED FAMILY

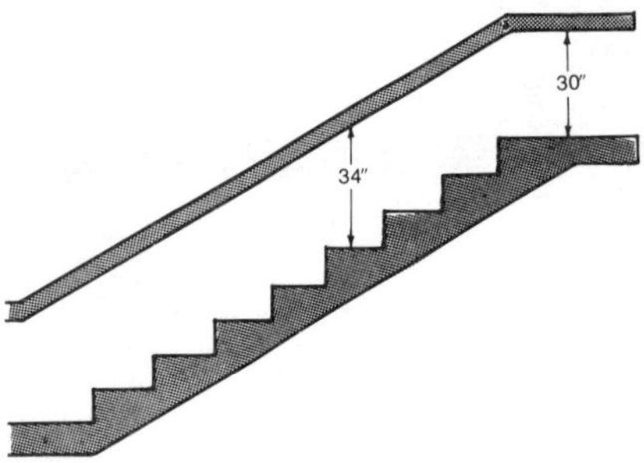

HANDRAIL

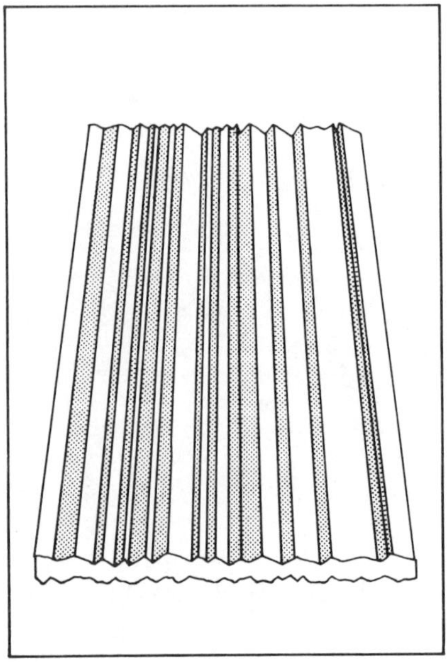

HANDSPLIT SHAKE OR SHINGLE

duration; (2) Substantially impedes his or her ability to live independently; (3) Is (are) of such nature that his or her ability to live independently could be improved by more suitable housing conditions.

HANDICAPPED FAMILY A family, the head of which (or his spouse) is handicapped.

HANDRAIL A rail placed next to a stair for support and safety. A handrail is typically attached to the wall by brackets or supported by posts called *ballusters*.

HANDSPLIT SHAKE OR SHINGLE An exterior covering material that dates back to colonial days. A properly applied shingle should last the life of a building. The difference between a shake and a shingle is that a shingle is sawed and a shake is split.

HANSEL AND GRETEL COTTAGE *See* Cotswold Cottage.

HARBOR A natural or manmade deep water inlet where ships can anchor and be safe.

HARDBOARD Layers of wood fiber compressed into sheets and used as building material.

HARD FINISH An outer coat of gypsum plaster that is troweled smooth.

HARDPAN A dense, hard soil made of silt or clay cemented or compacted together.

HARDWARE **1.** The metal fittings essential to building; doorknobs, locks, hinges, etc. **2.** The physical equipment that makes up a computer system.

HARDWOOD Wood from deciduous trees. Does not refer to the hardness of the wood. Oak, birch, and maple are commonly used in house construction for floors, cabinets, interior paneling, and furniture.

HARDWOOD FLOOR A floor made from the wood of a deciduous tree.

HARDWOOD PLYWOOD Plywood made from hardwood. It is used as decorative material and takes its name from whatever species is used for the face veneer, e.g., maple plywood.

HATCHWAY A door in a ceiling or floor that is used as an access to the story above or below.

HATHAWAY, ANN, COTTAGE *See* Cotswold Cottage.

HAZARD A dangerous condition that may potentially cause bodily injury or property damage.

H-BEAM A beam with a cross section shaped like a capital "H"

HEAD **1.** Generally, the uppermost structural member of a building. **2.** The top horizontal framing member of a door or window. **3.** A roofing tile used for forming the first course at the eaves. **4.** The upper part or source of a river or stream.

HEADER A framing member that goes across the top of an opening and carries the load above. In masonry, it is a brick, block, or stone laid with the end toward the face of the wall.

HEAD JAMB The top framing member of a door or window. *See also* Jamb.

HEAD ROOM The clear, vertical space measured from ceiling to floor.

HEADWAY *See* Head Room.

HEARTH The floor of a fireplace and the floor immediately in front of the fireplace.

HEARTWOOD The wood in the center of a log.

HEATER A self-contained heating device that is used to heat small areas.

HEATING SYSTEM A broad term used to describe any system used to heat a large area or entire building. It often consists of a central source of heat, such as a furnace or boiler. The heat is distributed by pipes or ducts into many areas or rooms.

HEAT LOSS CALCULATIONS Calculations that are made, usually by experts, to determine how much heat a building loses considering its design, construction, insulation, weatherstripping, etc.

HEAT PUMP A system employed to transfer heat into a space or substance. A condensor provides the heat while an evaporator picks up heat from air, water, etc. By shifting the flow of air or water, a heat pump system may also be used to cool the space.

HEAVY INDUSTRY Industries of a large or complex nature. Often they are unattractive, emit noise, and create pollution. A steel mill is a heavy industry.

HEDGE ROW PLANTING The planting of trees, vines, or shrubs in rows with space in between to allow easy harvesting or pruning.

HEDGING The act of trimming or pruning orchards or groves.

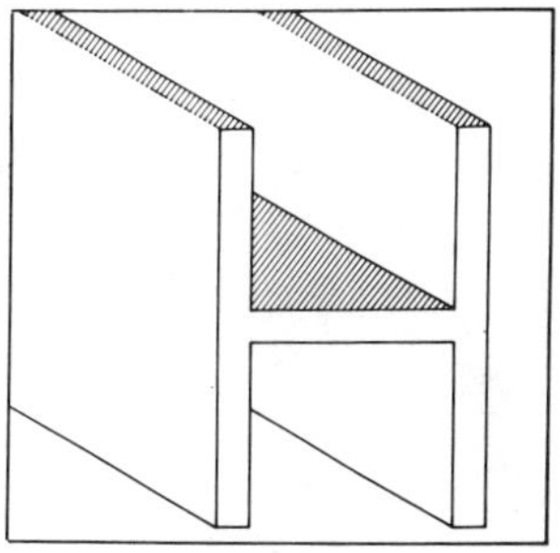

H-BEAM

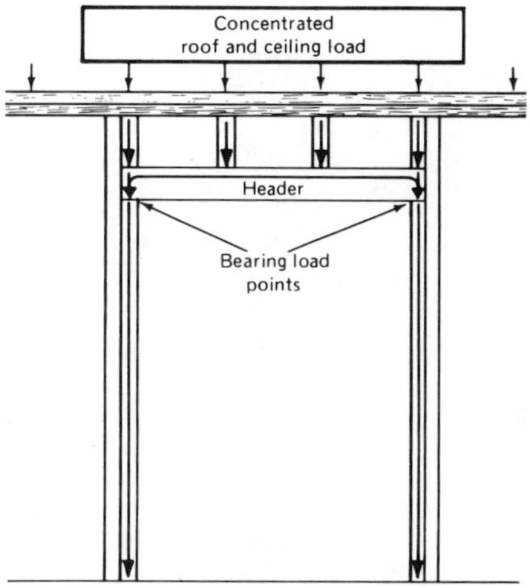

HEADER

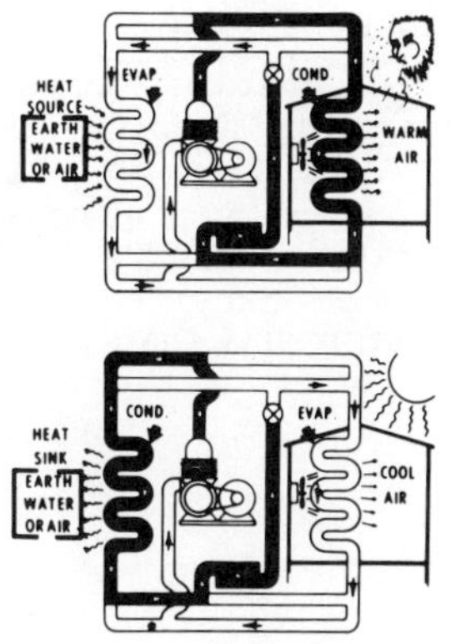

HEAT PUMP

HEEL

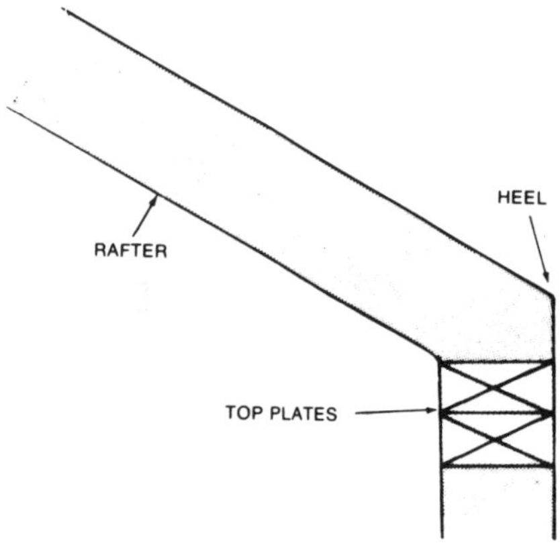

HEEL

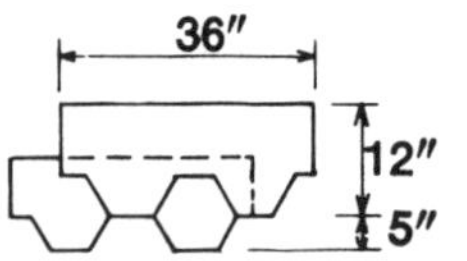

HEXAGONAL SHINGLES

HIGH VICTORIAN GOTHIC STYLE

HEEL A part of a framing member that rests on the wall plate.

HEIGHT DENSITY A zoning regulation that limits the maximum height of the structures within a designated area.

HEIR A person who inherits property. Also, the court-appointed recipient of an estate when someone dies intestate (without a will).

HEREDITAMENTS Everything capable of being inherited. It is a broad term that includes real and personal property, corporeal and incorporeal property, and a mixture of all these types of property.

HERRINGBONE WOOD FLOORING Flooring arranged in a zigzag pattern.

HEXAGONAL SHINGLES A common type of shingle that is six-sided.

HIGHEST AND BEST USE The utilization of a property to its best and most profitable use. It is that use, chosen from among reasonably probable and legal alternative uses, which is found to be physically possible, appropriately supported, and financially feasible to result in highest land value.

HIGH-RISE APARTMENT BUILDING **1.** An apartment building that is considered high in relation to those buildings surrounding it. **2.** A modern, elevator-equipped apartment building usually more than four stories high.

HIGH VICTORIAN GOTHIC STYLE A nineteenth-century American house style based on European Gothic styles. Most of the High Victorian Gothic houses were built after the Civil War. Pointed arches above the windows and doors are the distinguishing characteristic. The exterior wood trim is structural as well as decorative. The use of different stones, wood, and brick give a multi-colored effect.

CTS SYSTEM: Nineteenth Century American
High Victorian Gothic
(Hi Goth-705)

HIGH VICTORIAN ITALIANATE STYLE A nineteenth-century American Italian-based style that became popular in the United States after its rise in popularity in England in the early 1800s. Straight-sided, flat-topped, and rectangular window arches are the main distinguishing feature. The house has a square shape, ornate exterior, hip roof, and symmetrical bays.

CTS SYSTEM: Nineteenth Century American
High Victorian Italianate
(Vic Ital-706)

HIGH WATER LINE The line on the shore to which high tide rises under normal weather conditions

HIGHWAY **1.** A public roadway, street, avenue, etc., which everyone has the right to use. **2.** A large, paved road that has many lanes with high speed traffic. It is used to connect centers of population.

HIGHWAY CAPACITY The number of vehicles that can safely travel on a highway. The number reflects the size and type of vehicles, the allowable speed limit, and the road itself.

HIGHWAY EASEMENT An easement that is created for the purpose of the construction of a highway. Often, the abutting property owners own the title (fee) under the highway, and when the highway is abandoned, title reverts to these owners.

HIGHWAY FRONTAGE The portion of the land of abutting property owners that touches the highway right of way.

HIGHWAY LINE The outside limits over which a highway has right of way; not to be confused with the actual physical borders of the highway. It often includes extra land on each side of the highway.

HILLSIDE RANCH A type of house ideal for a sloping lot. The basement can be finished for additional living space complete with windows and doors.

HIP The junction of three sloping sides of a hip roof.

HIP RAFTER The rafter placed at the intersection of the sloping sides of a hip roof.

HIP ROOF A roof that rises by inclined planes from all four sides of the house.

HISTORICAL COST The actual cost of the construction of a structure when it was originally built; to be distinguished from the original cost—the cost to the present owner—which may be more or less than the historical first cost.

HISTORIC DISTRICT A district created within a community for the purpose of perpetuating the architectural heritage of the district.

HIGH VICTORIAN ITALIANATE STYLE

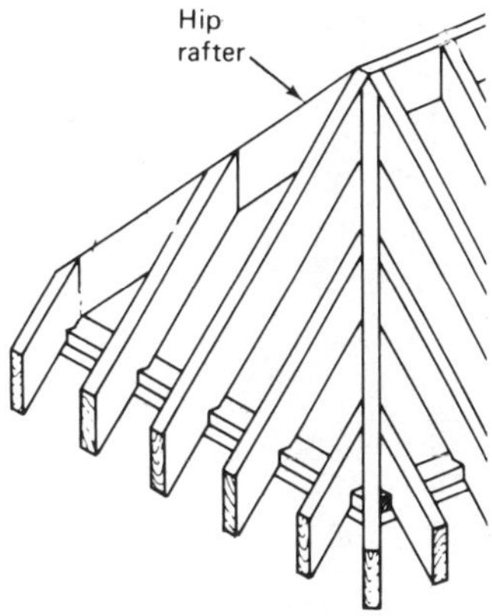

HIP RAFTER

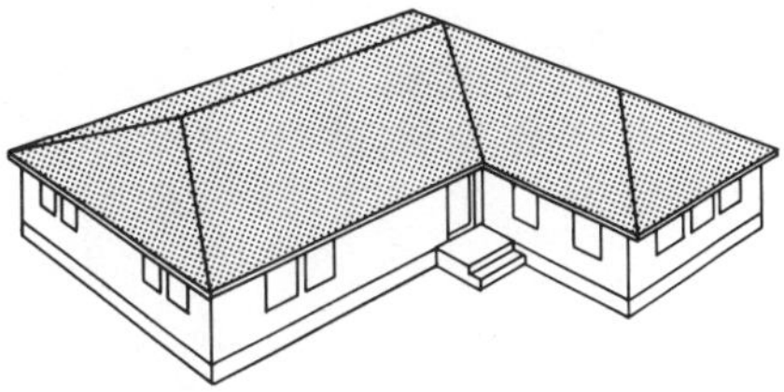

HIP ROOF

HISTORIC PRESERVATION A process of retaining the historical architectural characteristics of structures, sites, and areas through the establishment of regulations and by making structural restorations.

HISTORIC PRESERVATION LOAN A type of loan insured by the FHA. It is made by financial institutions for the purpose of preserving, rehabilitating, and restoring eligible residences.

HOLDBACK A portion of a mortgage loan that is withheld by the lender from the borrower at the time of the closing to be disbursed later, after the borrower has met specified conditions set forth in the mortgage document. Typical conditions are the construction, improvement, and repair of the property and the renting of it to a pre-specified level of occupancy.

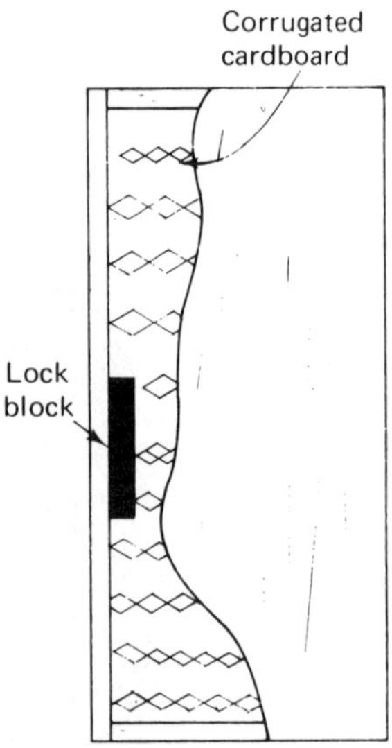

HOLLOW CORE DOOR

HOLDING OVER The act of maintaining possession of a property without the owner's consent after the lease has expired.

HOLDING PERIOD The duration of ownership for an investment set by the IRS to determine if the profit (or loss) from its sale will be taxed as a long-term or short-term capital gain (or loss).

HOLDING PERIOD YIELD The total yield of a bond held for less than its full term. It considers the gain or loss from the resale, as well as the regular interest income received, from the time the bond was purchased until it was sold.

HOLDOVER TENANT A tenant who retains possession of a leased property after his or her lease has expired.

HOLLOW CORE CONSTRUCTION A door or wall built with two facing panels with a space between them filled with air, insulation, or other filler.

HOLLOW MASONRY TILE A hollow masonry unit that has core holes which exceed 25 percent of the total tile volume.

HOLLOW WALL A masonry wall made of two layers of masonry separated by a small air space.

HOME IMPROVEMENT Additions and/or changes made to a residence that improve the structure and design, and therefore the value, of the home.

HOME IMPROVEMENT LOAN A mortgage loan, installment loan, or discount loan made by a lender for the stated purpose of making an improvement to a home.

HOMEOWNERS' ASSOCIATION **1.** An association of property owners in a residential area formed for the purpose of improving the area both physically and socially. The association may own or maintain some physical facilities. **2.** An association that is formed as part of the process of establishing the ownership of a property such as a condominium or planned unit development. The association is responsible for the regulation and maintenance of the commonly owned property.

HOMEOWNER'S INSURANCE A multi-peril policy that combines a group of insurance policies needed by homeowners. The coverage includes protection for the dwelling itself, protection for the contents, and protection against claims, such as liability claims from bodily injury and property damage claims caused as a result of ownership of the property or the activities of the owner and his family.

HOME OWNERSHIP Ownership in some form, as opposed to a tenant's or renter's status, is the American dream. Many feel that it is the foundation of our democratic way of life. *See also* Ownership.

HOMESTEAD **1.** The fixed residence of a family, including the surrounding land and buildings. **2.** An artificial estate giving certain statutory exemptions against the rights of creditors.

HOMESTEADER One who claims a homestead.

HOMESTEAD EXEMPTION LAWS State laws that allow a family to have a home and some land which are protected against the claims of general creditors.

HOME WARRANTY INSURANCE Insurance that protects the homeowner against mechanical system failures and structural failures. It is available for both new and used homes.

HOMOGENEOUS Similar or the same. In appraisal, it refers to an area having similar properties or properties of similar use. It is no longer axiomatic that maximum value is created by homogeneity.

HOOD A canopy placed over an opening or object to shelter it, such as a fireplace, chimney, or stove.

HOPPER A piece of material on the sides of an awning type of window that reduces the draft. An awning type of window has hinges at the top to permit the window to open horizontally to become an "awning."

Items Covered by a Typical Homeowners Insurance Policy

- Damage to your home
- Damage to ancillary buildings
- Damage to your seasonal dwelling
- Damage to your personal property
- "All Risk" coverage for scheduled items
- Watercraft and their trailers
- Loss of use (living expense insurance)
- Trees, shrubs, lawns and plants
- Debris removal
- Fire department service charge
- Credit card forgery
- Counterfeit money
- Glass breakage
- Premises liability
- Personal liability
- Medical payments to others
- Property damage of others

HOMEOWNER'S INSURANCE

HOPPER

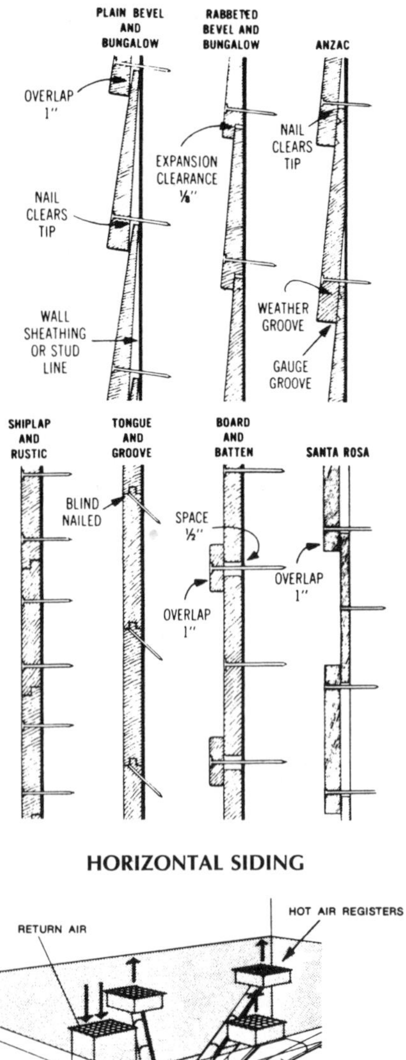

HORIZONTAL SIDING

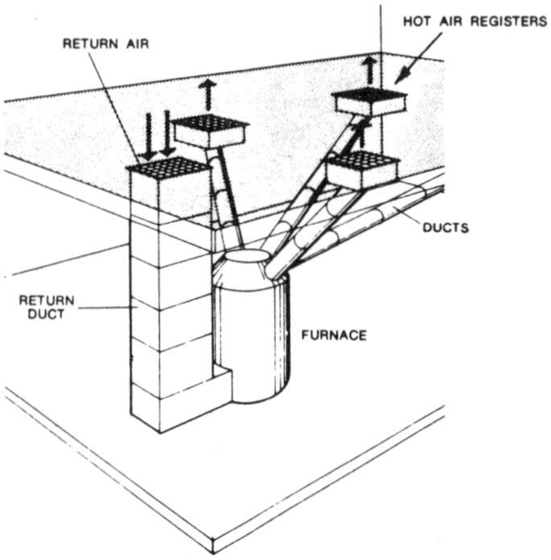

HOT-AIR GRAVITY SYSTEM

HOPPER WINDOW *See* Hospital Window.

HORIZON **1.** The line where earth and sky seem to meet.

HORIZONTAL PROPERTY ACTS Laws enacted by various states pertaining to the formation of condominiums. They permit ownership of layers of air space as real property ownership.

HORIZONTAL SIDING A group of siding materials that are attached to the sheathing in horizontal rows. Some common types are drop siding, bevel siding, and flush siding.

HOSE BIBCOCK *See* Bibcock.

HOSKOLD, H. E. An English mining engineer who originated the Hoskold method for valuation of real estate that has depleting assets, such as coal mines and timberland. He used a specially constructed set of tables.

HOSKOLD FACTOR A special multiplier made popular by H. E. Hoskold that is used to convert an income stream from a wasting asset into a value. It provides for a sinking fund that is assumed to be reinvested at a safe rate to compensate for the value of the asset that is being depleted. *See also* H. E. Hoskold.

HOSPITAL A place where the sick and injured receive care, nursing, and surgery, primarily as in-patients. A hospital may be publicly or privately owned (non-profit and proprietary).

HOSPITAL WINDOW A window that is hinged on the bottom, opens inward, and has hoppers (draft preventers) on the sides.

HOT-AIR GRAVITY SYSTEM A type of heating system where the air is heated in a furnace and distributed through ducts without the aid of fans. The circulation of the air depends on the fact that hot air will naturally rise and cold air will naturally settle downward.

HOT-AIR HEATING SYSTEM *See* Warm Air System.

HOTEL Today, hotels tend to be either in resorts or urban centers. They have sleeping rooms (most with private bathrooms), suites, meeting rooms, banquet facilities, restaurants, and many other amenities.

HOT-WATER HEATER A tank in which hot water is heated for domestic, commercial, or industrial use.

HOT-WATER HEATING SYSTEM A heating system that uses

hot water circulating from a boiler and flowing through a series of pipes to the areas to be heated and back to the boiler.

HOT-WATER PIPE A pipe that is part of a hot-water heating system, or a domestic hot-water system, that conveys the water away from the source of heat.

HOT-WATER SYSTEM *See* Domestic Hot Water System.

HOUSE **1.** A general term for a building that is designed for use as living quarters. **2.** All or part of a legislative assembly such as the House of Representatives of the United States Congress.

HOUSE PLANS Drawings, usually in scale, of a house showing all the design and construction details. A complete set of house plans consists of the following:

1. Orthographic projections of each floor and the basement
2. Electrical plan
3. Plumbing plan
4. Wall sections
5. Elevations of all sides
6. Plot plan
7. Door and window schedules
8. Specifications

HOUSE STYLE The exterior design of a house based on historic or contemporary fashions.

HOUSE TYPE The physical configuration of a house, not the style. Examples of terms describing a house style would be one, two, or three-story; Raised Ranch; Split-entry; etc.

HOUSING AND HOME FINANCE AGENCY (HHFA) A federal agency created in 1947. A forerunner of HUD, it had many of the same powers and duties. It is no longer in existence.

HOUSING AND URBAN DEVELOPMENT, DEPARTMENT OF The cabinet-level department of the federal government that is responsible for major government housing programs. Its functions include the broad operations of the Federal Housing Administration (FHA), urban renewal, model cities, nursing homes, sewer, and water facilities, etc. It also developed and implemented the Real Estate Procedures Act (RESPA).

HOUSING STARTS The number of residences on which construction has begun in a specified period at a designated location, which may be a community, region,

Major House Styles in the CTS System

- Colonial American
- English
- French
- Swiss
- Latin
- Oriental
- Nineteenth Century American
- Early Twentieth Century American
- Post World War II American

HOUSE STYLE

House Types in the CTS System

- One-story
- One-and one-half story
- Two-story
- Two-and one-half story
- Three or more stories
- Bi-level or
  Raised ranch or
  Split entry or
  Split foyer
- Split levels
- Mansion
- Other

HOUSE TYPE

HUDSON RIVER BRACKETS

state, or the whole nation. It is used as an economic indicator.

HOUSING STOCK The total inventory of dwelling units in a designated area, such as a community, region, state, or the nation. This includes both owned and rented units.

HUD *See* Housing and Urban Development, Department of

HUDSON RIVER BRACKETS Large brackets under the cornices common on the Italian Villa house style.

HUMIDIFIER A mechanism that raises the humidity by emitting water vapor into the air. It may be part of the heating system or a separate piece of equipment.

HUNDRED PERCENT LOCATION The location in the central business district that has the most potential for retail business because of the number of people who pass through it.

HUTCH **1.** A house for rabbits. **2.** A very small house, hut, or hovel that people live in.

HYDRAULIC CEMENT A cement that resists moisture and can harden under water.

HYDROELECTRIC PLANT A plant in which energy from flowing water is turned into electricity.

HYDRONIC SYSTEM A hot-water heating system.

HYDROSTATIC HEAD Water pressure on a surface due to the height of the water above a specific point.

HYDROSTATIC PRESSURE *See* Artesian Well.

HYPOCAUST An early Roman heating system consisting of small masonry flues in the walls and floors that distributed hot air from room to room.

HYPOTHECATE To pledge a property as security for a mortgage loan without actually delivering title.

I

I-BEAM A metal framing member whose cross section forms the letter "I."

I-GIRDER *See* I-Beam.

IGNEOUS ROCK Rock formed by cooling magma (molten volcanic material).

ILLEGAL CONTRACT An agreement that is contrary to existing law or public policy and therefore cannot be enforced in court.

ILLIQUIDITY An adjective which describes assets that cannot be easily liquidated (i.e., sold and turned into cash).

IMPACT INSULATION CLASS A single-figure rating that provides an estimate of the impact sound insulating performance of a floor-ceiling assembly. It is a measure of the structure's ability to reduce the transmission of noise.

IMPACT SOUND TRANSMISSION Sound that is caused in a structure from such sources as footsteps on a floor, dropped objects, slamming doors, or vibrations from mechanical equipment. Floor/ceiling constructions are prime sources of problems caused by this type of noise transmission.

IMPERVIOUS SURFACE Dense, compact, fine-grained soils that restrict the infiltration of water.

IMPLIED AGENCY An agency that, although not expressly set out either verbally or in writing, is created by the voluntary acts of the principal and the agent.

IMPLIED CONTRACT A contract that is created by the acts and conduct of the parties involved rather than verbally or in writing.

IMPLIED EASEMENT An easement of necessity.

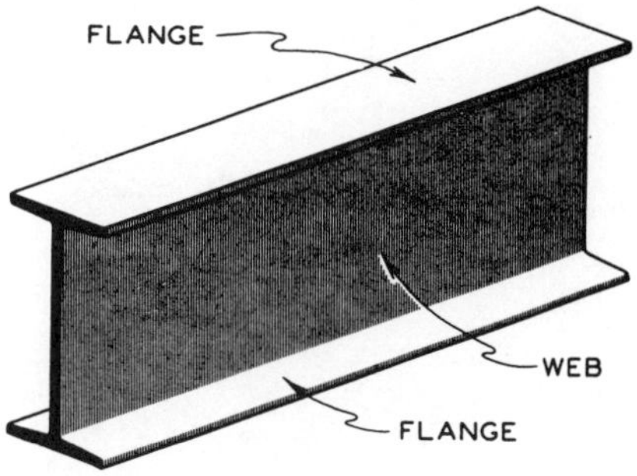

I-BEAM

IMPORTANT LAND FEATURES An outline that lists the significant features of a piece of land, such as topography, soil types, road location, etc.

IMPROPER IMPROVEMENT An improvement that does not conform to the highest and best use of a site.

IMPROVED LAND **1.** Land that has been improved by the creation of some structure (for example). **2.** Land ready for development that has been rough graded, has been drained as necessary, and has installed utilities.

IMPROVEMENTS Additions made to a property or utilities that are intended to increase the value of the property.

IMPROVEMENTS ON LAND *See* Land Improvements.

IMPROVEMENTS TO LAND *See* Land Improvements.

IMPUTED INCOME Savings that owners receive when they occupy their own buildings because they do not have to pay rent. When the value of owner-occupied buildings is estimated, this savings must be added to the rents received from the other tenants to give a true picture of the income potential of the property.

INADEQUATE IMPROVEMENT *See* Under-improvement.

INCHOATE DOWER A wife's interest in her husband's real property while he is living, which may become a right of dower upon his death.

INCHOATE INSTRUMENT An unrecorded instrument, such as a deed, which the law requires to be recorded. Until it is recorded, it is valid only between the parties who made it and others who know about it. However, it does not affect anyone who does not have notice of its existence.

INCINERATOR A furnace-type device for the burning of rubbish. It is often designed to give off a minimum of heat and smoke and to burn the rubbish as completely as possible.

INCOME The amount of money earned over a certain time period and caused by results of a person's or organization's activities, including the return on invested funds.

INCOME APPROACH One of the approaches to value used by real estate appraisers to estimate the value of property being appraised. It is based on the theory that the present value of a property is equal to the present value of its future capacity to produce income including the proceeds of a sale at a future date.

Steps of the Income Approach

- Estimate potential gross income
- Estimate and deduct a vacancy and collection loss allowance to derive effective gross income
- Estimate the stabilized operating expenses
  - Fixed expenses
  - Operating expenses
  - Reserves
- Deduct the expenses from the effective gross income to derive the net operating income (NOI)
- Develop an appropriate capitalization rate
- Divide the NOI by the capitalization rate to derive a value indication by the income approach

INCOME APPROACH

INCOME AVERAGING A method used in computing the amount of income tax that is due. The rate of tax is computed by a formula that averages the taxpayer's income over a period of several years. For example, if a real estate salesperson earns $20,000 a year for four years and then, in the fifth year, sells a skyscraper and earns $200,000, he or she could take the total income for five years ($80,000), divide by five, and then pay taxes at a rate based on $56,000 average income per year over the five-year period.

INCOME MULTIPLIER A reciprocal of the overall rate. *See also* Net Income Multiplier.

INCOME PARTICIPATION One of the new forms of mortgage whereby the morgagee shares in a percentage of the mortgaged property's income, usually over the term of the mortgage.

INCOME PREMISE The basis of the capitalization process used by real estate appraisers to estimate the value of a property. It is based on the assumption that, even though the future income installments of a property may fluctuate, their stabilized equivalent may be assumed. This assumed income stream is capitalized into a present value estimate.

INCOME PRICE RATIO The unadjusted ratio of net income to the selling price of a property.

Examples of Income Price Ratio Calculations

Sale price:	$325,000
Net income:	$ 37,000
Income price ratio = 8.78 ($325,000 ÷ $37,000)	
Sale price:	$1,375,000
Net income:	$ 125,000
Income price ratio = 11 ($1,375,000 ÷ $125,000)	
Sale price:	$ 73,000
Net income:	$ 8,000
Income price ratio = 9.125 ($73,000 ÷ $8,000)	

INCOME PRICE RATIO

INCOME PROPERTY Property that has the primary purpose of producing income, usually from rents. It may also produce income from business profits that can be segregated so that the portion directly attributable to the property can be estimated.

INCOME RISK The amount of risk estimated to exist that a future income stream projected for a property will occur as estimated.

INCOME TAX A tax levied by the federal, state, or local government on the income earned by a person, corporation, or other organization subject to being taxed according to the applicable tax legislation.

INCOME TAX LIABILITY As it refers to income-producing real estate, it is the income taxes that will be due on the net operating income produced by the property, less the mortgage interest and depreciation. It is the tax on that portion of a property's income that is unsheltered.

INCOME TAX LIEN *See* Tax Lien.

INCORPOREAL PROPERTY Any "invisible" interest in real property, such as rights of way or rights of use that have not been exercised.

INCREASE CLAUSE *See* Escalation Clause.

INCREASING AND DECREASING (DIMINISHING) RETURNS A valuation principle which states that an increase in such things as the amount of labor, materials, amenities, capital, or any other factor of production may not increase the value of the property equal to the cost of the added items. For example, the addition of a second story to a commercial building may increase its value more than the cost of adding the second story, while the addition of a third story to this same building may add value far less than the cost of the third story.

INCREASING ANNUITY A steadily increasing net operating income of a property forcasted over a long period of time. To be classified as an annuity, the income stream should be low risk, durable, and of high quality.

INCREMENT An increase, or growth, often used in reference to increases in land value and caused by factors such as population growth that have little to do with the activities of the property owner.

INCREMENT UNEARNED *See* Unearned Increment.

INCUMBRANCE *See* Encumbrance.

INCURABLE DEPRECIATION A defect of design, material, condition, etc., of a property that is not prudent to cure because the cost to effect the cure would be greater than the value added to the property caused by curing the defect.

INCURABLE FUNCTIONAL OBSOLESCENCE A defect in a property that reduces its value as a result of its design, materials, condition, etc., as opposed to its age or conditions off the premises. The cost to cure the defect is greater than the value added by effecting the cure.

INDENTURE BOND A deed that contains reciprocal agreements.

INDEPENDENT APPRAISAL **1.** An appraisal made by someone who has no relationship with the property and/or the people for whom the appraisal is made and who, therefore, has no vested interest in how high or low the estimated value is. **2.** An appraisal made by a single appraiser independently and without help from other appraisers.

INDEPENDENT CONTRACTOR A self-employed person who performs services without being controlled by the person or organization for whom the services are rendered. For a real estate salesperson to be an independent contractor, he or she must be free to act independently and without obligations such as floor time, meeting attendance, fixed hours, etc. The independent contractor should be paid gross amounts without tax deductions for his or her services.

INDEX LEASE *See* Escalation Clause.

INDEX NUMBER A number used to express the difference between the value, price, cost, etc., of a group of items at two or more different points of time. Traditionally, a base point in time is designated as 100, and the index number of other times reflects changes from the base. An example of an index is the Consumer Price Index issued by the United States Department of Labor.

INDIRECT CONSTRUCTION COSTS *See* Indirect Costs.

INDIRECT COSTS Costs to an owner to develop a property (other than site acquisition costs) that would not typically be included in a general construction contract, such as:

Appraisal and consulting fees;
Architectural, surveying, and engineering fees;
Legal and accounting fees;
Financing costs;
Insurance during construction;
Taxes during construction;
Interest during construction;
Owner's overhead during construction;
Losses, including a reasonable return on invested capital from the completion of the project until the project reaches an acceptable occupancy level.

INDIRECT LIGHTING Lighting with softened glare achieved by reflection of the light off the ceilings, walls, or other surfaces.

INDIRECT SUBSIDIES *See* Subsidy, Indirect.

INDIVIDUAL SYSTEM A utility system, such as water or sewerage, serving a single property.

INDORSE *See* Endorsement.

INDORSEMENT (ENDORSEMENT) *See* Endorsement.

INDUSTRIAL DISTRICTS Areas in which the major improvements are of an industrial nature such as factories, warehouses, etc.

Consumer Price Index
(1967 = 100)

Year	*Housing*	*All items*
1940	52.4	42.0
1945	59.1	53.9
1950	72.8	72.1
1955	82.3	80.2
1960	90.2	88.7
1965	94.9	94.5
1970	118.9	116.3
1975	166.8	161.2
1979	227.6	217.4
1980	263.2	247.0

INDEX NUMBER

INDUSTRIAL PARK A park-like area especially developed to accommodate industry with appropriate wider roads, water supply, sewage disposal, and other needed utilities.

INDUSTRIAL PROPERTY **1.** Land that is zoned for, and adaptable for, industry. **2.** Property suited for and specially improved for industrial use.

INDUSTRIAL SIDING A railroad track that runs alongside and serves an industrial building or park and is connected to a main railroad line.

INDUSTRIAL TAX EXEMPTION A property tax exemption given by local, county, or state governments in order to encourage industries to locate in a certain area.

INFILTRATION **1.** The gradual change in the make-up of the population or the use of the properties in an area. **2.** The seeping into a building of air or water through cracks and other unsealed openings.

INFLATION A general rise in prices throughout a wide area beyond the expected moderate increase in prices caused by a growing economy.

INFRASTRUCTURE The network of public facilities (such as schools, sewers, parks, etc.) located within a community.

INGRESS AND EGRESS A right to enter upon and pass through land.

INHARMONIOUS The opposite of harmonious. It refers to a property *not* suited to its surroundings.

INHERITANCE Property that is received or will be received by an heir from an estate.

INHERITANCE TAX Tax paid for the privilege of inheriting property rather than for the right to transmit property upon death.

INJUNCTION A court order that restrains a party from acting or continuing some action. It also applies to the agents and servants of the party. It may be temporary or permanent.

INLAID LINOLEUM A term applied to all types of "true" linoleum, including marbleized, jasper, plain, and molded types, as distinguished from the less expensive, inferior, enamelled or thin-faced felt sheets.

INLAID PARQUET *See* Parquet Floor.

INLAND WATERS All bodies of water exclusive of the open sea.

INLET A narrow waterway extending inland.

IN LIEU TAX Payments received by a community, county, or state from property owners who are not required to pay *ad valorem* because of an exemption they have. For example, a university not subject to property taxes may voluntarily pay a community for the services and protections it receives.

INNER CITY A general term for a low-income, high-crime area of a city. It is not necessarily the geographic center of the city.

INNER HEARTH The inner portion of a fireplace where wood, coal, or gas is burned.

INNOCENT PURCHASER FOR VALUE A bona fide buyer, one who buys in good faith with no prior knowledge of unrecorded interests in the property.

IN PERPETUITY Forever.

IN REM An action against a thing as opposed to an individual person.

INSIDE LOT A lot far enough away from an intersection so as not to be considered under corner influence.

INSIDE TRIM *See* Interior Trim.

INSOLVENCY A situation when someone or some organization cannot pay their debts.

INSOLVENT *See* Insolvency.

INSPECTION The examination of a property for a specific purpose, such as to determine its condition, whether it is termite infested, its interior layout, etc.

INSTALLMENT CONTRACT A type of real estate sale based on an agreement between buyer and seller wherein payment is made in specified installments (usually monthly). Equitable title and possession of the property pass to the buyer at the beginning of the contract, and legal title passes after all the required payments have been made. *See also* Land Contract.

INSTALLMENT LAND SALES CONTRACT *See* Land Contract.

INSTALLMENT SALE A term used by the Internal Revenue Service to describe a sale where sellers receive less than 100 percent of the cash due to them in the first

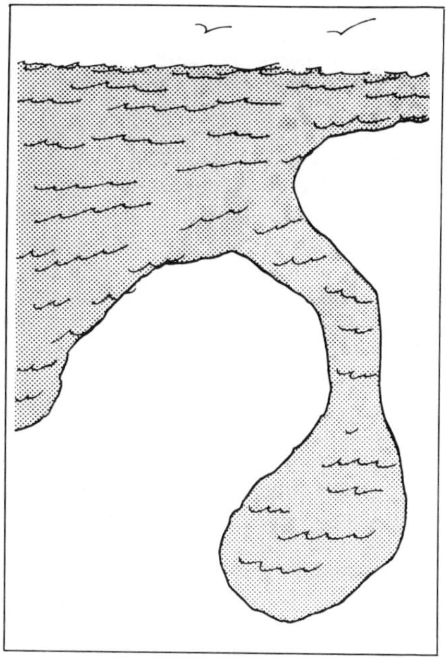

INLET

calendar year of the sale. Taxes are due yearly only on that percentage of the gain that is equivalent to the ration of cash received to the total amount of cash due.

INSTITUTE OF REAL ESTATE MANAGEMENT (IREM) One of the institutes of the NATIONAL ASSOCIATION OF REALTORS.® Its members specialize in property management. It confers the CPM (Certified Property Manager) designation.

IREM

INSTITUTE OF REAL ESTATE MANAGEMENT

INSTITUTIONAL ADVERTISING Advertising designed to improve the image of a person, company, or organization rather than to directly sell a product or service.

INSTITUTIONAL LENDER Banks, insurance companies, pension funds, savings and loan associations, and other non-profit institutions who, legally during the course of their ordinary business, make loans on a regular basis.

INSTITUTIONAL PROPERTY **1.** Property owned and run by nonprofit organizations such as schools or hospitals. **2.** Schools, hospitals, mental institutions, foundations, etc.

INSTRUMENT A formal, legal document such as a sales contract, deed, mortgage, etc.

INSULATING BOARD OR FIBERBOARD A board made of compressed plant fibers, such as wood or cane, used as a building material.

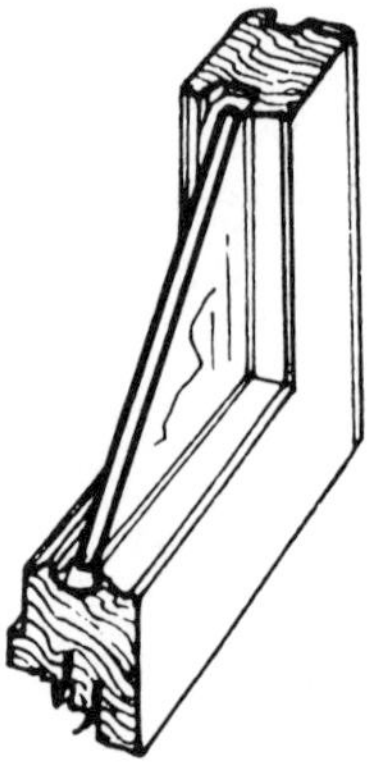

INSULATING GLASS

INSULATING GLASS Two pieces of double- or single-strength glass sealed together with an air space between them.

INSULATION **1.** Any material used to reduce the transmission of heat and cold or to reduce fire hazard. **2.** Material used to cover wire and act as a barrier to the transmission of electricity.

INSULATION BOARD *See* Insulating Board.

INSURABLE INTEREST An insurance term which expresses the concept that only people or organizations that have an interest in a property or who will suffer a loss in the event of its damage or destruction may insure the property and receive benefits as a result of these events.

INSURABLE (INTEREST) VALUE The value of property for insurance purposes. The value of those portions of a property that are considered to be insurable.

INSURANCE A contract between an insured (in real estate, a property owner or someone else with an insurable interest in a property) and an insurance company (the insurer) whereby the insurer agrees to indemnify the insured for damages or losses they incur as a result of perils or events specified in the contract (insurance policy).

INSURED MORTGAGE A mortgage in which payments to the mortgagee are guaranteed in the event the mortgagor fails to make them.

INTANGIBLE ASSET *See* Intangible Property.

INTANGIBLE PROPERTY Personal property that has value but cannot be physically touched. Examples are patents, copyrights, trademarks, the good reputation of a business, a franchise, etc.

INTANGIBLE VALUE The value of intangible property.

INTENSITY The amount of labor and capital put into the development of a parcel of land. For example, how many dwelling units per acre.

INTENSIVE FARMING The input of large amounts of labor and capital into land to produce maximum production of crops.

INTERCHANGE A system of ramps, overpasses, below-grade-level changes, etc., used to regulate highway traffic to reduce the need for controls such as lights and stop signs.

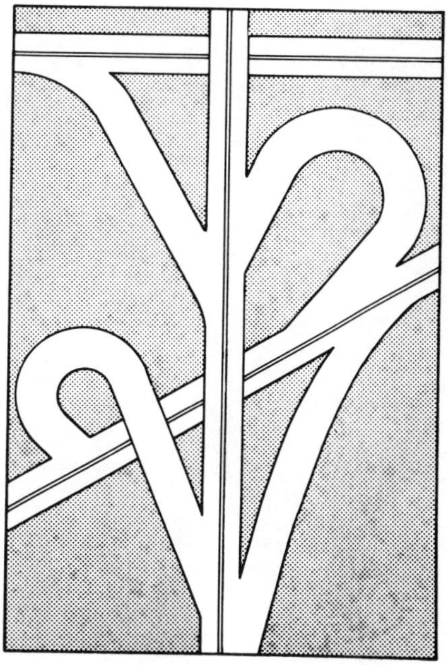

INTERCHANGE

INTER-COMMUNICATION SYSTEM An electrical system of microphones and speakers that uses low-voltage, hazard-free wiring and facilitates communication between rooms.

INTEREST **1.** A right or share in something. **2.** Money paid for the use of borrowed money. **3.** Money paid to savers by thirft institutions for keeping the money at that institution.

INTEREST ONLY LOAN A loan for which the lender is repaid the principal in one lump sum at the end of the loan term and is paid interest only during the term of the loan.

INTEREST RATE A percentage of a principal sum that is paid for by the borrower for its use.

INTERIM FINANCING A temporary or short-term loan usually secured by a mortgage.

INTERIM LOAN *See* Interim Financing.

INTERIM USE Temporary use of a property to produce some income during the period in which development is postponed.

INTERIOR LOT *See* Inside Lot.

INTERIOR TRIM The interior finish of a building, such as the casings, moldings, and baseboards.

INTERIOR TYPE PLYWOOD A plywood made with less expensive, soluble adhesives. It should not be used in areas where it will be exposed to water or humidity.

INTERNAL RATE OF RETURN The effective annual rate of return (interest) on an investment. It is generally a rate that is calculated when an investment is analyzed instead of being the stated or given rate.

INTERNATIONAL REAL ESTATE FEDERATION (FIABCI) An international real estate organization with headquarters in Paris, France. It has chapters in 37 countries. Its purpose is to exchange ideas and techniques. It holds an annual World Congress.

INTERNATIONAL STYLE An early twentieth-century American house style introduced in Europe in the 1920s by Walter Gropius, Ludwig Mies van der Rohe, and the architects of the Bauhaus. The design was introduced in the United States in the 1930s and is the basis of much modern architecture. The design is simple and has no ornamentation. The roof is flat, and wall surfaces are smooth and uniform. Windows appear continuous and often go around corners.

CTS SYSTEM: Early Twentieth Century American International (Internat-804)

INTERNATIONAL STYLE

INTERPLEADER An action filed in court by someone who holds funds in which they have no interest asking the court to instruct them as to what to do with the money. A court action that can be filed by a real estate broker holding a commission claimed by both the buyer and the seller.

INTERPOLATION The act of approximating a value between two known quantities within the range of available data. It is used with mortgage interest, depreciation, building costs, etc., tables when the amount to be looked up falls between two quantities on the table.

INTERSECTION A crossing, usually of lines or roads, at the same grade.

INTERSTATE Between two or more states.

INTERSTATE HIGHWAY SYSTEM The federal system of high-speed, limited-access roads that connects major cities and industrial areas from coast to coast across the United States. It also serves as part of the National Defense System.

INTERSTATE LAND SALES Offering of lots in subdivisions for sale to purchasers who are from different states than where the property is located. The buyers are, therefore, very dependent on the good will of the seller. Federal Disclosure Laws now give the purchaser three days after signing an agreement in which to withdraw.

INTESTACY *See* Intestate.

INTESTATE A person who dies without leaving a will or who leaves a will that is invalid.

INTESTATE LAWS Laws that control the distribution of an estate of someone who dies intestate.

INVENTORY **1.** A detailed list of all articles and items belonging to a person. **2.** A list of the stock on hand of a business. It usually contains, at a minimum, the name of each item, its stock number, its cost, and the quantity of the item on hand.

INVERSE CONDEMNATION A legal process wherein an owner of a property may sue for damages caused as a result of a condemnation that has been publicly announced but has not been performed by the condemning body within a reasonable period from the time of the announcement.

INVESTED CAPITAL The original capital invested in an enterprise plus profits that are put back into the company (or not withdrawn).

INVESTMENT Money placed in a property, business, stock, etc., with the intention of making a profit or receiving interest as well as ultimately recovering the invested money.

INVESTMENT ANALYSIS An analytical process used to estimate the attractiveness of an investment. It uses known benchmark ratios as tools for the analysis. It considers the goals of the investor, the investor's potential income tax liability, and other identifiable characteristics.

INVESTMENT PROPERTY Property acquired for the purpose of making a profit. The profit may consist of income resulting from the operation of the property, capital gains made on its sale in the future, or a combination of both.

INVESTMENT TRUST A company established specifically for the purpose of being used as a vehicle for investors to pool their money and make investments in stocks, real estate, or other types of investment. Capital is raised by the sale of the company's stock. Open-end investment trusts have no fixed number of shares. Their stock is bought and sold to investors by the company. Closed-end investment trusts have a fixed number of shares. Once sold, the company usually does not buy them back, so the investors must sell their stock to other investors should they wish to liquidate their shares. *See also* Real Estate Investment Trust (REIT).

INVESTMENT VALUE Value to an investor based on his or her individual needs and income tax bracket.

INVESTMENT YIELD The gain from a real estate investment expressed as an annual percentage that includes all of the income and the capital gain or loss from the resale.

INVOLUNTARY CONVERSION An income tax term that describes the conversion of real property into personal property (money) by condemnation. The owner is allowed to purchase another property within a specified period with the proceeds and postpone the payment of capital gains taxes.

INVOLUNTARY CONVEYANCE A transfer of real property without consent of the owner usually by the act of condemnation.

INVOLUNTARY LIENS A lien that is attached to a property without the consent of the owner such as a tax lien, judgment lien, or special assessment.

INWOOD ANNUITY The nickname for a set of present worth factors found in compound interest tables that can be used to convert a level stream of income into a lump sum current value.

INWOOD COEFFICIENT *See* Inwood Factor.

INWOOD FACTOR A factor that is a reflection of the present worth of one dollar per period for a specified number of periods discounted at a specified rate. It is one of the traditional six functions of a dollar.

INWOOD, WILLIAM An English architect and mathematician (1771–1843) who compiled "Tables for the Purchasing of Estates and for the Renewal of Leases Held Under Corporate Bodies."

IRA (INDIVIDUAL RETIREMENT ACCOUNT) A special type of savings program permitted by IRS regulations. Income (up to the limit specified in the current law) placed in this account is not taxed for the years it was earned nor is interest earned on the money as long as it remains in the account. When left in until the employee's retirement, the money can be withdrawn. It is then taxed at the current tax rate, which is usually lower because of the retiree's lower income. When money is prematurely withdrawn, substantial penalties are added to the regular tax.

IRONCLAD CONTRACT A slang term for a contract that is considered to be particularly binding because it is well written and therefore especially hard to break.

IRREVOCABLE That which cannot be annulled, abrogated, revoked, or withdrawn.

IRRIGATION The artificial watering of crops in times of drought or in dry areas. It is done by carrying water to the cultivated area through pipes.

IRRIGATION DISTRICT An agency established by a local government that is given the authority to build and run irrigation systems for an area. It levies taxes for that purpose.

IRRIGATION DITCH A ditch, channel, or canal used to carry water to crops that do not receive enough water naturally.

ISLAND **1.** Land surrounded on all sides by water. **2.** A space between oncoming lanes of a highway.

ITALIAN STYLE VILLA A Latin house style first built in the United States in 1837 and popularized by Andrew Jackson in the mid-1800s. The Italian Villa is a massive, two-to-three-story house with large, overhanging eaves supported by brackets. It has decorative iron work and may have square or octagonal towers.

CTS SYSTEM: Latin
Italian Villa
(It Villa-502)

ITALIAN STYLE VILLA

J

JACK RAFTER A short roof rafter.

JACK STUD An additional vertical framing member in a wall above or below a window opening that adds support.

JACOB'S LADDER A hanging ladder with rope sides and wooden steps.

JALOUSIES Windows and doors made of movable glass louvers that can be adjusted to slope upward to admit light and air yet exclude rain or snow.

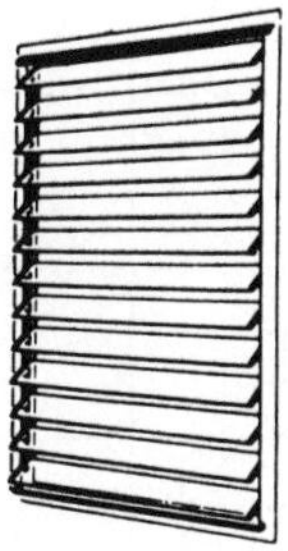

JALOUSIES

JAMB The framing pieces that line doors and windows. *See* Head Jamb and Side Jamb.

JANITOR A person who is paid to take care of a building, clean it, lock it up after closing, and perform minor repairs.

JAPANESE HOUSE An Oriental house style, first introduced into America in Hawaii and California, that has been increasing in popularity in the last 10 years. The classic Japanese house is remarkably similar to our modern homes. The Japanese house is distinguished by the use of exterior sliding panels *(shoji),* ornamental gardens, and a tile, thatch, or wood-shingle roof. The floors are covered by three foot by six foot *tatami* mats, and interior walls have sliding panels known as *fusuma.*

CTS SYSTEM: Oriental
Japanese
(Japan-601)

JAPANESE HOUSE

JERRY-BUILT Cheaply or poorly constructed.

JETTY **1.** A pier or other stone or pile structure placed in a body of water to protect a harbor by hindering currents. **2.** The projecting parts of a building such as a balcony, a bay window, or an overhanging second story.

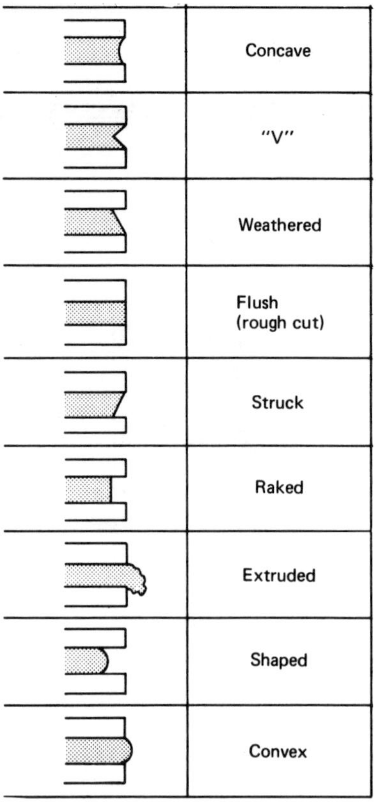

JOINTING

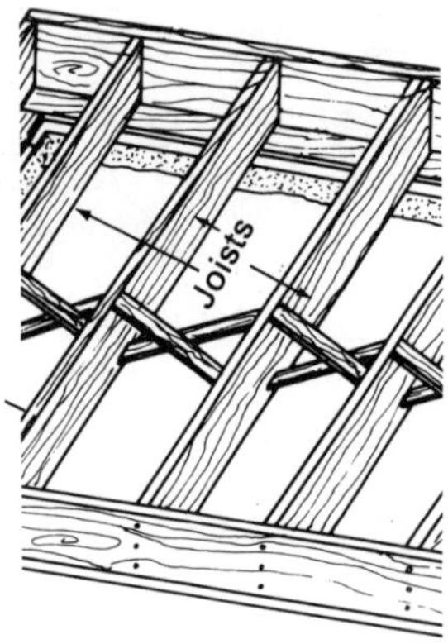

JOISTS

J FACTOR In the Ellwood method of mortgage equity analysis, the J factor is an income adjustment factor.

JOINT **1.** The space between two adjacent surfaces, e.g., between masonry units. **2.** The point of union where two members are attached by nails, fasteners, etc. **3.** Two or more, such as joint tenants.

JOINT ADVENTURE When two or more people combine their property, skills, and funds and become partners in a single business purpose.

JOINT AND SEVERAL A liability against two or more signers of a contract that allows the creditor to sue any one of the debtors or all together.

JOINT ESTATE *See* Joint Tenancy.

JOINTING Finishing off the surface of the motar between courses of brick or stone with a special tool called a *jointer*. Common joint types are flush joints, concave joints, tooled joints, weather joints, "V"-tooled joints, rabbet joints, cove joints, raked joints, stripped joints, and struck joints.

JOINT PROTECTION POLICY A type of title insurance that protects both owner and lender under one policy.

JOINT TENANCY An estate or tenancy shared equally by two or more parties with the right to survivorship. When a joint tenant dies, his or her interest goes to the surviving tenants rather than to his or her heirs.

JOINT TENANTS People holding under joint tenancy.

JOINTURE The arrangement for settling a freehold interest in a property for the benefit of the owner's wife to satisfy the wife's dower right.

JOINT VENTURE *See* Joint Adventure.

JOISTS A series of parallel timber beams used to support floors and ceilings. They are installed with the widest side vertical, and they are supported by large beams or walls.

JUDGMENT **1.** The final decision of a court after a trial or hearing. **2.** The opinion of a professional based on the data and other evidence available. **3.** An appraisal term meaning the ability to estimate the value of a property based on the data plus the skill and experience of the appraiser.

JUDGMENT LIEN A lien placed on a property as a result of the decision of a court. It is used as a guarantee that the owner of the property will comply with the decision of the court.

JUDGMENT PROOF An attempt by someone who thinks he will be subject to the placing of liens on his property as a result of court decisions to divest himself of all property that could be subject to a lien.

JUDICIAL SALE The sale of property to satisfy the debt in a mortgage foreclosure. The court orders and supervises the sale and distribution of the proceeds to the creditors.

JUNCTION BOX A metal box that houses the junction of electrical cables, wires, and circuits and has a removable cover for easy access.

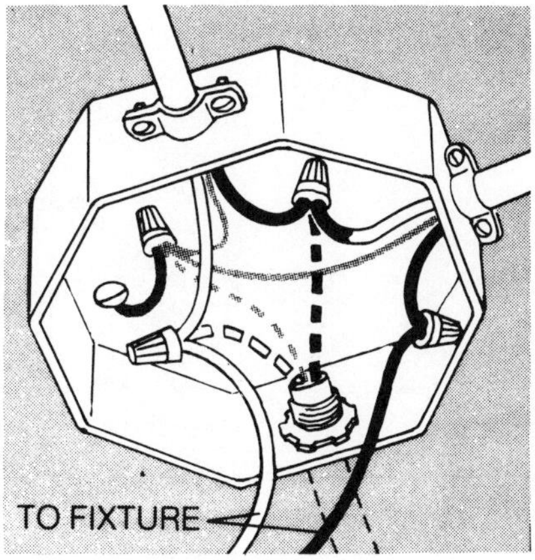

JUNCTION BOX

JUNIOR FINANCING Money which is loaned on real estate that is secured with mortgages which do not have first claim on the property (second, third, etc., mortgages). Because there is additional risk in this type of financing, the rate of interest is usually higher than the interest on the first (senior) mortgage.

JUNIOR LIEN A lien placed on a property that is subordinate to a lien that has been previously made and recorded.

JUNIOR MORTGAGE A mortgage that is legally subordinate to another mortgage.

JUST COMPENSATION The amount paid to a property owner when a property is condemned. In theory, the payment leaves the owner no richer or poorer than before the consideration.

JUTE (SISAL FIBER) A plant fiber that makes cheap, strong yarn used in canvas and carpet backing.

JUTE-BACKED CARPET Carpeting that has a jute back and which should be installed over a carpet pad.

K

KALAMEIN Galvanized, sheet-metal cladding of wood doors.

KEENE'S CEMENT A type of white, hard-finished, unusually tough gypsum that produces very durable walls used in commercial buildings and bathrooms.

KEEPING ROOM The predecessor to the family room, which, in the pilgrim's time, was a large room with an enormous fireplace where stoves were kept and the family gathered for food and warmth.

KELP-SHORE The land between the low and high water marks.

KEY LOT A lot that has one side adjacent to the rear of other lots. It is regarded as the least desirable of the lots in a subdivision.

KEYSTONE In masonry, the center, wedge-shaped piece of an arch.

KICK PLATE A protective strip placed on the lower edge of a door or stair to prevent damage by kicking.

KILN **1.** A large, oven-like chamber used for baking, drying, and hardening various materials such as lumber, brick, and lime. **2.** An oven made of special fire brick and used to cure ceramics.

KILN-DRIED LUMBER Lumber that has been dried in a kiln from two days to several weeks, depending upon its thickness and grade, to reduce its moisture content.

KILO A prefix meaning one thousand.

KILOGRAM 1000 grams (2.204 pounds).

KILOMETER 1000 meters. *See* Meter.

KILOVOLT 1000 volts.

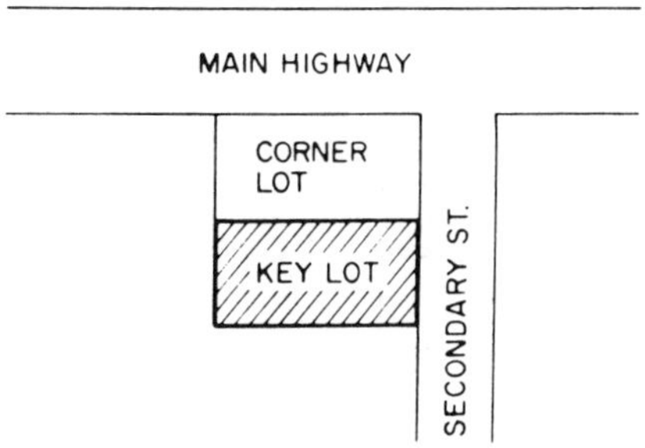

KEY LOT

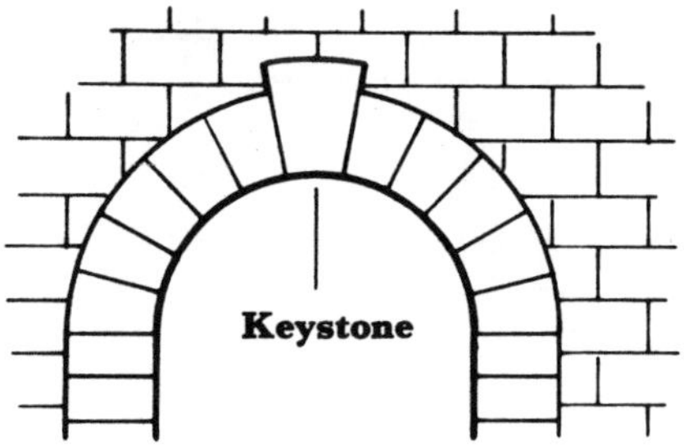

KEYSTONE

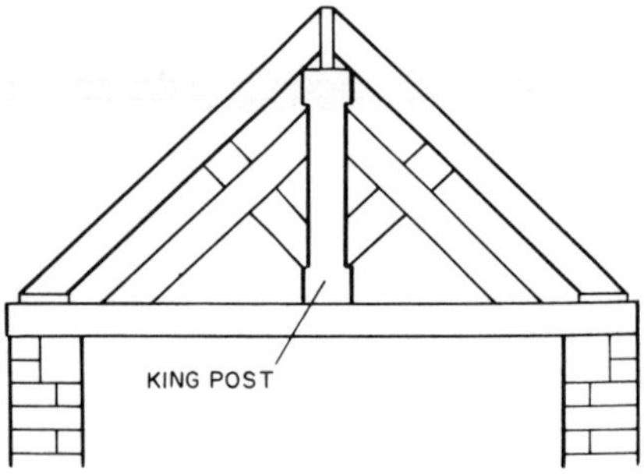

KING POST

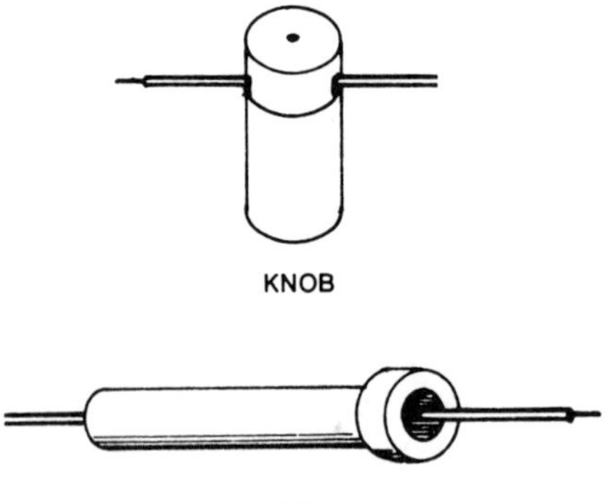

KNOB AND TUBE WIRING

KILOWATT 1000 watts.

KILOWATT HOUR 1000 watt-hours.

KING POST **1.** A vertical member of a truss that reaches from the apex of the inclined rafters to the tie beam between the rafters. **2.** A vertical post in a roof framing system that extends down from the apex of the roof rafters to a supporting beam.

KIP A unit of force equal to 1000 pounds.

KITCHEN A room or area used primarily for the preparation of food.

KITCHEN FIXTURES A variety of fixtures used for the preparation and storage of food.

KITE WINDER The kite-shaped steps in a stairway at the place where the stairway direction changes.

KNEE BRACE A brace placed across the angle between two members that are joined to provide extra strength.

KNOB AND TUBE WIRING An early method of electric wiring still used in some areas. Wire is attached to the house frame with porcelain knob insulators and porcelain tubes.

KNOB INSULATOR A porcelain knob where electric wires are fastened. It is rarely used in building today.

KNOCK DOWN The portions of a building that can be easily installed or removed, such as windows.

KNOLL A small, rounded hill.

KNOT The hard, irregular-shaped masses in lumber caused by cutting at a point where a tree branch meets the trunk.

KRAFTCORD Tightly twisted yarn made from wood pulp fiber and used to make carpet backing instead of the more common materials, such as cotton and jute.

L

LACUSTINE SOIL A heavy, fine-textured soil formed from materials deposited by the waters of lakes and ponds.

LAISSEZ FAIRE A French expression which states that the government should not interfere with free enterprise.

LALLY COLUMN A steel column usually cylindrically shaped and used as a support for beams or girders. Often, they are filled with concrete to increase their strength.

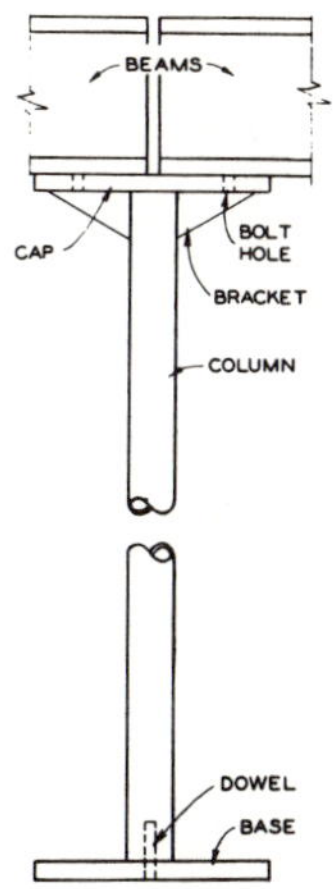

LALLY COLUMN

LAMELLA ROOF A roof framing system made up of lamella, which are reinforced concrete, metal, or wood members joined in a crisscross pattern so as to form an arch or vault.

LAMINATE A product that is fabricated by bonding together two or more layers of material such as wood, plastic, or metal.

LAMINATED WOOD A material made by bonding together two or more layers of wood.

LANAI A special kind of porch or veranda found in Hawaii and the West Coast of the U.S.A.

LAND As defined by appraisers, it is the solid portion of the earth's surface substantially in its undisturbed condition as distinguished from "site," which is land that has been increased in utility by the proximity of man-made improvements such as roads and utilities.

LAND CONTRACT A contract for the sale of real estate by which the buyer pays only a portion of the purchase price when the contract is executed. The balance of the purchase price is paid in installments over an extended period of time. Title remains with the seller until either the total purchase price or a stipulated portion of the purchase price is paid. The advantage to the seller is the ease of reclaiming title in the event the required payments are not made.

LAND COURT A special court that has jurisdiction over issues related to real property and interests in real property.

LAND DESCRIPTION *See* Legal Description.

LAND ECONOMICS A branch of economics that concerns itself with how land is used and with land as a resourse useful to society.

LAND GRANT A type of deed used by the federal government to convey title to an individual or individuals.

LAND IMPROVEMENTS One of many terms that indicates the physical alteration of land or the construction of improvements on land or improvements attached to the land. Generally, these alterations or improvements are of such a nature as to increase the utility and thereby the value of the property. This term includes both improvements to land and improvements on land.

LANDING **1.** One of the components of a flight of stairs. The platform at the bottom or at the top, or a platform between two flights of stairs that breaks the rise or changes the direction of the staircase. **2.** An area where a boat can dock to discharge passengers or freight.

LANDLOCKED A situation where a parcel of land is surrounded by other parcels of land in such a way as to be cut off without any access to a road or highway.

LANDLORD A person who owns real estate and rents it to another.

LANDMARK **1.** A prominent feature of the landscape. **2.** A building or site that has historical significance. **3.** A fixed marker or monument indicating a boundary line.

LAND PATENT *See* Land Grant.

LAND PLANNING The technique of designing how to use land areas by planning for roads, utilities, and the layout of the improvements.

LAND RECLAMATION The process of turning unusable or marginal land into productive, useful land by draining, filling, providing utilities, and other similar techniques.

LAND RESIDUAL TECHNIQUE A five-step process that is used to estimate the value of land. It is based on the

Example of the Land Residual Technique

Estimated improvement value:		$220,000
Estimated net operating income:		$ 43,000
Capitalization rate		
Risk rate	12%	
Recapture rate (25 yr. life)	4%	
Total rate	16%	
Portion of income attributed to the improvements = (220,000 × .16)		−35,200
Net income imputable to the land		$ 7,800
Land value (Risk rate × NOI imputable to land) ($7,800 × .12)		$ 93,600
Improvement value		+220,000
Total property value (land value + improvement value)		$313,600

LAND RESIDUAL TECHNIQUE

assumption that the income a property earns can be split between the land and the improvements.

LANDSCAPE Natural or manmade scenery particularly that which can be seen and enjoyed at one location. In a broader sense, it is the aspect of the land characteristic of a particular region, i.e., the Texas landscape.

LANDSCAPING Improving a property with lawn, shrubs, trees, flowers, and other natural growth.

LAND SURVEYING *See* Surveying.

LAND TRUST A device to hide the true owner of a property by having the title in the name of a trustee. The powers of the trustee are controlled by a trust agreement. Often the real control of the property is vested not in the trustee but in the real owners.

LAND TRUST CERTIFICATES Certificates issued to investors in land trusts as evidence of their share in the trust and its property.

LAND USE CAPABILITIES A cataloging of what the land is capable of being used for based on the type and amount of topsoil, and the topography and shape. These uses are primarily agricultural and include guides to crop rotation, cropping practices, and erosion control.

LAND USE MAP A map that is designed primarily to reveal the character of the various uses of the land and the density of each use.

LAND USE PLANNING The long-range development of plans for the use of land, taking into consideration the needs of the general public as well as what will most benefit the owners of the land.

LAND USE REGULATION A broad term which describes the public and private restrictions that control the uses to which land may be put. Public restrictions include zoning regulations, environmental regulations, building codes, etc. Private restrictions include deed restrictions and leases. *See* Bundle of Rights.

LAND UTILIZATION AND MARKETABILITY STUDY (LUMS) A study made of the potential uses of land that is to be acquired as part of an urban renewal project. The study considers the entire market to be served by the area included in the proposed renewal project. It also considers the effect of the entire project upon the area. The goal of the study is to determine what the highest and best use of the land being studied will be when the

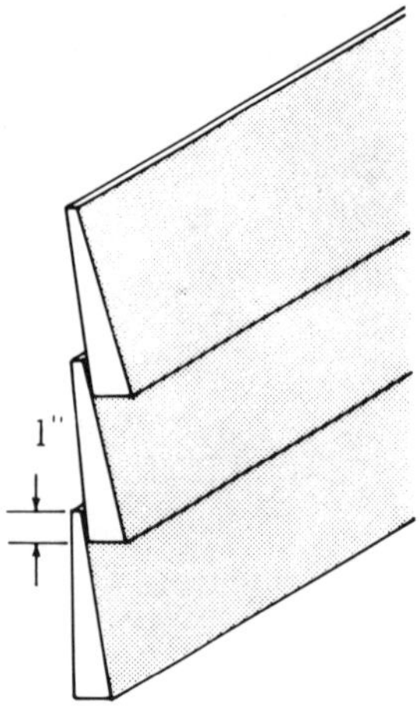

LAP JOINT

LATERAL SUPPORT

whole redevelopment project is completed. *See also* Highest and Best Use.

LAND VALUE MAP A map prepared by assessors indicating the use of the land and its value. The value is usually indicated in units of comparison, such as value per square foot, value per acre, or value per front foot.

LAP JOINT A joint formed by placing one board or piece of material partly over the other and fastening them together. *See also* Lap Siding.

LAP SIDING A type of siding commonly used on the exterior walls of houses. Each piece laps over the adjoining piece. *See also* Clapboard.

LARGER PARCEL A legal term used in condemnation. It refers to all the property affected by a condemnation including that portion which is not actually taken. It should be included for consideration of severance damages.

LATENT DEFECT An imperfection or flaw in a structural component or mechanical system that escapes initial detection.

LATERAL **1.** Of, relating to, or situated at or on the side or sides. **2.** An extension of a sewer line or septic system drain line.

LATERAL SUPPORT The right of a property owner (and the duty of his neighboring property owners) to have his land supported by the land of his neighbors. The restriction against using one's land in such a way as to undermine or cause the collapse of land of an adjoining property.

LATH Strips of wood, metal, or other material that are fastened to the frame of a building or the studs of an interior wall to act as a plaster or stucco base.

LATHING The process of installing lath. It is also synonymous with lath.

LATITUDE **1.** The distance in degrees north or south of the equator measured along a meridian on a map or globe. **2.** A degree of freedom from normal restraints, limitations, or regulations.

LATTICE A decorative, open framework made of strips of metal, wood, or the like, interwoven to form regular, patterned spaces. Often, it is used as a screen, window, or gate.

LAUNDROMAT A trademark for a commercial establishment equipped with coin-operated washing machines and dryers.

LAUNDRY A room used for washing clothes.

LAVATORY **1.** A room used for washing and equipped with a sink and sometimes a toilet. **2.** A sink, basin, or bowl usually permanently installed with water faucets and used for washing the hands and face.

LAW **1.** In mathematics, physics, and other sciences, a general principle that always applies when applicable. **2.** Rules established by society to control the actions of people and corporations. Generally, they are divided into federal laws, state laws, and municipal laws. Most laws are created by legislative bodies. **3.** *Real estate license laws:* Special laws enacted by each state to regulate the practices of real estate brokers and salespeople. **4.** Real estate laws are special laws generally evolved from English common law that regulate real estate such as zoning regulations and building codes.

LAW DAY A day established in a mortgage foreclosure proceeding on which a property owner or creditor must either pay a prescribed sum of money or lose his equity interest in the property being foreclosed.

LAWN An area that is planted with grass, or similar ground covering plants, and usually kept mowed to a short height.

LAY OF THE LAND A slang expression used to generally describe the topographical features of a parcel of land.

LAYOUT A sketch or plan of a building that shows the location of the rooms, walls, entrances, etc.

LEACHING The process of absorbing water into the ground from a waste disposal system.

LEACHING CESSPOOL A hole in the ground lined with stones. Water flows from a household waste disposal system into the hole. The solids sink to the bottom of the hole and the liquids flow into the ground through holes in the site. *See also* Cesspool.

LEACHING FIELD A part of a waste disposal system used to disburse the waste water into the ground. Often, it consists of a field of trenches dug into the ground and lined with tile, broken stone, gravel or sand and into which the waste water is distributed through perforated pipes.

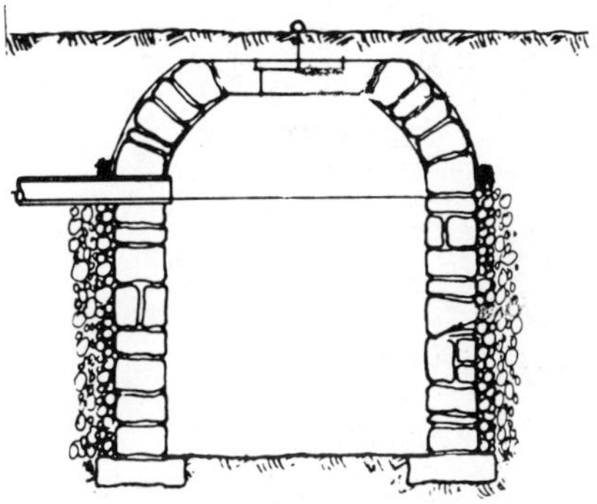

LEACHING CESSPOOL

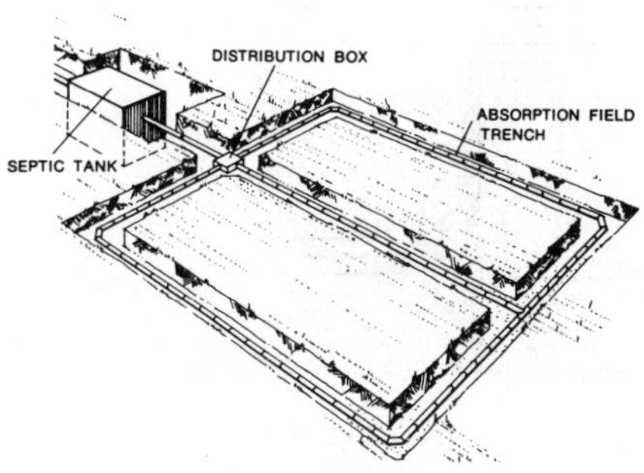

LEACHING FIELD

LEACHING TRENCHES *See* Leaching Field.

LEACH LINE A line of perforated pipe in a leaching field. *See also* Leaching Field.

LEADER *See* Downspout.

LEAN-TO ROOF A slanted, single-plane roof often attached to the side of building.

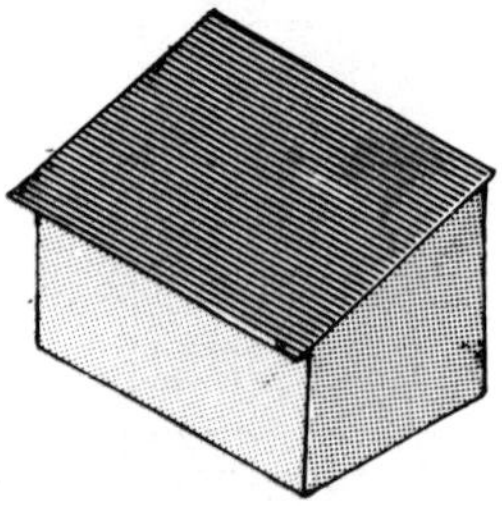

LEAN-TO ROOF

LEASE A contract that transfers the right to use or occupy a property from the owner to a tenant in exchange for payments by the tenant to the owner (landlord) called rent. A typical lease is for a specific period of time and spells out the terms and conditions of the agreement. In most states, a lease for a year or more must be in writing to be enforceable. *See also* Graded or Step-up Lease, Ground Lease, Index Lease, Leasehold Estate, Net Lease, Percentage Lease, Reappraisal Lease.

LEASEBACK *See* Sale-Leaseback.

LEASED FEE The interest in a property that remains with the owner after he has granted someone else the right to occupy the property. This right is usually granted by a lease for a specific period of time.

LEASED FEE ESTATE *See* Leased Fee.

LEASEHOLD The interest in a property of a tenant (lessee) created by a lease. It is usually the right to occupy and use the property for a stipulated period of time in exchange for the payment of rent. It is usually subject to terms and conditions that are set forth in a lease. *See also* Leasehold Improvements, Leasehold Estate, Leasehold Value.

LEASEHOLD ESTATE A non-freehold estate in a property created by a lease. *See also* Freehold Estate.

LEASEHOLD IMPROVEMENTS Additions, alterations, and improvements to a property made by a tenant (lessee) in anticipation of their use during the period the tenant has the right to use the property.

LEASEHOLD MORTGAGE A mortgage secured by the tenant's interest in a property. In the event of foreclosure, the lender takes over the tenant's rights to occupy and use the property as set forth in the lease, together with the obligation to continue to pay rent and comply with the other terms and conditions of the lease. Usually, a leasehold mortgage can be obtained only when the lease has been drafted with the special requirements of the lender in mind.

LEASEHOLD POLICY A special type of title insurance protecting the tenant's interest in the property. *See also* Title Insurance.

LEASEHOLD VALUE The value of a tenant's interest in a lease. When the value of the right to occupy the premises and the rent being paid are equal, there is no leasehold value. When the value of the right to use the property is greater than the value of the rent being paid for this right, the difference is the leasehold value. Appraisers estimate the value of the leasehold interest by calculating the rent savings over the term of the lease (the difference between the contract rent and the market rent) and discounting the difference into a present value.

LEASE INTEREST *See* Leasehold.

LEASE-PURCHASE AGREEMENT An agreement whereby a tenant can acquire ownership of a property through a series of payments specified in a lease. At the end of the lease term, title is transferred to the tenant. *See also* Land Contract.

LEDGER A horizontal framing member, supported by hangers or by upright posts, that supports the joists.

LEDGE STONE A type of stone mined in a quarry and used as a building material. A popular variety of the material is used extensively for building in Indiana.

LEDGE STONE

LEGACY A special gift of money or other personal property made in a will to a recipient called a *legatee.*

LEGAL ACCESS The inherent right of the owner of property immediately adjacent to a highway to enter onto the highway from the property. *See also* Access Rights.

LEGAL DESCRIPTION A method of identifying the boundaries of a property. There are a variety of different systems approved by the laws of different states. *See also* Geodetic System, Metes and Bounds, Public Land System, Recorded Map.

LEGAL INTEREST RATE The maximum rate of interest that can be charged for a loan according to state or local laws. *See also* Usury Laws.

LEGATEE The beneficiary of a will who receives a legacy. *See also* Legacy.

LENDER PARTICIPATION A situation in which a lender who gives a mortgage loan to a developer or property owner participates in a share of the income and equity

LESSEE–LESSOR

Example of How Leverage Increases (Decreases) Rate of Return

Example A (no leverage)	
Purchase price:	$100,000
Cash invested:	$100,000
Resale price:	$120,000
Profit:	$ 20,000
Rate of return: 20% ($20,000 ÷ $100,000)	
Example B (high leverage)	
Purchase price:	$100,000
Cash invested:	$ 10,000
Mortgage:	$ 90,000
Resale price:	$120,000
Profit:	$ 20,000
Rate of return: 200% ($20,000 ÷ $10,000)	

LEVERAGE

ownership in addition to receiving interest and principal payments.

LESSEE The party to a lease (tenant) who receives the right to use or occupy a property in return for the payment of rent. *See also* Lease Tenant.

LESSEE'S INTEREST *See* Freehold Estate, Leasehold, Leasehold Estate, Leasehold Value.

LESSOR The party to a lease (often a landlord) who owns the fee title and gives a tenant (lessee) the right to use or occupy the property in return for the payment of rent. *See also* Lease Landlord.

LESSOR'S INTEREST *See* Freehold Estate, Leasehold, Leasehold Estate, Leasehold Value.

LEVEE **1.** A raised embankment along the edge of a river that prevents the river from overflowing. **2.** A continuous ridge surrounding an irrigated field.

LEVEL ANNUITY A series of equal income payments from a property or other investment source forecasted to be received in the future. *See also* Annuity.

LEVERAGE A technique used by investors to increase the return on their equity. Investors invest only a small percentage of their own money and borrow the balance when they buy a property. Usually, they mortgage the property to secure the invested capital.

LEVY **1.** The imposition of a real estate tax by a legislative body for a specific purpose. **2.** The seizure of a property to satisfy a judgment.

LIABILITY A comprehensive term that includes all the obligations a person has as required by law or equity. *See also* Appraiser's Liability, Liability Insurance, Real Estate Agent's Liability.

LIABILITY INSURANCE Insurance that indemnifies owners and tenants against claims by third parties who suffer bodily injury or property damage due to causes attributable to the ownership or use of the property insured. The following are kinds of liability insurance:

Bodily Injury Liability
Contractor's Liability
Contractual Liability
Manufacturer's Liability
Personal Injury Liability
Products Liability
Property Damage Liability

LICENSE **1.** A permit or authorization issued by the government granting permission to do something that would otherwise be illegal. *See also* Real Estate License, Appraiser's License. **2.** A right granted by the owner of a property to someone to do some act or series of acts on the property without obtaining an interest in the property.

LICENSEE **1.** One who obtains permission from the government to practice a profession or engage in an enterprise that otherwise would be illegal without a license. *See also* Appraiser's License, Real Estate License. **2.** One who has permission to enter a property to perform some act or series of acts on the property. This permission does not grant an interest in the property.

LICENSE LAWS Laws created by legislative bodies that prohibit the practice of specified professions or business enterprises without obtaining a license from the government granting permission to practice the profession or conduct the business enterprise. *See also* Appraisal License, Real Estate License.

LICENSE YEAR The period of time for which a license is granted. It often is different from a calendar year.

LIEN A claim or charge upon property which encumbers the property and makes it security for the payment of a debt.

LIENEE The owner of a property that is encumbered by a lien. *See also* Lien.

LIENOR The person who has the right of lien against a property to secure the payment of a debt. *See also* Lien.

LIEN THEORY A legal distinction which states that the holder of a mortgage has only a lien against the mortgaged property rather than a true title interest. *See also* Lien.

LIEN THEORY OF MORTGAGE A legal theory which states that the true title of a property rests in the borrower and that the lender has only a lien on the property.

LIFE The duration of the existence of the improvements on a property. *See also* Economic Life, Physical Life.

LIFE ANNUITY A series of payments collectible at even intervals that last for the lifetime of a designated recipient. *See also* Annuity.

LIFE ESTATE An ownership interest in property that terminates upon the death of a designated person. *See also* Life Interest, Life Tenant.

LIFE INTEREST An interest in a property, other than ownership, such as occupancy, that terminates upon the death of a designated person.

LIFE TENANT A person who owns an estate in a parcel of real property that continues only during the lifetime of the person owning the estate or the lifetime of some other designated person.

LIFTING CLAUSE A clause put in mortgages to allow property owners to refinance their property without paying off the second mortgage. It allows the new mortgage to be put ahead of the other mortgages for redemption purposes.

LIFT SLAB A construction system for building concrete structures. The floor, walls, and roof sections are cast on the ground and lifted or jacked into place.

LIGHT **1.** A source of illumination and the illumination derived from such a source. **2.** Of low weight or density. **3.** A pane of glass.

LIGHTER A barge used to transport freight from large ships to the shore or over a short distance in shallow water.

LIGHTERAGE The transferring of freight from a large ship to or from the shore on a barge, small boat, or lighter.

LIGHTERAGE LIMITS A point in a harbor beyond which freight on lighters cannot be delivered.

LIGHTERAGE PIER A special pier for the transfer of freight from railroad cars and trucks to barges, lighters, and small boats that, in turn, load it onto larger ships.

LIGHT INDUSTRY A term used in zoning and planning to distinguish those types of industry that are relatively low producers of noise, odors, and pollution. *See also* Heavy Industry.

LIGHTING The various processes and systems used to provide illumination.

LIGHTING PANEL An electric panel that divides a main electric supply into branch circuits, each of which is protected with a fuse or circuit breaker. It may also have switches for controlling the lights and lighting circuits.

LIGHT SHAFT *See* Light Well.

LIGHT WELL A shaft within a building that is open at the top. Windows on the shaft receive their light and air through this opening.

LIME An ingredient made from burned limestone and used to make concrete, mortar, and plaster.

LIMITED ACCESS HIGHWAY A highway designed for the unimpeded flow of heavy traffic. Often an interstate highway, it has a limited number of entrances and exits.

LIMITED PARTNERSHIP The most common form of organization used for real estate syndications. It is a hybrid of a corporation and a general partnership. There are two classes of partners: (1) the general partners, who manage the partnership affairs and can be held personally liable for the partnership obligations; and (2) the limited partners, who may not take an active role in the running of the affairs of the partnership. Their personal liability is limited to the amount of money they have invested in the partnership.

LIMITING CONDITIONS A statement in an appraisal report setting forth a series of assumptions which have been made and which affect the validity of the value estimate.

LINE FENCE A fence that serves primarily to mark a boundary between properties.

LINEN STORAGE CLOSET A special closet in a home used for the storage of tablecloths, napkins, sheets, pillowcases, towels, and facecloths.

LINE-OF-SITE EASEMENT **1.** A right of a property owner to look over another property. **2.** An easement that restricts the obstructing of a view. *See also* Conservation Easement, Scenic Easement.

LINING Material that covers an interior surface, such as the framework around a door or window, interior surface boards, and flue.

LINKAGE As used in real estate, it is the time and distance relationship between a property and its supporting facilities.

LINOLEUM A floor-covering material made of linseed oil, powdered cork, resins, and colored pigments that are coated onto burlap and baked under pressure for curing.

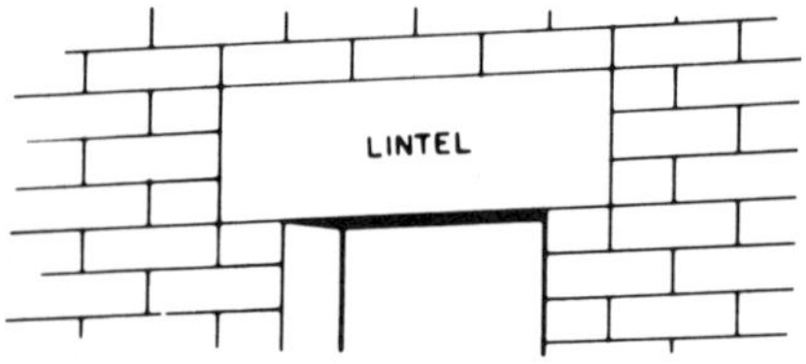

LINTEL

LITTORAL PROPERTY
LITTORAL RIGHTS

LINTEL A horizontal structural member often made of steel, stone, or wood, and placed over an opening to bridge that opening and carry the weight of the wall above it. *See also* Header.

LIQUID ASSETS Assets that are either cash or immediately convertible into cash, such as stocks and bonds or certificates of deposit.

LIQUIDATION DAMAGES A provision in a real estate sales contract that limits the liability of a designated party to the agreement to a specified sum if that party defaults on his obligation under the contract.

LIQUIDATION PRICE The price a property will bring if sold quickly in order to raise money.

LIQUIDITY A measurement of how quickly one's assets can be converted into cash. If the asset is property, it is how fast it can be sold.

LIS PENDENS Notice that a lawsuit is pending as applied to the doctrine of *lis pendens*. It is the jurisdiction, power, or control that courts acquire over property involved in a suit, pending the continuance of the action, and until its final judgment therein.

LISTING **1.** An agreement between a property owner and a real estate broker in which the owner authorizes the broker to offer the property for sale or rent and agrees to pay a commission if the broker's efforts are successful. **2.** A document that describes a property being offered for sale or rent. **3.** A property listed in a listing agreement.

LISTING CONTRACT *See* Listing.

LITER (LITRE) A liquid measurement in the metric system. It is two pints, 67.2 cubic inches, which is slightly more than a U.S. quart.

LITIGATION A contest in a court of justice for the purpose of enforcing a right.

LITTER **1.** The uppermost layer of forest floor consisting chiefly of decaying organic matter. **2.** The careless discharge of waste material.

LITTORAL *See* Littoral Property, Littoral Rights.

LITTORAL PROPERTY Property abutting a large body of water, such as an ocean, sea, bay, or large lake.

LITTORAL RIGHTS The rights of owners of littoral property to enjoy the use of the body of water to which their property abuts. *See also* Littoral Property.

LIVABILITY An overall rating of a property pertaining to its ability to satisfy the needs and desires of its occupants. *See also* Functional Utility.

LIVE A description of an electrical wire that has electricity in it, as opposed to "dead," which is a wire without electricity.

LIVE LOAD One of a variety of variable weight loads a house is subject to, such as snow on the roof and people on the floors. *See also* Dead Load.

LIVING ROOM A room in a house used by the family for entertaining and recreational purposes.

LIVING TRUST A trust that is established and made active during the life of the trust's creator.

LOAD **1.** The weight that is supported by load-bearing parts of a building such as load-bearing walls. **2.** An electrical term describing the power delivered by a motor, generator, or other power source. **3.** The electric current flowing through an electric circuit.

LOAD-BEARING WALL *See* Bearing Wall.

LOAD CENTER Either the main or branch electrical distribution center in a property. It is usually equipped with circuit breakers.

LOADING CHUTE A chute used for the handling of livestock. It permits the livestock to walk from the ground up to the loading docks.

LOADING SHED A shed used to provide temporary shelter for livestock.

LOAM A type of soil consisting mostly of sand, clay, or silt. Often, it also contains organic matter. A thin layer provides an excellent base for grass.

LOAN CONSTANT An annual payment expressed as a percentage of the original loan consisting of both interest and principal.

LOAN FEE A one-time payment made to a lender at the time of the initial loan and in addition to the regular loan interest. *See also* Points.

LOAN MATURITY The length of time the lender loans the money to the borrower. A 10-year loan has a 10-year maturity.

LOAN-TO-VALUE RATIO The percentage the amount of a loan is to the value of the property or other security pledged to secure the loan.

Examples of Loan-to-Value Ratios

Amount of loan: $60,000
Value of security: $100,000
Loan-to-value ratio: 60%

Amount of loan: $150,000
Value of security: $200,000
Loan-to-value ratio: 75%

Amount of loan: $40,000
Value of security: $80,000
Loan-to-value ratio: 50%

LOAN-TO-VALUE RATIO

LOBBY **1.** A room next to the entrance of a public building, theater, hotel, apartment building, etc. **2.** A room in which the public is permitted outside a legislative chamber. **3.** To seek to influence the way legislators vote.

LOCAL GOVERNMENT A division of government that has jurisdiction over a community, county, or some other territory within a state.

LOCAL HOUSING AUTHORITY (LHA) A public body, often in corporate form, that is created to operate on behalf of a community or state public housing and sometimes urban renewal programs. Often, housing authorities are empowered to raise capital by selling bonds, or by receiving subsidies and direct funds from local, state, and federal government.

LOCAL PUBLIC AGENCY (LPA) A public agency created specifically to contract with the federal government to plan, build, and administer an urban renewal project.

LOCATION **1.** The position of a property on the earth. **2.** An economic concept which relates to the unique characteristic of real estate—its immobility.

LOCATIONAL OBSOLESCENCE *See* Economic Obsolescence.

LOCATION ANALYSIS The study of the characteristics of a property or group of properties to determine potential uses.

LOCKED-IN PERIOD A mortgage clause that prohibits prepayment of the loan during a specified period of time.

LODGING A place to stay, usually on a temporary basis.

LOESS A type of soil that is fine-grained with a buff-to-grey color. It is probably deposits of wind-blown dust.

LOFT **1.** A large unpartitioned upper floor of a commercial or industrial building. **2.** A gallery or balcony in a church. **3.** The upper section of a barn used for the storage of hay. **4.** A coop in which pigeons are kept. **5.** A large room used for making sails.

LOFT BUILDING A multi-story building with few partitions used for manufacturing or storage. Many are being converted into other uses.

LOG **1.** A trimmed but unhewn piece of a tree. **2.** A permanent record book.

LOG CABIN A colonial American style of house made of either round or square logs.

CTS SYSTEM: Colonial American
Log Cabin
(Log Cab-115)

LOG CABIN

LOG RULES A table of measuring used to determine the number of board feet of lumber that can be obtained from unhewn logs.

LONGITUDE The distance in degrees east and west of the prime meridian at Greenwich, England, to the point on the earth's surface for which the longitude is being ascertained.

LONG-LIVED ITEMS Those parts of a building that typically last for the entire life of the building.

LONG-TERM LEASE By tradition, a lease 10 years or longer in duration.

LOOSE-FILL INSULATION Types of insulation that are in the form of shreds, flakes, powder, fibers, nodules, granules, etc.

LOT **1.** A parcel of land that is distinctly designated. **2.** A portion of a city block. **3.** The site on which a house is constructed.

LOT AND BLOCK DESCRIPTION A map that divides a parcel of land into lots.

LOT LINE The border of a lot as described in the title documents.

LOUISIANA A French house style also known as Creole. Many are found in and around New Orleans, Louisiana. *See also* Creole style.

LOUVER A series of overlapping slats that cover an opening in such a way as to let in air and light and keep out rain and snow. It is commonly used on doors and windows.

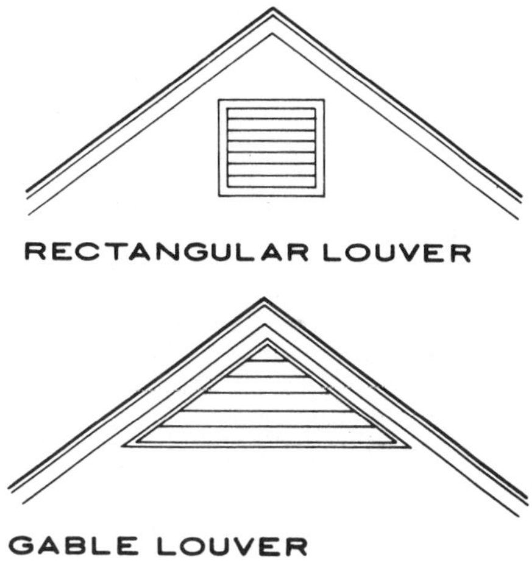

LOUVER

LOW VOLTAGE SWITCHING SYSTEM A series of switches, transformers, relays, and auxiliary devices used to control a number of lighting circuits from remote locations.

LOW VOLTAGE WIRING Wires that carry voltage low enough to not be dangerous to humans or to be a fire hazard. Often door bells, music systems, controls, alarm systems, and telephones have low voltage wiring.

LOW WATER LINE

LOW WATER LINE A line along the shore of an ocean, sound, bay, etc., that occurs at low tide. *See also* Mean Low Water Line.

LUMBER Timber that has been sawed and planed into boards, timbers, and various varieties of lumber, such as dimension lumber, dressed lumber, factory lumber, shop lumber, or yard lumber.

LUMEN A measurement of light. A 100-watt bulb emits about 1,600 lumens of light.

LUMINOUS CEILING A lighting system consisting of a large, continuous surface of light-transmitting material lit from above.

M

"MAGIC LOANS" Conventional mortgage loans insured by the Mortgage Guarantee Insurance Company; called "magic" because of the initials of the company (MGIC).

MAGNESITE FLOORING A finishing surface used on floors and made of powdered magnesite, magnesium chloride, and other fillers.

MAI (MEMBER APPRAISAL INSTITUTE) The designation given to members of the American Institute of Real Estate Appraisers.

MAIN BEARING BEAM AND COLUMN A beam that supports floor joists.

MAIN CIRCUIT The main electrical circuit that supplies current to other, smaller branches in the distribution system.

MAIN SWITCH An electrical switch between the point where the electric service enters the building and the main distribution box that can turn off the entire service either manually or automatically in the event of an emergency or a failure in the system.

MAINTENANCE The act of maintaining a property in adequate condition to efficiently perform its intended service; also, the expenditures necessary to do so.

MAINTENANCE FEE The sum charged to each unit owner in a condominium or planned development to maintain the common area.

MAINTENANCE RESERVE Money held to cover costs of maintenance.

MAKER A person who signs a note promising to pay a sum of money.

MAI
AMERICAN INSTITUTE • OF • REAL ESTATE APPRAISERS
®

MAI (MEMBER APPRAISAL INSTITUTE)

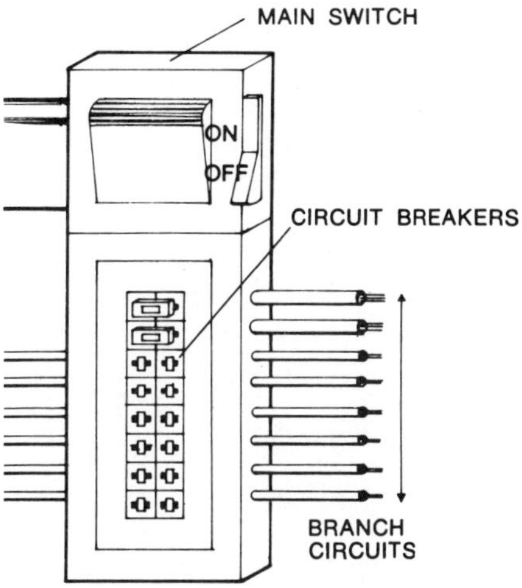

MAIN SWITCH

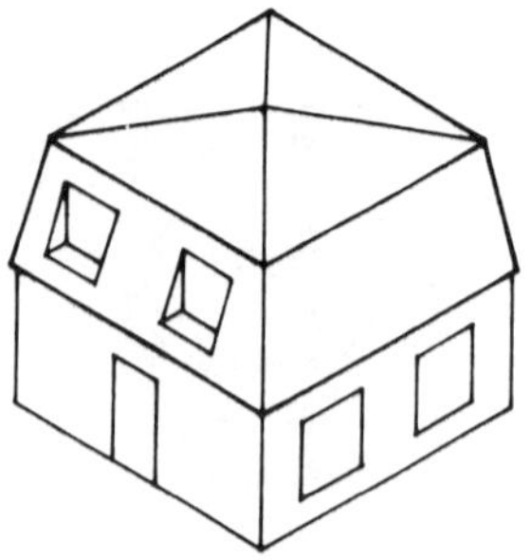

MANSARD ROOF

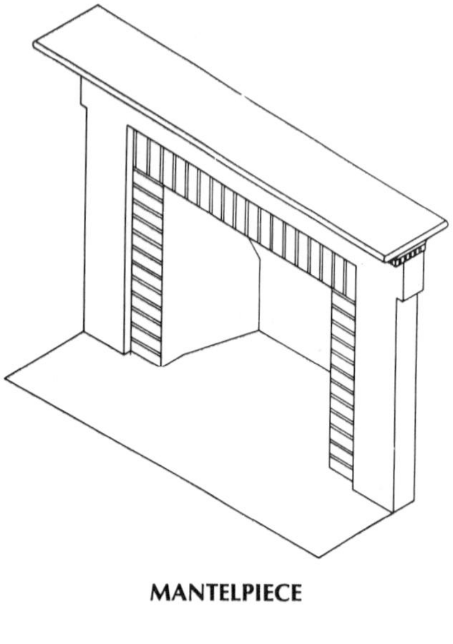

MANTELPIECE

MALL **1.** Originally, a shaded plaza or walk. In modern usage, it is an area in a shopping center intended for pedestrians only. **2.** A median strip.

MANAGEMENT The supervision of the use of money. *See also* Property Management.

MANAGEMENT AGREEMENT *See* Property Management Agreement.

MANAGEMENT CONTRACT *See* Property Management Agreement.

MANAGEMENT FEE Money paid for management.

MANAGEMENT PROGRAM A plan presented by a real estate management company to a property owner setting forth how they plan to manage the property.

MANDAMUS An order given by a superior court that forces an inferior court, public official, or other government employee to perform or refrain from certain acts. For example, the court could order a building inspector to issue a building permit even when the inspector did not want to do so.

MANIFOLD Having many parts, sides, features, etc.

MANSARD ROOF A roof with two slopes on all four sides. The lower slope is very steep. The upper slope is usually not visible from the ground. The lower slope is not really the roof but rather the wall of the upper story made to look like a roof. Originally designed by François Mansart (1598–1666) a French architect.

MANSION A house of considerable size or pretension. It usually has large rooms for entertaining and quarters for guests and servants.

MANTEL The decorative facing around a fireplace.

MANTELPIECE The shelf that protrudes over a fireplace.

MANTISSA The decimal portion of a logarithm.

MAP A drawn representation of physical features on the earth's (or moon's, etc.) surface.

MARBLE Metamorphic rock composed mainly of calcite or dolomite and, commercially, many dense limestones. In more expensive construction, marble is used in place of tile.

MARGINAL An investment that barely supports itself and is not considered strong.

MARGINAL LAND Land that barely produces enough income to meet the costs of operation.

MARGIN OF SECURITY The dollar difference between the amount of a mortgage loan and the appraised value of the property used to secure the mortgage loan.

MARINA A facility in a river, lake, or harbor that offers dockage, supplies, and maintenance for boats.

MARINE SOIL A type of soil formed by deposits from the oceans that later become exposed by the upward movement of the earth's crust.

MARITAL DEDUCTION Deduction allowed for tax purposes because a person is married.

MARKET A series of conditions that facilitates the bringing together of buyers and sellers. In a particular market, there is a free exchange of the product. Some markets, like the stock market, are regional and national. The market for residential real estate tends to be local.

MARKETABILITY The salability of a property at a specific time and price.

MARKETABILITY STUDY A study to discover how a particular piece of property can be marketed.

MARKETABLE TITLE A title which can be readily marketed that will not expose the buyer to litigation.

MARKET ANALYSIS A study made of general market conditions for the product proposed to be marketed. It takes into consideration the supply and demand of the product. It also considers the current attitudes of the buyers and sellers and the availability of financing.

MARKET AREA The geographic territory within which a product being marketed can reasonably expect to find a buyer.

MARKET DATA APPROACH *See* Market Value Approach.

MARKETING The process of developing ways to conceive, develop, and deliver goods and services in a manner that will satisfy customers and produce satisfactory sales of the goods or services.

MARKET PRICE The actual price paid for a property.

MARKET RENT The amount of rent a property should bring if it were being currently offered for rent under competitive market conditions.

MARKET SURVEY *See* Market Analysis.

Steps of the Market Data Approach

1. Find in market the sales and listings of properties most similar to the property being appraised.
2. Collect and verify data about each of the properties including their price, date of transaction, physical characteristics, locational characteristics and any special conditions and financing.
3. Analyze and compare each comparable property with the property being appraised.
4. Adjust the price of each comparable property for dissimilarities between it and the property being appraised.
5. Reconcile the adjusted prices of the comparable properties into an indicated market value of the property being appraised.

MARKET DATA APPROACH

Elements of Fair Market Value

- Buyer and seller are ready, willing and able to buy and sell
- Buyer and seller are informed
- Buyer and seller are acting under no unusual compulsion or duress
- Property is exposed to the market for a reasonable period of time
- Sale is for money with typical financing available

MARKET VALUE

MARKET VALUE The price (highest or most probable) that a property will sell for in a competitive market when all the conditions for a fair sale exist. These conditions include buyers and sellers who are knowledgeable of the property and the market and who are typically motivated and free of unusual stimulus and acting in their own best interests. It also assumes that there is sufficient time available to market the property and that typical financing will be available.

MARKET VALUE APPROACH An appraisal technique that compares the recent price paid for similar properties and considers the degree of similarity of these properties to estimate the value of a property being appraised. Significant differences between the comparable properties and the property being appraised are adjusted for so that each comparable property gives an indicated value of the property being appraised. The different value indications are reconciled into a value conclusion based on this approach.

MARQUEE A roof-like projection over the entrance to a building that is not supported by posts or columns.

MARSH A soft, wet, grassy area of ground.

MARSHALLING Lining up conflicting claims or interests in an order that is most fair to all concerned.

MASONRY A construction of units made of such materials as clay, concrete, shale, gypsum, or stone set in mortar.

MASONRY, HOLLOW Units in which the voids exceed 25 percent of the cross-sectional area.

MASONRY, SOLID Units in which the voids do not exceed 25 percent of the cross-sectional area at any plane parallel to the bearing surface.

MASONRY VENEER A masonry facing that is placed against a wall but not bonded to it. It does not add to the structural strength of the wall. It is primarily for decorative purposes and for protecting the exterior surface from wear. It may also increase the insulation rating of the wall.

MASONRY WALL A wall made of brick, stone, concrete, etc.

MASSACHUSETTS TRUST A special form of ownership that exists in Massachusetts. Legal title to property is vested in trustees, who act merely as figureheads for the real owners. Most of the original reasons for these trusts no longer exist. However, they are still used as they are convenient and have some limited state tax advantages.

MASS APPRAISING The process of appraising an entire area or district at the same time for the purpose of adjusting property taxes.

MASTER BEDROOM The largest bedroom of a house, usually where the head(s) of the family sleeps.

MASTER DEED One of the documents required to convert property in fee simple ownership into a condominium form of ownership. It is filed together with the condominium declarations to create the condominium ownership.

MASTER LEASE The lease that controls subsequent leases. *See also* Master Deed.

MASTER PLAN A long-term, comprehensive plan for the growth and development of a community that includes basic zoning and administrative controls necessary to obtain the planned objectives.

MASTER SWITCH A switch that controls several different fixtures or outlets.

MASTIC **1.** A thick adhesive material used to cement surfaces together. **2.** A sealant with elastic qualities.

MATCHED BOARDS *See* Tongue and Groove.

MAT FOUNDATION *See* Floating Foundation.

MATURITY The date when an instrument comes due.

MATURITY VALUE The value of a financial instrument at the time when it matures.

MAXIMUM RENT The maximum rent established by rent control regulations.

MEAN **1.** A point in the middle of two extremes. **2.** A statistical term for a measure of central tendency of a set of data. It is the average produced by adding together all the items of data and dividing this total by the number of data items.

MEANDER LINES Lines run in surveying along navigable rivers to measure the curves of the river.

MEAN DEVIATION *See* Average Deviation.

MEAN HIGH WATER LINE The level on the shore that an average high tide will reach.

Example of the Calculation of the Mean

Sale Prices
$ 40,000
40,000
42,000
42,500
50,500
51,000
51,000
51,000
60,500
63,500
90,000
130,000
135,000
$847,000

M = Mean
A = Sum of the variates
= $847,000
N = Number of variates
= 13

$$M = \overline{X} = \frac{A}{N} = \frac{\$847{,}000}{13} = \$65{,}200$$

MEAN

MEAN LOW WATER LINE

Examples of Calculating the Median

1. Odd number of variates
   Monthly Rent
   300
   325
   330
   360 ←Middle variate
   375 (the Median)
   375
   390
2. Even number of variates
   Monthly Rent
   425
   430
   470) Mean of middle
   490) Two variates
   500 $480 (the Median)
   510

MEDIAN

MEAN LOW WATER LINE The level on the shore that an average low tide will reach.

MECHANICAL SYSTEMS Systems which convert a building that would be a dead shell into a usable entity. They normally include the plumbing and heating systems, electrical systems, air conditioning, and other specialized systems.

MECHANIC'S AND MATERIALMAN'S LIEN *See* Mechanic's Lien.

MECHANIC'S LIEN A special lien created by state statutes to protect those who work on real estate and provide material and labor for construction, improvement, and repairs. In many states, mechanic's liens have priority over other liens and mortgages even when they are recorded after these prior liens. Many state statutes give the mechanics a specified time after the work is performed to record a mechanic's lien. This creates the possibility of a potential lien existing at the time of a sale that does not show on the land records.

MECHANIC'S LIEN SURETY BOND A bond provided by a security company, or some other acceptable bonding source, which guarantees that claims being made that resulted in a mechanic's lien on a property will be settled. This protects the buyer of the property from having to make any payments as a result of the mechanic's lien on the property.

MEDIAN A statistical term for the middle number of a set of numbers when the total number of items in the set is odd, and they are arranged in ascending or descending order according to their size (arrayed). When the number of items in the set of numbers is even, the median is the average of the two middle numbers.

MEDIAN STRIP A concrete buffer or landscaped strip that divides opposing lanes of traffic on a roadway.

MEDIUM-TEXTURED SOIL A broad term for a variety of loams ranging from fine, sandy loams to heavy, clay loams.

MEETING OF THE MINDS The mutual agreement necessary between two or more parties to enter into a valid contract.

MEETING RAIL *See* Check Rail.

MEGALOPOLIS A densely populated urban area containing many cities.

MELAMINE-LAMINATED A type of counter surface of which Formica is a popular brand. It is a smooth, durable surface that resists stains. It scorches and dents easily, however.

MELLOW Soil that can be easily worked and possesses loamy and friable characteristics.

MEMBER APPRAISAL INSTITUTE (MAI) *See* MAI.

MEMBRANE A waterproof sheet or film applied to floors or walls.

MERCANTILISM A classic enonomic theory from the sixteenth and seventeenth centuries. It states that gold is the basis of wealth. It also states that countries must export more than they import in order to collect wealth. The theory states that, if necessary, the government should control imports, exports, wages, prices, and whatever else is needed to produce a balance of trade in favor of the home country.

MERCHANTABLE TITLE A title to real estate that contains no encumbrances or other defects significant enough to prevent it from being sold.

MERGE LINE An appraisal term for the line that would split a lot that touches two parallel streets so that each new lot would have the highest value.

MERGER The combining of two or more businesses or interests into one.

MERGER OF TITLE The act of combining the ownership of two abutting properties that have been owned separately.

MERIDIANS Imaginary circles on the earth's surface that pass through both poles and are used for mapping purposes to describe the location of a point on the earth.

MESQUITE A type of vegetation found in the southwestern United States and Mexico where various types of mesquite (prosopsis) shrubs and small trees are predominant.

MESSUAGE A legal term for a residence and the land and buildings surrounding it.

METAL-CLAD BUILDING A building that is covered with metal.

METAL LATH A heavy, coarse metal base with slits at intervals on which plaster is spread.

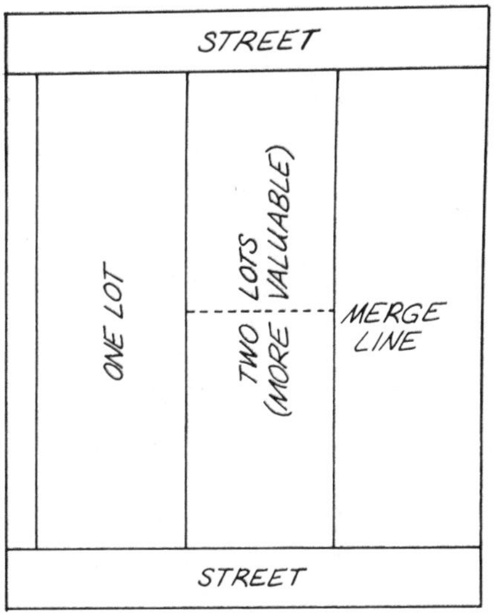

MERGE LINE

METAL VALLEY *See* Flashing.

METAMORPHIC ROCK Rock formed by metamorphosis (change) usually from combinations of the forces of heat, pressure, and water.

METER **1.** A metric unit of measurement equal to 39.37 inches. **2.** A measuring device for utilities.

METES Lineal measurements along a property boundary made to specify the exact quantity of land in a property. It is used chiefly in the phrase "metes and bounds."

METES AND BOUNDS The boundary lines of a property including terminal points and angles.

METRIC CONVERSION CHARTS Charts used to convert metric measurements and quantities of the metric system into the *standard* system used in the United States.

Metric Conversion Charts

Linear Measurements

1 inch	= 2.54 centimeters
1 foot	= 30.48 centimeters
	= .03048 meters
1 yard	= 91.44 centimeters
	= .9144 meters
1 mile	= 1.609347 kilometers
	= 1609.347 meters
1 centimeter	= 0.3937 inches
1 meter	= 3.2808 feet
1 kilometer	= .62135 miles

Square Measurements

1 sq. inch	= 6.4516 sq. centimeters
1 sq. foot	= .0929 sq. meters
1 sq. yard	= .83613 sq. meters
1 acre	= 40.467 sq. meters
1 sq. mile	= 2.59 sq. kilometers
1 sq. centimeter	= .1550 sq. inches
1 sq. meter	= 1550 sq. inches
	= 10.764 sq. feet
1 sq. kilometer	= .3861 sq. miles

METRIC CONVERSION CHART

METROPOLITAN AREA A major city and its surroundings.

METROPOLITAN AREA PLAN A community plan that is expanded to include the surrounding metropolitan area.

METROPOLITAN DISTRICT *See* Standard Metropolitan Statistical Area.

METROPOLITAN SHOPPING CENTER *See* Regional Shopping Center.

MEZZANINE **1.** An intermediate floor between two floors that does not have the same area as the rest of the floors. **2.** In a theater, the partial balcony between the main floor and the first balcony.

MGIC *See* Mortgage Guaranty Insurance Corporation.

MICRORELIEF A term used by farm appraisers to mean small surface features, such as channels or dunes, as opposed to hills or mountains.

MIDDLE RAIL The middle horizontal structural member of a door.

MILDEW Discoloring and surface coating and odor caused by fungi, particularly in damp conditions.

MILE A measurement equal to 5,280 feet on land. A nautical mile is 6,076 feet.

MILL **1.** A building equipped with machinery for grinding grain into flour. **2.** A building or group of buildings used to manufacture or process a wide variety of items. **3.** To process trees into various forms of lumber. **4.** One-tenth of a cent.

MILL CONSTRUCTION Construction built specifically to resist fire through the use of heavy timber and brick, masonry, and other fire-resistant materials and strategems such as incombustible fire stops and elevator hatches and the avoidance of corners and small projections that could ignite easily.

MILL-CUT ESTIMATES *See* Will-cut Cruise.

MILLWORK The portion of a building made of wood and manufactured in a mill. Some common items are doors, windows, mantels, panel work, stairways, and cabinets.

MINERAL FIBER PRODUCTS Products composed of a combination of asbestos fibers, Portland cement, and water. This combination forms a durable, fire-resistant, maintenance-free material. Its main drawback is low resistance to impact.

MINERAL RIGHTS The rights to minerals beneath the ground such as coal, iron, and gold with or without ownership of the surface of the land.

MINERALS In real estate terminology, minerals that may be mined, such as gold, silver, or iron. Mineral rights may be sold or leased separately from a property itself.

MINERAL WOOL A type of insulation made by sending steam through molten slag or rock. Common types are glass, wool, rock, wood, and slag wool.

MINIMUM LOT The smallest permitted lot for development as determined by local zoning ordinances.

MINIMUM RENTAL The minimum rental paid by the tenant who has leased premises with a percentage lease.

MINING LEASE A right to mine minerals.

MINOR A person who has not reached the age of majority (18).

MINUTE A unit of measurement equal to one-sixtieth of a degree or to 60 seconds.

MISPLACED IMPROVEMENT An improvement that does not contribute to the highest and best use of a property.

MISREPRESENTATION A statement that represents a fact which is false. When a property has certain defects, a broker, seller, or builder has a responsibility to inform a buyer or tenant of their existence. Failure to do so is a misrepresentation. A misrepresentation may be deliberate, negligent, or innocent.

MINERAL RIGHTS

MISSION STYLE

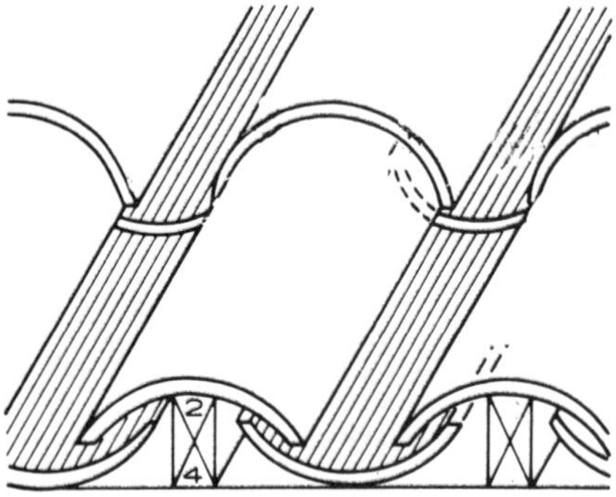

MISSION TITLE

MOBILE HOME

MISSION STYLE A nineteenth-century American house style developed in the West during the 1800s when people made an effort to become aware of their architectural past and popularized the Mission style as a reaction against the conventional Eastern styles. The houses resemble the old mission churches and houses of southern California. The Mission style house has arch-shaped doors and windows, stucco walls with no sculptural ornamentation, tile roofs, parapets, and towers and turrets with pyramid-shaped roofs.

CTS SYSTEM: Nineteenth Century American
Mission
(Mission-717)

MISSION TILE A type of clay roofing tile which is laid so that units have their convex side alternately up and down.

MITER To cut wood at an angle to form a miter joint.

M & M LIEN *See* Mechanic's Lien.

MOBILE HOME A post-World-War-II American home that is built in a factory and transported to its site. A home that is relocatable. That is, it may be put on wheels and pulled by a car or truck cab. Mobile homes are 12 feet wide and 60 feet long on the average. Mobile homes are now also called *manufactured housing*.

CTS SYSTEM: Post World War II American
Mobile Home
(Mobile-906)

MOBILE HOME PARK An area (sometimes park like) that has facilities such as plumbing and utilities, recreation centers, and security guards for mobile homes. Each mobile home is attached to a special pad constructed for that purpose.

MOBILITY The relative ease with which people can move from one place to the next.

MODE A statistical term for the most frequent number that appears in an array of numbers. Its advantage is that it is free from the influence of the extreme numbers in an array.

MODEL HOUSE A house that a builder exhibits to potential buyers in order to sell other houses.

MODERN ARCHITECTURE An architectural style that uses the contemporary functional design in order to combine utility and aesthetic quality in a house.

MODERNIZATION The process of bringing a property up to current standards of design and mechanical equipment. This may require changes in the exterior and interior and the replacement of mechanical equipment with current equipment.

MODERNIZE To restore a structure to its maximum utility and attractiveness without changing its function.

MODULAR CONSTRUCTION Prefabricated rooms that are built in a factory and shipped to their eventual location. Today, there is less and less difference between modular construction, mobile homes, and manufactured housing.

MODULAR HOUSE *See* Prefabricated House.

MODULAR PLANNING Designing structures to use modules.

MODULE A standard measure used in construction for components and design which allows easy repetition and saves material and labor costs.

MOISTURE BARRIER Material used to slow down or stop the build-up of condensation in walls.

MOISTURE EQUIVALENT A unit of measurement for the amount of water contained in soil. This is an arbitrary figure based on the amount of water that would be retained by soil at 1,000 times the force of gravity.

MOISTURE PROOFING The process of making a building moisture proof by the installation of moisture barriers.

MOISTURE PROTECTION Safe-guarding living units against the penetration or passage of water, water vapor, and dampness.

MOLDED BASE A two-member base that is composed of a common base with a molding on top or a three-member base that has a common base in the center, a base mold above, and a shoe mold below.

MOLDING Pieces of wood (or any building material) used to cover the crack between the meeting of a wall and ceiling or floor or simply used as decoration to introduce varieties of outlines and contours.

MONETARY CONTROLS The control the Federal Reserve System exerts over the level of economic activity by regulating the availability of money and interest rates.

MONEY Any accepted medium of exchange. *Money* usually refers to currency.

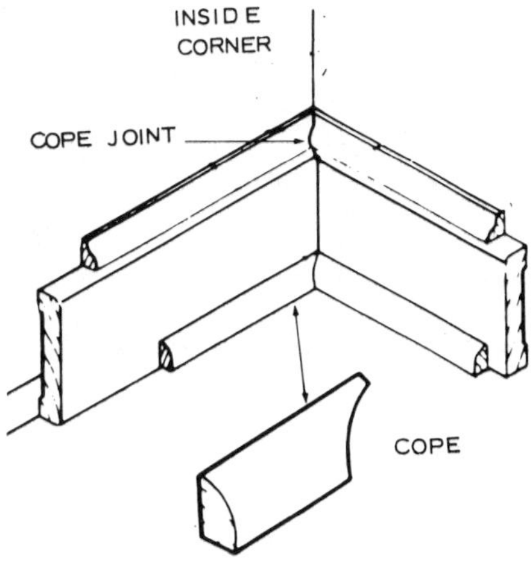

MOLDED BASE

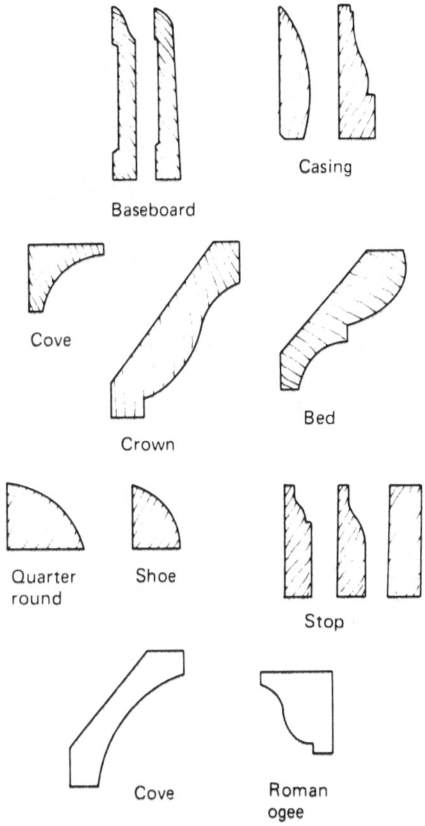

MOULDING

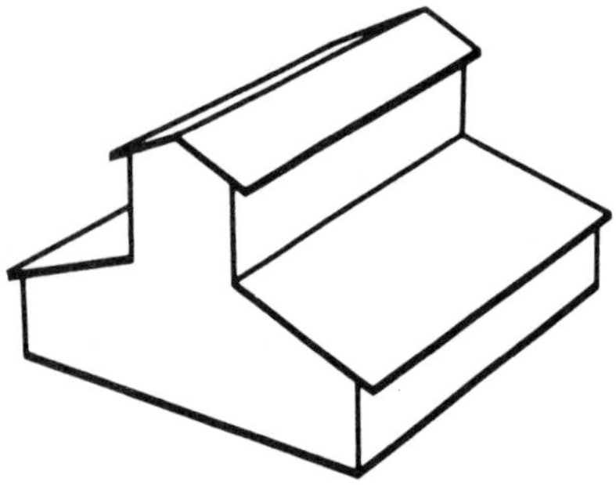

MONITOR ROOF

MONTEREY STYLE

MONEY MARKET A broad term for the market that exists where capital gets together with those who wish to borrow on a short-term basis. This market consists of the commodity markets that trade in money market instruments, commercial banks, corporations, finance companies, and others who are active in the use of short-term loans.

MONITOR An elevated structure on a roof that has louvers or windows to let light and air into the building.

MONITOR ROOF *See* Monitor.

MONOLITHIC One piece. A single block of stone or concrete.

MONOPOLY PROPERTY A property used by a business that has exclusive right to carry on certain enterprises.

MONTEREY STYLE A nineteenth-century American house style that originated in 1835, when Thomas Larlin, a Boston merchant, moved to Monterey, California, and built his version of a New England Colonial out of adobe brick. The Monterey is a two-story house with a balcony across the second-story level, with roof shingles, and with a fireplace. Most other houses in Monterey at that time were one story.

CTS SYSTEM: Nineteenth Century American
Monterey
(Monterey-715)

MONTH-TO-MONTH TENANCY Tenant rents for one month at a time.

MONTICELLO The home of Thomas Jefferson. *See also* Classic Colonial.

MONUMENTS Natural or artificial marks indicating real estate boundaries.

MONUMENT'S DESCRIPTION A manner of describing property by referring to natural or manmade objects.

MOP BOARD *See* Baseboard.

MORAINE A mass of material deposited by a glacier.

MORAL HAZARD A situation that is created when, because of the provisions of insurance policies, the insured person will gain from a loss caused by the hazards insured against. For example, when a person has disability insurance with benefits greater than the person's normal income, he or she might be tempted to try to claim the insurance rather than earn the income.

MORATORIUM In real estate, most commonly when a local agency suspends construction until it can determine the best use for the land involved.

MORTAR A mixture of plaster, or lime, or cement, sand, and water used to hold stones or bricks together that hardens in place.

MORTAR JOINTS Joints made of mortar. There are two types of mortar joints: troweled and tooled.

MORTGAGE The pledge of property to a lender to secure the payment of the debt. There are a variety of forms that are determined by custom and state statutes. They must be in writing and often are recorded in the land records. They are temporary in nature and end when the debt is paid off by the mortgagor.

MORTGAGE BANK CORRESPONDENTS The mortgage bankers who act as agents of lenders in order to place and service mortgage loans.

MORTGAGE BANKER A person or organization that makes loans secured by mortgages from their own funds and then sells the mortgages, usually in groups. Often, mortgage bankers continue to service the mortgages they sell for a fee.

MORTGAGE BANKERS ASSOCIATION OF AMERICA A trade organization whose members are mortgage bankers.

MORTGAGE BOND A type of bond issued by corporations and which are secured by a mortgage on the corporation's property (often both real and personal property).

MORTGAGE BROKER A person who brings together a borrower and lender, for a fee, and manages the necessary papers for a borrower to secure a loan against a property by giving a deed of trust or mortgage as security. He usually receives a percentage of the mortgage as commission for his services.

MORTGAGE BROKERAGE The enterprise of bringing a lender and borrower together and handling additional services, such as helping the closing of a loan.

MORTGAGE CERTIFICATE A certificate issued by the Federal Home Loan Mortgage Corporation. They are issued for an undivided interest in a large group of mortgages. The certificates are usually for 30 years and in $100,000 denominations. The payment of interest and principal is guaranteed by the Federal Home Loan Mortgage Corporation.

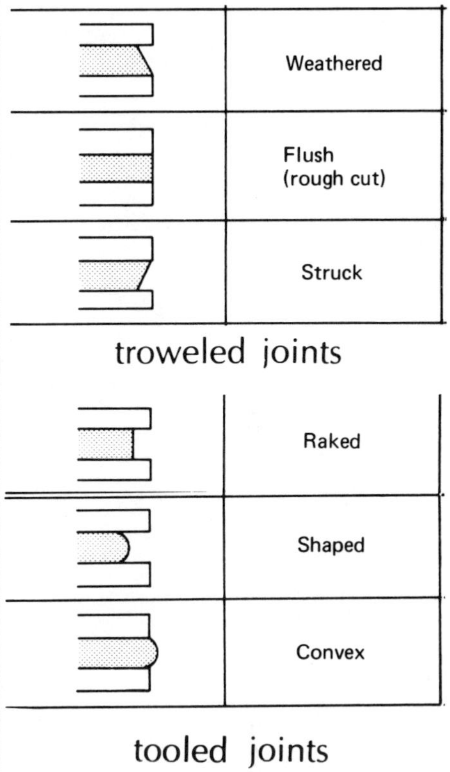

MORTAR JOINTS

MORTGAGE COEFFICIENT The multiplier used in the Ellwood Technique to find the overall rate "R".

MORTGAGE COMMITMENT A written notice given by a lending institution that promises a mortgage loan for the future and specifies the conditions and terms of the loan. It often contains a series of conditions that must be met by the borrower in order for the mortgage to be made.

MORTGAGE COMPANY A company which, for a fee, originates and services real estate loans.

MORTGAGE CONSTANT The percentage of the original loan balance that the annual payment represents. It consists of both principal and interest.

MORTGAGE CORRESPONDENT A person or company that acts as the representative of an institution that makes mortgage loans. Their function is to make mortgage commitments for the lender in the territory serviced by the correspondent. They often also service the loan for the lender.

MORTGAGE DEED A written document verifying that a real property has been given as security for a loan.

MORTGAGEE The lender who loans money, the repayment of which is secured by a mortgage.

MORTGAGE-EQUITY A technique used by appraisers as part of the income capitalization process. It recognizes the influence of mortgage terms and equity requirements.

MORTGAGE FORECLOSURE *See* Foreclosure.

MORTGAGE GUARANTY INSURANCE Insurance available to mortgage lenders from the Mortgage Guaranty Insurance Corporation that is issued against financial loss. Private insurance issued by companies, the largest of which is the Mortgage Guaranty Insurance Company, that insures the payment of mortgages. The insurance they issue is similar to VA and FHA mortgage insurance.

MORTGAGE GUARANTY INSURANCE CORPORATION (MGIC) An independent insurance company organized in 1956 that will insure a percentage of loans made by approved mortgage lenders to qualified buyers to help protect mortgage lenders from financial loss.

MORTGAGE INSURANCE PREMIUM The sum paid by a borrower for the insurance on a loan made by the FHA.

MORTGAGE LIFE INSURANCE A type of term life insurance (or a combination of term and whole life insurance) that is structured to pay off the balance of a mortgage in the event the borrower dies.

MORTGAGE NOTE A document which states that, in addition to the property being security for the repayment of the mortgage, the borrower also personally guarantees the mortgage repayment.

MORTGAGE POLICY (MORTGAGEE'S POLICY) A title insurance policy that guarantees to the mortgagee that the title to the property being used as mortgage security is a good title. It does not guarantee anything to the mortgagor.

MORTGAGE REDEMPTION INSURANCE *See* Mortgage Life Insurance.

MORTGAGE REQUIREMENT The regular payment that is necessary over a specified number of periods that is required to pay off a mortgage loan. Each payment consists of principal and interest.

MORTGAGE RISK RATING The process of analyzing all of the factors that affect the risk of a mortgage, such as the amount of equity, quality of the property, financial strength of the mortgagor, or economic conditions. Based on this analysis, the mortgage can be rated for its quality as an investment.

MORTGAGE SERVICING Maintaining the responsibilities of a mortgage, such as paying taxes and insurance and collecting payments. Servicing may be done by the lender or an intermediary for a fee.

MORTGAGE VALUE The value of the property for mortgage security purposes. It is often the market value of the property.

MORTGAGE WAREHOUSING The accumulation by a mortgage banker of a portfolio of mortgages in his own account for the purpose of selling them in a package to a lending institution.

MORTGAGOR The person who borrows money secured by a mortgage.

MORTISE A hole or notch cut into a piece of wood to receive a tenon (a bar of wood) in order to join the two or a lock.

MORTISE AND TENON A joint between two structures formed by fitting a tenon from one member into a mortise in another.

MORTGAGE DEED
MORTGAGEE
MORTGAGOR

MOSAIC Decoration using small chips of glass, ceramic, or stone pressed into mortar to form a design.

MOST APPROPRIATE USE *See* Highest and Best Use.

MOST PROBABLE SALES (SELLING) PRICE The price at which a property probably would sell under present market conditions if exposed for a reasonable length of time. This term is preferred by some appraisers instead of "highest price."

MOST PROBABLE USE Highest and best use in relation to market value.

MOST PROFITABLE USE *See* Highest and Best Use.

MOTEL Originally, a group of buildings located off a highway providing motorists a place to park and sleep. Now some motels have come to have almost all the services of a hotel, such as restaurants, recreation, and shops.

MOTOR HOTEL *See* Motel.

MPS (FHA) *See* Federal Housing Administration Minimum Property Standards.

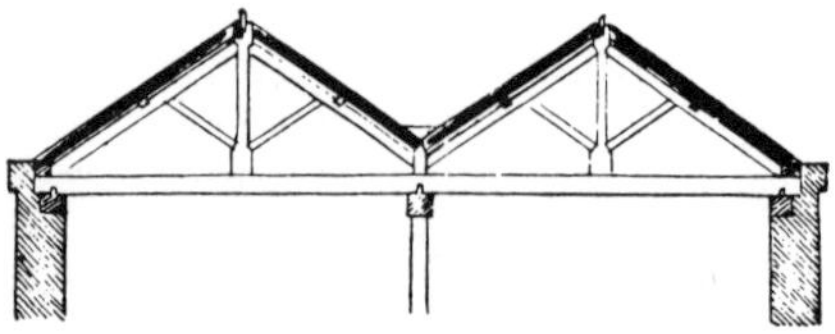

M ROOF

M ROOF A roof formed by the junction of two double-pitched roofs creating a shape that resembles an "M."

MUCK **1.** A type of soil composed of very soft, decomposed organic material. **2.** Material such as dirt, clay, or stone that must be excavated.

MUD ENTRANCE *See* Mud Room.

MUD ROOM A small room or vestibule containing an entrance from a yard or alley. It often contains a washer and dryer.

MULLION

MULLION Vertical bars between multiple window panes.

MULTI-FAMILY HOUSING **1.** A structure occupied by more than one family. **2.** Used by the FHA to refer to multi-family rental housing projects of eight or more units.

MULTI-FAMILY STRUCTURE A broad term used to describe residences that house more than one family. It has different meanings in different areas with respect to how many families there must be in order for the dwelling to be classified as multi-family.

MULTIPLE DWELLING *See* Multi-family Housing.

MULTIPLE LISTING (MLS) A system where a group of brokers agree to work together and cooperate to sell each other's listings. When a listing is taken, it is published through the multiple listing system, and the cooperating brokers are invited to become subagents of the listing broker.

MULTIPLE-NUCLEI A theory of land use development. It states that the automobile has become the primary factor in determining the use of land. Now, rather than having just a single center of economic activity in an area, there are many economic focal points that are accessible by automobile.

MULTIPLE REGRESSION ANALYSIS A statistical technique for measuring the effect that a number of independent variables have on one dependent variable. The technique is now being used by appraisers because of the availability of calculating equipment and computers capable of making the numerous calculations needed.

MULTIPLIER A figure used to estimate the value of a property based on its gross income. The multiplier is developed from comparable properties by taking their gross incomes and dividing them into their selling prices. The multiplier thus developed is multiplied by the gross income of the property whose value is being estimated to produce the value estimate.

MUNICIPAL CORPORATION A village, city, or town incorporated as a political corporation under state laws.

MUNICIPAL SEWER SYSTEM The sewer system owned and operated by the municipality.

MUNIMENTS OF TITLE Written documents that an owner holds as evidence of his title to a property.

MUNTIN Thin bars of wood or metal between lights of glass in a window.

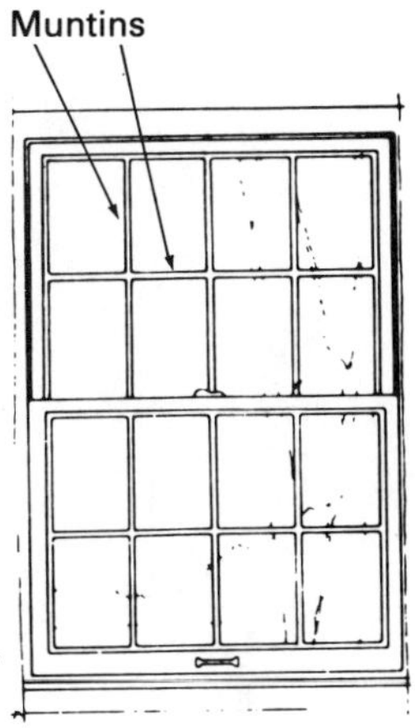

MUNTIN

MUSIC SYSTEMS Part of the electrical system of some buildings. It consists of a tuner or phonograph turntable or tape player and an amplifier, which is connected by wire to a series of speakers throughout the building.

MUTUAL OWNERSHIP A financial institution that is owned and operated under the control of its depositors.

MUTUAL SAVINGS BANK A form of thrift institution found primarily in the northeast. Most of them are in Massachusetts, Connecticut, and New York. They operate very similar to a savings and loan association. They are owned and controlled by their depositors, who deposit funds in the bank and receive interest. The banks invest the funds primarily in residential mortgages. Recently, they have expanded their services to include home improvement loans and checking accounts that pay interest (NOW accounts).

MUTUAL WATER COMPANY A water company that is organized and owned by the customers.

N

NAILS Thin, straight pieces of metal that usually have a head and are pointed. Nails are driven with a hammer and used primarily to hold pieces of wood together.

NATIONAL APARTMENT ASSOCIATION (NAA) A national trade organization of people associated with multi-family housing.

NATIONAL ASSOCIATION OF BUILDING MANUFACTURERS (NABM) A national trade organization for those associated with the industrialized housing industry.

NATIONAL ASSOCIATION OF HOME BUILDERS (NAHB) The largest trade association of builders who primarily build residences and others associated with the construction of residential property.

NATIONAL ASSOCIATION OF HOUSING AND REDEVELOPMENT OFFICIALS (NAHRO) A national trade organization of people and agencies involved in public housing, urban redevelopment, and housing code enforcement.

NATIONAL ASSOCIATION OF HOUSING COOPERATIVES A national organization of people who live in and own a cooperative apartment.

NATIONAL ASSOCIATION OF MUTUAL SAVINGS BANKS The national trade organization of mutual savings banks.

NATIONAL ASSOCIATION OF REAL ESTATE BROKERS (NAREB) An association dedicated to improving the real estate industry, specifically the role of blacks and other minorities in the industry. Many of the members call themselves Realtists.

NATIONAL ASSOCIATION OF REAL ESTATE INVESTMENT TRUSTS (NAREIT) A non-profit corporation with membership consisting of real estate investment trusts and

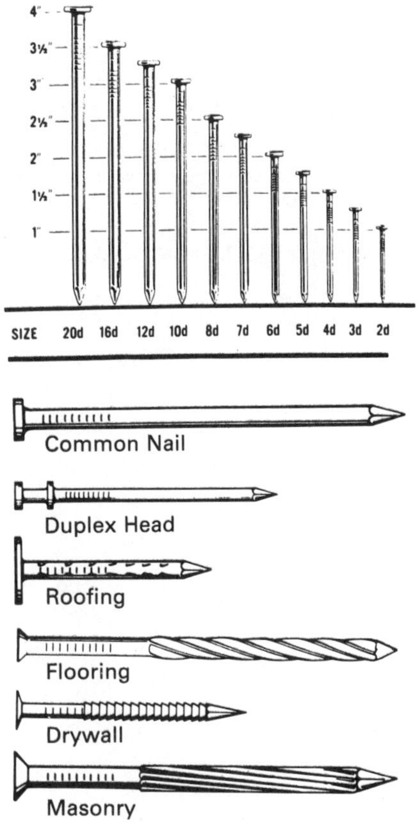

NAILS

NATIONAL ASSOCIATION OF REAL ESTATE LICENSE LAW OFFICIALS

Institutes, Societies and Councils

- Society of Industrial Realtors (SIR)
- Institute of Real Estate Management (IREM)
- Farm and Land Institute (FLI)
- American Institute of Real Estate Appraisers (AIREA)
- Real Estate Securities and Syndication Institute (RESSI)
- American Society of Real Estate Counselors (ASREC)
- Woman's Council of Realtors (WCR)
- American Chapter of the International Real Estate Federation (FIABCI)

NATIONAL ASSOCIATION OF REALTORS® (NAR)

people and companies associated with the field, such as lawyers, bankers, and accounting firms.

NATIONAL ASSOCIATION OF REAL ESTATE LICENSE LAW OFFICIALS (NARELLO) An association whose members are real estate commissioners and other officials and officers who enforce the license laws of various states, provinces, etc.

NATIONAL ASSOCIATION OF REALTORS® (NAR) An association that serves people in the real estate business. NAR is the largest business trade association in the world, having more than seven hundred thousand members. NAR is dedicated to raising the standards of real estate practice and preserving property rights through legislation and by promoting education and high ethical standards for its members. Only members of NAR can use the trademark REALTOR®.

NATIONAL INCOME The total net earnings of all the various businesses of a nation during a particular time period.

NATIONAL SAVINGS AND LOAN LEAGUE The national professional and trade association for the individual savings and loan associations.

NATURAL DISASTER *See* Act of God.

NATURAL FEATURES A term used to describe the elements in the world caused by natural events such as rivers, mountains, and valleys rather than those created or made by humans, such as roads and houses.

NATURAL FINISH A clear finish such as a varnish that does not significantly change the original surface, color, or grain.

NATURAL LAND CLASSIFICATION A classification of soil into groups that have common characteristics of position, texture, and drainage.

NATURAL RESOURCE PROPERTY A property that contains natural resources such as mineral deposits or oil and gas which may be commercially exploited.

NATURAL RESOURCES Resources created by nature such as minerals, oil, gas, timber, fish, water, and wildlife.

NATURAL SEASONING The drying of lumber by stacking it to allow the air to circulate around each timber.

NAVIGABLE **1.** Water that is capable of carrying commercial shipping. **2.** In some states, any waters put to public use.

NAVIGABLE WATERS A general term that may mean a body of water able to carry commerce or a body of water large enough to ebb and flow.

NECESSARIES A term referring to the necessaries of life, which are food, clothing, and shelter.

NEGATIVE CASH FLOW A negative cash flow comes into existence when the income from an investment does not pay for the expenses, and the owner must furnish the extra cash periodically to meet these expenses.

NEGATIVE LEVERAGE The increase in financial loss that results from borrowing when costs exceed returns.

NEGOTIABLE Something capable of being negotiated. It is commonly an item that is transferable, such as securities, notes, and negotiable bonds.

NEGOTIABLE INSTRUMENT A negotiable instrument, according to the Uniform Negotiable Instruments Act, is a written and signed instrument within which there is an order or unconditional promise to pay, on demand or at a definite future date, a specified sum of money to the bearer or to a named drawee.

NEIGHBORHOOD In modern usage, a neighborhood tends to be any separately identifiable cohesive area within a community with some community interest shared by its occupants. Some neighborhoods may have recognizable or manmade boundaries.

NEIGHBORHOOD LIFE CYCLE Every neighborhood is constantly changing, although sometimes the change is almost indiscernible. Neighborhoods often follow a four-phase life cycle. The phases are: **1.** *Growth:* The period when active construction takes place, new inhabitants are attracted, and the neighborhood gains favor and acceptance. **2.** *Stability:* A period of undefined length in which there are no major changes and no marked gains or losses. **3.** *Decline:* A period that begins when a neighborhood is less able to compete with other neighborhoods. Properties may change use and be in a poor state of maintenance. **4.** *Renewal:* A period of rejuvenation and rebirth of market demand.

Period	*Value Trend*
• Growth	Up
• Stability	Level
• Decline	Down
• Renewal	Up
• Stability	Level
• Decline	Down

NEIGHBORHOOD LIFE CYCLE

NEIGHBORHOOD SHOPPING CENTER A group of stores that service a limited area (or neighborhood). Usually, there are food and convenience stores and parking.

NET Money remaining after all deductions, outlays, losses, etc.

NET ACRE An acre that may be used for construction after space has been allowed for streets, sidewalks, and other off-site improvements.

NET AFTER TAXES The net income from property after income tax is paid.

NET BEFORE TAXES Net income before payment of income tax but after payment of property taxes.

NET CASH PROCEEDS OF RESALE The amount of money a property owner receives when his property is sold after the commission, other selling expenses, mortgages, and other debts that are outstanding at the time of the sale are paid. The expenses to be paid do not include income or capital gains taxes caused by the sale.

NET EARNINGS *See* Net Operating Income.

NET GROUND LEASE A lease of unimproved land in which the lessee agrees to pay the owner's expenses such as *ad valorem* taxes and assessments.

NET INCOME The balance remaining after deducting all operating expenses, maintenance, taxes, and losses from the gross income.

NET INCOME BEFORE DEPRECIATION (NIBD) *See* Net Operating Income.

NET INCOME BEFORE RECAPTURE (NIBR) *See* Net Operating Income.

NET INCOME MULTIPLIER A factor obtained by dividing the selling price by the net income. This factor can be used to estimate the value of other properties whose net income is known by multiplying the net income by the factor.

NET INCOME RATIO The ratio of net income to effective gross income.

NET LEASE A lease in which a tenant pays maintenance and operating expenses for the leased property in addition to rent. It is also called net net, net net net triple net, etc.

NET LISTING A listing under which the broker receives all monies above the minimum sales price predetermined by owners and broker. This form of listing is now illegal in many states.

NET LOSS The difference between expense and income when expense is larger.

NET NET; NET NET NET *See* Net Lease.

NET OPERATING INCOME (NOI) A term used by appraisers in the income approach to value. It is the gross operating income of the property less the fixed expenses, variable expenses, and reserves for replacement. It does not include deductions for depreciation or debt service or any expenses not directly related to the property.

NET PRESENT VALUE (NPV) A value used to rate the quality of an investment. It is the difference between the total cost of the investment and the present worth of all the future anticipated benefits of the investment. To be acceptable, the NPV should be a positive number.

NET PROFITS Money remaining after deducting all expenses and charges from income.

NET RENTABLE AREA The net rentable area of a multiple tenancy floor shall be the sum of all rentable areas of that floor. *See also* Rentable Area.

NET RENTAL Rental over and above the expenses of the property.

NET SALES Gross sales minus deductions for returns and allowances.

NET SALES AREAS The square footage in a retail or department store used only for the display and sale of goods.

NET SPENDABLE INCOME The cash income a property owner receives after paying all the expenses including the debt service and the income taxes that result from the property income.

NET USABLE ACRE *See* Net Acre.

NET WORTH The equity of a person, partnership, or corporation after subtracting all their debts and obligations.

NEWEL The central post in a circular stairway around which the steps wind. *See also* Newel Post.

NEWEL CAP An ornamental finish on the top of a newel post.

NEWEL POST The upright post at the bottom of a stairway that supports the handrail.

Example of the Calculation of Net Operating Income

Income	
Gross potential income	$83,500
Vacancy and collection loss	−4,000
Effective gross income	$79,500
Expenses	
Fixed expenses	$ 9,000
Variable expenses	39,000
Reserves for replacement	12,500
Total operating expenses	−$60,500
Net operating income (NOI)	$19,000

NET OPERATING INCOME (NOI)

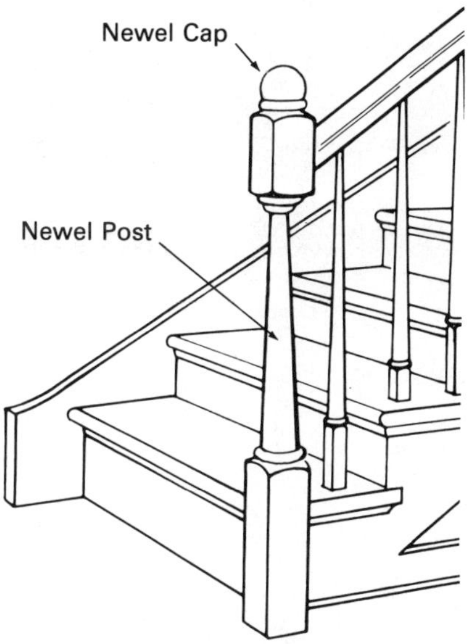

NEWEL CAP
NEWEL POST

NEW ENGLAND COLONIAL STYLE

NEW ENGLAND FARM HOUSE STYLE

NEW ENGLAND COLONIAL STYLE A colonial American house style that evolved from the Cape Cod style. The New England Colonial is a large, roomy, two-and-one-half story, rectangular or square, box-shaped house. It usually has side or rear wings and traditionally has clapboard siding and a shingled gable roof. Other distinguishing characteristics are double-hung windows with shutters the same size as the windows, elaborate cornices with dentals, and a central hallway on the first floor running from front to rear.

CTS SYSTEM: Colonial American
New England Colonial
(NE Col-107)

NEW ENGLAND FARM HOUSE STYLE A colonial American house style that originated in the New England countryside during the 1700s and 1800s. This simple, box-shaped house was a favorite among farmers because it was simple to construct and maintain. A steep, pitched roof is used to shed snow, and a central chimney helps to support the frame.

CTS SYSTEM: Colonial American
New England Farm House
(NE Farm-102)

NEW ORLEANS STYLE *See* Creole Style.

"NO BONUS" CLAUSE A provision in a lease that restricts the tenant from receiving any of the proceeds when the property is taken by condemnation. Without this clause, the tenant may be able to claim a portion of the compensation because he or she has a leasehold interest in the property.

NOGGING Used bricks placed between the timbers of wall construction. It is called covered nogging when covered with stucco and exposed nogging when visible.

NOMINAL INTEREST RATE The rate of interest stated in a contract. It may not be the effective rate or true rate of interest if there were financing charges or discount points.

NOMINAL SIZE The commercial size given a piece of lumber or other material by the trade, other than its actual size. For example, the actual size of a 2×8 can be $1\frac{1}{2} \times 7\frac{1}{4}$.

NOMINEE One who is designated to act for another person with specific limited authority. A nominee is often used to purchase property when the real buyers do not wish to be identified.

NOMOGRAM A chart or diagram that represents numerical relationships.

NON-BASIC ACTIVITIES The economic activities of a community that do not bring in money from outside the community.

NON-BASIC EMPLOYMENT Employment in those activities in a community that do not bring in money from outside the community.

NON-BEARING PARTITION *See* Non-bearing Wall.

NON-BEARING WALL A wall that supports only its own weight and does not carry any load.

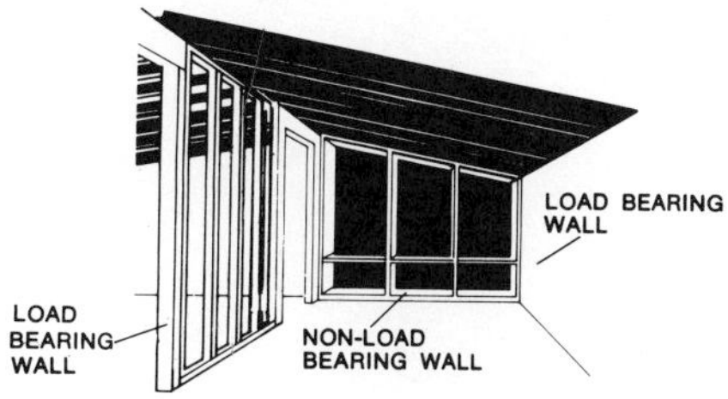

NON-BEARING WALL

NON-COMBUSTIBLE As applied to building construction material, it means a material which, in the form in which it is used, is either one of the following: **1.** Material of which no part will ignite and burn when subjected to fire in accordance with ASTM E-136 test Non-combustibility of Elementary Materials. **2.** Material having a structural base of non-combustible material as defined in item No. 1 above, with a surfacing material not over ⅛ inch thick which has a flame spread rating of 50 or less tested in accordance with ASTM-84 test Surface Burning Characteristics of Building Materials or ASTM E-162 test Surface Flammability of Materials Using a Radiant Heat Energy Source

NON-CONFORMING BUILDING *See* Non-conforming Use.

NON-CONFORMING USE A use that does not currently conform to the zoning regulations of an area. It is a use that was lawfully established prior to the zoning and maintained but does not now conform because of a change of zoning ordinance.

NON-CONFORMITY A property that does not conform in usage or physical appearance to its neighboring properties.

NON-DURABLE GOODS *See* Durable Goods.

NON-FREEHOLD ESTATE An estate in real estate without seisin (ownership). The most common form is a leasehold estate.

NON-METALLIC CABLE A cable whose wires, in addition to their own insulation, are wrapped with a paper

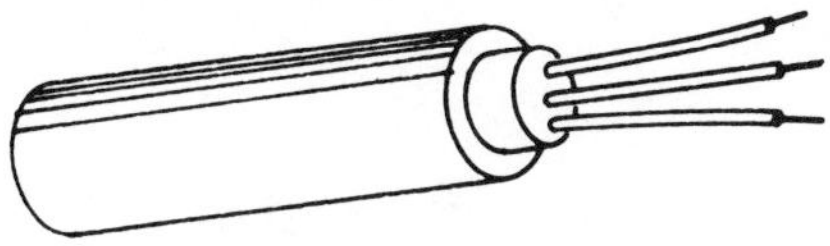

NON-METALLIC CABLE

tape, covered with a heavy fabric or plastic, and then treated to be made fire resistant.

NON-OPERATING INCOME Money that a business earns from sources other than the operation of the business itself; money from investments, capital gains, etc.

NON-PROFIT CORPORATION A corporation that is formed for a purpose other than making a profit. Such groups are often used for charity purposes or may be political, fraternal, or educational organizations. These corporations do not have shareholders or stock. They have members who elect a board of directors to run the affairs of the corporation. In many other respects, they operate like a regular corporation.

NON-RECOURSE LOAN A type of loan where the borrower is not held personally responsible for the repayment of the loan. The lender's security is limited to the property that is put up as security for the loan.

NON-RECURRING EXPENSE An expense that usually is not repeated, such as a loss by fire or theft.

NON-RESIDENT A person who does not reside within the state or is not from that particular state.

NON-ZONING Not restricting the use of land via zoning ordinances.

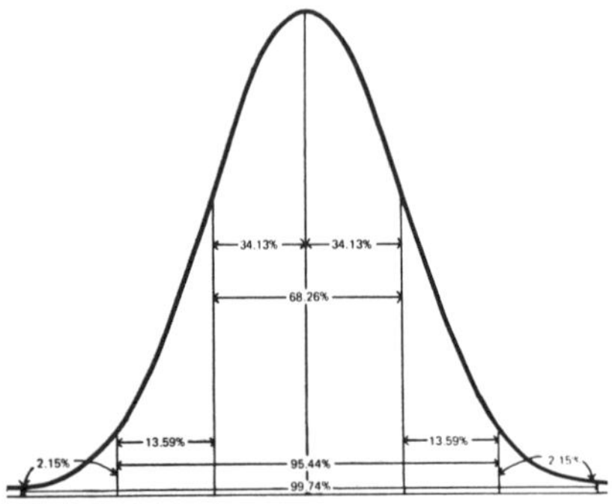

NORMAL CURVE

NORMAL DISTRIBUTION

NORMAL CURVE A statistical term meaning a bell-shaped curve which represents the normal distribution of certain measurements that might be drawn from any large sample of a population.

NORMAL DISTRIBUTION A statistical term. It refers to the distribution of data that can be expected in a large random sample. This distribution is usually represented by a normal curve. *See also* Normal Curve.

NORMAL WEAR AND TEAR *See* Wear and Tear.

NORTHWESTERN STYLE

NORTHWESTERN STYLE A post-World-War-II American house style. It was first developed in 1908 by Ellsworth Storey as a group of cottages on Puget Sound. The style did not really become popular until the 1950s. It is a low ranch house with generous overhangs. The exterior walls are often made of redwood and the roof has cedar shingles. Its principle distinguishing characteristic is the South Sea Island influence in the roof design.

CTS SYSTEM: Post World War II American
Northwestern or Puget Sound
(North W or P Sound-902)

NOSING The rounded outer face of a stair tread.

NOTARY PUBLIC A person who has a state or federal commission to attest and certify deeds, administer oaths, and attest to the authenticity of signatures.

NOTE A written and signed acknowledgement and promise to pay a debt.

NOTICE OF ACTION A recorded notice of a pending suit, such as notice that a property may be subject to a lien or that the title is defective.

NOTICE OF COMPLETION A recorded notice that a construction job is finished.

NOTICE OF DEFAULT A notice that is filed when a borrower is in default on a mortgage or a deed of trust.

NOTICE OF NON-RESPONSIBILITY A notice that an owner files in the event that work being done on his property has not been contracted for by the owner.

NOTICE OF RECISION A notice filed to void notice of default of a mortgage or deed of trust.

NOTICE TO QUIT A written notice given by a landlord to a tenant advising the tenant that the landlord wants possession of the premises at some stated time.

NOTORIOUS POSSESSION In order to obtain title by adverse possession, possession must be notorious, that is so open and exclusive that the owner is presumed to be aware of it.

NOVATION The substitution of a new obligation, contract, or debt for an existing one.

NUCLEAR ENERGY Energy derived from the fission of atoms.

NUISANCE Property used in such a manner as to interfere with the use and enjoyment of other property. It involves such things as creating excessive noise, fumes, or odors.

NUISANCE LAWS Laws that prohibit the conduct of obnoxious activities on one's land that would interfere with a neighbor's peaceful enjoyment of his property.

NUISANCE VALUE The amount that someone would pay for a property, not for its own sake but because, as it is currently owned and run, it is a nuisance or is actually damaging the prospective buyer.

NULL AND VOID Void. Not legally binding. *See also* Voidable.

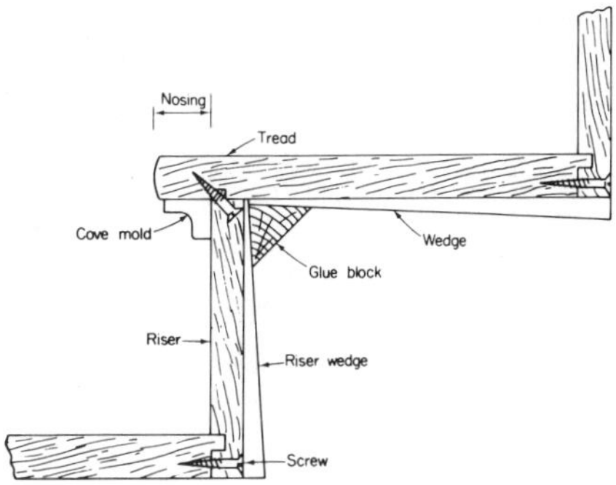

NOSING

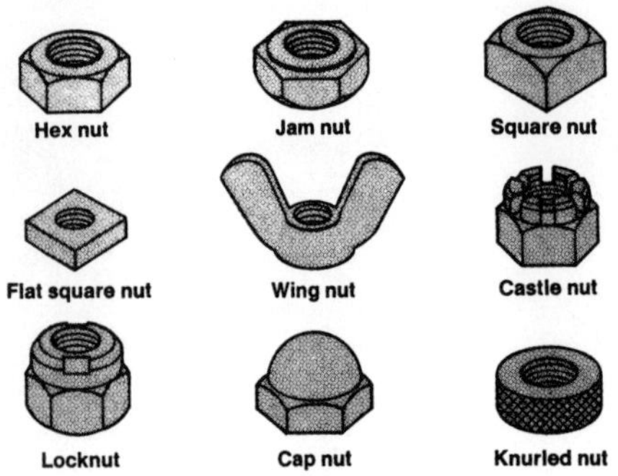

NUT

NULL HYPOTHESIS A statistical technique which starts with the hypothesis that there is no significant difference between two statistics and then proceeds to test the hypothesis.

NUT **1.** A slang term. *See also* Overhead. **2.** A metal block with a threaded hole that attaches to the end of a bolt, screw, or other threaded device.

NUTRIENTS Elements in the soil that nourish plant growth and are essential to soil development.

O

OAK FLOORING The most popular hardwood flooring.

OAKUM A caulking fiber obtained by pulling apart old hemp rope.

OATH A solemn attestation that the statements a person makes are true.

OBJECTIVE A word describing an opinion, decision, etc., made free of prejudice or bias.

OBJECTIVE VALUE *See* Value in Exchange.

OBLIGEE A person to whom a debt or favor is owed.

OBLIGOR A person who owes a debt.

OBSERVATORY *See* Belvedere.

OBSERVED CONDITION The physical condition of a property ascertained by a detailed inspection.

OBSERVED CONDITION METHOD An appraisal method of estimating depreciation. The appraiser makes three separate estimates—one each for physical deterioration, functional obsolescense, and economic obsolescense—based on his observations and then adds the three estimates together to produce a final estimate of depreciation.

OBSERVED DEPRECIATION The three forms of depreciation that are observed by the appraiser using the observed condition method of estimating depreciation.

OBSOLESCENCE Forms of depreciation that are caused by things other than physical deterioration. Often, obsolescence is divided into functional obsolescence and economic obsolescence.

OBSOLETE The condition of being no longer useful or desirable.

OBLIGEE
OBLIGOR

OCTAGON HOUSE

OCTAGON WINDOW

OFFEREE
OFFEROR

OCCUPANCY The state of being in possession of a property; to physically occupy a property.

OCCUPANCY, COST OF The cost of occupying a property, which usually includes rent, utilities, and repairs.

OCCUPANCY RATE The percentage of the total available units of a property that are actually occupied.

OCTAGON HOUSE A nineteenth-century American house style that originated in the 1850s as a result of an idea of the popular author Orson Squire Fowler. Fowler believed that a happy life could be found in an octagon-shaped house because this shape made for good heating, lighting, and interior circulation. The most distinguishing characteristic of this style is the octagonal shape. It is also characterized by flat roofs and a center chimney.

CTS SYSTEM: Nineteenth Century American
Octagon House
(Octagon-704)

OCTAGONAL WINDOW A window with eight sides. It is one of the design features of the Regency style.

OFFER A proposal subject to another's acceptance to do a specified deed when the other party in turn performs a specified deed. Part of the process of making a binding contract that consists of an offer and acceptance.

OFFER AND ACCEPTANCE One of the essential elements of a contract to transfer a real property.

OFFEREE The person to whom an offer is made.

OFFEROR A person making an offer.

OFFER TO PURCHASE *See* Purchase Agreement.

OFFICE **1.** A place of business where the type of work conducted consists primarily of professional activities or other activities that involve processing paperwork. **2.** A zoning designation which permits businesses that only do paperwork, such as accounting, law, or insurance firms, rather than those that sell or manufacture, to operate in a certain area.

OFFICE BUILDING A building that contains mostly offices rather than being used for residential, commercial, or industrial purposes.

OFFSET **1.** A ledge that makes a change in the thickness of a wall. **2.** To balance. **3.** A printing process.

OFF-SITE Not on the property.

OFF-SITE IMPROVEMENTS The development and construction of improvements, such as streets and sewers, to make adjacent property fit for construction.

OGEE MOULDING A type of ornamental molding.

OIL AND GAS LEASE A lease granting the right to extract oil and gas from land. Usually, the lessor is paid based on the oil and gas taken.

OLIGOPOLY A market controlled by a limited number of participants.

"ONCE IN A LIFETIME" TAX EXCLUSION An exclusion that may be taken only once by a senior citizen to forgive a part of the tax due on a sale of a residence.

ON CENTER A measuring term meaning the distance from the center of one structural member to the center of a corresponding structural member, such as studs or joists.

ONE-HOUR DOOR A door that is fire resistant and will contain a fire for a minimum of one hour.

ONE-HOUR WALL A wall that is fire resistant and will contain a fire for a minimum of one hour.

ONE-PIPE RETURN TEE FITTING A special fitting used in a hot-water heating system that keeps the water flowing in only one direction.

ONE-PIPE SERIES CONNECTED HEATING SYSTEM A simple hot-water heating system where all the radiators are connected in series, one after the other, and the water flows through each radiator and on to the next.

ON RAIL Property serviced by a railroad.

ON-SITE IMPROVEMENTS Improvements that are erected permanently for use on a site, such as a fence or building.

ON-SITE OFFICE A branch office of a real estate estate firm that leases or sells property for a particular development and is situated at said development.

OPEN AND NOTORIOUS POSSESSION *See* Notorious Possession.

OPEN-BEAM CONSTRUCTION A construction technique that eliminates the ceiling and ceiling joists and leaves the roof beams exposed, giving the room a spacious, rugged appearance.

OGEE MOULDING

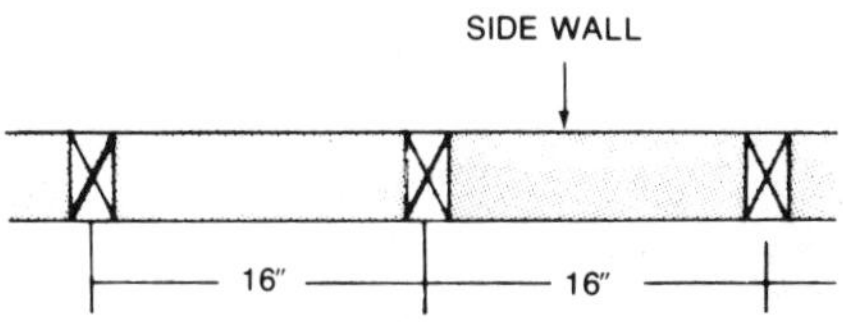

ON CENTER

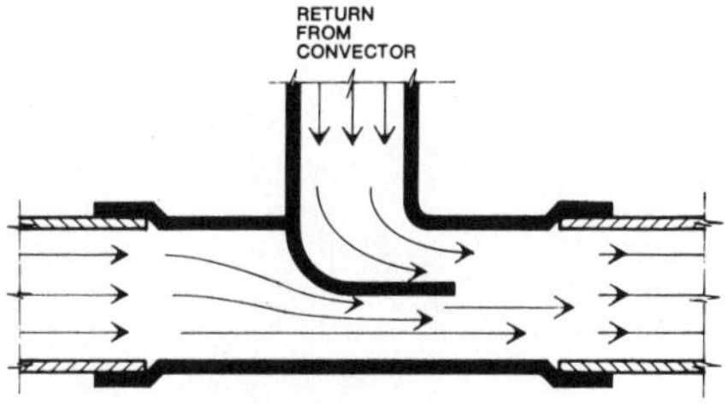

ONE-PIPE RETURN TEE FITTING

OPEN CHANNEL A drainage course designed to carry major storm sewer flow on the surface. It is generally used only where no other feasible method of drainage is possible.

OPEN-END CLAUSE A clause in a mortgage that permits the amount of the loan to be expanded during the life of the mortgage without the necessity of writing a new mortgage. It may also provide that the interest rate of the additional money be adjusted to the then current rate.

OPEN-END MORTGAGE A mortgage that contains a clause allowing the mortgager to borrow additional money under the same mortgage.

OPEN HOUSE A house that is open to prospective buyers to examine without an appointment during specified times during the week.

OPEN HOUSING Housing that is available to anyone without regard to sex, color, religion, race, or national origin.

OPEN LISTING A listing to sell or rent property that is given to more than one broker. The first broker who finds a party ready, willing, and able to buy or rent at the asking price, or at a mutually agreeable negotiated price, receives a commission that is specified in the listing agreement. Unless required by state law, an open listing does not have to be for a specified period of time.

OPEN MORTGAGE A mortgage that can be paid at any time. A mortgage that is overdue is also called an open mortgage or due on demand.

OPEN OCCUPANCY Residential property that is available to anyone without regard to race, sex, religion, or color. Under the U. S. Constitution, all property is open occupancy.

OPEN PLAN House design having a minimum of walls and partitions.

OPEN SPACE LAND Land designated on a map for recreation, watershed, wildlife, agriculture, etc.

OPEN SPACE RATIO The ratio of the site area to the floor area of an apartment building used to meet zoning requirements.

OPEN STEEL CONSTRUCTION Steel construction that is not fireproofed. It is the main steel frame carrying exterior walls on multi-story buildings. Usually, the steel framing is load bearing.

OPEN WEB JOIST An open, webbed, lightweight steel truss.

OPERATING EXPENSE RATIO Relationship between operating expenses and projected gross income, expressed as a percentage of the gross income.

OPERATING EXPENSES The expenses resulting from the production of income from a property, such as taxes, insurance, management, repairs, utilities, and rubbish removal.

OPERATING INCOME The income of a business that is comparable to the net operating income of a property. It is the direct operating income of the business minus the direct operating expenses.

OPERATING PROFIT The profit developed from the normal operation of a business enterprise as distinguished from income that comes from outside sources.

OPERATING STANDARDS Standards of performance set for a property based on the experience of similar properties.

OPERATING STATEMENT An accounting of the income and expenses of a business or property over a given period of time.

OPERATIVE PROPERTY (OPERATING PROPERTY) A property that is necessary for the conduct of a business.

OPERATIVE WORDS Words in a deed or lease that effect the transaction that is the subject of the document.

OPINION OF TITLE A legal opinion which states that a property is free and clear and marketable. *See also* Abstract of Title.

OPTIMUM USE *See* Highest and Best Use.

OPTION An agreement that grants the right to purchase or lease a property during a specified period of time at stipulated terms.

OPTIONEE A person who receives an option.

OPTION FOR ADDITIONAL SPACE An option granted to a tenant to rent additional space at a stipulated time and for stipulated terms.

OPTIONOR A person who, for a consideration, gives an option.

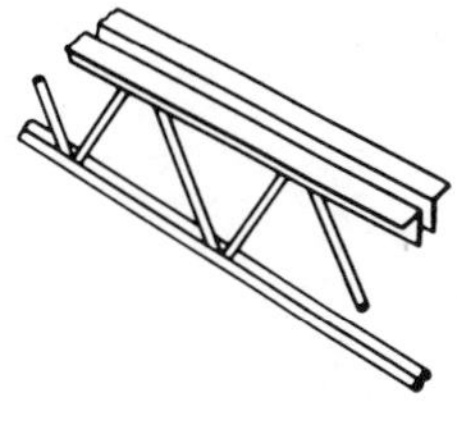

OPEN WEB JOIST

OPTION
OPTIONEE
OPTIONOR

ORDINARY HIGH WATER MARK

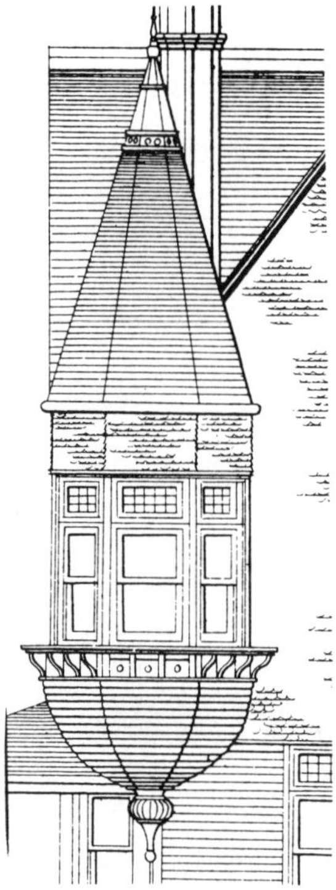

ORIEL WINDOW

ORAL CONTRACT A verbal agreement that may contain some or no writing. Every state now has a statute of frauds that makes verbal contracts for the sale of property non-binding.

ORCHARD A group of fruit- or nut-bearing trees that are planted in rows. The spacing of the trees in a well-planted orchard is such that maximum production is obtained from a given amount of land.

ORDER CONFIRMING SALE Court order that confirms the terms of a sale of property out of an estate.

ORDINANCE A law, regulation, or statute, usually made by a municipality.

ORDINARY ANNUITY A regular income stream of payments with each payment made at the end of a specified period.

ORDINARY HIGH WATER MARK The high water mark, which is distinguished by erosion, destruction of vegetation, etc.

ORDINARY INCOME For income tax purposes, a term which designates income that is taxed according to the regular graduated scale paid on income as opposed to capital gains or any other income that is taxed differently.

ORDINARY REPAIRS Repairs made to keep a property in good condition; repairs necessary to eliminate the results of ordinary wear and tear.

ORE A natural mineral containing enough metal, coal, or other useful materials to make mining it profitable.

ORGANIC MATTER The decomposed organic matter in the soil from plant and animal remains.

ORGANIC SOIL Soil that is predominantly formed of organic matter.

ORGANIZATION COST The basic cost incurred to start a business or real estate development. It consists primarily of legal and accounting expenses, and does not include the cost of raising capital, promotion costs, construction costs, or other ordinary business or development costs.

ORIEL WINDOW A window and bay projecting from an upper story that is supported by corbels or brackets rather than a foundation wall.

ORIENTAL HOUSE *See* Japanese House.

ORIENTATION The relation between a structure and its lot with regard to the points of the compass. The direction the improvements face on the site.

ORIGINAL COST The initial sum paid to build or purchase a property by its present owner, whether or not the present owner is the first owner. This is the cost that is normally used as a basis for depreciation (exclusive of that portion of the cost which is for the land).

ORIGINATION FEE A fee charged by a lender for making a loan or taking a mortgage. It is usually a percentage of the mortgage. One percent of the face amount of the mortgage is called a point.

OR MORE CLAUSE A clause in a deed of trust, note, or mortgage that permits additional payments to be made without penalty.

ORNAMENTAL GARDEN A formal garden that is often associated with oriental style houses.

ORTHOGRAPHIC PROJECTION A drawing of a building without perspective. The lines that are parallel in the building are parallel on the drawing. It is the type of drawing that is the basis for building plans.

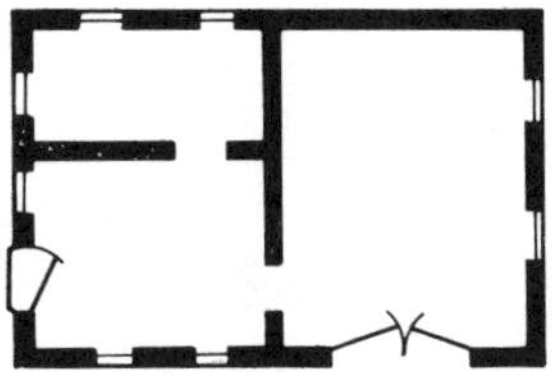

ORTHOGRAPHIC PROJECTION

OSTENSIBLE AGENCY An agency created through the force of law without the voluntary consent of the principal or agent. It is sometimes referred to as an agency of estoppel.

OUTDOOR LIVING The use of patios, porches, lawns, and extensive glass in an attempt to integrate the indoors and outdoors.

OUTDOOR STORAGE SHED A small, outdoor structure of wood or steel used to house bikes, yard equipment, lawn furniture, games, grills, ladders, etc.

OUTER BARK The dry, dead tissue of a tree that is the outermost layer.

OUTER HEARTH A continuation of the hearth that should extend at least 16 inches from the front of the fireplace and 8 inches beyond the side for protection against sparks. It must be fireproof and is usually made of tile, stone, or brick.

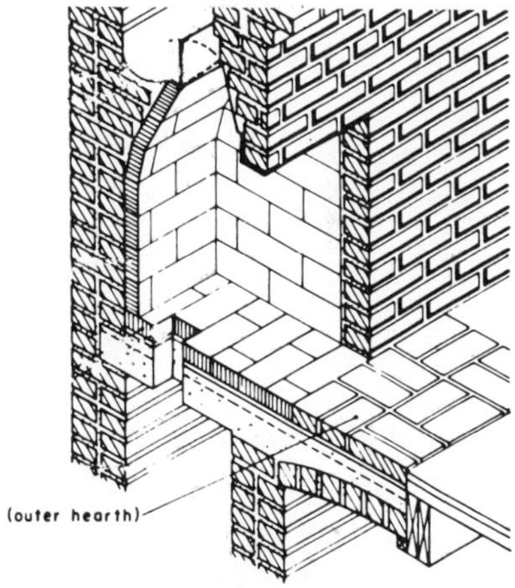

OUTER HEARTH

OVERAGE INCOME Rental income called for in a lease that is above the minimum rental. The tenant is required to pay this extra rent when specified conditions exist such as sales over a certain amount or profits over an agreed amount.

Example of the Calculation of an Overall Interest Rate

Safe rate	.12
Additional risk	.02
Money management	.01
Lack of liquidity	.01
Recapture (25 yrs.)	.04
Overall interest rate	.20

OVERALL INTEREST RATE

OVERALL INTEREST RATE The rate that includes interest on the land, interest on the building, and a recapture of capital.

OVERALL RATE The ratio between annual net operating income and value or sales price in the Ellwood formulation. It is designated by the symbol R or the following formula:

$$\text{appreciation} = \frac{r - R}{SFF}$$

OVERBUILDING The construction of many buildings of a particular type so as to create a surplus; building more structures than can be absorbed by the market.

OVERGRAZING Over stocking or use of a range in such a way that all the better forage is consumed. Eventually, a new type of forage will grow that is different in quality and quantity.

OVERHANG The part of a roof that extends beyond the exterior wall. *See* Cornice.

OVERHEAD The expenses of running a business or property.

OVERHEAD EASEMENT The right to use the area above the land for power lines, aviation, etc.

OVERHEAD IRRIGATION Sprinklers attached to poles or other supports that permit water to be delivered from above.

OVERIMPROVEMENT An improvement that is not the highest and best use for a property; an improvement that is excessive in cost or size in relation to the land value.

OVERPASS The bridging of one road or highway over a railway or other road or highway to avoid traffic congestion.

OVERRIDE A provision in a listing agreement which provides that the listing broker will be paid a commission if the property is sold to somebody who was shown the property during the term of the listing, even if the sale is made after the listing expires. Often, there is a time limit during which the provision is in effect.

OVERRIDING ROYALTY A royalty that is paid by the lessee to someone other than the lessor in return for some contribution of capital or services made to the exploration process.

OVERSTORY The part of a forest that has the tallest trees.

OVERT Open, public, manifest.

OWELTY OF PARTITION Money paid by one co-tenant to another when a property is split into pieces of unequal value. Often, the payment is ordered by the court as part of a partition proceeding.

OWNER One who has the right of ownership. *See also* Ownership.

OWNER OCCUPIED Property that is physically occupied by the owner.

OWNER OF RECORD The ownership of a property as shown in the land records. This owner may not be the true owner of the property.

OWNERSHIP A broad term that describes the ownership of property. There are many different forms of ownership. Some of the more common are joint tenancy, tenancy in common, tenancy by the entirety, tenancy in severalty, corporate ownership, and partnership ownership.

OWNER'S POLICY A type of title insurance policy that protects the owner of a property from a defective title. It is not as common as a mortgagee policy and is often written in conjunction with a mortgage policy at a small additional charge at the same time the mortgagee title insurance policy is issued.

P

PACKAGED CHIMNEY A complete, factory-built chimney usually made of metal and insulation. It is used primarily with prefabricated fireplace units.

PACKAGE MORTGAGE A mortgage, most often used for new homes, that finances both real and personal property, such as household appliances. One payment pays for the mortgage interest and principal, appliances and equipment, and taxes and insurance.

PACKAGE TRUST DEED *See* Package Mortgage.

PALLADIAN STYLE WINDOWS A window style found in many American Georgian Colonial style buildings. It is based on the windows designed by Andrea Palladio in Renaissance Italy.

PALLADIAN STYLE WINDOWS

PANE The glass portion of a door or window.

PANEL **1.** A section of a wall, fence, ceiling, etc. **2.** A thin sheet of lumber, plywood, gypsum, or other building material. **3.** A portion of a flat surface recessed below the surrounding area and often set off by molding or other decorative devices.

PANEL BOARD A portion of an electrical system onto which the electric meter, main switch, and protection devices are mounted.

PANEL HEATING A heating system that places the electric coils, steam pipes, and other heating devices into walls or ceilings to serve as heating panels and transmit heat by radiation.

PANELIZED FLOOR SYSTEM A type of floor system that is premanufactured in a mill or on the job site and then set in place over the joists as an integrated unit.

PANELIZED ROOF SYSTEM A type of roof system that consists of mill-manufactured or on-site prefabricated in-

PARAPET

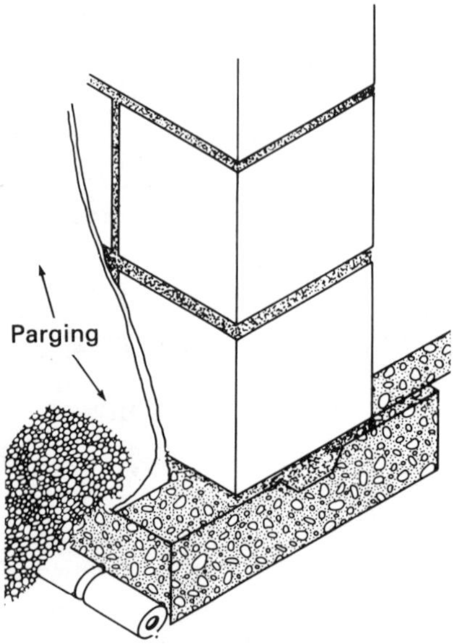

PARGING

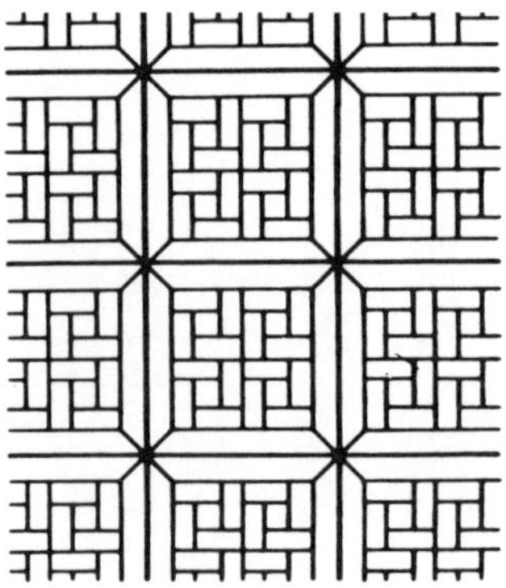

PARQUET FLOOR

tegrated units which are installed as part of the roof system.

PANEL WALL *See* Curtain Wall.

PANIC SELLING An illegal practice of telling residents of a non-integrated neighborhood that the neighborhood is about to become integrated and convincing them to sell their property "before it is too late." Historically, some operators would then buy the property and sell it to minorities at a profit.

PANTRY A small room near the kitchen where food, silver, china, linens, etc., are stored.

PAPER A broad term for mortgages, deeds of trust, and other security instruments. The term is used to refer to that portion of a sale price that is received by a seller in a form other than cash.

PAR A financial term for the face value of a negotiable instrument or mortgage as opposed to being sold at a discount or premium.

PARAPET The part of the wall of a house that rises above the roof line.

PARCEL A piece, portion, or any part of land.

PARCEL IDENTIFIER A number or code that serves as an abbreviation of a property's legal description.

PARGING A coating of cement applied to the surface of a masonry wall to waterproof it.

PARISH In Louisiana, a political division equivalent to a county.

PARKING AREA The portion of a property used to park cars.

PARKING GARAGE A building designed to hold parked cars.

PARKING LOT *See* Parking Area.

PARKING SPACE A space in which to park a car. It should be at least 10 feet wide and 22 feet long.

PARKWAY Traditionally, a highway for non-commercial vehicles. It often runs through a park or park-like area. In more modern usage, it is a freeway or expressway.

PARQUET FLOOR Hardwood flooring consisting of small pieces laid in a decorative pattern.

PARTIAL INTEREST Ownership in property that is less than fee simple; a fractional interest that is less than the whole.

PARTIALLY AMORTIZED MORTGAGE The combination of a term mortgage and an amortized mortgage. When the payments are made as scheduled over the whole term of the mortgage, there still remains an unpaid balance at the end of the term.

PARTIALLY DISCLOSED PRINCIPAL A situation where an agent reveals to a third party that the agent is acting for someone else but will not reveal who that person or organization is.

PARTIAL PAYMENT A level payment of a mortgage that provides a predetermined interest rate and rate of recapture. It is often called a mortgage constant when expressed on an annual basis.

PARTIAL RECONVEYANCE *See* Partial Release.

PARTIAL RELEASE The release by a mortgage of a portion of a property that is being used as mortgage security. It is usually done upon receipt of an amortization payment. It is common on land mortgages where individual lots are released as they are sold off.

PARTIAL TAKING The taking of a portion of a property by the government's power of eminent domain. The compensation received by the owner is the difference between the value of the whole property prior to the taking and the value of the remaining property after the taking.

PARTICIPATION *See* Equity Participation and Income Participation.

PARTICIPATION MORTGAGE **1.** A type of mortgage where the lender shares in the equity venture. **2.** A mortgage that is held by many lenders, who share the risk.

PARTITION **1.** The division of a property owned by several owners into individually owned interests. **2.** A wall used to divide a room or other area.

PARTITION ACTION A court action in which co-owners seek to dissolve their joint ownership into individual ownerships.

PARTNERSHIP An association of two or more persons who carry on a business for profit as co-owners.

PARTY WALL A common wall in a building that separates two units in separate ownership.

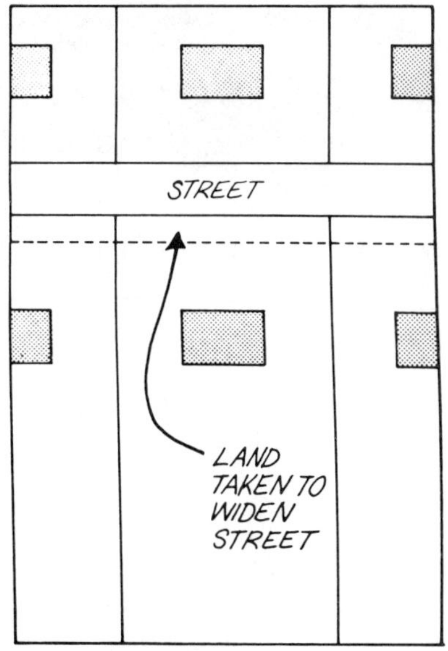

PARTIAL TAKING

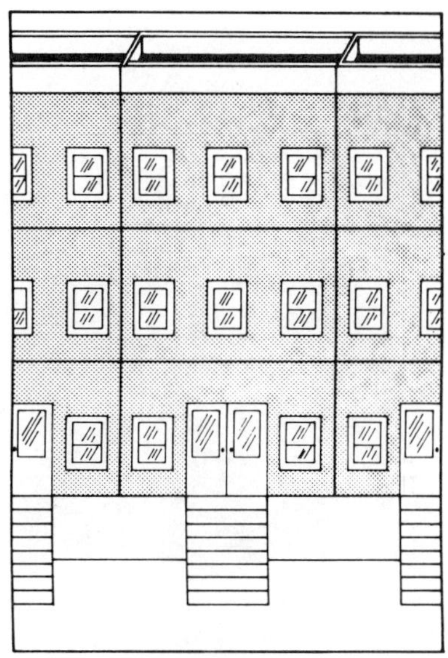

PARTY WALL

PASS-THROUGH SECURITIES PROGRAM

PENNSYLVANIA DUTCH COLONIAL STYLE

PENT ROOF

PASS-THROUGH SECURITIES PROGRAM A GNMA-mortgage-based security program wherein the principal and interest on the mortgages purchased by the investors are passed through to them as they are collected.

PATIO An open, paved area used for outdoor living. It might be all or partially surrounded by parts of the house.

PAYBACK PERIOD The period of time it takes investors to recover their initial cash investment from a real estate project, without interest.

PAYEE The legal word for the party to whom an instrument, such as a mortgage note, is made payable.

PAYOFF The repayment in full of a loan, mortgage, lien, or other outstanding debt.

PEDESTRIAN OVERPASS A bridge over a highway, railway, etc., for pedestrian traffic.

PEDESTRIAN TRAFFIC COUNT *See* Traffic Count.

PEDESTRIAN UNDERPASS A tunnel used for pedestrian traffic under a highway.

PENALTY **1.** An extra payment charged by the government to those who do not pay their taxes on time. **2.** A provision in a contract for extra payment (or reduced payment) if some action called for in the contract is not completed on time.

PENNSYLVANIA DUTCH COLONIAL STYLE A colonial American house style that was developed in the 1600s west of Philadelphia and in Lancaster, Pennsylvania. Its distinguishing characteristics are its gray ledge stone construction, multi-stories, a steep gable roof, and an unsupported hood over the front door.

CTS SYSTEM: Colonial American
Pennsylvania Dutch Colonial or
Pennsylvania German Farmhouse
(Penn Dut-110).

PENNSYLVANIA GERMAN FARMHOUSE *See* Pennsylvania Dutch Colonial.

PENTHOUSE **1.** A condominium or apartment on the roof of a building, used as a residence. **2.** A small building on a roof that houses elevator machinery, ventilating equipment, etc.

PENT ROOF A short, hood-like roof between the windows of the first and second floor.

PER ANNUM Yearly, annually.

PERCENTAGE LEASE A lease which contains a provision that the rental (or a portion of the rental) is based on a percentage of the gross sales, income, profit, etc., of the tenant.

PERCENTAGE RENT *See* Percentage Lease.

PERCOLATION RATE The speed at which water is absorbed by the soil.

PERCOLATION TEST A test made to determine the capacity of the soil to absorb water. It is often required to establish the location of the leaching fields of a septic system.

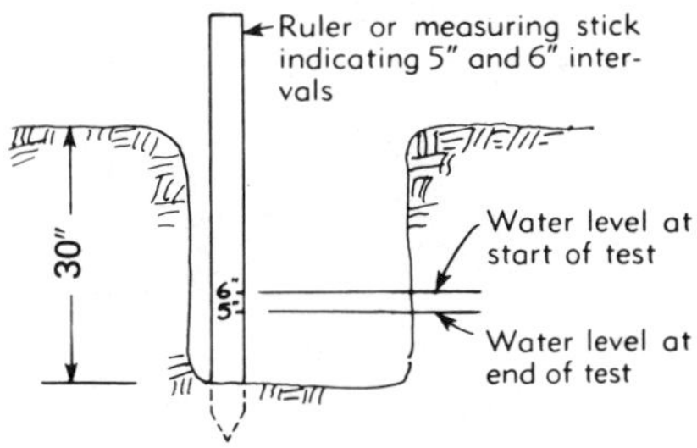

PERCOLATION TEST

PER DIEM Daily.

PERFORMANCE BOND A bond used to insure the completion of an effort in accordance with an agreement. It is commonly used to guarantee the construction of roads by subdividers and the completion of buildings by contractors.

PERFORMANCE STANDARDS Tests applied to a piece of property to determine if the proposed or existing use is in accord with the zoning regulations.

PERIL An insurance term for the exposure of property to a hazard that may damage the property, such as fire, flood, wind, or earthquake.

PERIMETER The total boundary of a site or the distance around a building.

PERIMETER HEATING *See* Baseboard Heating.

PERIMETER LOOP HEATING SYSTEM A type of heating system in which warm air is fed from the furnace through feeder ducts into a duct that runs around the exterior wall of a house.

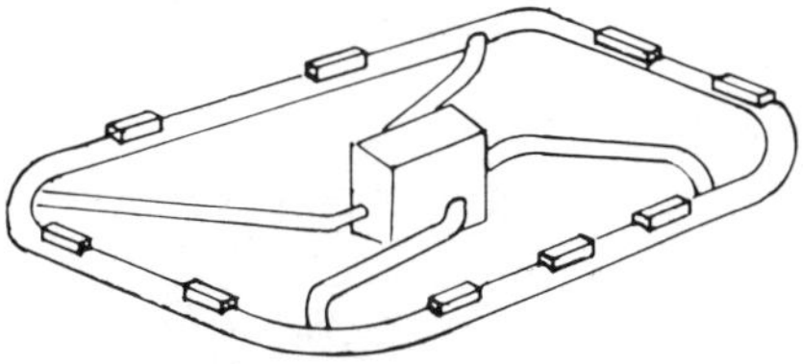

PERIMETER LOOP HEATING SYSTEM

PERIMETER RADIAL DUCT HEATING SYSTEM A heating system in which ducts extend directly from the furnace under the floor joists or concrete floor slab to registers along the outside walls.

PERM The unit of measurement of the water vapor permeability of a material. Value of one perm is equal to one grain of water vapor per square foot per hour per inch of mercury vapor pressure difference.

PERMANENT MORTGAGE A long-term mortgage on completed construction.

PERMEABILITY The ability of soil to absorb water.

PERPETUITY Going on or lasting forever.

PERSONAL PROPERTY One of the two broad classifications of property, the other being real property, from which it is distinguished by its movability versus being permanently affixed. The precise difference varies from state to state. In making the distinction, the manner of annexation, intent of the parties who annexed it, and the use must all be considered.

PERSONALTY Property that is movable, not real property. *See also* Personal Property.

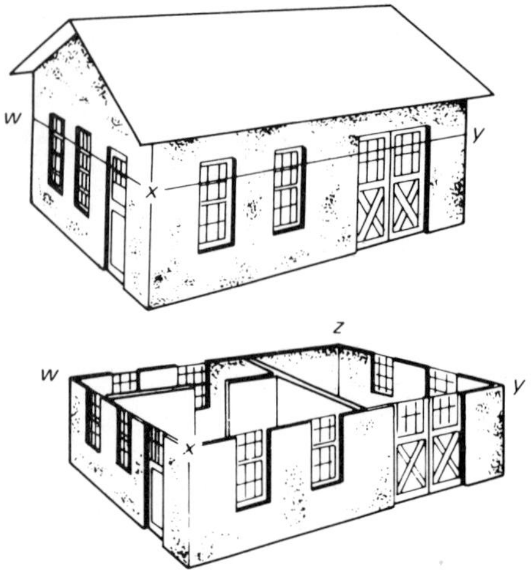

PERSPECTIVE DRAWING

PERSPECTIVE DRAWING A drawing in which the lines are drawn to appear as the eye sees them in real life.

PERVIOUS SOILS Loose, porous, coarse-grained soils that allow the infiltration of water.

PHYSICAL ASSETS Tangible assets, such as land, machinery, furniture, or buildings.

PHYSICAL CURABLE DETERIORATION Items of physical deterioration in a property that should be cured by a prudent owner because the value added to the property by making the repairs is greater than the cost of the repairs.

PHYSICAL DESCRIPTION A description of the tangible portions of a property, such as size, shape, elevation, design, style, materials, construction details, condition, and layout.

PHYSICAL DETERIORATION Loss in value of a property caused by wear, tear, age, and use. It is also an appraisal term for one of the three broad categories of depreciation.

PHYSICAL INCURABLE DETERIORATION Items of physical deterioration in a property that a prudent owner would not cure either because it is not physically possible to do so or because the cost of making the repair would exceed the increase in value of the property as a result of the repair.

PHYSICAL LIFE The projected typical life of an improvement that is correctly maintained and cared for.

PHYSICAL POSSESSION The state of occupying a property by an owner, tenant, or anyone else.

PICTURE WINDOW

PICTURE WINDOW A large window often facing an interesting view, the street, or used to let in light. It usually does not open.

PIER A masonry or concrete column supporting foundations of the floor structure in basementless spaces. A pier may be freestanding or bonded at its sides to other masonry or concrete.

PIERHEAD LINE *See* Bulkhead Line.

PIGGYBACK MORTGAGE A mortgage loan made by two or more lenders on the same property. One lender is usually an institution, and the other lender is a private lender. Together, they are permitted to loan a greater percentage of value than the institution is permitted to make alone. The position of the private lender is junior to the institutional lender. Both positions are usually insured by private mortgage insurance.

PIG PARLOR A farm building designed for and used to raise and breed hogs and swine.

PILASTER A rectangular column attached to the exterior side of a wall, often of the same color and material.

PILE A timber; a concrete-filled, steel tube; or some other vertical support member driven into the ground to serve as a foundation.

PILINGS A foundation system made of steel, timber, or concrete members that extend into the ground to help support a structure that the soil cannot bear alone.

PIPELINE A series of concrete pipes used for the transportation of gas or liquids.

PIPELINE EASEMENT The right to build a pipeline on, over, or under land owned by others.

PIPES Hollow tubes used to carry liquids, gases, or wires.

PITCH **1.** The slope of a roof, road, or other surface. **2.** A black substance made of resins and used for waterproofing.

PITCH POCKET A natural defect in wood caused by a separation of the layers, which become filled with resins.

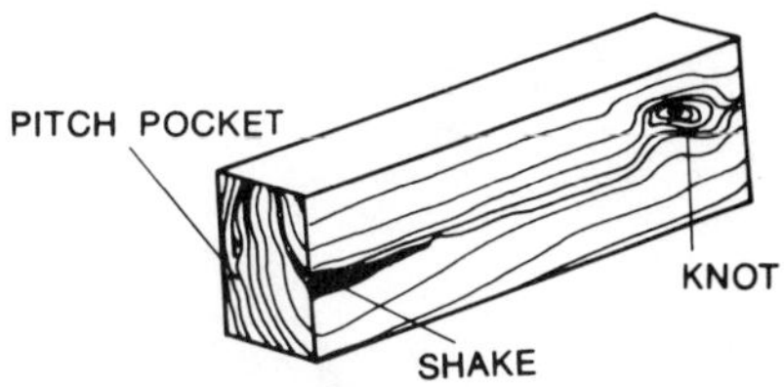

PITCH POCKET

PIVOT SPRINKLER A type of automatic irrigation system consisting of a mechanically moved pipe connected to a water source around which it rotates. A typical system consists of 1,320 feet of pipe, which irrigates an area of 128 acres.

PLANK A heavy piece of unfinished lumber that is typically two inches to four inches thick and at least eight inches wide.

PLANK AND BEAM CONSTRUCTION

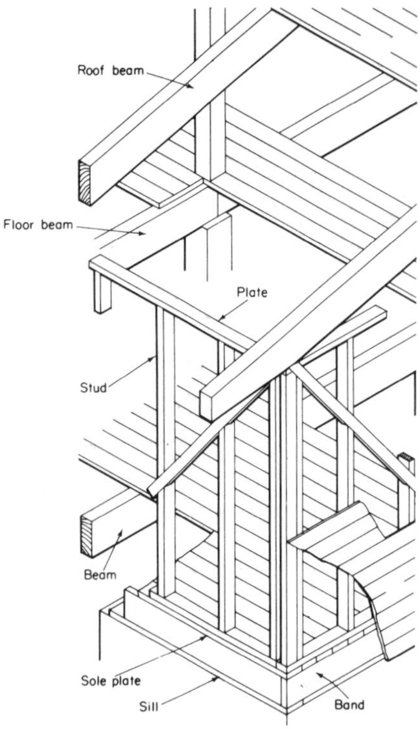

PLANK AND BEAM CONSTRUCTION

PLASTIC HOUSE

PLANK AND BEAM CONSTRUCTION One of the three common methods of framing in which beams are placed up to eight feet apart and covered with planks.

PLANK FLOORING A type of flooring that is made from planks of lumber.

PLANNED UNIT DEVELOPMENT (PUD) A type of land development that is specially provided for in a community's zoning regulations. Typically, it allows the developer more flexible use of the land. Part of the land is divided into lots, which are individually owned. The balance is set aside for use by all the owners of lots within the subdivision and is owned either by the community or by an association formed of the lot owners in the subdivision.

PLANNING CENTER An area in the kitchen designated for desk, cookbooks, menus, stationery, telephone, etc.

PLANS **1.** Two-dimensional drawings that are a representation of a structure. **2.** A complete set of plans for the construction of a project. They often consist of drawings of each floor and the basement, electric plans, plumbing plans, wall sections, elevations of all sides, plot plan, door and window schedules, and specifications.

PLANT In real estate, a very general term that may include the land, buildings, and machinery. It is usually of an industrial nature.

PLANTING EASEMENT An easement for the growing and maintaining of plants for safety and beautification on property owned by others.

PLASTER A material consisting of lime, gypsum, or portland cement mixed with water and sand that has a paste-like quality until it hardens.

PLASTER BOARD *See* Gypsum Wallboard.

PLASTER WALLS Walls constructed by applying three coats of plaster over lath that has been attached to the studs or furring strips.

PLASTIC HOUSE A post-World-War-II style of experimental house, built of fiberglass or other plastic material, which has clean, modern lines and little or no ornamentation. Often, it has curved walls and ceilings.

CTS SYSTEM: Post World War II American
Plastic House
(Plastic-907)

PLAT (PLAT MAP) A map that indicates the boundary lines of real estate, usually of land that has been subdivided.

PLAT BOOK A record book that holds the plat maps together with the names of the owners of the property in a designated area.

PLATE A horizontal structural member placed across the top of the studs in a frame wall. On the top floor, it also serves as the place where the attic joists and roof rafters rest and are fastened.

PLATE GLASS A high-quality glass sheet used as window glass.

PLATFORM FRAME CONSTRUCTION One of the three common methods of framing (also called Western platform framing). It is characterized by subflooring that extends to the outside edges of the building and which is used to provide a platform upon which exterior walls and interior partitions are erected. It is the most common type of framing system used for houses.

PLAYROOM *See* Recreation Room.

PLENUM A large duct or air chamber in which hot air from the furnace builds up pressure, which forces the air out through the ducts to the registers.

PLOT A parcel of land, consisting of one or more lots or portions thereof, which is described by reference to a recorded plat or by metes or bounds.

PLOT PLAN A drawing that indicates the position of the improvements on a lot. It may also show the contours of the land and the location of underground pipes.

PLOTTAGE The increase in value that takes place when two or more small lots under different ownership are assembled into one common ownership to produce a larger lot that has increased utility over the separately owned smaller lots.

PLUMBING *See* Plumbing System.

PLUMBING FIXTURES Parts of a plumbing system consisting of lavatories, washbasins, tubs, showers, toilets, sinks, urinals, bidets, etc.

PLUMBING SYSTEM One of the mechanical systems that is a part of most buildings. It consists of all the pipes, drains, and fixtures involved in bringing water into a building, using the water, and removing waste water and sewage.

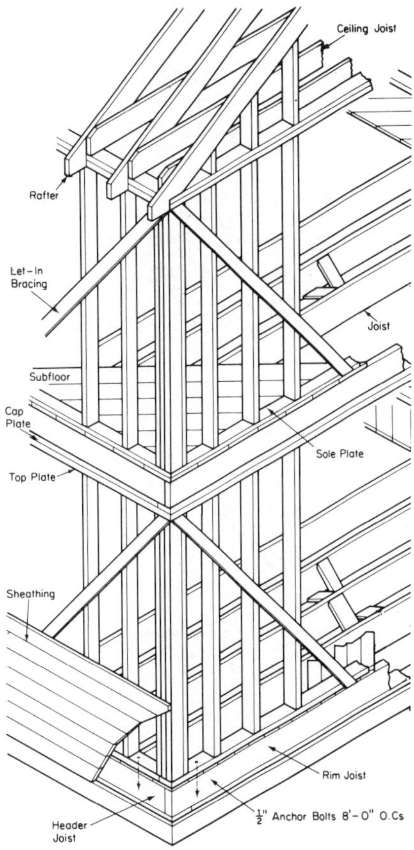

PLATFORM FRAME CONSTRUCTION

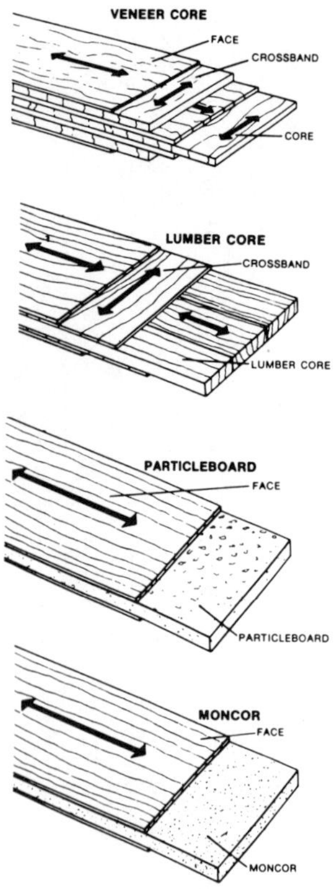

PLYWOOD

STATE OF CONNECTICUT
DEPT. OF CONSUMER PROTECTION
Connecticut Real Estate Commission
Know all men by these presents that pursuant to the General Statutes of Connecticut, the person and/or firm named below is hereby duly licensed to transact business as a:

CONTROL NO. 03556 REAL ESTATE BROKER

HENRY S HARRISON
315 WHITNEY AVE
NEW HAVEN CONN

SERIAL NUMBER | DATE OF ISSUE | 04-30-82 EXPIRATION DATE

Issued by the Connecticut Real Estate Commission

POCKET CARD

PLY A term that denotes the number of layers of plywood, built-up roof surfaces, veneers, etc.

PLYWOOD A building material consisting of thin sheets of wood glued together under pressure.

PLYWOOD SHEATHING The first layer of tight covering made of plywood that is applied to the outside of a building. It serves as a base to which the outside siding is fastened.

PLYWOOD SUBFLOORING A layer of plywood that is laid on top of the floor joists to which the finished flooring is attached.

PMI (PRIVATE MORTGAGE INSURANCE) Mortgage insurance that is written by companies not part of the federal government. It insures that the borrower will make timely mortgage payments on conventional mortgages.

POCKET CARD A card given by the state to a licensed broker or salesperson to show that the person is licensed.

POINT One percent of the face amount of a mortgage that is charged by a lender at the time of the closing as a fee for making the mortgage loan. It may be paid by the buyer, seller, or both.

POINTING **1.** A process of troweling mortar into the joints between bricks. **2.** The material used to fill the joints.

POINT OF BEGINNING (POB) A term used in metes and bounds descriptions to designate where the description starts.

POLE CONSTRUCTION A construction method that uses poles and timbers installed at intervals for support.

POLE GUTTERS A type of gutter consisting of wooden strips nailed perpendicularly to the roof and covered with sheet metal.

POLE LINE EASEMENT An easement for the construction and maintenance of a pole line (such as for electric or telephone wires) over the property owned by others.

POLICE POWER The power of the government to control the use of real estate for the general welfare of the public. It does this through zoning regulations, building codes, environmental regulations, etc. It also includes the government's right to acquire property by condemnation.

POLLUTION The contamination of water, air, soil, and food supplies. Excessive noise is also considered pollution.

PORCH A structure that is attached to a building, often in connection with an entrance. It is roofed, and it may be open, screened, or glassed in.

POROSITY *See* Soil Porosity.

PORT AUTHORITY An agency that has the authority to develop and control land, air, and water traffic in and about a port.

PORTICO An open space covered with a roof that is supported by columns.

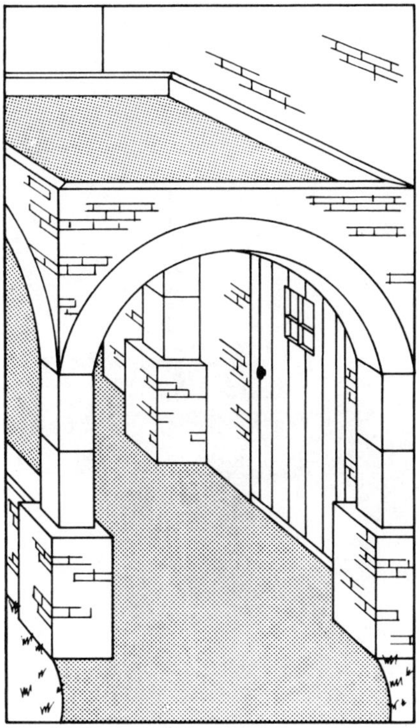

PORTICO

PORTLAND CEMENT A compound of lime, silica, aluminum, and iron that is obtained from limestone, oyster shells, clay, marl, iron ore, silica sand, and blast furnace slag. The ingredients are mixed together in the proper portions and heated to approximately 2,700 degrees in a rotary kiln. The resulting clinkers are ground into powder. It is the primary ingredient of concrete.

PORTLAND CEMENT MORTAR Mortar made of portland cement, sand, and water. It hardens at a quick, constant rate and develops high compressive strength and good freeze-thaw resistance but has poor workability and low water retention.

POSSESSION Having physical control of land or personal property. It may be by the owner, tenant, or someone else. It may be legal or illegal.

POST **1.** A stiff, vertical support that may be of stone, metal, or wood. **2.** To give notice by attaching notices in a public place, such as a mall. **3.** To make entries into bookkeeping records.

POSTS AND TIMBERS Large pieces of lumber with cross sections of five inches by five inches of grades suitable primarily for use as columns and posts.

POSTSTRESSED CONCRETE Concrete that has been given extra strength by imbedding cables in metal sheaths in wet concrete. When the concrete hardens, the cables are stretched, and the casing filled with grout. When the grout sets, the cables are released, and the stress is transmitted to the concrete.

POTENTIAL GROSS INCOME The amount of rent a property will produce when 100 percent rented for a whole year.

POTENTIAL VALUE A value projected in the future that is based on the assumption that projected future probabilities take place as projected.

POWER FEED WIRING The main power line that supplies electricity to a building.

POWER OF ATTORNEY Written instrument that gives one person the authority to act for another either in a general or limited way.

POWER OF SALE A clause used in mortgage deeds, wills, deeds of trust, etc., giving someone or some organization the authority to sell specified property under certain conditions, such as default on loan payments that are secured by a mortgage on the property.

PRAIRIE HOUSE

POWER PLANT A plant that generates power from either gas, water, coal, or oil. The power can be either for an industry's own consumption or for sale to the public.

PRACTICAL CAPACITY The maximum number of vehicles (cars or trucks) that can safely travel over a given roadway during one hour under normal driving conditions.

PRAIRIE HOUSE An early-twentieth-century American house style designed by Frank Lloyd Wright with a long, low, roof line and continuous rows of windows. The house is made up of individual areas of different sizes, lighting, and functions designed to satisfy the physical and psychological needs of the inhabitants.

CTS SYSTEM: Early Twentieth Century American
Prairie House
(Prairie-801)

PRECAST CONCRETE A plain or reinforced concrete element cast in other than its final position in the structure.

PRE-ENGINEERED BUILDING A building made of prefabricated parts that are assembled at the construction site.

PREFABRICATED HOUSE A house made of prefabricated components that are sometimes partly assembled before delivery to a site. It is also called a modular or "pre-fab" house.

PREFABRICATION The construction of building components in a factory for later assembly (on site).

PRE-HUNG DOOR A door that is purchased already attached to its frame, eliminating the difficult step of hanging the door at the site.

PRELIMINARY TITLE REPORT A report of a title search made prior to the sale of a property which shows the condition of the title.

PREMISES A broad term for a distinct and definite locality. It may be just a room or building, or it may include a group of buildings together with their site and site improvements.

PREMIUM **1.** Money paid by an insured to an insurance agent or insurance company for an insurance policy. **2.** A lump sum paid as part of the rent by a tenant to obtain a lease. **3.** An extra payment made in excess of the value of a property.

PREPAID INTEREST Interest that is paid before it is actually due.

PREPAID ITEMS Expenses relating to property, such as taxes, insurance, and rent, which are paid in advance. If the property is sold, these items are often prorated between the buyer and the seller.

PREPAYMENT The act of making a mortgage or note principal payment before it is due.

PREPAYMENT PENALTY A penalty imposed on a borrower for repaying a loan, note, or mortgage before it is due.

PREPAYMENT PRIVILEGE The right of a borrower to pay off a loan, note, or mortgage before it reaches maturity without paying a penalty.

PRESCRIPTION The act of acquiring an easement to use a property by long, continuous use.

PRESCRIPTIVE EASEMENT The right to use another's property acquired by long, continuous use. The use must have been continuous, open, exclusive, and for a period of time set by state statute.

PRESENT OPERATOR A farm term for an individual who is actually cropping the land. It may be a tenant or the property owner.

PRESENT VALUE The current value of a series of payments to be received in the future from an investment, including the proceeds from its sale at a future date.

PRESENT WORTH OF ONE The present value of a lump sum payment to be received at some specified time in the future based on an appropriate discount rate.

PRESERVATIVE A chemical product used to prevent insect destruction in wood and rust on metal.

PRESERVATIVE

Example of the Calculation of the Present Value of an Investment from a Series of Future Payments and the Proceeds of the Future Sale of the Investment

Yr.	Payment	Discount	Present Value
1	$ 10,000	.13	$ 8,850
2	10,300	.13	8,066
3	10,300	.13	7,138
4	11,000	.13	6,747
5	11,000	.13	5,970
6	12,000	.13	5,764
7	12,000	.13	5,101
8	13,300	.13	5,003
9	8,000	.13	2,663
10	6,000	.13	1,768
	Sale of investment		
10	$120,000	.13	35,351
Total present value of investment			$92,421

PRESENT VALUE

Examples of the Present Value of a Future Payment

Amount of Future Payment	When Received	Interest Rate	Present Value
$100,000	1 year	10%	$90,909
100,000	5 years	10%	62,092
100,000	10 years	10%	38,554
100,000	1 year	15%	86,957
100,000	5 years	15%	49,718
100,000	10 years	15%	24,718
100,000	1 year	20%	83,333
100,000	5 years	20%	40,188
100,000	10 years	20%	16,151
100,000	25 years	20%	1,048

PRESENT WORTH OF ONE

PRESERVATIVE TREATMENT Preservative treatment is, unless otherwise noted, impregnation under pressure with a wood preservative. Wood preservative is any suitable substance that is toxic to fungi, insects, borers, and living, wood-destroying organisms.

PRESTRESSED CONCRETE Concrete that is given extra strength by imbedding wire that is stretched up under tension in the unset concrete without the use of casings. When the concrete hardens, the cables are cut, and they release their tension and compact the concrete into a stronger product.

PRICE In real estate, the sum of money for which a property is sold or listed (asking price).

PRICE SUPPORTS Government programs to help keep market prices from sinking to certain levels. The supports may involve purchasing above actual value or outright subsidies.

PRICE TAKE-OFF METHOD *See* Quantity Survey Method.

PRIME COST Those costs of a real estate project that consist of labor and materials.

PRIME LENDING RATE The lowest interest rate on short-term loans charged by a commercial bank to its most creditworthy customers.

PRIMER A first coat of sealant or paint that is applied to a surface to seal and fill wood, plaster, or masonry.

PRIME RATE *See* Prime Lending Rate.

PRIME TENANT The major tenant of a large building, shopping center, etc. Often, a prime tenant must be obtained before permanent financing can be obtained.

PRINCIPAL **1.** The capital portion of a debt or investment as distinguished from interest, income, or profit. **2.** In an agency relationship, the one who employs another (the agent) to act in his behalf. **3.** The head of a real estate company. **4.** A party to a transaction acting for himself.

PRINCIPAL RISK The risk consideration in an investment that the invested principal will not be totally recovered or will be worth less at the end of the investment period.

PRIORITY The order of liens on a property that is established by the time they are filed and by statutes which give some liens preference.

PRIVATE COVENANTS Agreements made between property owners to restrict the use of their properties, resulting in mutual advantage. The restrictions are binding on future owners of the property.

PRIVATE LAND GRANT A grant of public land to an individual.

PRIVATE PROPERTY Property that is owned by a person, partnership, corporation, or other organization but not by the government.

PROBABILITY A statistical term for the likelihood that an event will take place represented by a number between 0 and 1.

PROBATE Originally *probate* described anything related to proving a will was valid. In modern usage, it has come to mean all actions over which probate courts have jurisdiction.

PROBATE COURT The court that has jurisdiction over those matters concerning the estate of a minor, a deceased person, or an incompetent person.

PROBATE SALE Property that is sold from an estate under the supervision of the probate court.

PROCURING CAUSE Being the direct cause of a real estate transaction. In order to be entitled to a commission, a broker or salesperson must often prove he was the direct cause of the transaction being consummated.

PRODUCTION *See* Factors of Production.

PROFESSIONAL APPRAISER A person who is properly qualified to make a real estate appraisal. The appraiser should be able to assemble and evaluate pertinent data and should have the necessary knowledge, experience, integrity, judgment, and willingness to work as well as a thorough familiarity with market stimuli and techniques and methods of presentation.

PROFILE, SOIL A cross section that shows different layers of the soil.

PROFIT **1.** A broad term for income produced by an investment or business enterprise. **2.** The difference between the cost of an item and what it is sold for. **3.** Excess of revenues over expenses for a transaction.

PROFIT AND LOSS STATEMENT A statement made from the books and records of a business or other profit-

Example of a Progressive Tax

Income Up To	*Tax*	*Tax Rate on Excess*
$ 5,000	$ 400	10%
10,000	1,500	15%
15,000	2,150	20%
20,000	3,300	23%
25,000	4,800	30%
30,000	6,600	36%
35,000	8,800	44%
40,000	11,100	46%
45,000	13,500	48%
50,000	16,000	50%

Examples:

Income	*Total Tax*
$21,500 (3,300 + 1,500 × .23)	$ 3,645
$37,800 (8,800 + 2,800 × .44)	$10,032
$80,000 (16,000 + 30,000 × .50)	$31,000

PROGRESSIVE TAX

PROMISEE
PROMISSOR
PROMISSORY NOTE

making enterprise that shows its income, expenses, and profits or losses.

PROGRESSIVE TAX A tax that is a percent of income, and the percentage rate increases as the income increases.

PROJECTION The use of extrapolation or extension of the past into the future by means of a mechanical formula based on the assumption that past conditions will continue on into the future.

PROJECTION PERIOD A future period of time during which the income, expenses, and net operating income of a property or business are estimated.

PROMISEE A lender who has been promised the payments required by a note.

PROMISOR A person, partnership, corporation, or other organization who makes a promise to make the payments required by a note.

PROMISSORY NOTE A document that is a promise by one party to pay a specified amount to a second party.

PROPER INTEREST RATE The rate of interest that will attract capital into the investment market.

PROPERTY **1.** A broad term for an area of land under one legal ownership together with all the buildings and other improvements. **2.** The rights or interests in land or chattels. **3.** Anything that is owned by a person, partnership, corporation, or other type of organization.

PROPERTY BRIEF Information pertinent to a property that is submitted to a prospective buyer.

PROPERTY DESCRIPTION Identification of real estate.

PROPERTY INSURANCE Insurance that covers loss to physical property from damage either from individual actions or natural forces.

PROPERTY LINE The recorded boundary of a property.

PROPERTY MANAGEMENT The day-to-day operation of real property. The duties of management range from leasing space and collecting rents to responsibility for repairs, upkeep, and renovation.

PROPERTY MANAGEMENT AGREEMENT The contract between a property owner and property manager that determines responsibilities and fees.

PROPERTY MANAGER A person or organization who performs specified functions on behalf of a property's owner. These functions relate to the management of the property and often include renting, collecting rents, making repairs, and any other functions an owner would be expected to perform.

PROPERTY OWNERS' ASSOCIATION *See* Homeowners' Association.

PROPERTY RESIDUAL TECHNIQUE An appraisal technique that is part of the income approach to value. The technique combines all of the income produced by the property rather than dividing it between income produced by the site and income produced by the improvements. The whole income stream is capitalized into a single property value.

PROPERTY TAX A tax levied by the government on real and personal property. The amount of the tax is determined by multiplying the assessed value of the property by the tax rate.

PROPRIETARY LEASE A specific type of lease used in properties that are held in a cooperative form of ownership. It gives a shareholder in the cooperative corporation exclusive use of a portion of the property. For example, in a cooperative apartment, the lease gives each shareholder exclusive use of a specified apartment.

PROPRIETORSHIP A form of business ownership. It is usually unincorporated and is owned by one person.

PRORATE The process of dividing prepaid or unpaid expenses, such as taxes, insurance, and rent, proportionately between buyers and sellers at the time of closing or some other agreed-upon time.

PRORATION *See* Prorate.

PROSCENIUM The portion of the stage in front of the curtain.

PROSPECT A potential tenant, seller, or buyer.

PROSPECTUS A document that describes the details and the characteristics of a specific property, company, or partnership. It may be a simple document used for private offerings or a complex, detailed document used when shares of the offering are being sold to the public and are subject to strict government disclosure regulations.

Example of the Property Residual Technique

Estimated improvement value:		$220,000
Estimated net operating income:		43,000
Capitalization rate		
Risk rate	12%	
Recapture rate (25 yr. life)	4%	
Total rate	16%	
Less recapture on improvement value ($220,000 @ 4% recapture rate)		−8,800
Annual net income imputable to the property (land and improvements)		$ 34,200
Property value ($34,200 capitalized at 12%) ($34,200 ÷ 12)		$285,000

PROPERTY RESIDUAL TECHNIQUE

PROXIMITY DAMAGE A portion of the damages to a property that result when some other part of the property is taken by condemnation. Specifically, it is the damages to the remaining untaken property arising from being near whatever is being constructed on the portion that is being taken, such as a noisy highway, high-voltage power line, gas or oil transmission line, etc.

PRUNING The selective cutting of branches from a tree, vine, or shrub.

PUBLIC DOMAIN *See* Public Domain Land.

PUBLIC DOMAIN LAND Land that is owned by the federal government.

PUBLIC HOUSING Housing that is owned by the government which is usually used to accommodate low-income or elderly families.

PUBLIC LANDS Land owned by the federal government that is not intended for use by the government and is subject to sale or lease.

PUBLIC LAND SYSTEM *See* Government Survey.

PUBLIC RECORDS Records which the government is required to keep in order for someone or some organization to give notice that is required by law. Deeds, mortgages, and other real-estate-related documents are required to be filed in order to satisfy a variety of statutory requirements.

PUBLIC REPORT A written report about the cost and condition of an area given to prospective buyers of houses in a new subdivision. It is required in some states by statute.

PUBLIC SALE The sale of property at an auction that is open to the public, such as a tax or foreclosure sale. These sales usually require public notice (in the form of advertising) and must be accessible to the general public.

PUBLIC SPACE A legal, open space on the premises accessible to a public way or street, such as a yard, court, or open space permanently devoted to public use and abutting the premises.

PUBLIC SYSTEM A public utility system, such as water or sewerage, which is owned, operated, and maintained by a local government authority or by a local utility company adequately controlled by a government authority.

PUBLIC TRUSTEE The public officer to whom title to real property is conveyed in some states in a deed of trust for the benefit of a specified beneficiary.

PUBLIC UTILITY A company that supplies a necessary service, such as electricity, water, gas, or telephones. These companies may be privately owned, but they are subject to the control of a Public Utilities Commission.

PUBLIC UTILITY PROPERTY Property used by public utilities.

PUD *See* Planned Unit Development.

PUEBLO STYLE An early-twentieth-century American house style based on the houses of Indians of New Mexico and Arizona. It became popular in the Southwest in the early 1900s. The buildings are made of adobe brick (or material that looks like adobe brick). They have flat roofs, are massive looking, and are supported by protecting beams called *viga*.

CTS SYSTEM: Early Twentieth Century American
Pueblo or Adobe
(Pueblo or Adobe-803)

PUEBLO STYLE

PUFFER A person hired to make false bids at an auction in order to raise the price of the property being sold.

PUFFING The act of exaggerating the qualities of something that is being offered for sale or rent. It usually is something less than an outright misrepresentation of facts.

PUGET SOUND STYLE *See* Northwestern

PUR AUTRE VIE A legal term for an estate held for the duration of the life of another person often not directly connected with the property, such as a famous person or a member of a royal family.

PURCHASE AGREEMENT An agreement between the buyer(s) and seller(s) of real property that defines the terms of the sale.

PURCHASE AND LEASE-BACK *See* Sale-Leaseback.

PURCHASE MONEY MORTGAGE A mortgage given by the seller(s) of a property to the buyer(s) to reduce the amount of cash needed to complete the sale.

PURCHASE MONEY TRUST DEED *See* Purchase Money Mortgage.

PURCHASE ON CONTRACT *See* Land Contract.

PURCHASER'S POLICY *See* Owner's Policy.

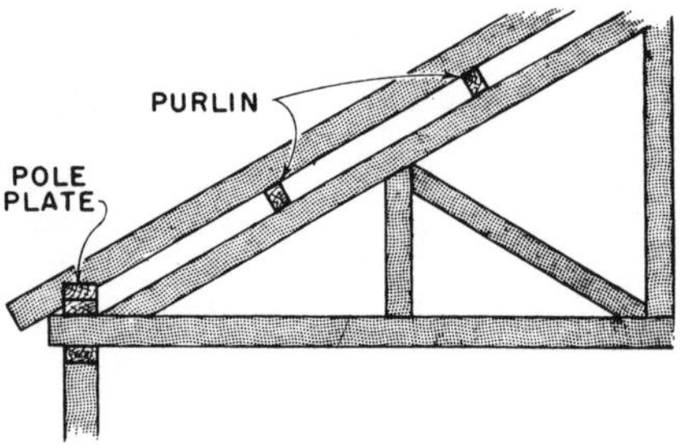

PURLIN

PYRAMID ROOF

PURLIN An intermediate supporting member at right angles to a rafter or truss framing.

PURPOSE OF APPRAISAL An appraisal term for the type of value being estimated in an appraisal, such as market value, insurable value, salvage value, or investment value.

PUTTY A paste used to fill cracks, holes, and joints and to install window panes.

PYLON **1.** The gateway to an Egyptian temple. **2.** In modern usage, any tower, post, or gateway.

PYRAMID ROOF A roof type that resembles a pyramid. It has four, triangular-shaped, sloping sides that meet at a point in the middle.

PYRAMID ZONING A type of zoning ordinance which permits all the uses in the most restricted classification in those classifications that are considered to be lower. For example, *residential* is often the highest classification, below which are *commercial* and then *industrial* zones. Residential and commercial uses would be permitted in the lower industrial zone.

Q

QUAD *See* Quadrant.

QUADRANGULAR SURVEY SYSTEM *See* Legal Description, Township, and Range Survey System.

QUADRANT **1.** A pie-shaped, 90-degree quarter of a circle. **2.** One of the four areas created by intersecting roads.

QUADRATIC MEAN *See* Standard Deviation.

QUADRO A house having four separate units connected by party walls. Each unit has a front entrance. Often, the front entrances face in different directions.

QUANTITY SURVEY *See* Quantity Survey Method.

QUANTITY SURVEY METHOD A method of estimating the cost of a new building or the replacement cost of an existing building by making a detailed estimate of quality and quantity of necessary materials as well as labor costs to install them.

QUARRY TILE An unglazed, machine-made ceramic tile.

QUARTER In public land survey, a quarter of a full section of 640 acres, having 160 acres.

QUARTER ROUND A popular style of molding in the shape of a quarter of a circle.

QUARTER SECTION *See* Quarter.

QUASI-CONTRACT An implied contract; an obligation similar to a contract, which is invoked by the courts to prevent undue enrichment of either party to a transaction.

QUAY A wharf built parallel to navigable water and used for loading and unloading ships.

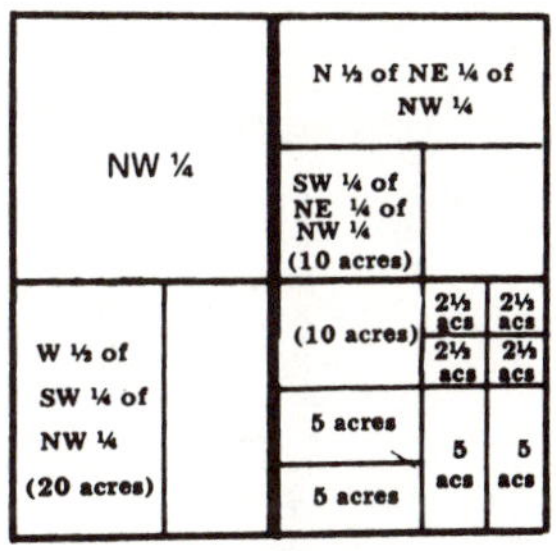

QUARTER

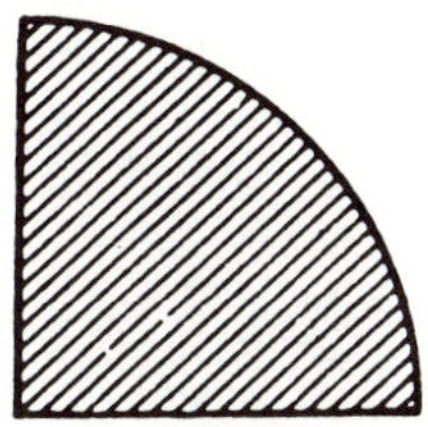

QUARTER ROUND

QUEEN ANNE STYLE

QUEEN ANNE STYLE

QUOIN

QUEEN POST

QUEEN ANNE STYLE The nineteenth-century American Queen Anne style was first designed in England by Richard Norman Shaw. It was started in the United States in the 1870s by architect Henry Hobson Richardson. The name Queen Anne has come to be applied to any Victorian house that cannot be otherwise classified. They are unique looking houses. Most are multistoried and are irregular in shape. They have a wide variety of surface textures, materials, and colors. Many Queen Annes also have big chimneys, half timbering, turrets, and bay windows.

CTS SYSTEM: Nineteenth Century American
Queen Anne
(Q Anne-712)

QUEEN POST One of the two vertical posts in a roof truss.

QUICK ASSETS *See* Liquid Assets.

QUIET ENJOYMENT The right of owners to the use and possession of their property without interference.

QUIET TITLE *See* Quiet Title Action.

QUIET TITLE ACTION A court action that settles the title of a property when there is a cloud on the title.

QUILT INSULATION A type of insulation that comes in blankets that are stitched like a quilt to give them added strength.

QUITCLAIM DEED A deed that conveys all of the ownership of the seller to the buyer without guaranteeing the quality of the title.

QUOIN A square, or nearly square, cut stone with beveled edges set in the corners of masonry and stone houses.

QUOTIENT The result obtained by dividing one number by another.

R

RACEWAY A conduit, usually made of metal or plastic, that carries electric wires. It has outlets at frequent intervals.

RACIAL STEERING The process of influencing a minority's choice of housing. The agent recommends neighborhoods that he feels would be best for the prospective minority buyer. The process is often illegal, no matter how well-intentioned the agent is.

RADIANT HEAT A heating system that consists of pipes or wires embedded in the walls, floors, and ceilings. Heat from these pipes or wires is transmitted into the room by radiation rather than by convection.

RADIATOR An exposed fixture, usually made out of cast iron, that transfers heat from the heating system by means of convection and radiation.

RAFTERS A series of roof framing members that are inclined and to which roof covering is fixed.

RAFT FOUNDATION *See* Floating Foundation.

RAFT OR MAT FOUNDATIONS A foundation system consisting of a number of spread footings that have been joined to form a monolithic unit foundation.

RAIL A horizontal member used as a guard, such as a porch rail. It is also part of a door or window that runs horizontally. Based on its position, it is known as a bottom rail, middle rail, or top rail. It is synonymous with stile.

RAILROAD SIDING AGREEMENT A contract between a railroad and an industry for the erection and maintenance of a side track. It can be located on either the railroad's or the industry's property.

RAISED RANCH *See* Split Entry.

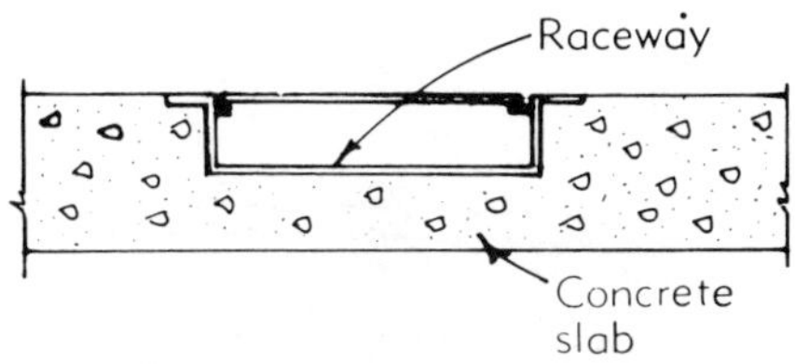

RACEWAY

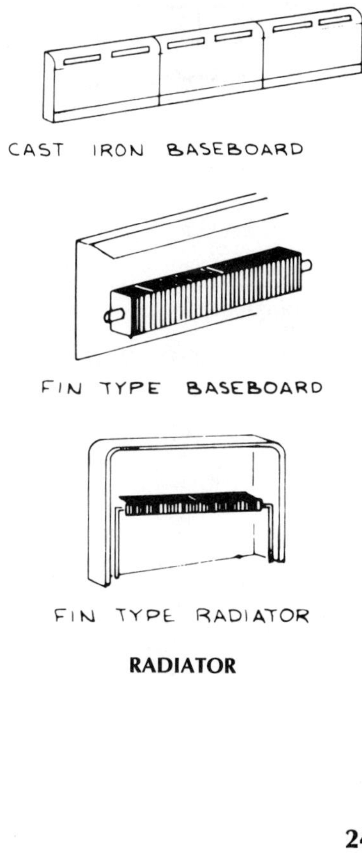

RADIATOR

RAKE

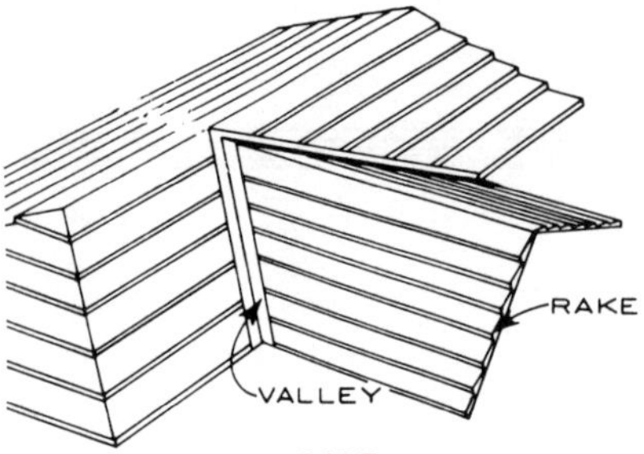

RAKE

RANDOM SHINGLE

$$\text{range capacity} = \frac{\text{density} \times \text{use factor} \times \text{surface acres}}{\text{forage acre requirement}}$$

RANGE CAPACITY FORMULA

RAKE The outer edge of a sloped roof; the angle or slope of a roof rafter, known as the "rake of the roof."

RAMP **1.** An inclined walkway or passageway that has no steps. It is often used to provide access for handicapped people. **2.** An exit or entrance to a limited access highway.

RANCH **1.** A place for raising livestock consisting of range lands, housing for the owners and employees, and ancillary buildings used in the livestock operation. **2.** A broad term used to describe many types of rural properties.

RANCH HOUSE A word which is now broadly used to describe many single-story houses that are wider than they are deep. *See also* California Ranch.

RANDOM SHINGLES Shingles of uniform lengths but different widths.

RANDOM WIDTH PLANK WOOD FLOORING Flooring made of planks of different widths.

RANGE **1.** As used in the government survey system of the United States, a six-mile-wide row of townships running north and south. **2.** Land used for feeding livestock. **3.** The area or region over which something occurs or is distributed. **4.** In a statistical distribution, the difference between the smallest and largest numbers. **5.** A cooking device with burners to heat pots and pans. **6.** A row of stones or other objects.

RANGE CAPACITY FORMULA The grazing capacity of an area expressed as a number. (Formula shown at left.)

RANGE HOOD A hood that collects air and smoke from an oven or range. The air is then either filtered and returned to the room or vented to the outside.

RATE OF INTEREST **1.** The amount of interest (on an annual basis) paid on borrowed money. **2.** The amount of interest paid (on an annual basis) for money deposited in a lending institution.

RATE OF RETURN The annual net income from an investment, enterprise, or other source expressed as a percentage of the invested capital or appraised value. It may include consideration of all of the income received over the forcasted life of the investment, including the proceeds of the ultimate sale of the investment.

RATE SURCHARGE An amount that is added to the discount rate to provide the investor compensation for the return of the invested capital or the risk of loss of all or part of the invested capital.

RATIFICATION The confirmation of an act committed on someone's behalf that might be voidable if not affirmed. For example, a salesperson in a real estate office makes some decisions that are beyond his or her authority. Afterwards, the owner of the office approves the decisions.

RAT WALL (STOP) A small barrier that rises a few inches above ground but extends further below (according to local specifications) and is used to prevent infestation by rats.

RAW LAND Land in an untouched, natural state. It is away from roads and without utilities or any significant improvements.

RAZE To demolish the improvements (such as old buildings) on a property.

READY, WILLING, AND ABLE A term often used or implied in a listing agreement which describes the buyer that must be produced by the broker in order to earn a commission. For the commission to be earned the ready, willing, and able buyer must offer the full listing price without unfilled contingent conditions. The commission is earned even if the offer is rejected.

READY, WILLING, AND ABLE

REAL ESTATE The physical land together with all improvements that are permanently affixed to it, such as buildings, walls, fences, courts, pools, and walks. Improvements that are not permanently affixed are classified as personal property.

REAL ESTATE ANALYST A real estate professional who acts as a consultant to owners, investors, lenders, and others who are interested in investment alternatives, investment desirability, analysis of potential uses, and other problems not directly linked to the valuation process.

REAL ESTATE APPRAISAL *See* Appraisal.

REAL ESTATE BOARD A local trade organization whose members consist of real estate brokers, salespeople, appraisers, representatives from lending institutions, title companies, etc. Usually, it is affiliated with a state association and the NATIONAL ASSOCIATION OF REALTORS.® Often, they operate a multiple listing system.

REAL ESTATE BROKER A person, partnership, corporation, or other type of organization that is employed as an agent to make sales, rentals, and other real-estate-related contracts for compensation. All 50 states require that a real estate broker be licensed.

REAL ESTATE CLOSING *See* Closing.

REAL ESTATE COMMISSION A regulatory body of a state that has the function of regulating specific real estate activities within the state. It often has the function of licensing real estate brokers and salespeople.

REAL ESTATE DEVELOPING A general term for the developing of raw land to a point where it is ready for construction of buildings. The process often consists of building roads, providing utilities, and grading the land.

REAL ESTATE INVESTMENT A device created to permit a group of investors to pool their funds and invest them primarily in real estate. Like mutual funds, the trust provides management and is not subject to the double taxation that would be incurred by an ordinary corporation or trust.

REAL ESTATE INVESTMENT TRUSTS (REIT) A trust or association set up to invest capital in real estate or real estate mortgage loans. It is accorded special federal tax treatment if the organization meets strict federal requirements.

REAL ESTATE LICENSE A license granted by a state to a person or organization permitting them to engage in a wide variety of real estate activities including sales, rentals, management, etc. Usually, the licensee must pass an examination and fulfill specified educational requirements.

REAL ESTATE MARKET The place of commercial activity in which real estate is bought, sold, rented, exchanged, etc. The area of the market varies depending upon the type of real estate and the characteristics of the market. The market for a type of single-family home may be limited to one neighborhood, whereas the market for some types of investment properties is international.

REAL ESTATE OPERATOR A person in the real estate business acting for himself and not as an agent for someone else.

REAL ESTATE SALESPERSON A person associated with a real estate broker who helps the broker with selling, buying, managing, and other real-estate-related activities. He or she may be an employee or an independent contractor.

REAL ESTATE SECURITIES AND SYNDICATION INSTITUTE (RESSI) An institute of the NATIONAL ASSOCIATION OF REALTORS® that serves members who are specialists in the promotion, creation, analysis, and marketing of real estate securities.

REAL ESTATE SETTLEMENT PROCEDURES ACT (RESPA) A federal law designed to protect buyers of real estate. It requires that lenders provide single- to four-family residence buyers with detailed information about closing and financing costs prior to the closing.

REAL ESTATE SYNDICATE A partnership in a real estate investment or venture. It may consist of both general and limited partners.

REAL PROPERTY *See* Real Estate.

REALTIST A member of the National Association of Real Estate Brokers.

REALTOR® A registered trademark for the exclusive use of real estate professionals who are members of a local real estate board and of the NATIONAL ASSOCIATION OF REALTORS.®

REALTOR ASSOCIATE® A registered trademark for the exclusive use of real estate professionals who are not owners or officers of their organizations which are members of a local real estate board and of the NATIONAL ASSOCIATION OF REALTORS®

REALTORS NATIONAL MARKETING INSTITUTE An institute of the NATIONAL ASSOCIATION OF REALTORS® whose main purpose is to better the professional competence of real estate professionals through publications and educational programs.

REALTY *See* Real Estate.

REAPPRAISAL LEASE A lease containing a provision that allows for a periodic readjustment of rents.

REASSESSMENT The systematic re-evaluation, for tax purposes, of all properties in a given area.

RECAPTURE CLAUSE **1.** A clause in a lease providing for retaking or recovering possession. **2.** A provision in a percentage lease that requires the tenant to pay, as

REALTOR®

REALTOR

REALTOR®-ASSOCIATE

REALTOR ASSOCIATE

REALTOR NATIONAL MARKETING INSTITUTE

additional rent, a portion of his earnings or profits over a specified base amount.

RECAPTURE RATE A portion of the income of a property that is allocated to provide the investor a return of the original invested capital. The annual rate is calculated by dividing the annual amount being recaptured by the amount of the original investment.

RECEIVER A person appointed by the court to hold and control property that is pending litigation or a final action by a court.

RECIPROCITY In real estate, an agreement between states that allows attorneys, real estate brokers, and salespeople to practice in a state other than the one in which they are licensed.

RECLAMATION The changing of unusable land into developable sites. It may be done by irrigation, draining wetlands, replanting forests and ranges, etc.

RECONCILIATION A series of steps throughout the appraisal process of selecting the most significant data from a variety of data and forming it into value conclusions.

RECONSTRUCTED OPERATING STATEMENT An operating statement prepared by an appraiser for use in the income approach of an appraisal. It includes all items of income and expense that directly relate to a property, with the exception of interest on borrowed money and depreciation.

Example of a Reconstructed Operating Statement

Income	
Estimated potential annual rent	$485,000
Other income	18,000
Gross potential income	$503,000
Vacancy and collection loss (5%)	25,150
Effective gross income	$477,850
Expenses	
Fixed expenses	
Taxes	$ 73,500
Insurance	6,200
Total fixed expenses	$ 79,700
Variable Expenses	
Management (4%)	$ 19,400
Electricity	4,300
Heat	23,050
Water	3,680
Gas	4,128
Air conditioning	6,050
Maintenance payroll	35,300
Cleaning	22,000
Maintenance and repairs	43,500
Decorating	22,300
Alterations	18,500
Grounds maintenance	6,850
Elevators	4,200
Security	12,000
Supplies	6,500
Rubbish	6,000
Extermination	1,200
Total variable expenses	$238,958
Reserves for Replacements	
Appliances	$12,000
Laundry equipment	2,000
Furniture	1,500
Carpeting	3,250
Roof	6,000
Elevators	8,500
Total reserves	$33,250
Total operating expense	$351,908
Net operating income (NOI) ($477,850–$351,908)	$125,942

RECONSTRUCTED OPERATING STATEMENT

RECONVEYANCE An instrument used to return property that has been held as collateral to its equitable owner.

RECORDED MAP A map or survey of a property that is recorded. It often includes a whole subdivision.

RECORDER *See* Registrar of Deeds.

RECORDING The process of recording a copy of certain legal instruments, such as deeds, mortgages, leases, liens, etc., to make public record of the document to benefit all concerned.

RECORDING ACTS State laws that govern the public recording of deeds, mortgages, liens, etc.

RECORD OWNER *See* Owner of Record.

RECOURSE The right of a lender to seek payment personally from a borrower or endorser of a note secured by a mortgage.

RECREATION ROOM A room used for recreation (game playing, TV watching, etc.) by the family in a house or apartment.

RECTANGULAR SURVEY The U. S. government survey method that uses meridians and base lines to form quadrangles, ranges, and townships.

REDEMPTION The regaining of a property lost in a foreclosure sale or other legal process by the original owner upon payment of the debt plus interest and costs.

REDEMPTION PERIOD A time period after a foreclosure, during which a land contract, deed of trust, or mortgage can be redeemed by the original owner upon payment of the debt, interest, and costs.

REDEVELOPMENT The razing, renovation, reconstruction, and improvement of blighted areas as part of an urban renewal project.

RED LINING A technique (which is now illegal in many states) of drawing lines on a map designating areas that are considered to be high risk for purposes of making mortgages or writing insurance.

REDUCTION SCALES Scales used on plans and maps by architects, engineers, or surveyors to indicate how much difference there is between the actual item and the drawing on the plan.

RE-ENTRY The right of a property owner to enter a property he owns that has been leased or rented and take back possession of it. Often, it requires a court action.

REFERRAL In real estate, a former customer recommending a broker or salesperson to another buyer or seller. Also, any recommendation of one agent to another is for a fee.

REFINANCE **1.** The renewal of an existing loan by the same borrower or lender. **2.** The obtaining of a new mortgage by a property owner, the proceeds of which are used to pay off an existing mortgage.

REFORMATION An action to reform or correct an error in a deed, mortgage, or other instrument. It may be to correct a simple mistake or an error that is a result of fraud.

REGENCY STYLE An English house style that reached its peak of popularity in England in the early 1800s. Many were built in the U.S. in the late 1800s, throughout the 1900s, and well into the twentieth century. It is a two-

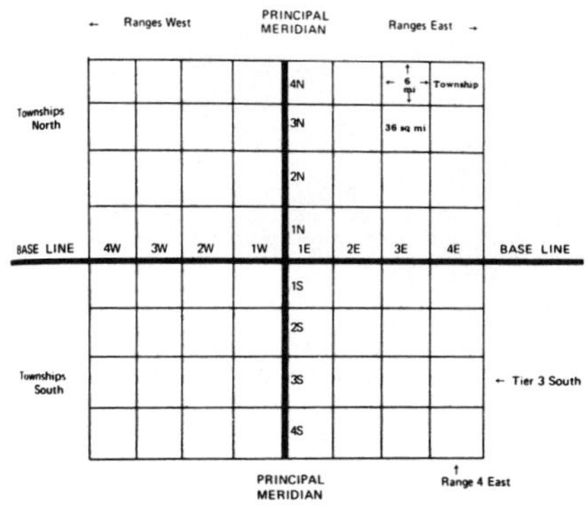

RECTANGULAR SURVEY

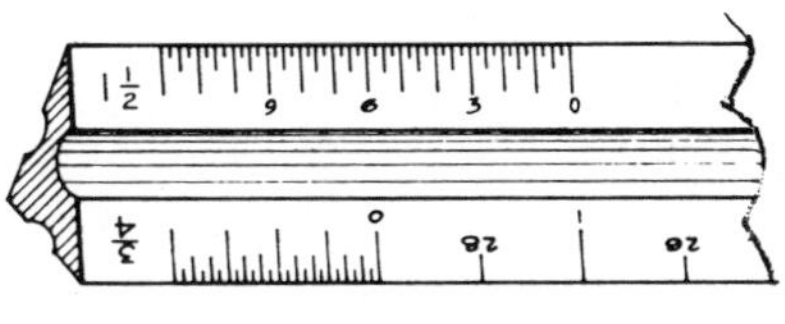

1/4 INCH = 1 FOOT

1″ = ├—— 4′ ——┤

1/8 INCH = 1 FOOT

1″ = ├—— 8′ ——┤

ARCHITECTS SCALE

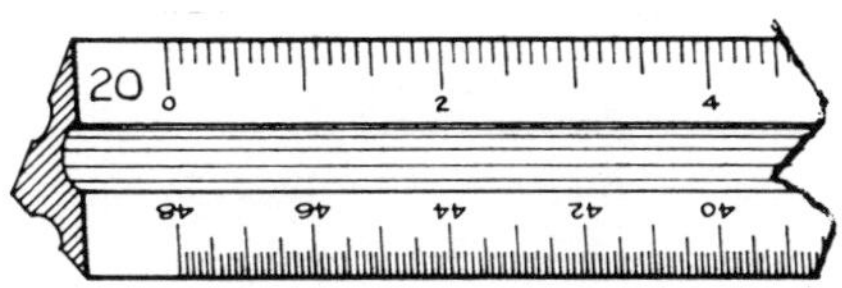

1 INCH = 10 FEET

1″ = ├—— 10′ ——┤

1 INCH = 1 FOOT

1″ = ├—— 1′ ——┤

ENGINEERS SCALE

REDUCTION SCALES

REGENCY STYLE

or three-story house with a hip roof. An octagonal window over the front door is traditional.

CTS SYSTEM: English
Regency
(Regency-205)

REGIONAL ANALYSIS In real estate, an analysis made of economic conditions in a region and how they affect real estate in that region.

REGIONAL SHOPPING CENTER The biggest type of shopping center. It has at least one large department store, many satellite stores, restaurants, lending institutions, and service businesses. It also has a large parking area and is commonly controlled and managed.

REGISTER A fixture installed at the end of an air duct that directs and controls the flow of air into the room.

REGISTERED LAND Land whose title has been registered in a special land court found in states that use the Torrens System of title registration.

REGISTRAR OF DEEDS The person in charge of recording title instruments; often called a *recorder*.

REGISTRY LAWS *See* Recording Acts.

REGRESSION ANALYSIS A statistical technique used (with the aid of a computer) to analyze the effect independent variables (size, number of rooms, location, etc.) have upon dependent variables (sales price). It is now being used to predict the sales price of houses.

REGRESSIVE TAX A tax that is relatively equal and at rates which do not increase in relationship to the income or wealth of the taxpayer. It tends to place a heavier tax burden on the poor than on the rich. A tax that does the opposite is a progressive tax.

REGULATION "Z" Federal Reserve Board regulation connected to the Truth-In-Lending Act. It states that all credit purchasers must be informed, in writing, of all costs associated with the credit portion of the purchase.

REHABILITATION **1.** The removal of blight and the restoration of deteriorating properties and public facilities in an urban renewal area. **2.** Restoring and renovating a property without destroying existing improvements and without changing the form or style of property.

REINFORCED CONCRETE Concrete reinforced and

strengthened by the addition of steel bars, mesh, rods, etc.

REINFORCED CONCRETE CONSTRUCTION Construction that uses reinforced concrete in its load-bearing members.

REINFORCING The adding of additional material to provide more strength. *See also* Reinforced Concrete.

REINSTATEMENT Payment of a deed of trust, note, or mortgage that carries it from default to good standing.

REINVESTMENT RATE The rate of return obtained by an investor on capital repayments of an existing investment.

REJECTION The non-acceptance of an offer on the terms in which it is presented. Acceptance based on any changes constitutes a new offer that must be accepted or rejected by the other party.

RELEASE The giving up of a claim or right by a person or company who possesses it; an instrument stating the right or claim that is abandoned.

RELEASE CLAUSE A clause in a mortgage, lien, or other encumbrance that discharges the instrument upon payment of specified amounts of money or upon other specified conditions being fulfilled.

RELEASE OF LIEN An instrument that discharges a lien when payment of the debt is made together with interest and costs.

RELICTION An increase in land by a gradual and permanent recession of water in a lake, sea, river, etc.

RELIEF MAP A map that shows the topography of an area.

RELOCATION The moving of people, businesses, and personal property by a local, state, or federal agency when the property in which they are located is taken for public use.

RELOCATION PAYMENT Money paid to people and companies to move them and their personal property when the building in which they are located is taken for public use.

RELOCATION PLAN The government plan that is part of an urban renewal program which regulates the relocation of occupants and their personal property displaced by the taking of their building for public use.

REMAINDER A future estate in real property created in any person other than the grantor that commences in

RELICTION

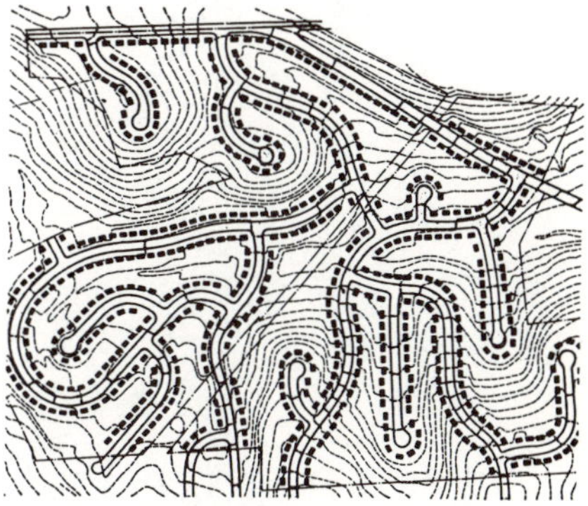

RELIEF MAP

the future after the end of another estate. It is the estate that starts at the end of a life estate.

REMAINDER ESTATE *See* Remainder.

REMAINDERMAN Anyone who has the rights to an estate after prior interests in the estate have expired.

REMAINING ECONOMIC LIFE The period of time from the date of appraisal until the improvements become economically valueless and contribute no value to the property.

REMISE To discharge, remit, or give up. It is also synonymous with *quit claim*.

REMNANT In real estate, a piece of land left after a taking by condemnation that is so small or irregularly shaped that it has very little or no value.

REMODEL To physically change for the purpose of improving the function, plan, or style of the interior or exterior of a building.

RENEGOTIATION The process of trying to agree on new terms to an existing contract, lease, mortgage, etc. It requires agreement by both parties.

RENEWAL **1.** To continue a lease for a new term. **2.** Redevelopment, replacement, or rehabilitation of urban blighted areas.

RENEWAL OPTION A provision in a lease that gives the tenant the right (but not the obligation) to extend the lease for a specified period of time.

RENOVATION A general term for substantially improving a property through rehabilitation, modernization, and remodeling.

RENT Money paid to a landlord (property owner) in return for the right to use the property.

RENTABLE AREA The rentable area of an office on a multiple tenancy floor shall be computed by measuring to the inside finish of permanent outer building walls, to the office side of corridors and/or other permanent partitions, and to the center of partitions that separate the premises from adjoining rentable areas. No deductions shall be made for columns and projections necessary to the building.

RENTAL AGENT A real estate professional who specializes in renting properties. He or she may act as an agent for the landlord and receive compensation in the form of fees or commissions. He or she also may help tenants find a property and be paid by the tenant.

RENTAL VALUE The amount of money a tenant is warranted in paying for the right to occupy or use a property for a given time under certain prescribed or assumed conditions.

RENT CONTROLS The control by a government agency of the amount of rent a landlord can charge for a property.

RENT MULTIPLIER Part of a technique used by appraisers and investors to estimate the value of property based on the ratio of rent (either monthly or annually) to value expressed as a multiplier. To estimate the value, the rent is multiplied by the selected multiplier.

RENT SUBSIDY A payment made by a government agency or charitable organization on behalf of people who are unable to pay the total amount of rent for a property.

REPAIRS The general upkeep of a property to maintain its condition and efficiency without major replacement or alteration of characteristics.

REPLACEMENT The substitution of an original part of a structure with something newer or in better condition that is substantially the same.

REPLACEMENT COST An appraisal term for total cost to replace an improvement at current costs with modern materials and using current design standards. The result is the estimated current cost of improvements with similar utility as those being appraised.

REPLACEMENT RESERVES **1.** Money set aside for the replacement of equipment and short-lived building components by landlords. **2.** Estimated reserves needed for replacement of short-lived items calculated by appraisers as an operating expense in the income approach to value.

REPOSSESS The act of a landlord retaking possession of his property after a lease has been violated or when a purchaser fails to keep up mortgage payments.

REPRODUCTION COST An appraisal term for the total cost to reproduce an exact replica of an improvement at current costs using the same materials and the same design as the original structure.

REPRODUCTION COST APPROACH See Cost Approach to Value.

Example of How to Estimate Property Value Using a Rent Multiplier

The multiplier is developed from the sales of similar properties by dividing their sale prices by their gross annual rents.

The multiplier is then multiplied by the rental of the property being appraised to give an estimate of its value.

Example:
Multiplier: 7.85
Annual Rent: $63,850.
Indicated Value: $501,225.
(7.85 × $63,850 = $501,225)

RENT MULTIPLIER

Typical Items for Which Reserves Are Commonly Established

Appliances
Furniture
Carpets
Roof, boilers, elevators
Store fronts
Linens, dishes and silverware
Other chattels

REPLACEMENT RESERVES

RERECORDING The second recording of a deed to correct a mistake made in the first recording; also called a *correction*.

RESCISSION The cancelling of a contract; the annulling or abrogating of contract and the return of the parties to their original positions. It may be done by agreement of all the parties or by one party who claims that there are legally sufficient reasons for the contract to be void.

RESERVATION **1.** A clause in an instrument or conveyance that allows the grantor to keep for himself some portion of the interest or profit in the granted estate. **2.** Public land set aside for a specific and special purpose, such as an Indian reservation.

RESERVE Money set aside from earnings for future taxes, maintenance, or to pay future claims or possible liabilities.

RESERVE FOR DEPLETION An amount that is set aside to compensate for the reduction in value of property from which minerals or other valuable components have been extracted.

RESERVE FOR DEPRECIATION An amount that is set aside to compensate for the anticipated reduction in value or the recapture of investment in real estate improvements.

RESERVE FOR REPLACEMENT Money set aside to provide for the necessary replacement of short-lived items that wear out from normal wear and tear, such as stoves, carpets, or refrigerators, before the main structure wears out.

RESERVOIR A natural area, such as a lake or pond, or an artificial one, such as a tank, where water is collected and stored for a community power plant or irrigation.

RESIDENCE **1.** The place where a person lives without the immediate intention of moving elsewhere. **2.** The physical structure in which people live.

RESIDENTIAL BUILDING RATE A unit of measurement of the rate of residential construction. It is the number of new residences that are started per 1,000 population over a specified period of time.

RESIDENTIAL MEMBER (RM) Designation awarded by the American Institute of Real Estate Appraisers of the NATIONAL ASSOCIATION OF REALTORS®.

RESIDENTIAL MEMBER

RESIDENTIAL PROPERTY Property that is intended primarily for use as a residence. Often, the use is controlled by zoning regulations and deed restrictions.

RESIDUAL PROCESS An appraisal technique that is part of the income approach to value. A portion of the net operating income is allocated either to the site or the improvements. The remaining income is capitalized into an estimated value of that portion of the property the remaining income is attributed to.

RESIDUAL SOIL Soil created by the decomposition of rock caused by weathering.

RESIDUAL TECHNIQUES *See* Residual Process.

RESILIENT TILES Tiles with dense, non-absorbent surfaces that spring back into place when dented. Popular types are linoleum, vinyl asbestos, pure vinyl, rubber, cork, and asphalt.

RESORT MOTEL A motel in a resort area geared to guests staying for periods longer than overnight. Often, resort motels have access to golf and tennis facilities, ski lifts, pools, beaches, etc.

RESORT PROPERTY Property that people go to for vacations.

RESPA (REAL ESTATE SETTLEMENT PROCEDURES ACT) *See* Real Estate Settlement Procedures Act.

RESTRICTION Limitations on the use and transfer of property. Public restrictions are made by the government through its police power, and use is regulated through zoning ordinances, building codes, environmental regulations, etc. Private restrictions are set forth in deeds by agreement between prior owners and bind future owners of the property.

RESTRICTIVE COVENANT A type of private restriction on the use or transfer of property.

RESUBDIVISION The process of creating a new subdivision out of a property that has already been subdivided.

RETAINING WALL A wall used to confine dirt, water, mud, etc.

RETURN ON INVESTMENT Interest earned by investors for the use of their money for a period of time.

RETURN TEE FITTING A type of fitting used in an individual take-off hot-water heating system that directs water flowing from the convectors in the direction of the flow of water in the pipe connecting the convectors or radiators to each other.

RETAINING WALL

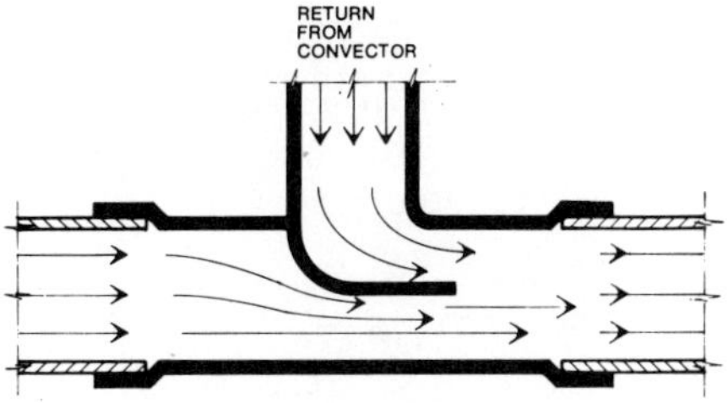

RETURN TEE FITTING

REVENUE STAMPS

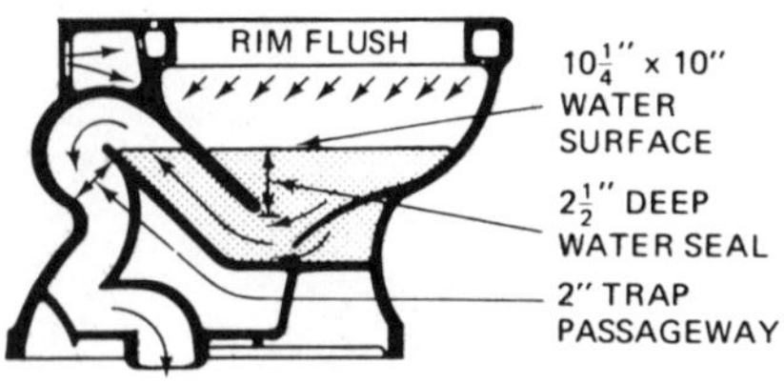

REVERSE TRAP TOILET

REUSE APPRAISAL An appraisal, the purpose of which is to estimate the projected resale value of property in a redevelopment project. It considers the effect of the redevelopment project upon the value and the planned permitted uses of the property after the redevelopment project is completed.

REVALUATION *See* Reassessment.

REVALUATION CLAUSE A clause in a type of lease that provides for specified periodic adjustments of the rent based on the appraisal of the property at the designated time.

REVALUATION LEASE A type of lease which contains a provision that requires specified periodic revaluation of leased property and a proportionate change in rent based on revised estimated market value of the property.

REVENUE STAMPS Formerly, federal tax stamps required to be affixed to any conveyancing instrument used for the sale or transfer of real property. They have been replaced by stamps issued by some state governments for the same purpose.

REVERSE LEVERAGE *See* Negative Leverage.

REVERSE TRAP TOILET A common type of toilet. The inside water level covers about two-thirds of the interior surface. It is flushed by creating a siphon action in the trapway.

REVERSION The return to the owner of real estate of rights granted to others for a specified period. An example would be the right of possession and use of the property at the end of a lease.

REVERSIONARY RIGHT The right of an owner of property to the use of the property at the end of a lease or to recover some other right to the property that was granted to a third party for a limited period of time, such as an easement, or right of way.

REVERSION FACTOR A factor that is used to discount the value of a single payment received in the future to present value. It reflects an appropriate discount rate and the specified time period. It is also known as the "present worth of one" factor.

REVERTER CLAUSE A clause in a deed that attempts to enforce private restrictions in the deed by stating that title reverts back to the grantor when the grantee violates the deed restriction. Such a clause is often considered to be a major cloud on the title that severely restricts the marketability of the property.

RIBBON DEVELOPMENT *See* Roadside Development.

RIBBON DRIVEWAY A driveway paved with two concrete strips the same distance apart as the wheels of an automobile.

RIDER *See* Addendum.

RIDGE The horizontal line where two sloping roof surfaces meet.

RIDGE BOARD The top structural member to which the rafters are nailed.

RIDGE TILE A tile that is partially curved and used to cover the ridge of a roof.

RIDGE VENT Ventilator opening at the ridge of a roof.

RIGHT OF ACCESS *See* Access Right.

RIGHT OF FIRST REFUSAL *See* First Refusal Right.

RIGHT OF REDEMPTION *See* Redemption.

RIGHT OF SURVIVORSHIP In a joint tenancy, the right of the surviving partner to automatically acquire the interest of a decreased joint owner.

RIGHT OF WAY **1.** The right granted by the owner of a property to somebody or something to pass over, on, or under the property. Some examples are the rights of utilities to run wires, pipes, tracks, etc., across the property. **2.** The roadbed of a street, highway, railroad, walkway, etc.

RIGHTS As applied to real estate, legally enforceable claims to any interest or title in property.

RIGID CONDUIT A stiff pipe used to cover and protect electric wiring. The pipe is installed first, and the wire is drawn through it.

RIGID FOUNDATION *See* Floating Foundation.

RIGID INSULATION A type of insulation that is manufactured in sheets and other non-flexible forms. It may be either structural or non-structural.

RILL EROSION Erosion of freshly cultivated ground caused by heavy rains.

RIPARIAN Relating to or belonging to the banks of a stream, waterway, river, etc.

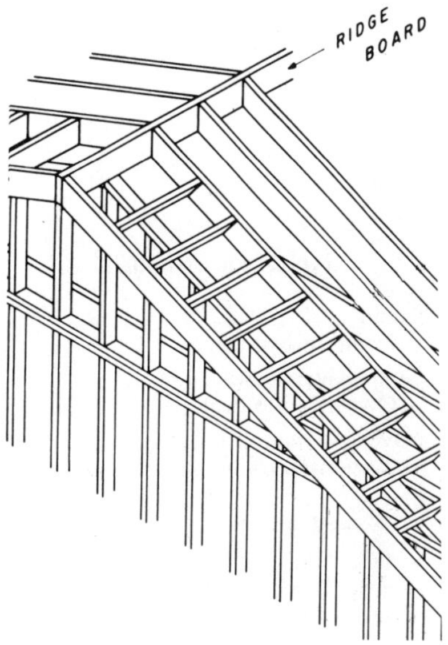

RIDGE BOARD

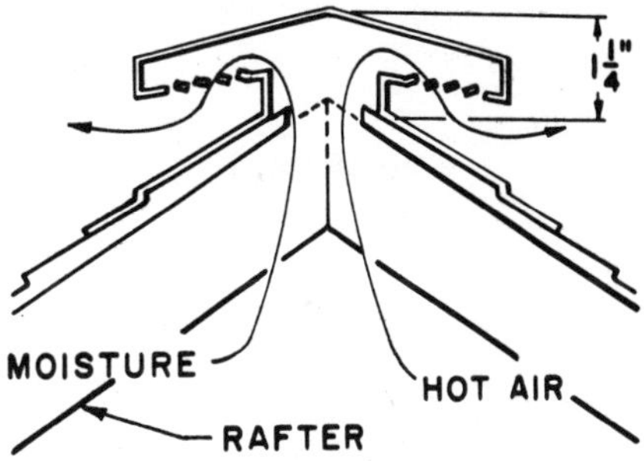

RIDGE VENT

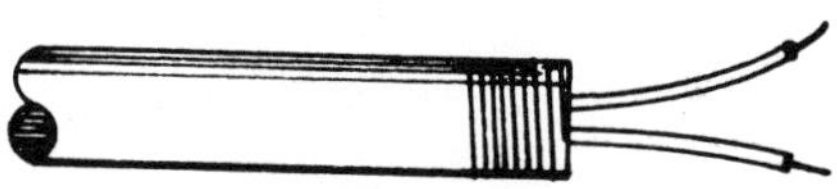

RIGID CONDUIT

Typical Riparian Rights

- Stream
  Ownership to center
- Non-navigable river or lake
  Ownership to center
- Navigable river or lake
  Ownership to low water mark
- Ocean
  Ownership to high water line
- Surface Water
  Each owner must take fair share of the run-off
  Owner cannot block run-off so as to flood neighbor
  Owner cannot divert surface water onto neighbor's property
- Underground water
  Each owner can use only their fair share
  Owner cannot take water from under neighbor's property

RIPARIAN RIGHTS

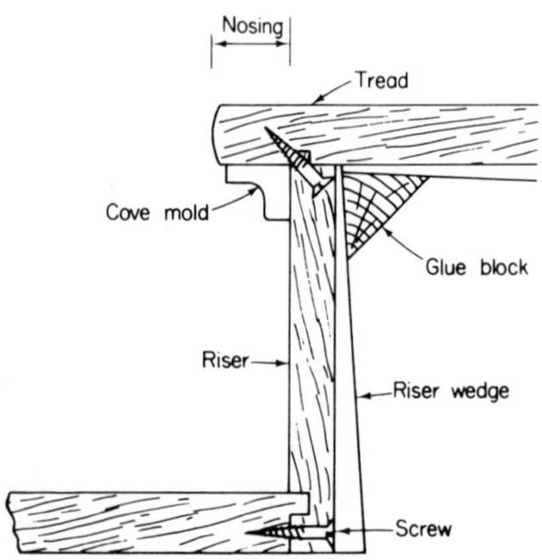

RISER

RIPARIAN GRANT The transfer of riparian rights from one owner to another.

RIPARIAN OWNER A person or organization who owns land that is adjacent to a watercourse, river, stream, etc.

RIPARIAN PROPERTY Land within the natural watershed or a watercourse, stream, river, etc.

RIPARIAN RIGHTS The rights of owners of property that is bounded or traversed by a river, stream, or waterway to use the water for such things as piers, boathouses, boating, or fishing as long as such use does not unreasonably interfere with the rights of the other owners of riparian rights on the same river, stream, or waterway.

RIPARIAN WATER Water within the normal bounds of a river, stream, or waterway. Flood water is not riparian water.

RIPRAP A wall of loosely placed rocks, stones, wood, or concrete beams used to prevent erosion by hindering the flow of water.

RISE The measure of a slope; its vertical ascent in relation to a horizontal measurement. For example, a road might rise two feet for each 100 feet of horizontal distance (a two percent rise).

RISER **1.** The part of a stair that is the vertical board under the stair top. *See also* Stairs. **2.** In plumbing systems, the vertical pipe that supplies steam to the radiators in the upper rooms.

RISK A measurement of the degree of possibility of financial loss of income or capital in an investment.

RISK FACTORS That portion of the return on an investment that is attributed to the investment risk. It is extra return sought by an investor as compensation for whatever risk of loss of invested capital or projected income there is in the investment.

RIVER A large, permanent, natural stream of water that empties into a sea, bay, ocean, lake, or other body of water.

RIVER BED The land between the banks of the normal course of a river.

RM *See* Residential Member

ROAD A "travelway" for pedestrians and vehicles.

ROADSIDE DEVELOPMENTS The residential, commercial,

and industrial developments that are found on properties with highway frontages. Usually, they line highways leading into urban communities.

ROCK A solid, naturally formed mass of mineral matter. Rocks vary in both size and composition.

ROCK WOOL *See* Mineral Wool.

ROD A linear measure of 5½ yards or 16½ feet.

ROLL *See* Tax Roll.

ROLLOVER (RENEWABLE) MORTGAGE A mortgage that is technically written for a short period of time (usually a few years), with a provision that the lender may offer to extend it for a series of renewable periods without the need of another closing or title search. The purpose is to allow the lender to adjust the interest rate to the then current rate.

ROLL ROOFING Roofing material that consists of fiber that is saturated with asphalt. It is commonly supplied in 36-inch-wide rolls that contain a total of 108 square feet. Sometimes it is coated with mineral aggregates.

ROMAN BRICK A brick with nominal dimensions of 2 inches by 4 inches by 12 inches that is narrower than a standard brick.

ROMANESQUE STYLE A nineteenth-century American house style that is characterized by its massive stone structure with semicircular arched openings with one or more towers or domes. It has a pyramidal roof. The style was popular in the 1800s for public buildings and churches. Only a few Romanesque houses were ever built in the United States.

CTS SYSTEM: Nineteenth Century American
Romanesque
(Roman-711)

ROMAN TILE A roofing tile that is tapered and channel shaped.

ROMAN TUSCAN MODE A nineteenth-century American house style brought from Italy in the 1800s. The style is box-like and fills an entire lot, leaving no yard space. Windows on each floor are treated differently. The roof is flat with a massive cornice. The house is usually built of stone.

CTS SYSTEM: Nineteenth Century American
Roman Tuscan Mode
(Ro Tusc-703)

ROMANESQUE STYLE

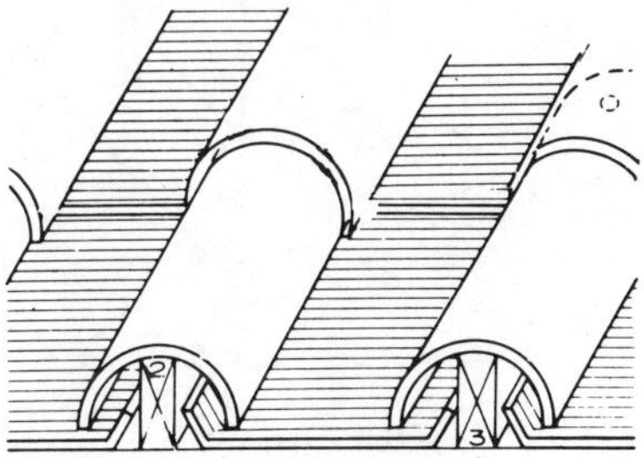

ROMAN TILE

ROMAN TUSCAN MODE

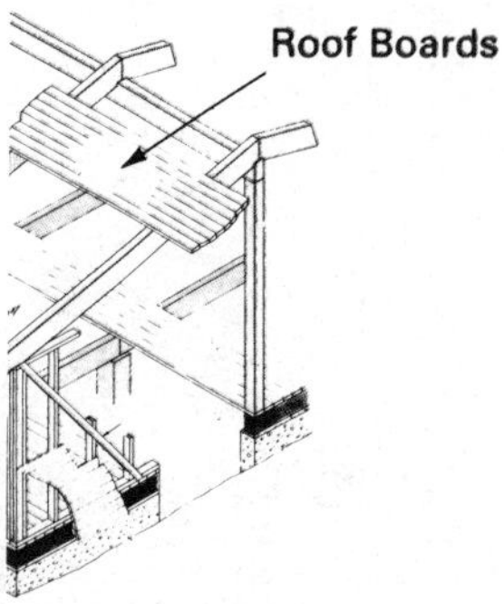

ROOF BEAMS, ROOF BOARDS

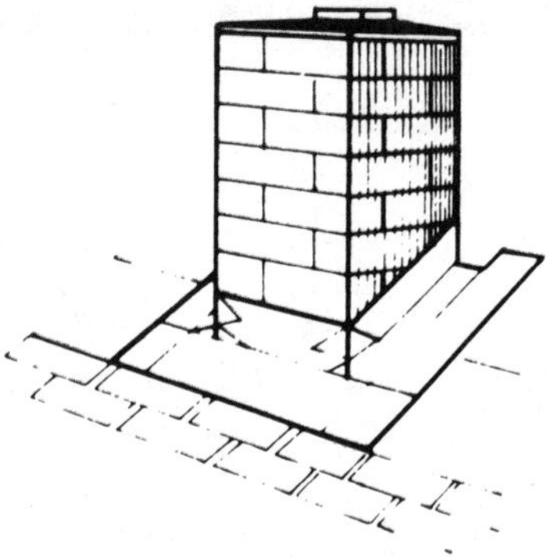

ROOF FLASHING

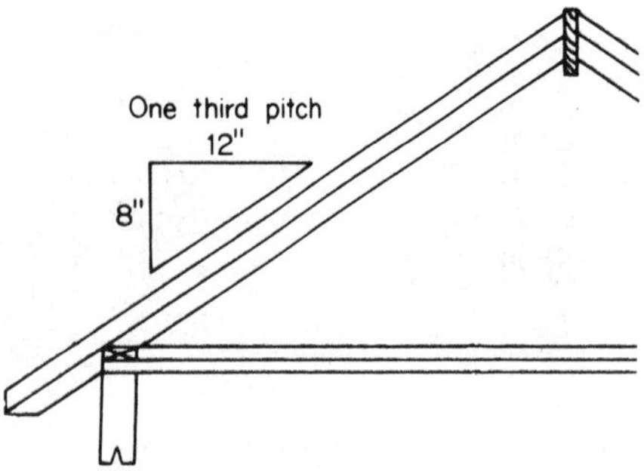

ROOF PITCH

ROOF The top of a house. The most common house roof types are gable, gambrel, hip, mansard, and flat.

ROOF BEAMS Framing members in a plank and beam framing system that support the roof planks. They run from the ridge beam down to the top of the outside wall.

ROOF BOARDS Boards or sheathing that are nailed to the rafters and to which are fastened the roof covering or shingles, tiles, or other material. *See also* Sheathing.

ROOF EDGE FLASHING Special flashing that seals the opening between the edge of the gutter and the edge of the roof.

ROOF FLASHING Flashing placed over roof intersections and where chimneys, vent pipes, and other items protrude through a roof. It seals the joint and makes it weathertight.

ROOFING Material used to cover the upper exterior portion of a house to make it watertight.

ROOF PITCH The slope of the roof, which is expressed in a ratio of vertical drop to horizontal distance. A 6-inch pitch or 6 in 12 pitch or 6 to 12 pitch means the roof rises 6 inches for each 12 inches of horizontal distance.

ROOFER'S CEMENT A special, elastic cement used by roofers to waterproof holes caused by nails and screws.

ROOF SHEATHING *See* Sheathing.

ROOF VENT A ventilation mechanism for an attic or roof cavity.

ROOM An enclosed interior subdivision of a building that is accessible usually through a doorway. Many types of rooms are named specifically, such as bedroom, bathroom, living room, and dining room.

ROOM COUNT The number of rooms in a structure. There currently is no standard system for counting rooms in residential buildings. Generally, bathrooms are counted separately. For example, the room count of a typical house might be seven rooms and two baths.

ROOM HEATER A freestanding, non-recessed, comfort heating appliance installed in the space being heated and not connected to ducts.

ROOT OR VEGETABLE CELLAR An underground area used for storing roots and vegetables during the nineteenth century. It is very uncommon in modern homes.

ROTATION The raising of two or more different crops on the same piece of land in different years in order to maintain productivity of the soil.

ROTCH HOUSE *See* Early Gothic Revival.

ROTUNDA A circular room or building, usually having a domed roof.

ROUGH HARDWARE In construction, hardware (such as bolts, spikes, and other metal fittings) intended to be concealed from view when the structure is finished.

ROUND TIMBER Timber left in its natural round form, such as poles, log siding, and piles.

ROW CROP Crops planted in rows to facilitate cultivation during growth.

ROW HOUSES Houses that are architecturally similar and have common sidewalls. Usually, they face in the same direction.

ROYALTY In real estate, money paid to a land owner for the right to farm, mine, or extract natural resources (such as oil, gas, sand, or timber).

"R" THERMAL RESISTANCE A measure of ability to retard heat flow. "R" is the numerical reciprocal of U (a measure of heat flow).

Formula for Calculating "R" Thermal Resistance

R = Thermal resistance
U = Heat flow

$$R = \frac{1}{U}$$

"R" THERMAL RESISTANCE

RUBBER-BACKED CARPETING Carpeting with rubber backing that is attached with a special glue directly to the floor. Removal would damage both floor finish and carpet.

RUBBER TILE A type of tile containing natural or synthetic rubber that is relatively flexible, burn resistant, durable, resilient, and sound absorbing.

RUBBLE Rough stones of irregular shape and size; also called *fieldstone*.

RUBBLEWORK Masonry walls made of rubble.

RULE AGAINST PERPETUITIES A principle, which has become a statute in some states, that a property interest is void unless it must vest, if at all, not later than 21 years plus period of gestation, after some life or lives in being at time of creation of interest.

RUNNING WITH THE LAND A covenant that passes with the transfer of the land is said to be running with the land. It is applied to either a liability or interest that passes to the next owner of a piece of property. Valid deed restrictions are common covenants that are binding on all owners of the land.

RURAL Pertaining to the country as opposed to the city.

RURAL-URBAN FRINGE Land on the outskirts of a city that is undergoing transition from rural to urban.

RURBAN **1.** Applied to rural areas that are close enough to a city to permit commuting. They have characteristics of both urban and rural land. **2.** Areas that are changing from rural to urban.

RUSTIC SIDING A type of siding especially designed to look rustic.

"R" VALUE (RESISTANCE TO HEAT FLOW) A standard measurement for the effectiveness of insulation. R= resistance to heat flow. The higher the "R" value, the better the insulation.

S

SADDLE The threshold of a door. A strip that is fastened to the floor under the door to cover the joining of the flooring.

SAFE RATE The interest rate on an investment that has maximum safety with a minimum of risk, such as bonds or bank savings.

SAFETY CLAUSE A clause in a listing which states that, if a property is sold during a specified time after the expiration of the listing to a buyer furnished by the broker during the listing period, the commission must still be paid to the broker. This prevents a buyer and seller from waiting until the listing expires to avoid paying the commission.

SAFETY GLASS **1.** Glass made by laminating two sheets of single- or double-strength glass to a strong plastic sheet. **2.** Glass that contains wire mesh to prevent shattering. **3.** Tempered glass.

SAFETY HAZARDS Items or situations that could potentially cause injury or damage to personal property.

SALE The transfer of a property title in exchange for some sort of payment.

SALE-LEASEBACK The sale of a property to an investor whereby the investor leases the property back to the original owner.

SALE PRICE The price for which a property actually sells.

SALES APPROACH *See* Market Data Approach.

SALES-ASSESSMENT RATIO The ratio of the assessed value of a property to its selling price.

SALES CONTRACT A contract that contains the terms to which a buyer or seller have agreed in order to transfer the title of a property.

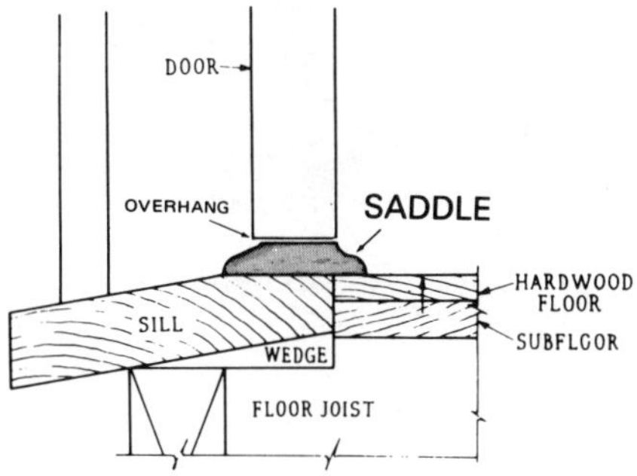

SADDLE

SALES EXPENSE Costs involved with the sale of a real property, such as advertising costs and broker's commissions; the sum spent to prepare the house for sale.

SALES KIT Materials used and carried by a salesperson to help with sales and listings, such as forms, maps, plans, tape measure, and amortization schedules.

SALESPERSON A person who is licensed to work in real estate under a broker.

SALTBOX COLONIAL STYLE

SALTBOX COLONIAL STYLE An American house style that is a colonial New England Farm House with a lean-to added to the back of the house so that snow can easily slide off. Its name comes from the fact that the house resembles the saltbox found in old country stores. The Saltbox is a two- to two-and-one-half story square or rectangular house that has a steep gable roof extending down to the first floor in the rear. Traditionally, the rear faced North to ward off winter winds. Exterior walls are usually clapboard or shingles. The Saltbox Colonial has a large central chimney, and the shutters are the same size as the windows.

CTS SYSTEM: Colonial American
Salt Box Colonial or
Catslide (in South)
(Salt Box or Catslide-109)

SALTBOX ROOF A roof style that has a short roof pitch in front and a long roof pitch in back, coming close to the ground.

SALVAGE VALUE The value of a building or a portion of the building, such as a plumbing fixture, if it were to be removed from the premises to be used at another site. The value of a property after full depreciation.

SAND Granular rock or mineral fragments resulting from natural abrasion of rock. Sand granules have a diameter ranging from 1mm (coarse sand) to .005mm (very fine sand). It also refers to soil composed of 90 percent or more of various grades of sand.

SANDWICH BEAM *See* Flitch Beam.

SANDWICH LEASE The second in a series of three leases. It is a sublease that, in turn, creates another sublease when the right to occupy the property is transferred by the original sublessee to another sublessee. Thus, the original sublease ends up between the original primary lease and the sublease of the tenant who occupies the premises.

SANDWICH LEASEHOLDER The lessor under a sandwich lease. *See also* Sandwich Lease.

SANDWICH PANEL Insulation "sandwiched" between two layers of concrete, asbestos, or metal.

SANITARY SEWER The pipe system that carries the domestic waste to a sewage treatment plant or other disposal area. *See also* Combination Sewer, Storm Sewer, Septic System.

SASH A framework into which window frames are set.

SASH CORD, SASH CHAIN The cord or chain that attaches the counterbalance weights to each double-hung window sash.

SATELLITE CITY A small city in the surroundings of a major city that leaves a deliberate space between itself and the major city to help stop urban sprawl.

SATISFACTION The completion of an obligation such as a mortgage by the payment of the amount due. It is also the document that is issued by the mortgagee when a mortgage is paid off.

SATISFACTORY RATE OF RETURN The risk, interest, or yield that will attract capital and satisfy the investor.

SAVINGS AND LOAN ASSOCIATION A state or federally chartered association that holds savings and specializes in residential mortgages. Savings and loan associations are federally regulated and insured.

SAVINGS BANK A lending institution that is chartered as a bank by the state in which it exists. Its primary purpose is to accept time deposits from the public and lend the money to property owners, accepting mortgages on the property as security for the loan. Most savings banks are mutual institutions. *See also* Mutual Savings Banks.

SAW LOG A log that is big enough to use in the production of sawed lumber or other sawed products.

SAW-TOOTH ROOF A series of single pitched roofs that used to be used in factories. The series resembled the sharp edge of a saw. A window was usually placed in each for light and ventilation. It is not used in modern construction.

SBA (SMALL BUSINESS ADMINISTRATION) A federal agency that makes loans to small businesses provided the borrower has been refused a loan by a private lender.

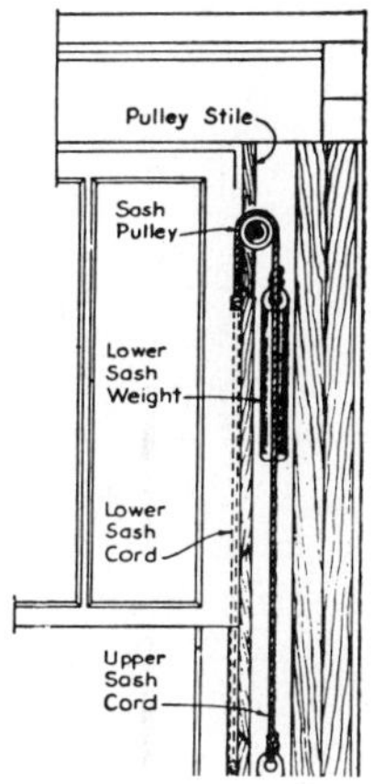

SASH CORD

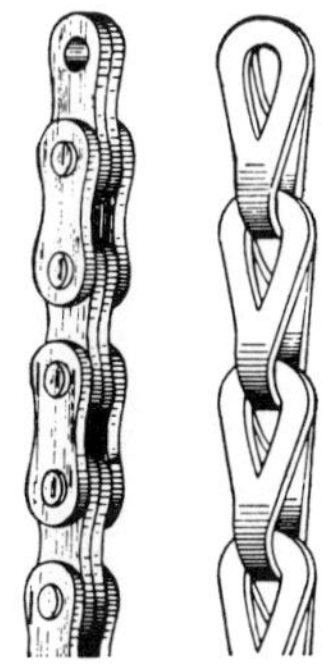

SASH CHAIN

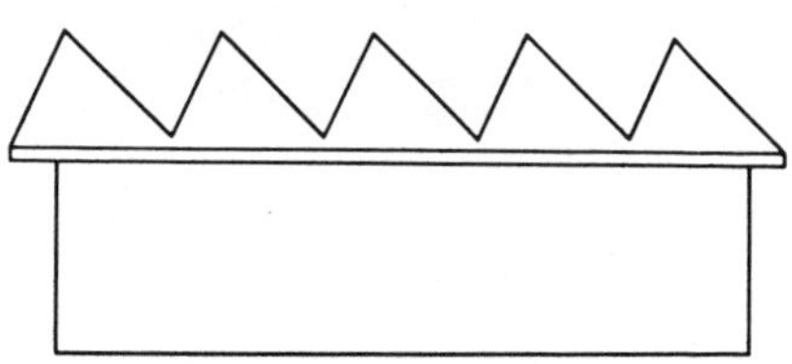

SAW TOOTH ROOF

SCALE

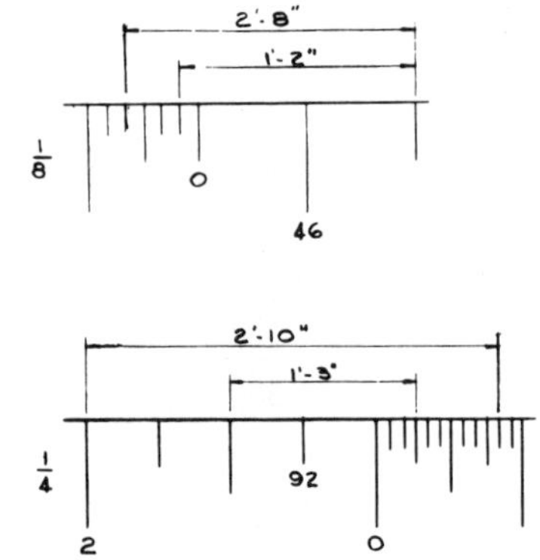

ARCHITECT'S SCALE

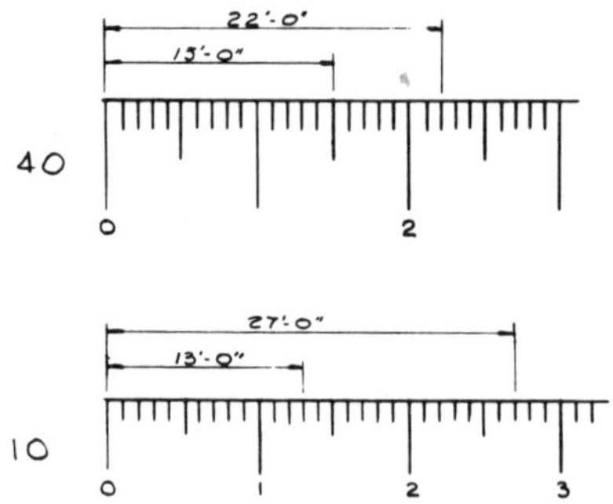

ENGINEER'S SCALE

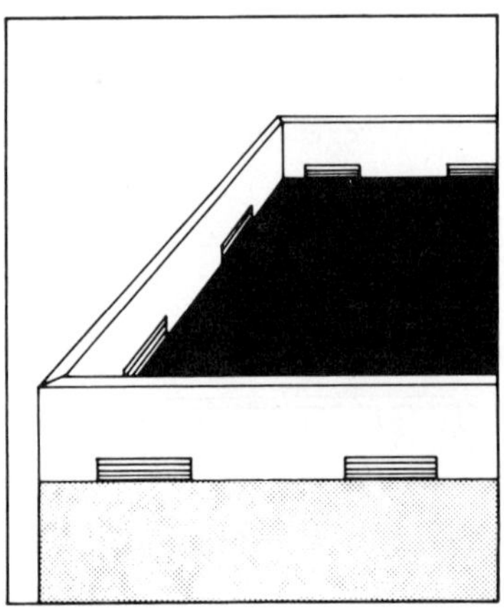

SCUPPERS

SCALE The proportion between a representation (map, blueprint, etc.) and that which it represents. For example, one inch on a blueprint equals 10 feet in actual distance. This ratio is the scale.

SCANTLING LUMBER Lumber two inches thick and less than eight inches wide.

SCARCITY Limited availability of real estate in relation to its demand.

SCARE SELLING To falsely convince someone to sell his property below market value because the area will be infiltrated by minorities.

SCENIC EASEMENT An easement granted to nearby property owners which restricts construction on the property to those improvements that will not detract from the attractiveness of the area. Often, such easements prohibit the construction of advertising signs or improvements that do not conform to the historic look of the area.

SCRAP VALUE The value of a building based on the value of the material alone. For example, walls have value for their bricks and wood.

SCRATCH COAT The first coat of plaster applied to the lath which is scratched to provide a bond for the next coat.

SCR BRICK Brick with the nominal dimensions of $2\frac{2}{3}$ by 6 inches by 12 inches used in places where a single layer of such bricks is sufficient.

SCREEN **1.** An improvement whose primary purpose is to hide or conceal something from view. **2.** A sheet of woven fabric or metal material that is used to cover doors and windows to keep out insects.

SCRIBING The cutting of wood to fit an irregular surface.

SCULPTURE Decorative shapes cut from wood, marble, or stone.

SCULPTURING The regrading of a piece of land in order to increase its beauty and privacy and to restrict sound.

SCUPPERS Openings in the wall above the roof that allow water to run off the roof.

SCUTTLE *See* Hatchway.

SEAL A physical sign placed on a document to indicate that the instrument was signed and executed in a formal manner.

SEALANTS Any material used to seal joints or openings against the intrusion or passage of any foreign substance, such as water, gas, air, or dirt.

SEA LEVEL The level of the sea at mean tide.

SEALING *See* Seal.

SEARCHING THE TITLE *See* Title Search.

SEASONAL FLUCTUATIONS Fluctuations in economic activity that occur every year at about the same time.

SEASONAL HOMES Homes intended for seasonal or other than year-round occupancy.

SEASONED MORTGAGE A mortgage that has been in existence for a period of time during which the borrower has a record of making timely payments.

SEC (SECURITIES AND EXCHANGE COMMISSION) The federal agency that regulates the stock market.

SECONDARY EMPLOYMENT Employment in a non-base activity.

SECONDARY FINANCING A loan secured by a mortgage or trust deed which is secondary to another deed or mortgage.

SECONDARY LOCATION A location that is not the prime location for the intended construction but is surrounding or adjacent to the prime location; a second-best location.

SECONDARY MORTGAGE MARKET The selling of first mortgages and trust deeds by primary lenders, such as banks, savings and loan associations, and credit unions, to Freddie Mac, Fannie Mae, Ginnie Mae, and other organizations who raise their capital in the bond market. The mortgages are often sold at a discount. Usually, the primary lender continues to service the mortgage or trust deed.

SECOND EMPIRE *See* American Mansard.

SECOND MORTGAGE A mortgage with a security interest in a property that is junior to another mortgage on the same property.

SECRET INTEREST An interest that is kept secret from a third party.

SECTION In the Rectangular Survey System, a section of land one mile square containing 640 acres; one thirty-sixth of a township.

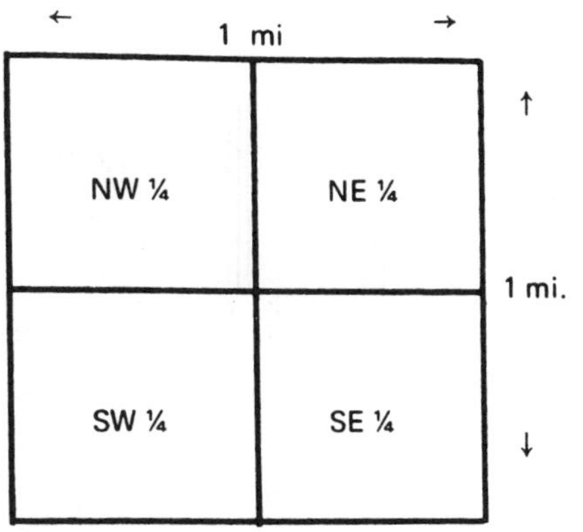

SECTION

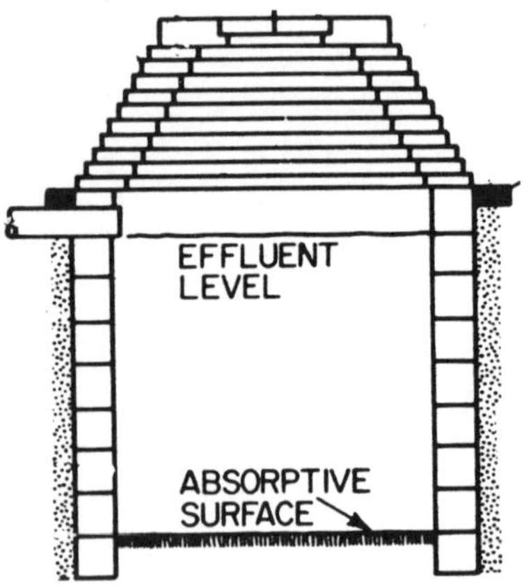

SEEPAGE PIT

SECTION 8 A federal program sponsored by HUD for leasing housing to lower-income families.

SECTORS The wedge-shaped areas that point to the center of a city. They are recognized as patterns of urban growth.

SECURED PARTY A party, such as a pledgee or mortgagee, that has a security interest.

SECURITY Real property or personal property pledged by a debtor to a creditor with power to sell if the debt is not paid; an additional protection for the lender's interest.

SECURITY AGREEMENT A general term for many types of legal instruments that describe the relationship between debtors and creditors where something of value is offered by the debtor to guarantee payment of a debt to a lender.

SECURITY DEPOSIT A deposit that a landlord requires of a tenant as security for payment of rent.

SECURITY INTEREST The special interest a debtor gives a creditor in property to secure the interest of the creditor.

SEDIMENTARY ROCK Rocks formed from sediment, such as sandstone, limestone, or shale. It is one of the three major classifications of rocks.

SEED MONEY The funds needed to start a project, such as money needed for acquiring or controlling a sale, making studies, or obtaining zoning.

SEEPAGE PIT A covered pit with open-jointed lining through which septic tank effluent may seep or leach into surrounding porous soil.

SEISIN A feudal term for the right of possession of real property under the claim of freehold estate.

SELECT LUMBER Lumber that is chosen for color and grain and relative lack of imperfections.

SELF-SUPPORTING WALLS Walls that only support their own weight and are not load bearing.

SELLER'S MARKET An economic situation whereby a seller can sell his property at higher prices than properties sold in a recent preceding period. It is a market where there is a large demand and a limited supply.

SELLING AGENT In a cobrokerage sale, the agent who

obtains the buyer and effects the sale rather than the agent who listed the property for sale.

SEMICIRCULAR ROOF A curved roof that resembles an extended arch. It is used on barns or barracks type buildings.

SENIOR MORTGAGE The mortgage that has higher priority to that of another mortgage.

SENTIMENTAL VALUE The emotional investment an owner has in his property.

SEPARATE PROPERTY Property that is owned by a married person in which the other spouse has no legal interest or ownership.

SEPARATION A permanent open space between a building's exterior walls and the lot line or the center line of a facing street or alley. Where two or more buildings are on a lot, it is the horizontal separation of the exterior walls.

SEPTIC FIELD *See* Leaching Field.

SEPTIC SYSTEM A sewage system consisting of a septic tank, distribution box, and field. It is used in areas where sewers have not been installed.

SEPTIC TANK A covered, watertight sewage settling tank intended to retain the solids in the sewage flowing through the tank long enough for satisfactory decomposition of settled solids by bacterial action to take place.

SEQUESTRATION, WRIT OF The seizure of one's property to force compliance with a court order.

SERVICE Notice given to a person involved with a court action, such as a defendant or witness, through delivery of a writ, subpoena, injunction, etc.

SERVICE INDUSTRY An industry that markets a service rather than a tangible product.

SERVICE LINES The various conduits that provide channelized space for either the collection or distribution of sewage, water, electricity, steam, gas, storm water, or other utility services.

SERVICE PROPERTY A property designed and used for a special purpose, such as a school, theatre, or hospital, that cannot be used for another purpose without major renovations.

SEMICIRCULAR ROOF

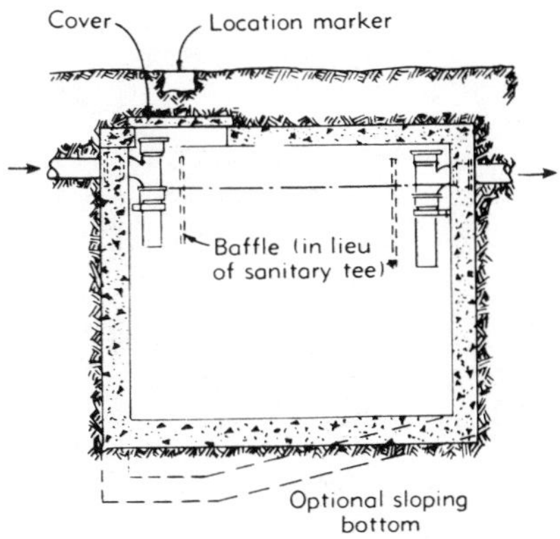

SEPTIC TANK

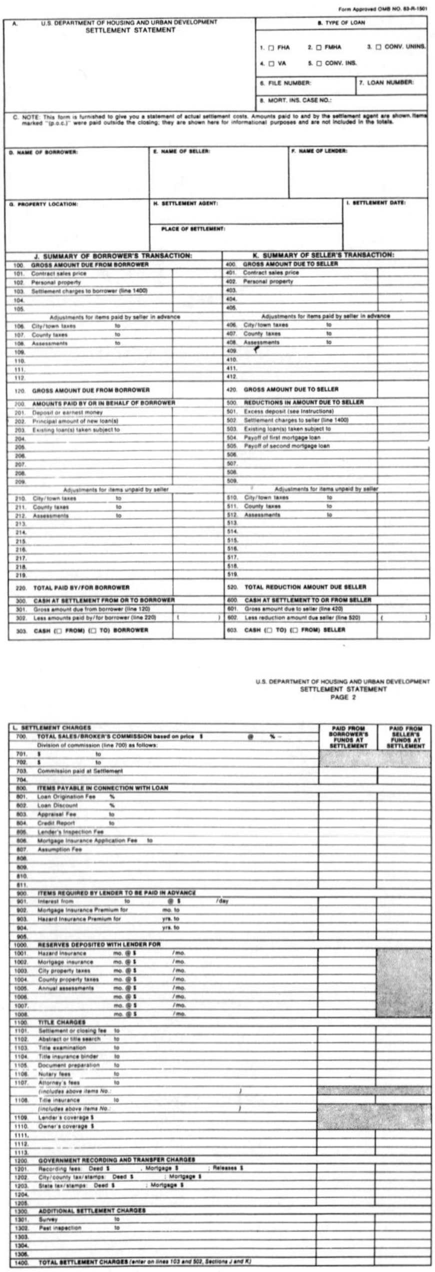

Form Approved OMB NO. 63-R-1501

A. U.S. DEPARTMENT OF HOUSING AND URBAN DEVELOPMENT
SETTLEMENT STATEMENT

B. TYPE OF LOAN
1. ☐ FHA 2. ☐ FMHA 3. ☐ CONV. UNINS.
4. ☐ VA 5. ☐ CONV. INS.
6. FILE NUMBER: 7. LOAN NUMBER:
8. MORT. INS. CASE NO.:

C. NOTE: This form is furnished to give you a statement of actual settlement costs. Amounts paid to and by the settlement agent are shown. Items marked "(p.o.c.)" were paid outside the closing; they are shown here for informational purposes and are not included in the totals.

D. NAME OF BORROWER: E. NAME OF SELLER: F. NAME OF LENDER:

G. PROPERTY LOCATION: H. SETTLEMENT AGENT: I. SETTLEMENT DATE:
PLACE OF SETTLEMENT:

J. SUMMARY OF BORROWER'S TRANSACTION:		K. SUMMARY OF SELLER'S TRANSACTION:	
100. GROSS AMOUNT DUE FROM BORROWER		400. GROSS AMOUNT DUE TO SELLER	
101. Contract sales price		401. Contract sales price	
102. Personal property		402. Personal property	
103. Settlement charges to borrower (line 1400)		403.	
104.		404.	
105.		405.	
Adjustments for items paid by seller in advance		Adjustments for items paid by seller in advance	
106. City/town taxes to		406. City/town taxes to	
107. County taxes to		407. County taxes to	
108. Assessments to		408. Assessments to	
109.		409.	
110.		410.	
111.		411.	
112.		412.	
120. GROSS AMOUNT DUE FROM BORROWER		420. GROSS AMOUNT DUE TO SELLER	
200. AMOUNTS PAID BY OR IN BEHALF OF BORROWER		500. REDUCTIONS IN AMOUNT DUE TO SELLER	
201. Deposit or earnest money		501. Excess deposit (see Instructions)	
202. Principal amount of new loan(s)		502. Settlement charges to seller (line 1400)	
203. Existing loan(s) taken subject to		503. Existing loan(s) taken subject to	
204.		504. Payoff of first mortgage loan	
205.		505. Payoff of second mortgage loan	
206.		506.	
207.		507.	
208.		508.	
209.		509.	
Adjustments for items unpaid by seller		Adjustments for items unpaid by seller	
210. City/town taxes to		510. City/town taxes to	
211. County taxes to		511. County taxes to	
212. Assessments to		512. Assessments to	
213.		513.	
214.		514.	
215.		515.	
216.		516.	
217.		517.	
218.		518.	
219.		519.	
220. TOTAL PAID BY/FOR BORROWER		520. TOTAL REDUCTION AMOUNT DUE SELLER	
300. CASH AT SETTLEMENT FROM OR TO BORROWER		600. CASH AT SETTLEMENT TO OR FROM SELLER	
301. Gross amount due from borrower (line 120)		601. Gross amount due to seller (line 420)	
302. Less amounts paid by/for borrower (line 220)	( )	602. Less reduction amount due seller (line 520)	( )
303. CASH (☐ FROM) (☐ TO) BORROWER		603. CASH (☐ TO) (☐ FROM) SELLER	

U.S. DEPARTMENT OF HOUSING AND URBAN DEVELOPMENT
SETTLEMENT STATEMENT
PAGE 2

L. SETTLEMENT CHARGES	PAID FROM BORROWER'S FUNDS AT SETTLEMENT	PAID FROM SELLER'S FUNDS AT SETTLEMENT
700. TOTAL SALES/BROKER'S COMMISSION based on price $ @ % =		
Division of commission (line 700) as follows:		
701. $ to		
702. $ to		
703. Commission paid at Settlement		
704.		
800. ITEMS PAYABLE IN CONNECTION WITH LOAN		
801. Loan Origination Fee %		
802. Loan Discount %		
803. Appraisal Fee to		
804. Credit Report to		
805. Lender's Inspection Fee		
806. Mortgage Insurance Application Fee to		
807. Assumption Fee		
808.		
809.		
810.		
811.		
900. ITEMS REQUIRED BY LENDER TO BE PAID IN ADVANCE		
901. Interest from to @ $ /day		
902. Mortgage Insurance Premium for mo. to		
903. Hazard Insurance Premium for yrs. to		
904. yrs. to		
905.		
1000. RESERVES DEPOSITED WITH LENDER FOR		
1001. Hazard insurance mo. @ $ /mo.		
1002. Mortgage insurance mo. @ $ /mo.		
1003. City property taxes mo. @ $ /mo.		
1004. County property taxes mo. @ $ /mo.		
1005. Annual assessments mo. @ $ /mo.		
1006. mo. @ $ /mo.		
1007. mo. @ $ /mo.		
1008. mo. @ $ /mo.		
1100. TITLE CHARGES		
1101. Settlement or closing fee to		
1102. Abstract or title search to		
1103. Title examination to		
1104. Title insurance binder to		
1105. Document preparation to		
1106. Notary fees to		
1107. Attorney's fees to		
(includes above items No.:)		
1108. Title insurance to		
(includes above items No.:)		
1109. Lender's coverage $		
1110. Owner's coverage $		
1111.		
1112.		
1113.		
1200. GOVERNMENT RECORDING AND TRANSFER CHARGES		
1201. Recording fees: Deed $; Mortgage $; Releases $		
1202. City/county tax/stamps: Deed $; Mortgage $		
1203. State tax/stamps: Deed $; Mortgage $		
1204.		
1205.		
1300. ADDITIONAL SETTLEMENT CHARGES		
1301. Survey to		
1302. Pest inspection to		
1303.		
1304.		
1305.		
1400. TOTAL SETTLEMENT CHARGES *(enter on lines 103 and 502, Sections J and K)*		

SETTLEMENT STATEMENT

SERVICE ROAD *See* Frontage Road.

SERVICE STATION A gas station; a place where trucks and automobiles are serviced.

SERVICING *See* Mortgage Servicing.

SERVIENT TENEMENT An estate that owes a servitude; usually a piece of land that has an easement attached to it.

SETBACK ORDINANCE The zoning ordinance which regulates the distance that a building must be set back from the street or the point where improvements may be constructed.

SET-OFF **1.** A construction term relating to the reduction of the thickness of a wall or any recess or sunken panel of the wall. **2.** In condemnation, the benefits to the remaining property in a partial taking may, in some jurisdictions, be "set-off" against the value of the land taken. For example, part of some land is taken for a freeway, and the residue is now more valuable because of the freeway. The increased value is "set-off" against the value of the land taken.

SETTING BED The bed into which tiles are placed and then mortared in place.

SETTLEMENT *See* Closing.

SETTLEMENT STATEMENT A statement drawn up by a broker, escrow agent, etc., that provides a breakdown of all the costs involved in a real estate sale.

SETTLING Compression of the soil due to the weight of the newly built structure upon it. If the compaction is extreme, cracks in the structure may result.

SEVERALTY A property owned by one person alone.

SEVERALTY OWNERSHIP Sole ownership; owned by one person only.

SEVERANCE Partition or separation.

SEVERANCE DAMAGE The decrease in value of a property caused by separation. It commonly results from the taking of a piece of the property for subsequent construction of a road or building.

SEWAGE Liquid or solid waste of humans, animals, or industry.

SEWER LINE EASEMENT An easement for the construction and operation of a sewer.

SEWERS, SEPTIC TANKS, AND CESSPOOLS A pipe or conduit used to carry waste or excess water to a point of disposal.

SHAKE A thick, hand-split shingle used as roofing or siding.

SHARE CROP A crop grown by a tenant farmer who gives a "share" as rent.

SHARECROPPER A person who farms and gives a "share" of the crop for rent.

SHAREHOLDER Commonly, one who owns stock (shares) in a corporation.

SHEATHING The wallboard, plywood, or other structural covering placed over the exterior studding or rafters of a house.

SHEATHING LINE The exterior, vertical plane of wall sheathing.

SHED ROOF A single-pitch roof; a roof that has only one sloping plane.

SHEET EROSION The removal of soil in even amounts over a given area by erosion.

SHEET METAL A flat, rolled metal product that is between .006 and .249 inches thick and has sawed, slit, or sheared edges.

SHEET PILING A barrier made of sheet piles used to stabilize foundations, prevent erosion, etc.

SHEETROCK A trade name for gypsum wallboard.

SHELTER BELT A row of trees or large shrubs planted to protect a building from blizzards, snow, storms, and prevailing winds.

SHELTER TUBE (TERMITE) Tubes constructed by termites of a mud-like substance between the ground and the wood above the ground in which the termite feeds. It is used to protect the termite from the light.

SHERIFF'S DEED A deed given to a buyer at a sheriff's mortgage foreclosure sale. There is a period after the granting of the deed that the owners being foreclosed may redeem the property by paying the debt, interest, and costs.

SHERIFF'S SALE A sale of property that is made by a sheriff as a result of a court order in a foreclosure proceeding.

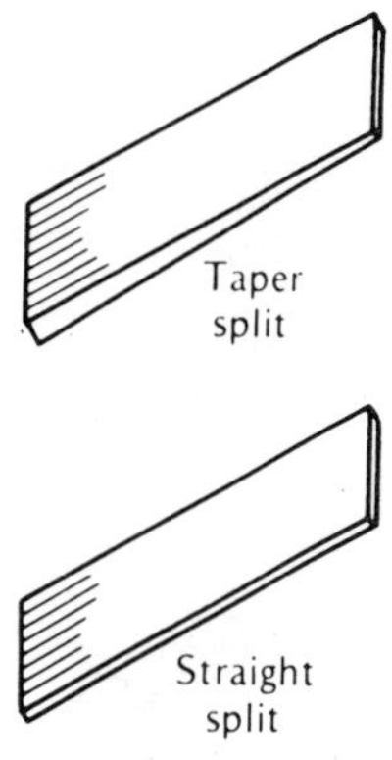

SHAKE

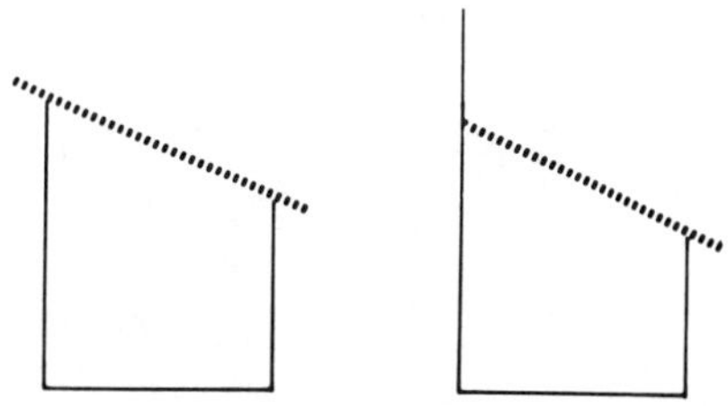

Freestanding **Porch**

SHED ROOF

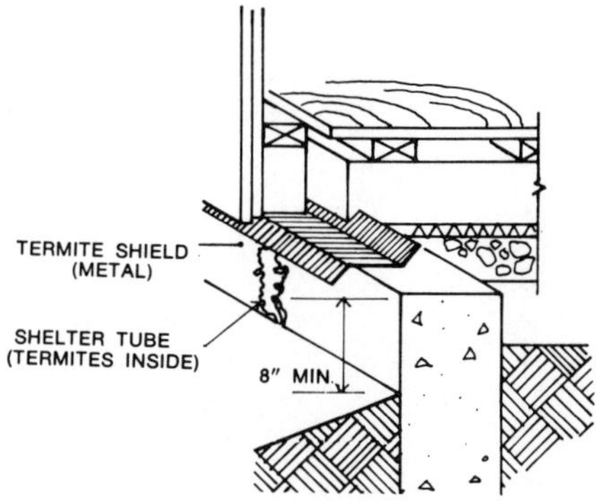

SHELTER TUBE (TERMITE)

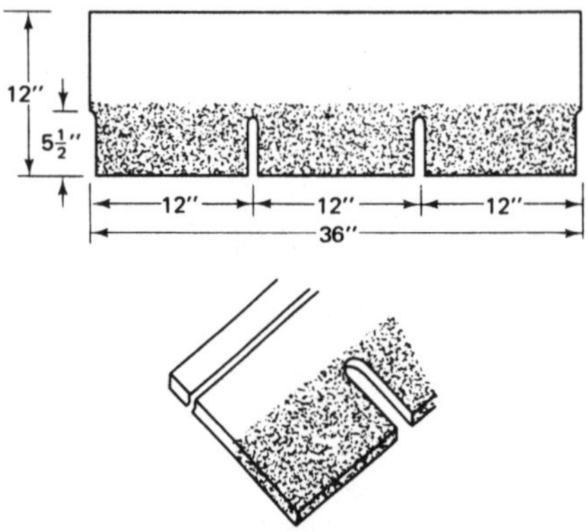

SHINGLES

SHINGLE STYLE

SHINGLES Thin pieces of wood or other material that are tapered and oblong in shape. They are used as wall and roof coverings.

SHINGLE STYLE A nineteenth-century American house style developed and popularized in New England in the 1880s that eventually spread throughout the United States. The Shingle Style house is big and box-like with a gable roof, double-hung windows, and several chimneys. As the name suggests, the roof and exterior walls are covered with stained or darkly painted shingles.

CTS SYSTEM: Nineteenth Century American Shingle Style (Shingle-710)

SHIPLAP A type of close, rabbeted joint used to join two boards together. *See* Joints.

SHIPLAP SIDING A type of wooden board siding material with rabbeted edges to make overlapping joints.

SHOE OR SOLE The bottom framing piece of a stud wall laid on top of the rough flooring in platform framing. It is also a type of molding trim used to cover the junction of the floor and wall.

SHOJI The Japanese word for sliding exterior wall panels.

SHOPPING CENTER A group of retail stores with a common parking area or enclosed walkway connecting them.

SHORE LINE The land between the high and low water mark.

SHORING Temporary beams and braces used during construction.

SHORT-LIVED ITEMS The portions of a structure that have a shorter expected economic life than the rest of the structure.

SHORT-TERM CAPITAL GAIN Profit from the sale of a capital asset that is bought and sold within a short period of time and so is not eligible to be treated as a long-term capital gain and, therefore, taxed at a lower income tax rate. The time period is set by Congress and varies from time to time. Usually, it is between six months and one year.

SHORT-TERM LEASE A general term for a lease with a term under five years (in some states) and usually not over ten years.

SHOTCRETING Concrete conveyed at relatively high velocity by pneumatic pressure through a conduit, discharged at high velocity, and forcibly deposited on the receiving surface.

SHOULDER The land, paved or unpaved, along a paved highway for vehicles to use if they must stop.

SHOWER AND TUB ENCLOSURES Enclosures to contain the water from the tub or shower. They should be made of safety glass.

SHOWER HEAD The device in a shower through which water is sprayed.

SHOWERS Devices to spray the body with water, usually from above from a shower head.

SHOWER STALL LIGHTING Lighting in the shower stall. The switches should be out of arm's reach from the shower or tub to avoid a shock hazard.

SHUTTERS Movable covers used to cover a window or other opening.

SIDE The longitudinal wall of a structure.

SIDE DITCH A water course alongside a highway that may be paved with portions of pipe or simply made of dirt or grass.

SIDE JAMB The vertical piece that forms the side of a door opening.

SIDE LIGHTS Pieces of glass at the sides of the front entrance door.

SIDEWALKS Pedestrian walks paved with cement along a driveway, leading to a house or leading to the street.

SIDING **1.** Lumber, aluminum, asphalt, etc., used to surface exterior walls. **2.** Railroad track connected to the main track and used for loading and unloading storage, etc.

SIDING PRODUCTS Materials used for siding, such as wood, shingles, stucco, masonry, and asphalt.

SIGHT LINE The line of vision in a theater, auditorium, or other spectator seating between a seat and the stage area. The seat is characterized as restricted when this line of sight is blocked by a column, overhang, or anything else impeding the vision of a spectator in the seat.

SHUTTERS

SIDE LIGHTS

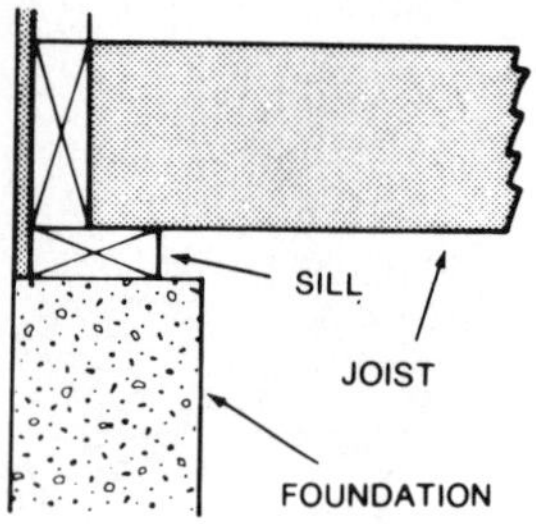

SILL

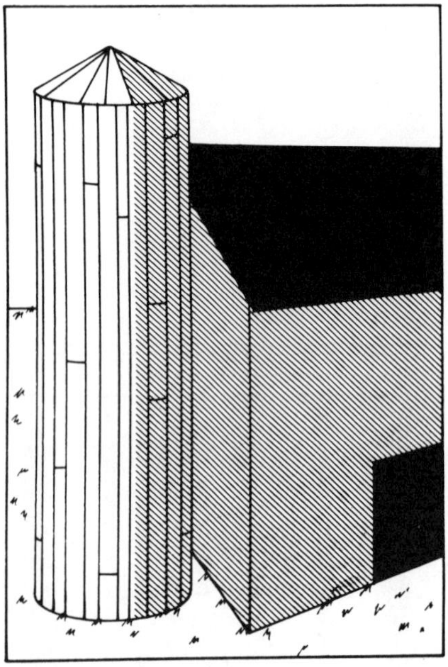

SILO

SIGHT LINE EASEMENT An easement that protects the line of sight over an adjoining property from being obstructed by a building or other obstruction, such as a tree or shrub.

SIGN Advertisement put on a property to indicate the property is for sale, lease, etc. Signs are the second best form of advertising and are only slightly behind classified newspaper ads in effectiveness.

SIGNATURE A person's name written on an instrument.

SIGNED, SEALED, AND DELIVERED A phrase meaning that everything necessary to convey has been performed by the grantor. Commonly, only governments, corporations, and notaries use seals.

SILAGE *See* Ensilage.

SILL A framing member placed on top of the foundation wall that serves as a level base for the wall studs and floor joists. *See also* Window Sill and Door Sill.

SILL COCK *See* Bibcock.

SILL PLATE *See* Sill.

SILO Generally, a tall, cylindrical structure used for storage of corn, etc.

SILT Minute soil grains ranging from .05 to .002 mm in diameter. The individual grains cannot be distinguished by touch.

SIMPLE INTEREST The interest computed on the original principal alone, not on accrued interest.

SIMPLE LISTING *See* Open Listing.

SIMULATION The use of a controlled experimental model to simulate actual conditions.

SIMULTANEOUS ISSUE The writing of two title insurance policies on the same property at the same time by a title insurance company, one for the property owner and one for the mortgage lender.

SINGLE A person who is not presently married.

SINGLE-FAMILY HOUSE A building designed to house one family only.

SINGLE-PIPE INDIVIDUAL TAKE-OFF HEATING SYSTEM A type of hot-water heating system where the radiators are connected by a single pipe in a loop. Each radiator is connected to the loop with an individual take-off pipe and shut-off valve.

SINGLE-PITCH ROOF A single-plane roof pitched at more than 20 degrees.

SINGLE-PURPOSE PROPERTY *See* Special Purpose Property.

SINK A plumbing fixture that consists of a basin, drain, and water supply.

SINKING FUND Money set aside to be used for necessary replacement of improvements.

SINKING FUND FACTOR A factor that is used to calculate the amount per period that will have to be deposited at a given interest rate in order to obtain a specified amount in a given number of years. The amount per period is determined by multiplying the desired amount by the factor.

SINKING FUND METHOD A way to recover the value of an asset by establishing a sinking fund.

SIPHON A tube used to carry water from an irrigation ditch to a field.

SIPHON ACTION TOILET A toilet in which the flushing action is assisted by a jet of water.

SITE A plot of land that is improved or is suitable for building purposes.

SITE ANALYSIS The study of a site and its surroundings to determine its suitability for a specific purpose.

SITE DEVELOPMENT Improvements, such as utility installation, that must be made to a site to make it suitable for construction.

SITE DEVELOPMENT COST The cost involved in preparing a site for use.

SITE WORK Productive effort designed to improve an area or tract of land, a part of which is the exact plot upon which a building or service facility is, has been, or is to be located.

SITING The placement of a house in relation to its lot.

SITUS Location, place.

SIX FUNCTIONS OF ONE DOLLAR The compound interest functions in the standard set of compound interest tables:

SKELETON The frame of a house or other construction.

SKELETON STEEL CONSTRUCTION A type of construction that transmits loads and stresses to the foundations through a steel framework of columns and beams.

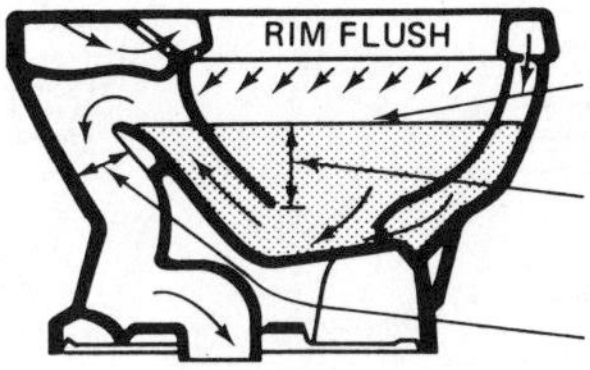

SIPHON ACTION TOILET

Six Functions of a Dollar

1. Amount of one
   (the future worth of one dollar with compound interest)
2. Amount of one per period
   (the future worth of per period with compound interest)
3. Sinking-fund factor
   (the amortization rate)
4. Present worth of one
   (the reversion factor)
5. Present worth one per period
   (inwood coefficients)
6. Partial payment
   (ordinary annuity)

SIX FUNCTIONS OF ONE DOLLAR

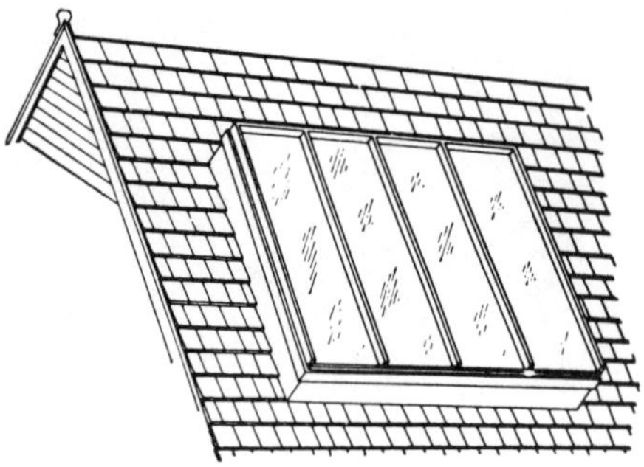

SKYLIGHT

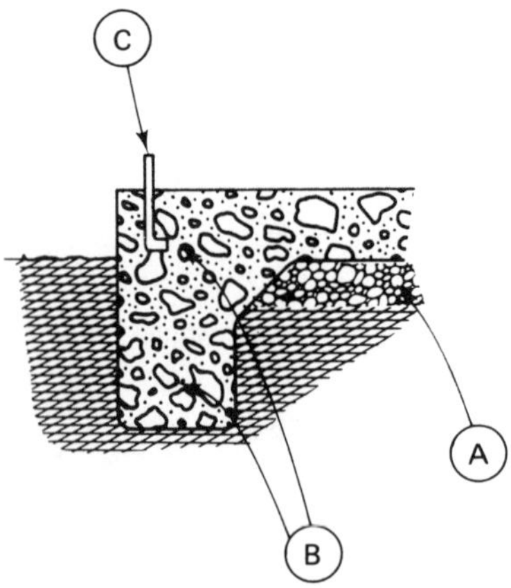

A Firm Subbase of Crushed Rock
B Continuous Reinforcement Rods
C Anchor Bolt

SLAB

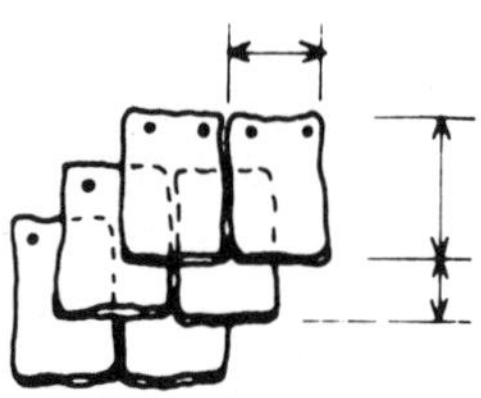

SLATE SHINGLE

SKEWNESS In a distribution, the amount of deviation from symmetry.

SKIN Any outer layer or coating. In construction, it is the outer covering of a building.

SKIN WALL An external wall covering.

SKYLEASE A long-term lease for the air and space above a real property.

SKYLIGHT An opening in a ceiling covered with plastic or glass, and used to admit light to the space below.

SLAB **1.** A concrete, ground-level floor that is part of the foundation. **2.** Any concrete floor.

SLAB-ON-GROUND A type of basementless foundation made by pouring concrete directly on the prepared ground surface and over the top of the footings.

SLAG A molten mass of fluxes and impurities that floats to the surface and is removed during the making of steel.

SLAG WOOL *See* Mineral Wool.

SLANDER OF TITLE The making of false, malicious statements regarding a person's interest in a property that cause damage to the third person against whom the statements were made.

SLASH The debris left on the ground after logging such as bark, stumps, branches, etc. It is also the debris resulting from wind or fire.

SLASHING A forest area upon which branches and tops of trees have been left after logging or a forest that is full of debris caused by fire and wind.

SLATER'S FELT An asphaltic paper that is laid over sheathing to be an underlayment for slate.

SLATE SHINGLE A shingle made of slate.

SLEEPER **1.** A horizontal timber to which flooring is nailed. **2.** Any horizontal timber used to distribute and support weight.

SLIDING WINDOW *See* Traverse Window.

SLIP Space between two docks or piers. It is generally where small boats are kept.

SLOPE The degree of deviation from a horizontal surface.

SLOPE EASEMENT An easement that permits the sloping of the land that adjoins a highway.

SLOPE RATIO The incline of a slope expressed in terms of horizontal distance per unit of vertical rise or fall. For example, 2 feet horizontal to 1 foot vertical would be designated as 2 to 1 or 2:1.

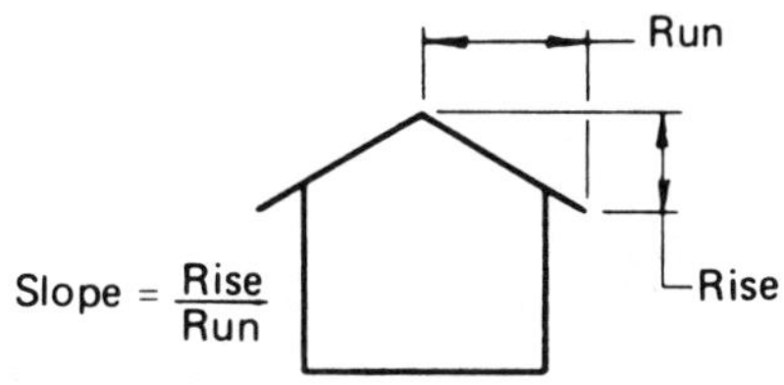

SLOPE RATIO

SLOPING FLOORS Floors that are no longer level because of settling of the building or defects in the framing system.

SLOW-BURNING CONSTRUCTION Mill construction.

SLUM AREA An area marked by overpopulation, poverty, and blight.

SLUM CLEARANCE The elimination of blighted improvements by the destruction of the improvements.

SLUMP Degree of wetness of concrete related to workability, i.e., a consistency measurement.

SLUMP TEST A rough measure of the consistency of concrete.

SMOKE CHAMBER A large space over the damper that prevents smoke from backing up into the fireplace.

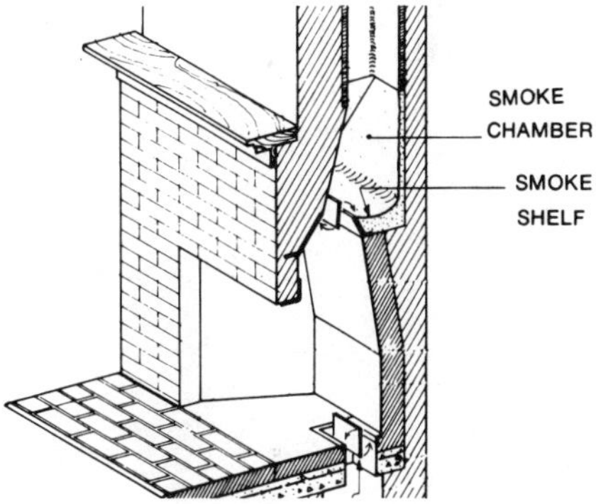

SMOKE CHAMBER

SMOKE SHELF A part of a fireplace that prevents cold air from flowing down the inside of a chimney into the fireplace.

SNOW FENCE A temporary fence placed alongside a road during the winter to keep snow from drifting onto the road.

SOAP HOLDER A bathroom fixture to hold soap bars over the sink, shower, and tub.

SOCIETY OF INDUSTRIAL REALTORS (SIR) A society that serves Realtors® who specialize in marketing industrial property and meeting the real estate needs of industry.

SOCIETY OF REAL ESTATE APPRAISERS A large, international trade organization of real estate appraisers. It awards the SRA (Senior Residential Appraiser), SRPA (Senior Real Property Appraiser), and SREA (Senior Real Estate Analyst) designations.

SOFFIT The exposed undersurface of an arch, stairway, balcony, lintel, or vault.

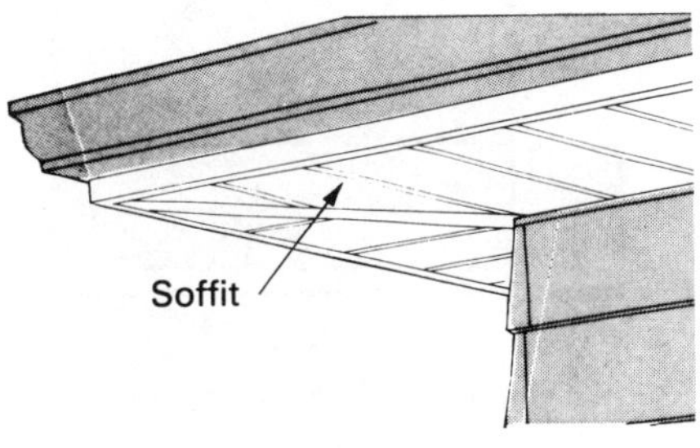

SOFFIT

SOFTWOOD Wood from trees known as conifers or coniferous because they have cones and usually needlelike leaves, which are always green. It does not refer to the softness of the wood. Pines, cedars, and firs are commonly used in house construction for structural and framing lumber, sheathing, and exterior siding.

SOFTWOOD PLYWOOD A type of plywood used extensively in house construction.

SOIL The top layer of earth. It is composed of organic and mineral materials in which plants grow.

SOIL BANK A federal program administered by the Commodity Stabilization Service that pays farmers for not growing crops or growing non-commercial vegetation in order to avoid surpluses and conserve the soil.

SOIL EROSION *See* Erosion.

SOIL LINE A vertical wastepipe that receives waste from the toilet.

SOIL MAP A map that shows the location and type of soils in a given area.

SOIL PIPE A sewer pipe that carries waste from a building to the sewer main.

SOIL POROSITY The degree to which soil is porous, expressed as the percentage of the total volume that is unfilled by solid materials.

SOIL PRODUCTIVITY The capacity that a soil has to produce crops in its own environment and under a specific farming system.

SOIL SATURATION A soil mass may be visualized as a compressible skeleton containing voids, which, in the case of saturated soils, are filled with water.

SOIL STACK The vertical pipe that receives waste from all the plumbing fixtures and appliances.

SOLAR ENERGY Energy derived from the sun. The sun's energy is collected by pipes or flat metal sheets that are painted or treated to increase their ability to absorb heat. The heat is then distributed through a standard heating system or one built especially for solar energy.

SOLAR HEAT Heating through the harnessing and use of the sun's energy.

SOLAR HEATING SYSTEMS Heating systems that rely on solar energy for an energy source.

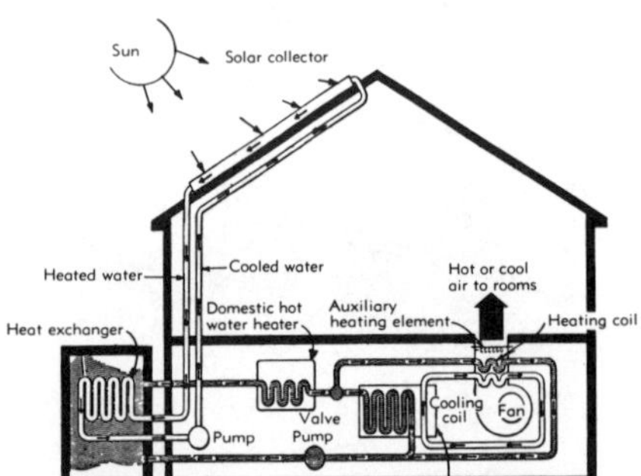

SOLAR HEATING SYSTEMS

SOLAR HOUSE A post-World-War-II American house that is designed to utilize the high summer and low winter sun. Solar houses use glass windows in a great portion of the exterior walls and overhanging eaves on the windows of both floors.

CTS SYSTEM: Post World War II American
Functional Modern or
Contemporary
(Fun Modern or Contemp-903)

SOLAR HOUSE

SOLE PLATE, SOLE PIECE, SOLE The bottom horizontal framing member of a stud wall that rests on rough floor in brace framing.

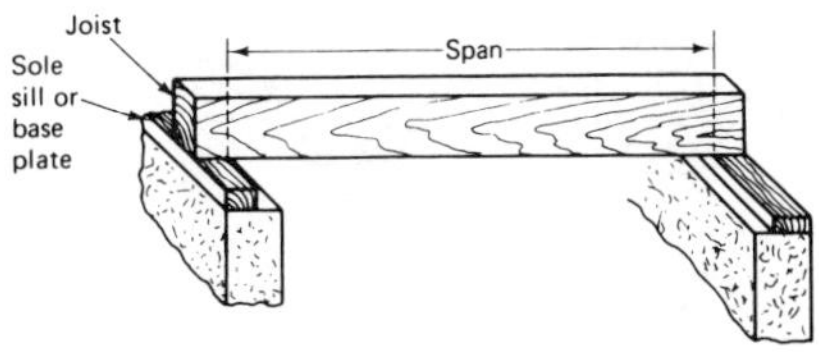

SOLE PLATE, SOLE PIECE, SOLE

SOLID CONCRETE MASONRY UNITS Another name for bricks.

SOLID MASONRY WALLS. A type of masonry wall, which, if well constructed, is durable and easily maintained.

SOLID VINYL TILE A type of tile that is durable, quiet, and has good resistance to stains and grease and fair resistance to cuts and burns. Solid vinyl tiles are easy to maintain. They tend to be more expensive than vinyl asbestos tile.

SONIC Pertaining to sound.

SOUND VALUE In fire insurance evaluation, sound value is synonymous with depreciated costs.

SOUTHERN COLONIAL A colonial American house style that combines both Georgian and New England Colonial in a way to suit the warmer southern climate. The Southern Colonial is a large, two-to-three story house with a colonnade extending across the front. The classic example of a Southern Colonial is Mount Vernon, built in the 1700s. Other distinguishing characteristics of the Southern Colonial are a shingled hip or gable roof, cornices with dentils, a symmetrical shape, a second-story balcony, a balustrade, and belvederes.

CTS SYSTEM: Colonial American
Southern Colonial
(South Co-113)

SOUTHERN COLONIAL

SPACE DESIGN The designing of the interior space of a building to meet the needs of the user.

SPACE HEATER A small heater with a powerful fan used to heat a room or supplement existing heating.

SPACER

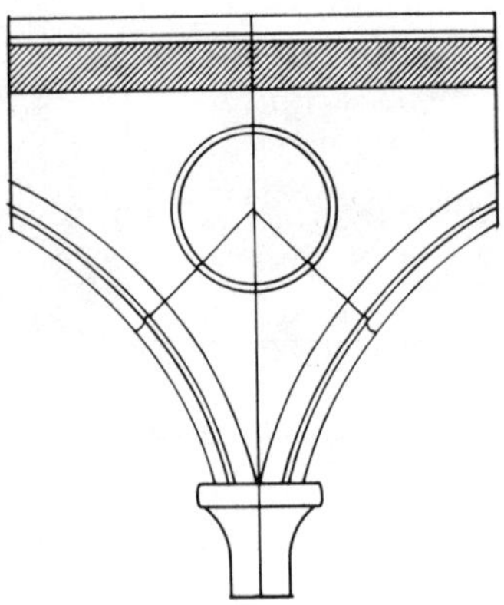

SPANDREL

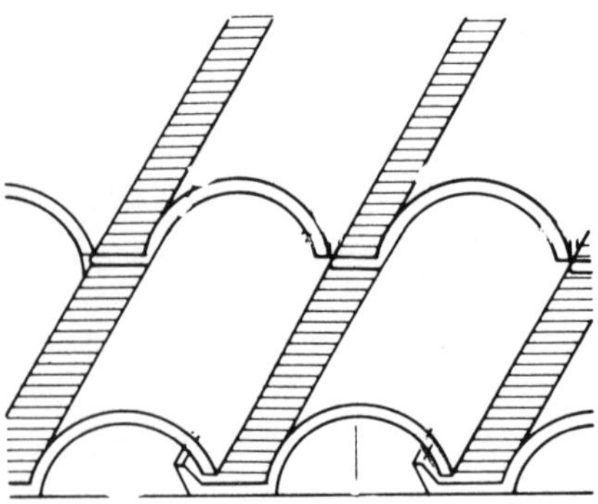

SPANISH TILE

SPANISH VILLA STYLE

SPACER A small piece of wood or other material placed on the edges of glass to help center it during installation and to maintain uniform width of sealant beads while preventing sealant distortion.

SPAN **1.** The distance between two terminals of a construction. **2.** The distance between structural supports, such as walls, columns, girders, and piers.

SPANDREL **1.** The triangular area between two adjacent arches and the line connecting their crowns. **2.** The space, in a multi-story building, between the top of a window in one story and the sill of the window in the story above. **3.** The triangular space below a stair string.

SPANDREL STRIP A triangular step such as that found in a circular staircase.

SPANISH TILE A type of interlocking tile. *See also* Mission Tile.

SPANISH VILLA STYLE A house style greatly influenced by Spanish architecture that is very popular in the warmer regions of the United States and is found with surprising frequency in the North, too, considering that it is really not suitable for cold climates. The Spanish Villa is an asymmetrical, one-to-three story house with painted stucco exterior walls and a red tile roof. Other distinguishing characteristics are oval top windows and doors and patios completely enclosed by exterior walls.

CTS SYSTEM: Latin
Spanish Villa
(Sp Villa-501)

SPECIAL ASSESSMENT A charge against a real estate made by a public authority to help pay for improvements, such as sidewalks and sewers, from which the real estate benefits.

SPECIAL BENEFITS The benefits received by the remaining untaken portion of a property that has been condemned for a public improvement. The benefits are caused by the construction of the improvement.

SPECIAL BRANCH CIRCUITS Circuits for appliances, such as heaters, air conditioners, ovens, and dishwashers, that use a large amount of electricity.

SPECIAL EXCEPTIONS (ZONING) Special exceptions in typical zoning codes acknowledge that it may be in the community interest to allow certain uses in a zone that do not fit the predominant permitted use. For example, a school, drugstore, food shop, or religious facility might be desirable exceptions in a one- or two-family zone. A special exception *must* be granted unless the zoning board can show that the proposed use may be harmful. A variance, on the other hand, is only granted when hardship can be proven.

SPECIALIST IN REAL ESTATE SECURITIES (SRS) Designation awarded by the Real Estate Securities and Syndication Institute.

SPECIAL PURPOSE OUTLET An electric outlet connected directly to the distribution box on its own circuit. It often has higher voltage and amperage than the regular outlets in the building.

SPECIAL PURPOSE PROPERTY A building, such as a hospital or church, that is limited by its design to one purpose and cannot be used for other than the original purpose without extensive remodeling.

SPECIAL USE PERMIT A permit provided for in many zoning regulations to allow uses that are in the community interest. In order to obtain this type of permit, the owner must demonstrate that there is a community need. However, unlike a variance, it is not necessary to prove that a hardship exists.

SPECIAL WARRANTY DEED A type of deed with a limited warranty by the grantor instead of a general warranty against all claims against the grantee. Generally, the warranty is limited to claims made by the grantor and people acting through him or her.

SPECIFICATIONS Detailed instructions to show a contractor how to proceed with construction. They contain details about materials, methods of installation, and other data that are not shown on the building plans.

SPECIFIC PERFORMANCE An action taken in a court to require one of the parties to a contract to perform as agreed to in the contract as opposed to paying damages for failure to perform.

SPECIFIED DENSITY The measurable control of the voids in a material by identification of the ratio of mass or weight per unit of volume. The specified density should be both a density that can be obtained practicably in construction and can be maintained during the life of the structure.

SPECIALIST IN REAL ESTATE SECURITIES

SPECIMEN TREE

SPLASHPAN

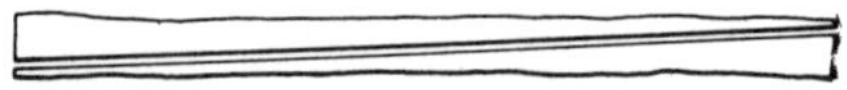

SPLIT AND RESAWN SHAKE

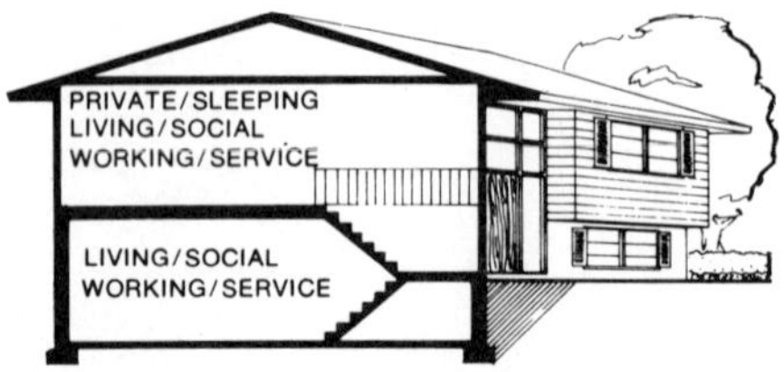

SPLIT ENTRY

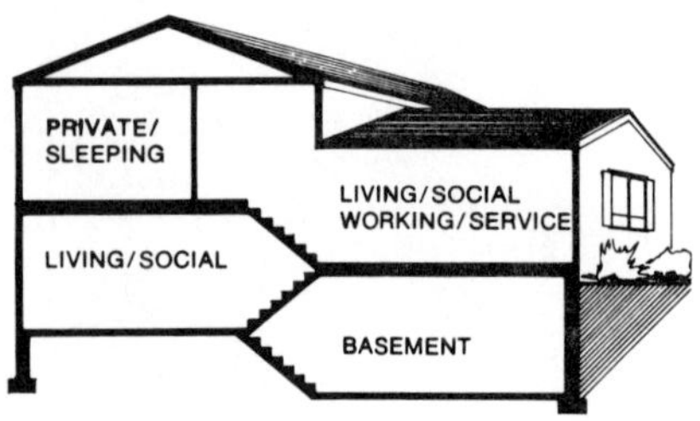

SPLIT-LEVEL HOUSE

SPECIMEN TREE A tree that is planted in a prominent position in a yard due to its special shape or species, such as a weeeping birch, magnolia, or other ornamental tree.

SPECULATION VALUE *See* Potential Value.

SPECULATOR A person who buys real estate in order to make a profit through a rise or fall in price.

SPENDABLE INCOME Net income after taxes.

SPIGOT *See* Faucet

SPITE FENCE A fence built solely for the purpose of annoying a neighbor. The fence may make parking difficult, ruin the view, or just be ugly.

SPLASHBACK A solid masonry block placed below a downspout to carry away water and prevent erosion.

SPLASHPAN A masonry slab that is placed at the bottom of a downspout to divert the flow of water away from the side of a building.

SPLIT AND RESAWN SHAKE A shake that is made from a block of wood that is sawn into two shakes. One side is rough, and one side is smooth.

SPLIT ENTRY A house type in which the basement is raised out of the ground several feet in order to give the basement greater light and make it usable as living space. The layout usually keeps traffic out of the living room. A common problem with this type is that the basement may be cold and damp and difficult to keep at even temperatures.

SPLIT-LEVEL HOUSE A house that has different levels but no level is one complete story higher than another.

SPLIT RATE An appraisal term for a capitalization rate that is made up of two different rates. One rate is for the land portion of the property, and the other is for that income that is produced by the improvements.

SPLIT RATE CAPITALIZATION *See* Split Rate.

SPLIT RATE INTEREST *See* Split Rate.

SPOTLIGHT A light with special bulbs or reflectors that focus the light into a limited area.

SPOT SURVEY A survey that shows the location and size of buildings on a property.

SPOT ZONING A change in zoning that permits non-conforming use in an area zoned for a different specific purpose.

SPOUSE One's wife or husband.

SPREADER DAM A dam designed to divert water to either side, spreading it over a given area.

SPRINKLER SYSTEM **1.** In reference to residential property, an underground system for watering grass. **2.** In commercial or industrial buildings, a system of pipes and heat-sensitive valves that automatically release water or a chemical in case of fire.

SPUR TRACK A piece of railroad track that is usually only connected at one end to a main track and services an industrial plant or site that has no regular train service.

SQUARE **1.** In the Rectangular Survey System, an area sometimes called a *check,* which measures 24 miles by 24 miles. **2.** In roofing or siding, 10 feet × 10 feet (100 sq. ft.)

SQUARE FOOT COST A unit cost that is obtained by dividing the total cost of a building or site or combination of both by the number of square feet in the same unit.

SQUARE FOOT METHOD A method for estimating the cost to reproduce or replace improvements where the square foot area of the improvements is multiplied by their cost per square foot.

SQUATTER A person who inhabits another's land without authority of the owner or right to possession.

SQUATTER'S RIGHTS The right to occupy land created by long and undisturbed use. In the nature of common law, a squatter does not have any legal title or arrangement and cannot acquire any because the squatter claims no interest adverse to the owner. It is not to be confused with adverse possession.

SRA (SENIOR RESIDENTIAL APPRAISER) A designation awarded by the Society of Real Estate Appraisers to members who are skilled in making residential appraisals.

SREA (SENIOR REAL ESTATE ANALYST) A designation awarded by the Society of Real Estate Appraisers to members who are skilled in making real estate analyses.

SRPA (SENIOR REAL PROPERTY APPRAISER) A designation

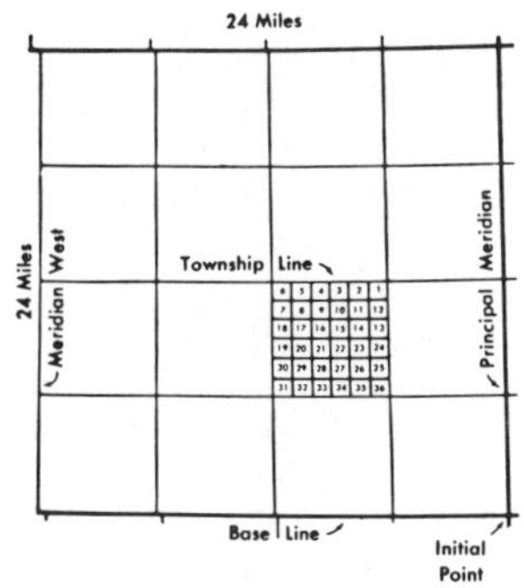

SQUARE

SENIOR RESIDENTIAL APPRAISER

SENIOR REAL ESTATE ANALYST

SENIOR REAL PROPERTY APPRAISER

awarded by the Society of Real Estate Appraisers to members who are skilled in making appraisals of all classes of property.

STABILIZED EXPENSES An appraisal term for the projected expenses shown in the operating statement that is used by the appraiser in the cost approach to value. They are adjusted to show the typical expenses for a year rather than the expenses for a specified year.

STABILIZED INCOME An appraisal term for the projected income of a property in a typical year rather than in any specific year.

STABILIZED VALUE A projected value over a period of normal conditions which does not consider any special conditions that exist at the time of the appraisal that may temporarily affect the value of the property.

STACK Any vertical pipe, such as a wastepipe or vent.

STAGFLATION An economic condition where economic growth is stagnant and there is a large price inflation.

STAGING A temporary platform to hold work, people, and materials during construction.

STAIN A paint applied to wood to enhance the grain.

STAINLESS STEEL A strong alloy of steel that has a large percentage of chromium to which nickel or other alloys may be added. Stainless steel is highly resistant to rust and corrosion.

STAIR **1.** One step in a staircase. **2.** A series of steps attached by landings connecting two or more floors.

STAIR CARRIAGE *See* Stringer.

STAIRCASE A flight of stairs from one floor to the next one above or below. It is also used to refer to all the stair parts.

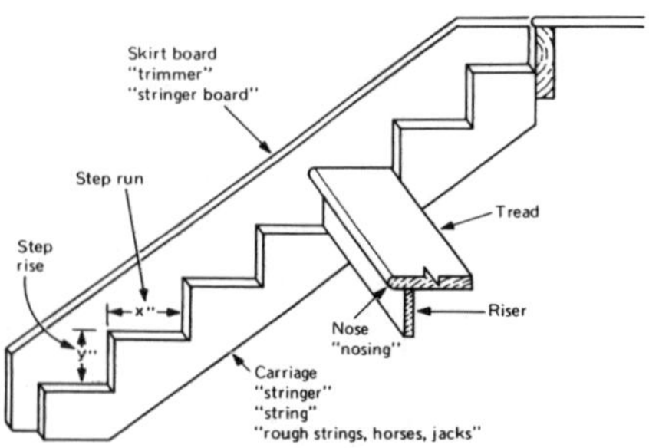

STAIRCASE

STAIR LANDING A platform between two flights of stairs.

STAIRS *See* Staircase.

STAIRWAY One or more flights of stairs and any landings or platforms connected therewith to form a continuous passage from one floor to another.

STANDARD DEPTH The depth of a lot regarded as normal or average for appraisal purposes. It is usually different for particular use categories, such as central business lots, commercial, or residential. Usually, 100 feet is the standard depth for a residential lot.

STANDARD DEVIATION A statistical term used to describe the extent of dispersion in a frequency distribution. It describes how far apart or different the items in a sample are from the average (mean) item.

STANDARD METROPOLITAN STATISTICAL AREA (SMSA) According to the Bureau of Census, a city or cities and their suburbs that have a population of 50,000 or more.

STANDARD PARALLELS East-West survey lines, which establish township boundaries at 24-mile intervals and correct inaccuracies in the government survey due to the curvature of the earth.

STANDARD SHEET GLASS The most common window glass used in houses. The most common types are single strength (single thickness) and double strength (double thickness).

STAND-BY COMMITMENT A commitment made by a lender who makes long-term permanent mortgages to make such a mortgage on a property under construction when it is completed and rented to an agreed-upon level. It is used by the builder to obtain construction financing.

STANDING MORTGAGE A mortgage that demands interest payments only, with the entire principal due in one payment at the maturity of the mortgage.

STANDING TIMBER Uncut timber; trees.

STARTER COURSE The first row of shingles or shakes.

STARTER FELT UNDERLAYMENT The first layer of felt underlayment on a shingle roof that is installed at the edge of the roof under the first row of shingles.

STARTER STRIP The first layer of roofing material attached along a line adjacent to the eaves.

STARTS The number of houses or other classes of real estate on which construction has begun in a specific period of time.

STATE ROAD A road under the jurisdiction of the state.

STATUTE A law enacted and established by the legislative body of government rather than by court cases.

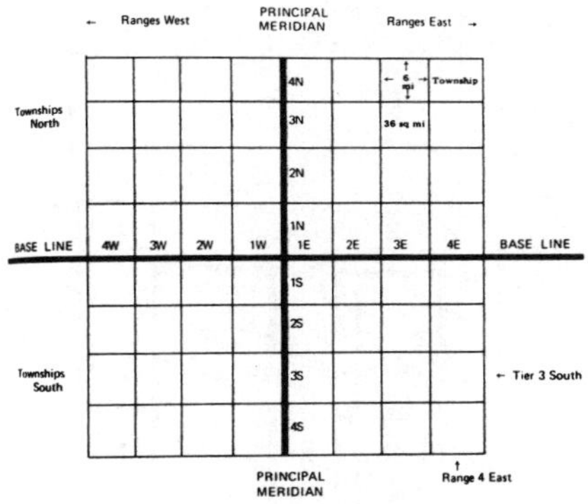

STANDARD PARALLELS

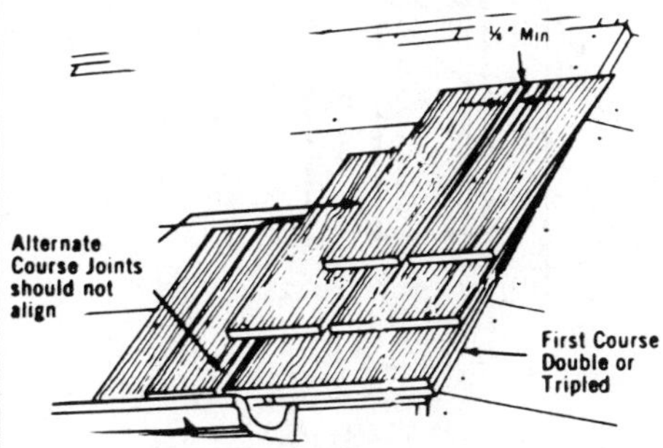

STARTER COURSE

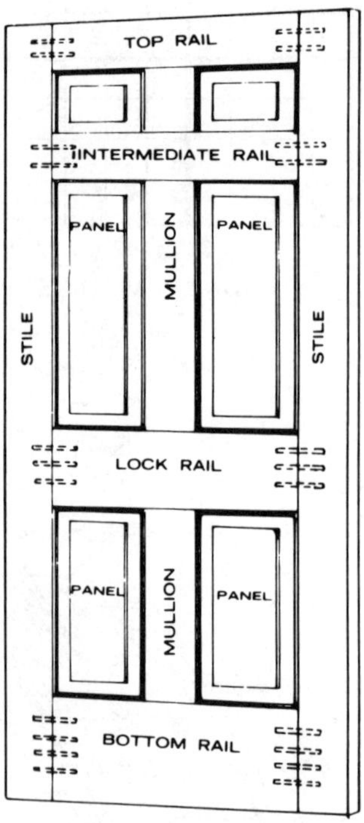

STILE

STATUTE OF FRAUDS State laws that require certain contracts to be in writing to be enforceable. All contracts for the sale of real property and leases for more than one year must be in writing.

STATUTE OF LIMITATIONS Statutes that prevent all right of court action (civil or criminal) after a certain specified period of time from the time when the action occurred.

STATUTORY LIEN An involuntary lien against a party by the operation of a statute, including tax, judgment, and mechanic's liens.

STATUTORY RESERVE Reserve funds that banks, savings and loans, and similar businesses must keep by law to insure their capacity for meeting demands for funds.

STEAM HEATING SYSTEM A type of heating system that produces heat by using a boiler with a firebox beneath it. The water boils, and its steam is forced by pressure through pipes into the radiators.

STEEL BEAMS AND COLUMNS Beams and columns made of steel. Because of their great strength, steel beams can be used to span great distances, but they have relatively low resistance to heat.

STEEP LAND Land that has slopes ranging from 30 percent to 45 percent.

STEP LEASE *See* Step-up Lease.

STEP-UP LEASE A graded lease; a lease that permits increases and decreases in rent at set, predetermined intervals.

STICK STYLE *See* Carpenter Gothic.

STILE **1.** An upright structural member of a frame, door, or window sash, synonymous with a rail. **2.** A series of steps for crossing a fence or wall.

STOCK COOPERATIVE *See* Cooperative.

STONE MULLIONS A vertical stone member that separates and often supports windows, doors, and panels set in a series.

STONE SIDING Siding made of stone.

STOOL A shelf-like support base of wood at the bottom of a window.

STOPCOCK *See* Bibcock.

STORE A place where goods are stocked and sold to customers by a merchant, who is engaged in buying the goods in wholesale quantities and selling them in retail quantities.

STORM DRAINAGE SYSTEM Facilities, structures, appurtenances, pipes, channels, and natural watercourse improvements to collect, convey, and dispose of surface run-off to an outlet.

STORM SASH (STORM WINDOW) A window placed on the outside of another window for additional protection against the weather.

STORM SEWERS A sewer used to carry off excess rainwater. Sometimes, a storm sewer will carry industrial wastes, although this practice is now forbidden in many areas.

STORM WATER, STORM WATER RUN-OFF Excess water from precipitation that flows along the surface due to gravity. It is absorbed through infiltration or remains in puddles or pools.

STORM WINDOWS *See* Storm Sash.

STORY That portion of a building between a floor and the next floor above or the roof.

STORY, FIRST (FIRST FLOOR) The lowest story, which is primarily above exterior grade on one or more sides, containing at least 50 percent living accommodations or related non-residential uses. Stories below grade used for storage, parking, mechanical equipment, or other services are considered basement stories. Related non-residential uses include laundry space, recreation or hobby rooms, commercial use, and related corridor space.

STORY, HALF A story finished as living accommodations located wholly or partly within the roof frame and having a floor at least half as large as the story below. Space with less than five feet of clear headroom shall not be considered as floor area.

STORY, TOP The story between the uppermost floor and the ceiling or roof above.

STRAIGHT LEASE A lease for a fixed period of time at a set rental that is not subject to adjustment or escalation.

STRAIGHT LINE CAPITAL RECAPTURE *See* Straight Line Recapture.

STRAIGHT LINE DEPRECIATION A method of depreciating assets over their estimated life in equal annual amounts.

STRAIGHT LINE METHOD *See* Straight Line Depreciation.

STRAIGHT LINE RECAPTURE A method of recovering the capital invested in an asset over a specified period of time. The annual amount to be recaptured is calculated by dividing the total capital to be recovered by the number of years over which the capital is to be recovered. Each recovery amount is equal.

STRAIGHT-TERM MORTGAGE A mortgage in which the principal is due in one lump sum at maturity.

STRAW MAN A person who acts for another, but not openly, to hide the identity of the person or party for whom he or she is acting.

STREAM Water that flows through a channel or bed, such as a river or brook.

STREET Technically, the distance between property lines. Commonly, it is a term that means any paved, urban road.

STREET IMPROVEMENTS Improvements concerning a street that are usually provided and maintained by local government, such as paving, sewers, or sidewalks.

STRESS The forces (pressures) that act on a structural member.

STRESSED SKIN Design that joins frame and skin or sheathing so that the skin helps in resisting strains.

STRESSED-SKIN FLOOR PANELS Floor panels that are made by bonding plywood skins to framing members.

STRETCHER A brick, stone, or block laid in a wall so that its side is facing outward and is the exposed surface.

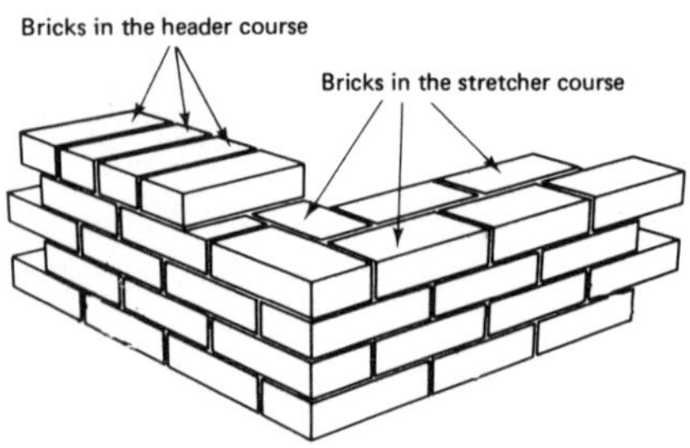

STRETCHER

STRIATED PLYWOOD A type of plywood.

STRICT FORECLOSURE A type of foreclosure action taken by a court which determines that, after a period of redemption, all the interests of the property owner terminate, and the property is turned over to the creditors.

STRINGER An inclined structural member that is shaped to support the treads and risers of a staircase.

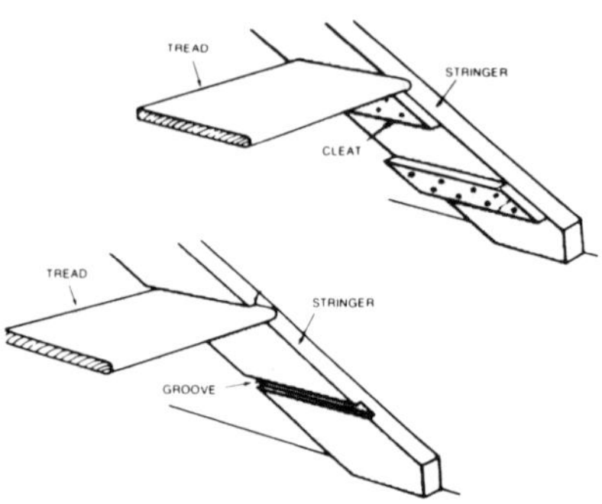

STRINGER

STRINGPIECE A long timber used as horizontal support.

STRIP CENTER A small shopping area consisting of a row of stores with a common parking area. A strip center does not usually have a major department store or large chain grocery store.

STRIP DEVELOPMENT The commercial development of city thoroughfares when the street is lined by a nearly continuous strip of stores and services. It also refers to a strip center. *See also* Strip Center.

STRIP FLOORING Hardwood flooring consisting of narrow, tongue and groove strips. Commonly used woods are maple, oak, and mahogany.

STRIP LUMBER Lumber cut less than two inches thick and eight inches wide.

STRUCK JOINT **1.** A masonry joint made by removing excess mortar with a stroke of a trowel. **2.** A masonry joint in which the mortar slopes downward and inward from the bottom edge of the upper brick. **3.** A weather-struck joint.

STRUCTURAL CLAY TILE A hollow masonry unit formed from mixtures of burnt clay, shale, and fire clay. Structural clay tile has parallel cells or cores within it.

STRUCTURAL CONCRETE Concrete that is specifically mixed and poured to bear a structural load.

STRUCTURAL FACING TILE Ceramic masonry tile used in exterior and interior unplastered walls, partitions, etc.

STRUCTURAL LUMBER Lumber more than two inches thick and four inches wide.

STRUCTURE A building or edifice.

STRUT A wooden brace placed between two other pieces to support a vertical load or horizontal pressure.

STUCCO A cement or plaster wall covering that is installed wet and dries into a hard surface coating.

STUDS A series of vertical wall or partition framing members spaced not more than 24 inches on center.

STYLE Used in the CTS System to describe the design of a house based on historical or contemporary fashion.

SUBBASE **1.** The lowest part of a structural base containing two or more horizontal pieces. **2.** The bed of crushed rock, sand, or gravel used as a base under a slab or roadway.

SUBCHAPTER "S" CORPORATION An entity receiving the

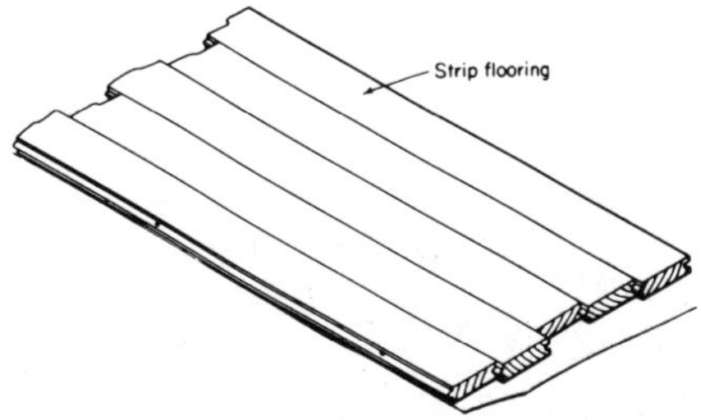

Side Matched Strip Flooring

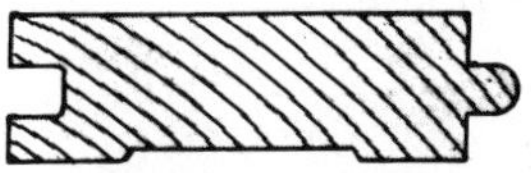

Section of Matched Strip Flooring

STRIP FLOORING

List of Common House Styles

- Colonial American
- English
- French
- Swiss
- Latin
- Oriental
- Nineteenth Century American
- Early Twentieth Century American
- Post World War II American

STYLE

protection of the corporate form but being taxed as a partnership.

SUBCONTRACTOR A contractor who contracts from another (most often a general contractor), such as a cement contractor or a plumbing contractor.

SUBDIVIDER *See* Developer.

SUBDIVIDING Division of a large parcel of land into smaller parcels.

SUBDIVISION An area of land that has been subdivided into parcels suitable for building.

SUBDIVISION MAP A map that must be submitted to the proper authority for approval in order to establish a subdivision.

SUBFLOOR A floor laid over the floor joist. The finish flooring is attached to the subflooring.

SUBGRADE SUPPORT STRENGTH The measurable capacity of the prepared earth surface to sustain weight, loading, pressure, strain, and wear without failure in accordance with design assumptions relative to its serviceability as a foundation for buildings, structures, pavement bases, or pavements and walks.

SUBJACENT SUPPORT

SUBJACENT SUPPORT An owner's right to have the surface of his land supported by the land under it to prevent collapse. Mining, excavating, etc., on adjoining land might infringe upon this right.

"SUBJECT TO" CLAUSE A clause in a deed which says that title is subject to an existing mortgage. Unlike under an assumption clause, the new owner is not responsible for the mortgage payments. However, if the mortgage is not paid, the mortgagee can foreclose on the property but cannot look to the new owner for a deficiency payment.

SUBLEASE A lease executed by the lessee of a property to a third person for a period of time shorter than the lessee holds it.

SUBLESSEE A person who subleases. *See also* Sublease.

SUBLET *See* Sublease.

SUBMARGINAL LAND Land that is so poor for the purpose of producing crops that the crops produced on it would not pay for their cost of production even if the land were free.

SUBORDINATE To make subject or junior to.

SUBORDINATION To relegate someone, or some legal instrument or security, to a lesser position in respect to a right or security.

SUBORDINATION AGREEMENT A clause in a contract, mortgage, lease, etc., that agrees to make the rights granted by the document subordinate to some other existing rights.

SUBORDINATION CLAUSE A clause in a lease that makes the lease subordinate to a mortgage that is placed on the property after the date of the lease.

SUBROGATION The substitution of one person for another to acquire another's legal rights and remedies. It is used mainly if there is a surety relationship, such as in insurance.

SUBSIDENCE The sinking and settling of the ground surface. Subsidence may be caused by a lowering of the water table due to drought or mining, etc.

SUBSIDIZED HOUSING Housing for low- to moderate-income families for which the families pay for part of the rent, and the government pays for part or else the government aids the developer with his loan interest cost so that the developer can charge lower rents.

SUBSIDY A payment made by the government to a farmer, real estate owner, or tenant to help the party pay part of the cost to produce a product, finance a project, or use a product or property.

SUBSOIL The soil that is immediately below the surface soil.

SUBSTITUTION, PRINCIPLE OF A basic economic principle which states that, all other things being approximately equal, a prudent buyer will purchase the product offered at the lowest price when there is a choice of products available.

SUBSTRUCTURES The foundations of a building that support the superstructure.

SUBSURFACE EASEMENT *See* Subsurface Rights.

SUBSURFACE RIGHTS The rights to minerals and oil, gas, or coal located at specified depths below the ground. The owner of these rights need not be the same as the owner of the fee title to the above surface of the prop-

Example of the Sum of the Years' Digits Method of Depreciation

Example: Remaining useful life: 10 years
(Long Formula)
1st Year:

$$\frac{10}{10+9+8+7+6+5+4+3+2+1} = \frac{10}{55} = 18.18\%$$

2nd Year: $\frac{9}{55} = 16.36\%$

5th Year: $\frac{5}{55} = 9.09\%$

10th Year: $\frac{1}{55} = 1.82\%$

(Short Formula)
(especially useful for long life property)

$$\frac{\text{Useful life} \times (1 + \text{Useful life})}{2} = \text{fraction denominator}$$

Example: 10 Years

$$\frac{10 \times (1+10)}{2} = \frac{110}{2} = 55$$

1st Year: $\frac{10}{55} = 18.18\%$

Example: 30 Years

$$\frac{30 \times (1+30)}{2} = \frac{930}{2} = 465$$

1st Year: $\frac{30}{465} = 6.45\%$

SUM OF THE YEAR'S DIGITS METHOD

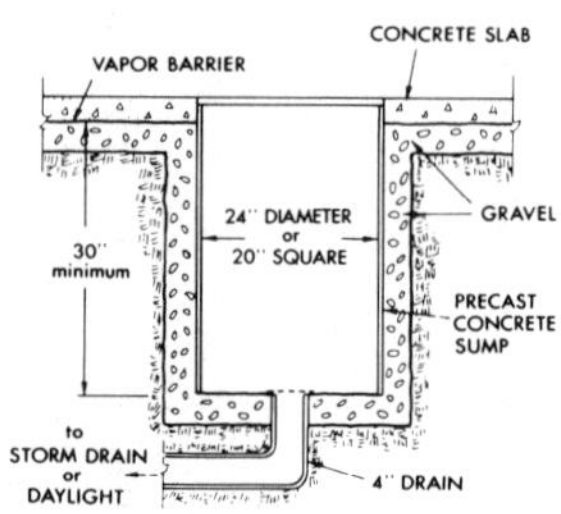

SUMP

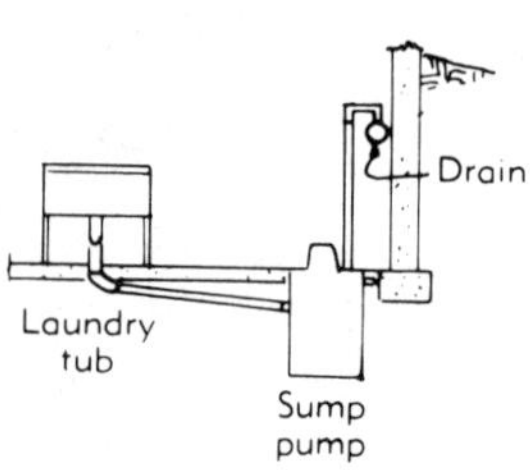

SUMP PUMP

erty. These rights may be in the form of ownership or easements.

SUBTERRANEAN TERMITE *See* Termite.

SUBURBAN The area around a city that is usually residential and blends the urban and the rural.

SUBURBS Areas that develop on the peripheries of a city.

SUCCESSION The transmitting of real property by will or inheritance as opposed to passing it by grant, deed, or other method of purchase.

SUFFERANCE *See* Tenancy at Sufferance.

SUGAR MAPLE FLOORING A flooring made from sugar maple trees, which produce some of the hardest and most wear-resistant wood.

SUITE A group of rooms in a hotel that contain a minimum of a bedroom, a bathroom, and a sitting room. The rooms are rented as one unit.

SUMMATION An old term still used for the cost approach to value. It is one of the three approaches to value in the appraisal process. The value of the land is added to the depreciated value of the improvements.

SUMMATION APPROACH *See* Cost Approach To Value.

SUMMER COOLING HOURS Operating hours per season (considered to be all hours when the outdoor temperature is 80°F or higher).

SUM OF THE YEAR'S DIGITS METHOD A method of calculating depreciation for tax purposes. The percentage of annual depreciation is calculated by making a fraction. The numerator of the fraction is the years of remaining useful life. The denominator is the sum of the individual years of remaining life. For example, if a property had an estimated remaining useful life of five years, the fraction would be constructed as follows:

$$\frac{5}{5+4+3+2+1} = \frac{5}{15} = 33.3\%$$

The percentage is multiplied by the cost of the improvements to be depreciated to give the first year depreciation.

SUMP A hole or depression to collect water. It is usually found in the basement floor.

SUMP PUMP An automatic electric pump installed in a sump hole that activates as the water in the hole reaches an excessive level and pumps it out to a drainage area.

SUN ANGLES The angles at which the sun's rays hit a house.

SUNDAY LAWS Laws in certain states or localities that forbid business activity on Sunday and that void contracts calling for performance on Sundays.

SUPERADEQUACY Those improvements made to a property that add less value than their cost because they result in an overimprovement of the property in the existing economic market.

SUPERHIGHWAY A limited access highway designed for high-speed traffic.

SUPERMARKET A grocery store that has 20,000 to 40,000 square feet, is often free standing, and is designed so that a wide variety of goods are conveniently displayed for patrons to select without clerical assistance.

SUPERSESSION The changing of use, e.g., parking lot to skyscraper. The economic death and rebirth of a property.

SUPERSTRUCTURE The portion of a structure above the foundation.

SUPPLY Amount available for sale.

SUPPLY AND DEMAND, LAW OF A theory which holds that price varies directly with supply, although not necessarily proportionally.

SUPPORT *See* Lateral Support, Subjacent Support.

SURETY A person or company that agrees to pay money to a third party in the event another party (the principal) fails to act as agreed.

SURETY BOND A bond provided by an individual or company that guarantees to a third party that another party (the principal) will act as agreed.

SURFACE EASEMENT The right to use the surface, and the surface only, of the land, such as for flowage or rights of way.

SURFACE RACEWAY A metal cover placed over wires that run along the floor to protect them from damage.

SURFACE RIGHTS Easements that allow owners of such rights to use the surface of the land in order to obtain access to subsurface elements. They include the right to drill through the surface for oil or to drive a mineshaft to minerals below the surface.

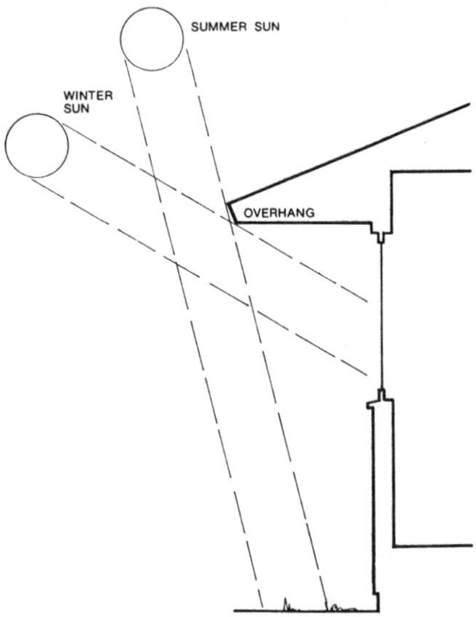

SUN ANGLES

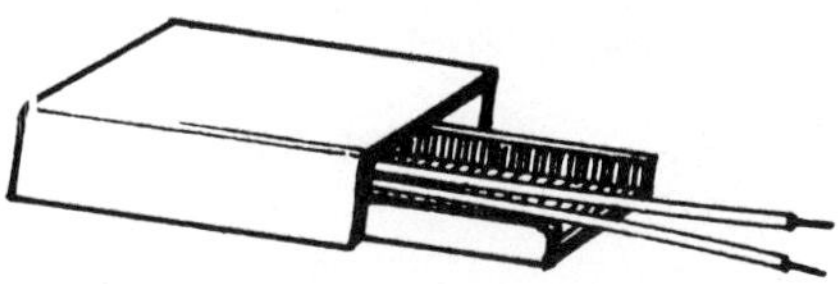

SURFACE RACEWAY

SURFACE WATER Water from any source that appears in a diffused state with no permanent, continuous source of supply or regular course to flow along. It should be distinguished from surface water run-off, which flows along a regular watercourse or drainage facility or has collected into lakes or ponds.

SURPLUS INCOME *See* Excess Rent.

SURPLUS PRODUCTIVITY An economic concept which states that any profit that remains after payment of labor, organization and management, and capital is surplus and is imputable to the land.

SURPLUS PROFITS Extra profit from a business or property that is above what is usually earned by similar properties or businesses. Often, these excess profits are temporary in nature.

SURRENDER The cancellation of a lease through mutual agreement of the lessor and lessee.

SURVEY The process of measuring the size of a piece of land and its quality, i.e., physical features such as grades, contours, structures, etc.

SURVIVORSHIP The gaining of sole interest in a joint interest by outliving the other who had an interest.

SWALE A shallow, open channel for the collection and disposal of excess surface water formed by intersecting slope bases.

SWAMP Boggy, wet land that is heavily vegetated and is often under water.

SWEAT EQUITY A program that allows a purchaser or borrower to do work on the property.

SWIMMING POOL A permanently installed, artificial pool of water, including all appurtenances to its use for swimming or bathing, over 24 inches in depth, with a surface area exceeding 250 square feet.

SWISS CHALET

SWISS CHALET A house style that is a direct copy of the mountain chalets in Switzerland. Swiss Chalets are built mostly as ski lodges in the United States. The Swiss Chalet is a one and one-half to two and one-half story house. It has a gable roof, open porches, and extensive natural woodwork on the exterior.

CTS SYSTEM: Swiss
Swiss Chalet
(Swiss Ch-401)

SWITCHES **1.** Devices that turn electric current on and off. **2.** Devices used to change the direction of railroad trains from one track to another.

SWITCH SITE A property that holds railroad switching facilities or has the right geography and topography to install such facilities.

SYNAGOGUE A Jewish house of worship.

SYNDICATE A group of people, companies, or organizations who join together for the purpose of making an investment.

SYNDICATION The process of joining together people, companies, or organizations into a group that makes investments for the benefit of their mutual interests.

T

TACKING In the process of adverse possession, it is the adding together of successive periods of occupancy by different parties to accumulate sufficient time to establish a claim of adverse possession.

TACKLESS STRIPS Metal strips with hooks placed under the edge of carpeting and fastened to the floor, stairs, etc.

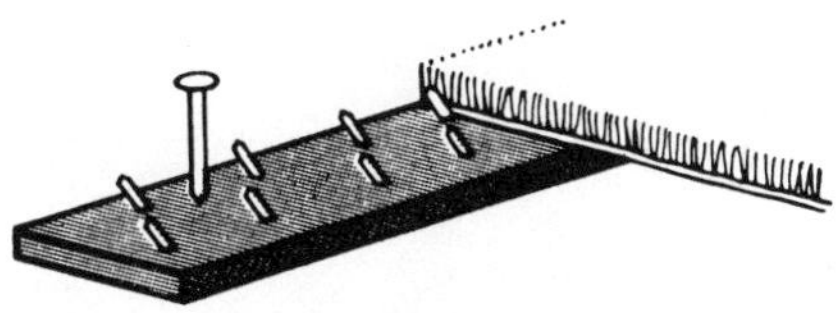

TACKLESS STRIPS

TAIL RACE The channel through which water flows from a mill after it has generated power.

TAKE OUT COMMITMENT An agreement made by a lender to grant a long-term loan on a property after its construction is finished.

TAKE OUT LOAN The long-term financing of real estate when its construction is completed.

TALUS Rocks and rock fragments that slide and roll down a slope, because of the effects of wind, gravity, and rain, and accumulate at the foot of a hill.

TANDEM PLAN A secondary mortgage market arrangement to make more money available for home financing whereby GNMA (Government National Mortgage Association) purchases mortgages at face value (par) and sells them to FNMA (Federal National Mortgage Association), a private corporation, at a discount.

TANGIBLE Property that is of a physical nature and capable of being moved.

TANGIBLE PERSONAL PROPERTY *See* Tangible Property.

TANGIBLE PROPERTY Physical property that may be perceived by the senses, i. e., land, furnishings, merchandise, and cash.

TANGIBLE VALUE The appraisal value of the physical

Example of Tax Free Cash Flow from a Property

Sale price:	$425,000
Downpayment:	$100,000
1st Mortgage:	$325,000
(20 years 14%)	
Income:	
Rents:	$104,300
Other income:	3,400
Total income:	$107,700
Expenses:	
Taxes:	$ 10,500
Insurance:	4,600
Management	2,700
Utilities:	3,100
Maintenance:	3,200
Elevators:	1,200
Heat:	8,200
Air-conditioning:	2,300
Rubbish and snow:	1,800
Reserves:	4,500
Total expenses:	$ 42,100
Net operating income:	$ 65,600
Mortgage payments:	−48,493
Cash flow:	$ 17,107
Operating statement for tax purposes	
Total income:	$107,700
Total expenses:	42,100
Net operating income:	$ 65,600
Mortgage interest:	−45,300
Depreciation:	−31,000
Bookkeeping Profit (Loss)	($17,000)

Note: In this example the property owner received $17,107 tax free cash flow plus a $17,000 loss.

TAX FREE CASH FLOW

property, such as land and buildings, to be distinguished from intangible value, such as a favorable lease.

TAP A faucet; a connection to the water supply.

TATAMI MATS Thick straw mats about three feet by six feet used as floor covering in a Japanese house.

TAX A monetary charge levied on persons or property to support the federal, state, or local government.

TAX ABATEMENT The decrease in the amount of tax improperly levied.

TAXABLE INCOME Income that is subject to income tax.

TAXATION The process whereby the government imposes taxes.

TAX BASE The sum of all the assessed values of properties in a community.

TAX DEED The type of deed in some jurisdictions that is given when a property is sold for unpaid taxes.

TAX EXEMPTION Exemption or partial exemption from the payment of taxes granted to educational, religious, and similar groups. In certain states, partial property tax exemptions are given to veterans and senior citizens.

TAX FREE CASH FLOW Cash income produced by a property that is tax free because it is sheltered by paper losses caused by depreciation.

TAXING DISTRICT The geographical area over which a taxing authority can levy taxes.

TAX LEVY The total income produced by a specified type of tax, such as a real estate tax.

TAX LIEN A lien taken for non-payment of property taxes.

TAX LIST *See* Assessment Roll.

TAX MAP An assessment map; a map that shows the boundaries of individual lots within an assessment jurisdiction.

TAX PARTICIPATION A condition in a lease which states that the lessee pays all or part of the property taxes.

TAX PARTICIPATION CLAUSE A clause in a lease that requires the tenant to share tax increases levied against the property during the term of the lease.

TAXPAYER **1.** Someone who pays taxes. **2.** A structure erected that does not represent the most profitable use of the land and is built for the primary purpose of producing revenue to help meet the taxes on the property.

TAX PENALTY A sum to be paid due to non-payment of taxes.

TAX RATE The ratio of dollars of tax to the value of the tax base.

TAX ROLL A list of every taxpayer subject to a property tax and a description of the taxed parcels, including assessed value and the tax amount.

TAX SALE The sale of property for unpaid taxes. It is usually done through a public auction by a government authority after a certain duration of delinquent payment.

TAX SHELTER Property that provides the owner with income tax deductions because it entails a financial loss of some sort.

TAX STOP A provision in a lease that sets the maximum amount of property tax an owner will pay. Taxes in excess of the specified amount are paid by the tenant.

TAX TITLE A title that is bought by the purchaser at a tax sale.

TEAM TRACK A track on which a railroad places cars for loading and unloading. It is open to use by the public, unlike industrial siding, which is private.

TEMPERED GLASS Glass that is two to four times as strong as regular glass because it has been prestressed by heat and then quenched.

TEMPLE A place of worship for people of Jewish, Christian, or other faiths.

TENANCY **1.** An interest of a tenant in real property consisting of the right to use the property. **2.** A general term for any interest in real property by any type of title.

TENANCY AT SUFFERANCE A tenancy that is created when a tenant fails to vacate the premises at the end of a lease and remains in possession with the landlord's consent. A tenant at sufferance is not a trespasser and cannot claim title by adverse possession.

TENANCY AT WILL A tenancy that can be cancelled at any time by either party giving notice to the other. It is

Example of the Calculation of a Community Tax Rate

Formula:

$$\frac{\text{Budget}}{\text{Total tax base}} = \text{Tax rate}$$

Example:

Total tax base:[1]	$32,565,140
Total budget (to be raised from property taxes)	$912,540

$$\frac{\$912{,}540}{\$32{,}565{,}140} = .028^{2} \text{ Tax Rate}$$

Note 1: The tax base is the total assessment of all the taxable property in the community.

Note 2: In many communities, a tax rate is expressed in Mills (10ths of a cent per dollar of assessment). Therefore, .028% would be 28 Mills

TAX RATE

for an unspecified period of time and often for an unspecified amount of rent. It is created by the owner giving the tenant permission to occupy the property.

TENANCY BY THE ENTIRETY A special tenancy specifically created for ownership by a married couple of property acquired after their marriage. Both spouses have an equal, undivided interest in the property. When either spouse dies, the surviving spouse gets ownership of the entire property without probate and without consideration of the rights of other heirs and creditors.

TENANCY FOR LIFE *See* Life Estate.

TENANCY FOR YEARS *See* Leasehold Estate.

TENANCY IN COMMON A tenancy shared by two or more parties with separate and distinct titles. Each owner has an undivided interest in the whole property. Each owner (co-tenant) is entitled to the undivided possession of the whole property. The interest of each owner does not have to be equal. There is no right of survivorship.

TENANCY IN PARTNERSHIP A form of ownership specifically created by state statutes that permits partnerships to own property in the name of the partnership. In states without this special legislation, title of partnership property is vested in the partners as individuals, not in the partnership.

TENANCY IN SEVERALTY Ownership of the property is vested in only one person. Corporations often hold title this way.

TENANT A person who uses and occupies a real property with the owner's permission, usually under a lease or other rental agreement.

TENANT AT SUFFERANCE *See* Tenancy at Sufferance.

TENANT AT WILL A tenancy of unspecified duration with permission of the property owner at an agreed-upon rent. Either party can terminate the tenancy by giving the other party proper notice.

TENANT CHANGES *See* Tenant Improvements.

TENANT FOR LIFE *See* Life Estate and Life Tenant.

TENANT IMPROVEMENTS Changes or improvements made to suit the needs of tenants. The cost may be paid for by the tenant or the landlord or shared by both.

TENANT IN SEVERALTY *See* Tenancy in Severalty.

TENANT IN TAIL *See* Fee Tail.

TENEMENT The buildings and other improvements on a property.

TENEMENT HOUSE A rundown apartment house. Often, it is overcrowded and has substandard mechanical systems.

TENTATIVE MAP A map of a subdivision that a subdivider submits to a local planning commission for approval and study.

TERM A length of time, such as the term of a mortgage.

TERMINABLE INTERESTS Interests that are liable to end, such as leaseholds.

TERMINAL A point where something can enter or leave. For example, data enter and leave a computer system via a terminal, and vehicles and people enter and leave from a bus terminal.

TERMITE An insect that resembles, but can easily be distinguished from, an ant. It lives underground, migrates into houses, and eats wood. Ants have "elbowed" antenna, stigma on their wings, narrow middles on their bodies, and dissimilar-shaped wings.

TERMITE BARRIER There are five basic types of termite barrier:

1. Specially treated lumber;
2. Properly installed termite shields;
3. Chemical soil treatment;
4. Poured, concrete foundations where no cracks greater than 1/64th of an inch are present;
5. Poured, reinforced concrete caps with cracks no greater than 1/64th of an inch.

TERMITE INSPECTION In certain kinds of sales, a required inspection to determine if termites are present in a structure.

TERMITE RESISTANT WOOD Woods that are naturally termite resistant, such as bald cypress, redwood, and Eastern red cedar.

TERMITE SHIELD A shield made of incorrodible metal or other inorganic material used on top of the foundation wall or around pipes to prevent the infiltration of termites.

TERM MORTGAGE *See* Straight-term Mortgage.

TERMS The considerations and conditions in a contract

differences between winged adult ants and termites

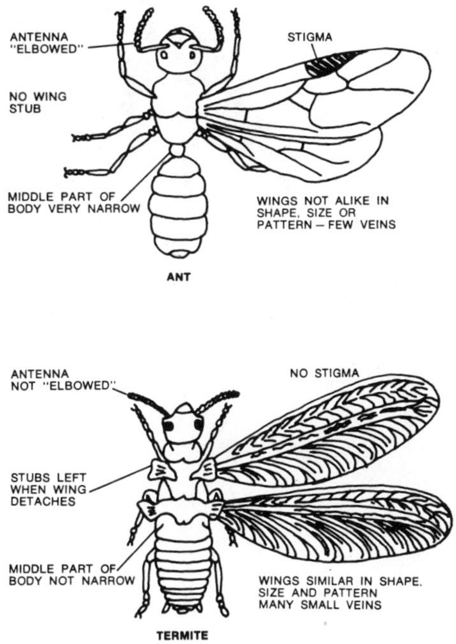

TERMITE

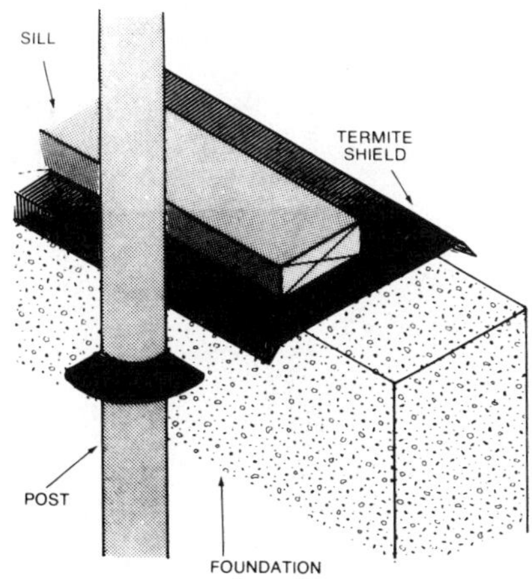

TERMITE SHIELD

THATCHED ROOF

THREAD OF THE STREAM

or mortgage, such as the manner in which the money will be paid or the time to take possession.

TERNEPLATE A roofing material made of an alloy of tin and lead.

TERRACE Commonly, a synonym for balcony.

TERRA COTTA A hard, unglazed, baked ceramic material used for ornamentation and roof and floor tile.

TERRAZO A floor covering of portland cement into which is poured marble or stone chips that are polished to a smooth surface after the mixture has hardened.

TESTAMENT A will; more technically, the disposition of personal property.

TESTATE A person who dies and has made a will is said to have died testate.

TESTIMONIUM CLAUSE The clause in a deed that recites the date on which the instrument was executed and by whom.

THATCHED ROOF A roof made of bundles of straw or shingles shaped to appear as if the roof were made of thatch.

THERM A unit of heat equivalent to 100,000 British Thermal Units.

THERMAL PROTECTION Safeguarding of living units against more heat loss or gain than necessary for winter and summer comfort.

THERMOSTAT An electric, temperature-sensitive instrument that controls a heating or air-conditioning unit by turning it on and off as the temperature varies from the preselected setting. Automatic ones also turn the units off or on at preset times.

THICKENED EDGE SLAB A type of concrete floor slab foundation where the slab is constructed integrally with the foundation wall.

THIRD PARTY Someone who is not a party to an agreement but is affected by the agreement.

THREAD OF THE STREAM The line half way between the banks of a stream. The center line of the stream.

THREE-PHASE WIRING A type of wiring that permits the simultaneous use of a series of heavy machines without overload. It is used in industrial buildings.

THREE-PRONG DUPLEX GROUNDING OUTLET An outlet that accepts two three-pronged plugs.

THREE-PRONG PLUG A plug that has three prongs, one of which serves as grounding.

THREE-WAY SWITCHES Switches that are used to control a fixture from two different places. The outlet is turned from "on to off" or from "off to on" whenever either switch is flipped. Thus, the top position is not necessarily the on position and vice versa.

THRESHOLD A strip attached to the floor underneath a door to cover the joint where two different types of floor materials meet. It particularly refers to a strip attached beneath an exterior door, over the threshold, that provides weather protection.

THRUST BLOCK A part of a wooden stair. It is the horizontal framing member at the bottom which supports the carriage beam.

TIDAL BASIN A bay, dock, or inlet where the water level changes directly with the ebb and flow of the tide.

TIDE LANDS Coastal land between the high-tide water line and the low-tide water line. Often, these lands are owned by the state.

TIE Any structural member, piece of metal, or other material used to hold two separated members together, such as two beams or two layers of a masonry wall.

TIE BEAM **1.** A beam on pile caps or spread footing used to distribute horizontal loads to other footings or pile caps. **2.** A beam that connects and ties together other structural members. *See also* Collar Beam.

TIER A group of townships that run east-west across a map.

TILE A wide variety of building materials made of fired clay, cement, plastic, vinyl, stone, glass, or other material used for floors, walls, drains, and a number of other purposes.

TILE FIELD *See* Disposal Field.

TILE GROUT Mortar that has a nearly liquid consistency and is poured between tiles.

TILT-UP CONSTRUCTION A method of construction of concrete wall panels where the panels are cast hori-

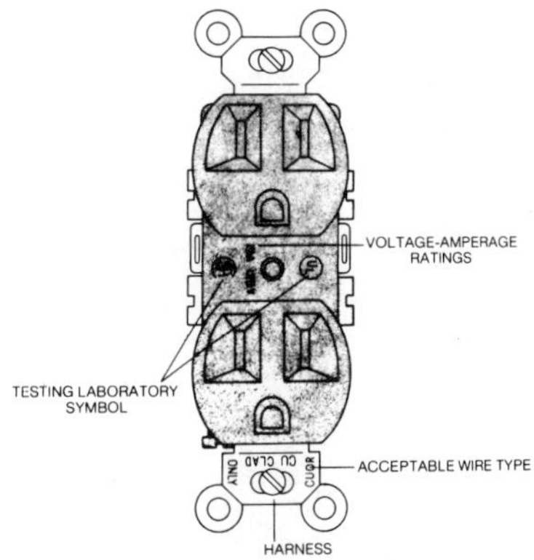

THREE-PRONG DUPLEX GROUNDING OUTLET

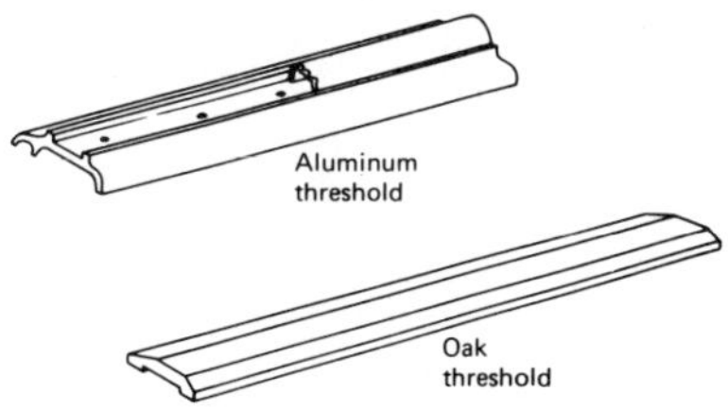

THRESHOLD

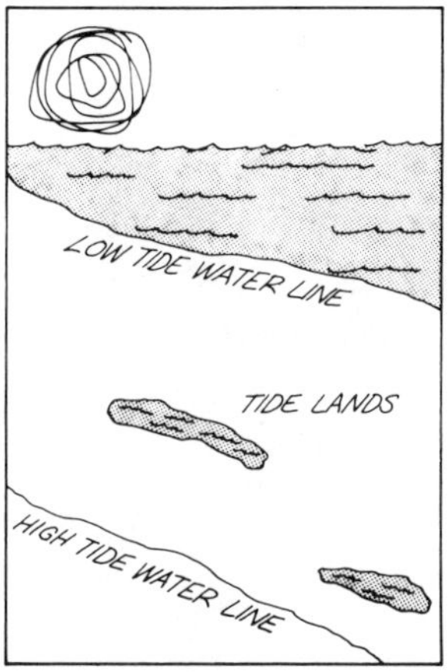

TIDE LANDS

zontally and then "tilted up" to the vertical position in which they are meant to harden.

TIMBER A large piece of lumber; trees that are still growing.

TIMBER CRUISING *See* Cruise.

TIME CERTIFICATE OF DEPOSIT (TCD) *See* Certificate of Deposit.

"TIME IS OF THE ESSENCE" A clause placed in a contract to indicate that timely performance is a condition, and performance not at that time can be entirely rejected.

TIME-SHARING A relatively new concept of ownership that is increasing in popularity. It is the purchase of an undivided interest for a fixed or variable time period.

TITLE **1.** Evidence of ownership of property. **2.** A name denoting the rank of a person or a distinction the person has earned. **3.** The name of a book or other literary work.

TITLE COMPANY A corporation whose basic function is to insure and issue title to real property.

TITLE GUARANTEE *See* Title Insurance.

TITLE INSURANCE An insurance policy issued to a property owner or mortgagee that indemnifies him against losses caused by defects in the title that are discovered after the closing.

TITLE INSURANCE COMPANY A company that provides insurance regarding title to real property.

TITLE REPORT A report made prior to the issuance of title insurance that states the condition of said title.

TITLE SEARCH A procedure of reviewing all public records and legal proceedings pertaining to a real property to determine the current state of the property's ownership.

TOE-NAILED A method used to drive in nails so that their heads will not be visible when the installation is complete.

TOILET **1.** A plumbing fixture (known as a water closet [W.C.] in the plumbing trade) used to collect human waste and convey it to the wastelines of the plumbing system. **2.** The room containing the water closet.

TOILET PAPER HOLDER A holder, usually attached to a bathroom wall, for toilet tissue.

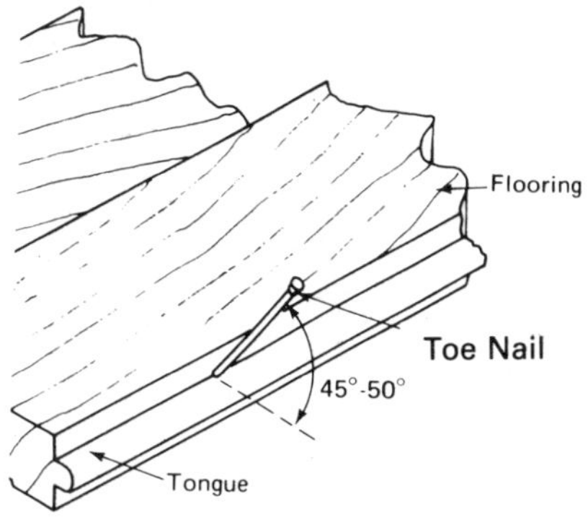

TOE NAILED

Wall Hung

Two-Piece Wall Hung Tank

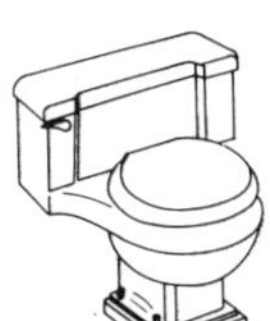

One Piece

TOILETS

TOILET ROOM (HALF BATH) Enclosed space containing one or more water closets and a lavatory.

TON **1.** A unit of weight equivalent to 2,000 pounds. **2.** A measure of capacity for an air conditioner. One ton equals 12,000 British Thermal Units.

TONGUE AND GROOVE A type of joint where one half has notches cut into it (grooves) and the other matching piece has tongues that fit into the grooves.

TONGUE AND GROOVE BOARDS Lumber that is cut with a tongue on one edge that fits into a groove on another piece of lumber.

TONGUE AND GROOVE SIDING Siding made out of tongue and groove boards. *See also* Tongue and Groove Boards.

TOOLED JOINT A masonry joint that is created with a tool before the mortar hardens.

TOPOGRAPHIC MAP A map of the slope, contour, and other physical features of an area of land.

TOPOGRAPHIC SURVEY A survey that shows the differences in grade level of a piece of land in relation to sea level.

TOPOGRAPHY The contour, elevation, and surface of land.

TOP PLATE The top horizontal piece of building frame to which rafters are attached.

TOP RAIL The top horizontal portion of a section of framing.

TOPSOIL The top layer of soil, whose quality determines if an area is suited for farming.

TORRENS CERTIFICATE In states that convey property according to Torrens Law, a document issued by the registrar that states the identity of the current owner of a property.

TORRENS SYSTEM A system used in some states to register the title of real property. It is also used to record liens on the property. The system was first used in the United States in Massachusetts in 1889.

TORRENS TITLE A system for keeping track of land titles invented by Sir Robert Torrens in Australia in 1858.

TORT A civil or private wrong committed against a person or property.

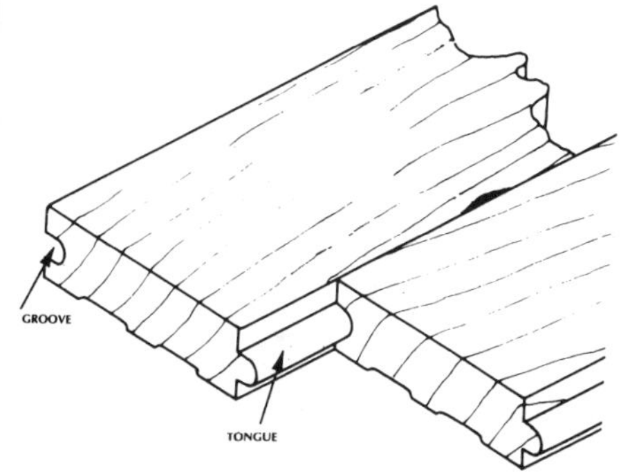

TONGUE AND GROOVE

TOPOGRAPHIC MAP

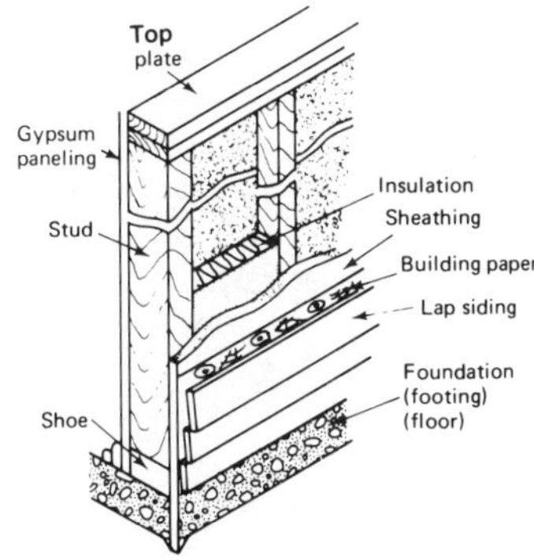

TOP PLATE

TOTAL LOAD Live load plus dead load; the total weight that must be supported in design.

TOWEL BAR A bar on which towels are hung in a bathroom.

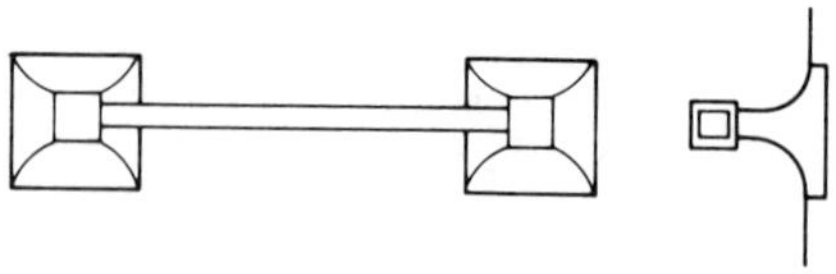

TOWEL BAR

TOWN A small, unincorporated city. A term that changes meaning from area to area.

TOWNHOUSE *See* Western Townhouse, Western Row House, Brown Stone, Brick Row House, or Eastern Townhouse.

TOWNSHIP A subdivision used in the Rectangular Survey System that is 6 miles long, 6 miles wide and has 36 sections, each 1 mile square.

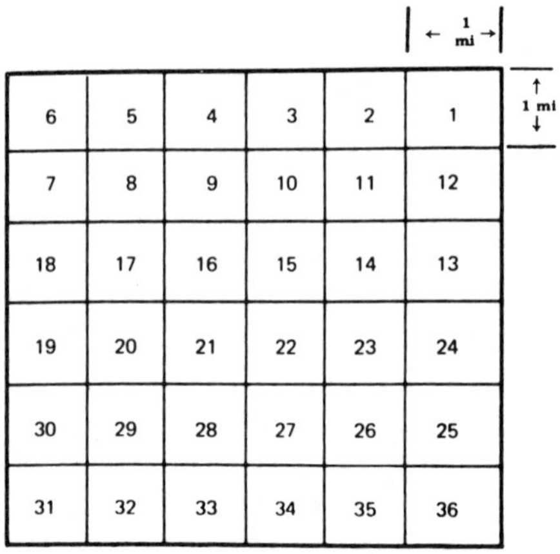

TOWNSHIP

TOWNSHIP LINES Lines that divide townships at their northern and southern borders.

TOWNSHIP ROAD A road that is under a town's or township's jurisdiction and control.

TRACERY The wood or stone shapes that create patterns in gothic windows or similar openings. It is usually in the shape of a mullion.

TRACT A piece of land.

TRACT HOUSE One of many similar houses built using the plan of a builder to be distinguished from a custom house.

TRADE *See* Exchange.

TRADE AREA The geographical area from which commercial developers will ordinarily expect to find customers for their goods and services.

TRADE ASSOCIATIONS A group of people and/or companies in the same or related businesses who join together in an organization to promote their businesses and improve their business skills. They also lobby for favorable legislation affecting their common interest. The NATIONAL ASSOCIATION OF REALTORS® is a trade association of people in the real estate business.

TRADE FIXTURES Articles of personal property employed in a business that are attached to the property. They are movable on the sale of the business but not on the sale of the real estate.

TRADE-IN A technique used by some real estate brokers in which the owner of a property who is buying another property through the broker is guaranteed that he will receive a specified amount for the property which he needs to sell in order to make the purchase.

TRADES *See* Exchange.

TRADING ON EQUITY The employment of borrowed financing to try to increase the rate of return on the equity investment.

TRAFFIC **1.** Goods that are transported in a trade or business. **2.** The movement of animals, people, or vehicles along a route or way.

TRAFFIC COUNT The number of vehicles or pedestrians that go by a certain point during a given time period. The statistics are used to figure business potential and effective street design.

TRAFFIC DENSITY The number of vehicles that cross a piece of road during a given time. It is expressed in vehicles per mile of street or road.

TRAFFIC SURVEY A survey that explores the nature of the trips people are taking at a specified time.

TRAILER PARK A site containing space and water, sewer, laundry, electricity, and bathing for two or more trailers. The more modern trailer parks, usually called *mobile home parks,* have all the conveniences that a regular apartment complex would have.

TRANSFER The conveyance of title to property from one person to another.

TRANSFER TAX A tax imposed by the government on the transfer of real property. It is usually based on the value of the property being transferred.

TRANSOM BAR A horizontal bar that divides a window or other opening into two parts.

TRANSOM, TRANSOM WINDOW A small window over a door or another window.

TRAP A bend in a wastepipe that remains filled with water, making a water seal that prevents sewer gases from backing up into the house.

TRAVERSE WINDOW A window which has two sashes on separate grooves that open horizontally—sliding past each other.

TREADS The upper horizontal board on each step of a flight of stairs *See also* Stairs.

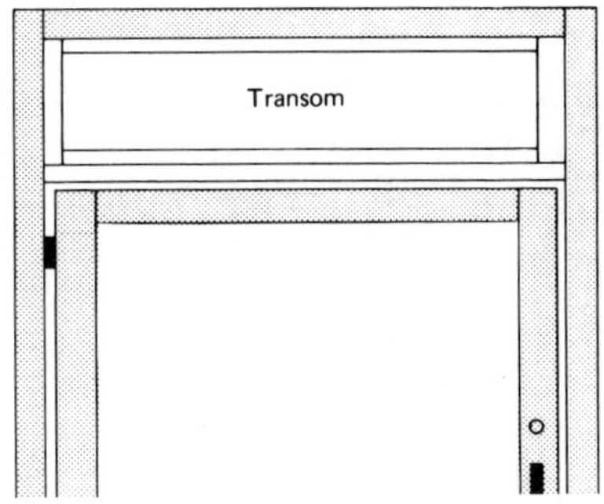

TRANSOM WINDOW

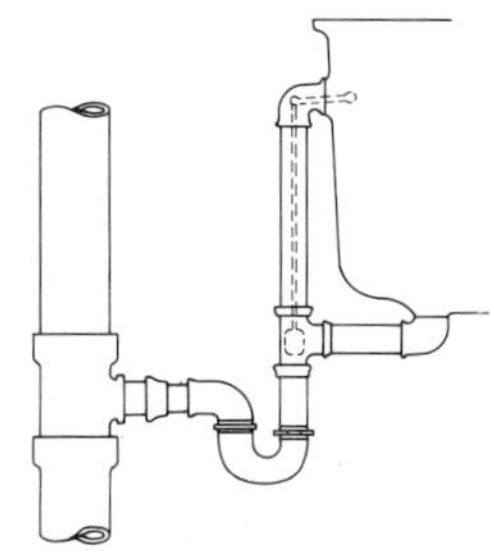

TRAP

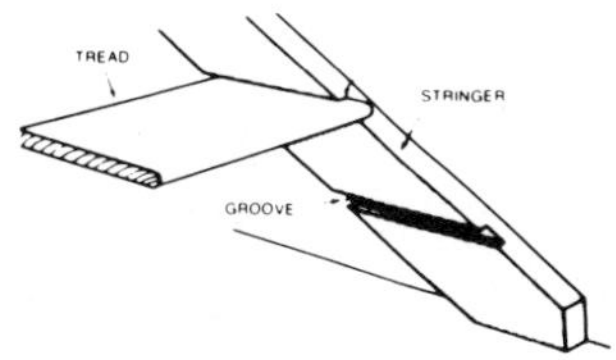

TREADS

TREATED WOOD

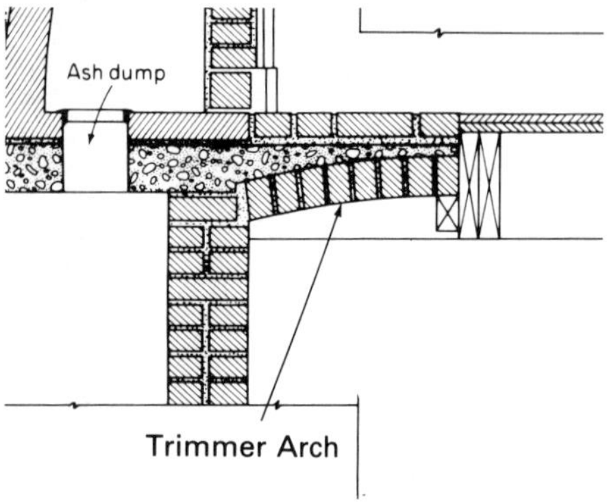

TRIMMER ARCH

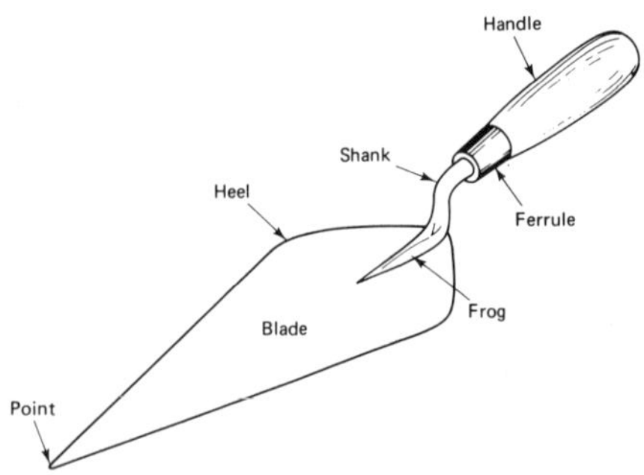

TROWEL

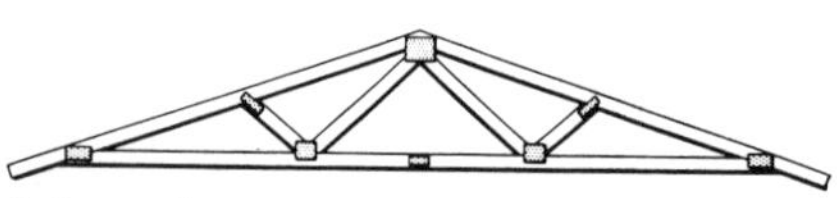

light roof truss

bowstring truss

TRUSS

TREATED WOOD Wood treated to resist termites or wood that has been waterproofed.

TREND An observable tendency of behavior, such as stable economic direction over extended periods of time despite temporary fluctuations.

TRESPASS Legally, any violation of law or any wrong against a person or property. Commonly, the unlawful entry, even if unintentional, on another's property is a trespass.

TRESPASSER A person who trespasses.

TRIM Wood or metal interior finishing pieces, such as door and window casings, moldings, and hardware.

TRIMMER A beam or joist into which another wood member is framed around a chimney, stairway, or other opening.

TRIMMER ARCH A nearly flat arch that is used to support a fireplace hearth.

TROWEL A tool used to spread cement, plaster, or adhesive.

TROWEL JOINT A joint that is made by squeezing excess mortar out of a joint after the brick or tile is laid in place.

TRUCK HIGH The height of a loading dock or platform (about four feet) that is about level with the unloading area of most standard trucks.

TRUCK WELL A area that is dug into the ground behind a loading platform and into which the rear wheels of a truck roll so as to lower the back of the truck to be level with the platform.

TRUSS A triangular arrangement of framing members usually pre-assembled and lifted intact into place. It is used to support loads over long spans.

TRUSSED RAFTER A truss where the chord members are also serving as rafters and ceiling joists and are subject to bending stress in addition to direct stress.

TRUSS HEIGHT The distance from trusses (roof beams) to the floor.

TRUST Rights in real estate or other property held by one party for the benefit of another party. The party that holds the title is the trustee and the party for whom the title is held is *cestui que trust.* A trust cannot be created for any purpose that is illegal, or against public policy.

TRUST ACCOUNT An account in which a broker is required by state law to deposit all monies that he or she is holding in trust for another. It is held separate from a broker's personal funds.

TRUST DEED A deed that conveys title of a property to a trustee. It is the deed that establishes a trust.

TRUSTEE **1.** A person or organization that holds property in trust for another party. **2.** In a broad sense, anyone acting in a fiduciary or confidential relationship to another party.

TRUTH-IN-LENDING ACT (TIL) The part of Public Law 90-231 (Consumer Credit Protection Act) that requires the borrower to be informed of true credit costs being charged.

TUB-SHOWER COMBINATIONS An arrangement where the shower is placed at the end of the tub. It saves space because a separate shower enclosure is eliminated.

TUCK POINTING The completion of masonry joints with putty or mortar. It is usually done as repair after the joints are cleaned out.

TUDOR STYLE A house style that originated in England in the late fifteenth century. It became popular in the United States in the late 1800s. The Tudor is an imposing-looking house that resembles a fortress. It is usually two and one-half stories high, and its siding is mainly made of stone and brick. Tudors are characterized by bays and turrets, casement windows with leaded glass, and high chimneys. A Tudor's interior is usually filled with nooks and crannies, large fireplaces, and beamed ceilings.

CTS SYSTEM: English
Tudor
(Tudor-203)

TURNKEY A arrangement between a contractor and a property owner whereby the contractor takes complete responsibility for the design and construction of a property and turns it over to the owner ready to be used.

TURRET A small, decorative tower.

TWO-HOUR DOOR A door specially built so that it would take a fire two hours to burn through it.

TWO-HOUR WALL A wall specially built so that it would take a fire two hours to burn through it.

TUDOR STYLE

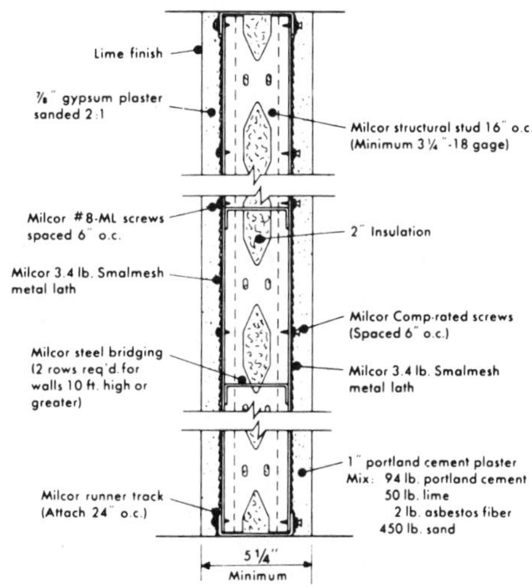

2-hr. fire-rated wall (O.S.U. T-4410)

TWO-HOUR WALL

TWO-PIPE REVERSE RETURN HEATING SYSTEM

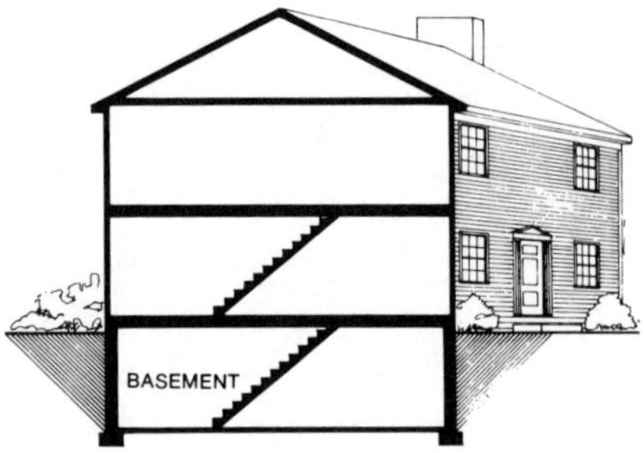

TWO-STORY HOUSE

TWO-PIPE REVERSE RETURN HEATING SYSTEM A hot-water heating system in which one pipe delivers the hot water and another returns it to the furnace.

TWO-STORY HOUSE A house with two stories. A two-story house is economical because of the small ratio of exterior walls, roof, and foundation to total living area, and it is well liked because of the privacy a separate sleeping floor provides. Disadvantages are the continuous need for the use of stairs and the fact that upstairs bedrooms and playrooms do not have direct access to the outside. *See also* House Types and Story.

TYPE Used in the CTS System to denote the structural nature of a house.

TYPES OF HOUSES *See* House Types.

U

"U" KITCHEN A kitchen in which counters and appliances are arranged in the shape of a "U".

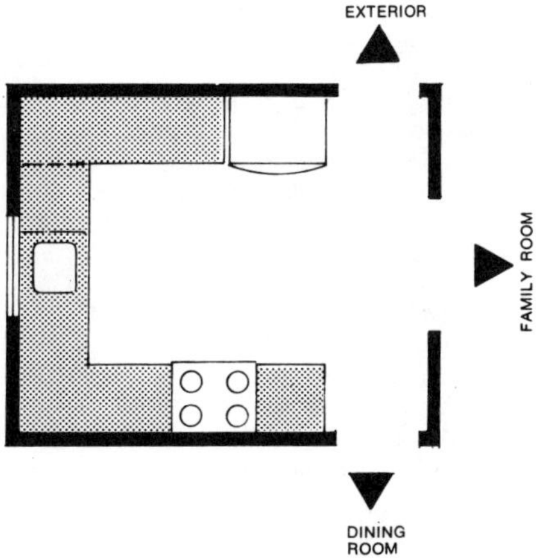

"U" KITCHEN

UNBALANCED IMPROVEMENT An improvement that does not conform with the surrounding area; an underimprovement or overimprovement.

UNDERCOATING The first or prime coat of paint that improves the seal and serves as a base for the topcoat of finish.

UNDERFLOOR WIRING SYSTEM Electrical wiring built into the floor and housed in ducts, raceways, and conduits.

UNDERGROUND CONDUIT PIPE An underground pipe for the containment of electrical wires.

UNDERIMPROVEMENT An improvement which is deficient in that it does not serve the highest and best use for the site on which it is located, i.e., the improvement is deficient in quality and/or size.

UNDER-LEASE A sublease for less time than that remaining on the master lease or for less property than covered by the master lease.

UNDERPASS A passageway under a street, road, or railway for pedestrians or automobiles or, in rural areas, for animals or farm equipment.

UNDERPINNINGS Supports added to increase the load-bearing capacity of a foundation.

UNDISCLOSED PRINCIPAL A principal whose identity is not revealed by an agent dealing with third persons nor is the fact that an agency relationship exists.

UNDIVIDED INTEREST Fractional ownership. It occurs when two or more people have an interest, equal or unequal, in the same property.

Example of Unit Cost in Place Method of Cost Estimating

Example: 1888 sq. ft. 1 story house

Component	Quantity Unit	Unit Cost	Total
General expense	1888 sq. ft.	1.40	$ 2,643
Foundation	1888 sq. ft.	1.95	3,682
Basement	1888 sq. ft.	2.35	4,437
Floors	1888 sq. ft.	3.42	6,457
Exterior walls	1812 lin. ft.	5.26	9,531
Roof	1888 sq. ft.	3.08	5,815
Interior walls & ceilings, doors, cabinets, trim, accessories	1888 sq. ft.	5.26	9,931
Stairways	2 outside	375	750
Heating	1888 sq. ft.	2.22	4,191
Electric system	1888 sq. ft.	2.60	4,909
Plumbing system	1888 sq. ft.	5.25	9,912
Fireplaces & chimneys	1 fireplace 1 chimney	1500 900	1,500 900
Doors	12	210	2,520
Windows	13	125	1,625
Site Improvements	lump sum	1100	1,100
Indirect costs	1888 sq. ft.	8.00	15,104
Total			$85,007

Note: These are not actual costs but are an illustration of how costs might be approximately allocated in an $85,000 house.

UNIT COST IN PLACE METHOD

UNDULATING LAND Land composed of two or more slopes of different grades.

UNEARNED INCREMENT An increase in property value due to a natural cause, such as an increase in population, rather than to an improvement in the property itself.

UNECONOMIC A term applicable to a process that does not increase the total sum of useful products or an action that produces goods at an unprofitable rate.

UNENCUMBERED Free and clear.

UNENFORCEABLE CONTRACT A contract that is valid but will not be enforced by the courts because of some special barrier.

UNFINISHED BUILDING SPACE Uncompleted building space that may need paint, minor completions, or major completions (such as plumbing and electricity).

UNGLAZED TILE A ceramic tile that is hard and dense and used for floors and walls.

UNIMPROVED A term usually used to describe land without buildings, land returned to nature, or land lacking in essential improvements necessary to serve a useful purpose.

UNINCORPORATED AREA A portion of a county that has not become a city.

UNIT **1.** A single thing. **2.** A condominium, apartment, or unit in a subdivision.

UNIT COST IN PLACE METHOD An appraisal method of estimating construction costs by figuring the cost of each component section, including labor cost and overhead.

UNITED STATES GOVERNMENT SURVEY SYSTEM *See* Geodetic System.

UNITED STATES SAVINGS AND LOAN LEAGUE A trade association of savings and loan associations.

UNITIES Four things necessary to create a joint tenancy under common law. They are unity of interest, time, title, and possession.

UNIT IN PLACE METHOD *See* Unit Cost in Place Method.

UNIT RULE A general rule used in condemnation proceedings to determine what constitutes the whole property and, therefore, what property may potentially suffer severance damages. In order to be considered part of a property being taken, it must have a unity of ownership, use, and physical location.

UNITS OF COMPARISON An appraisal technique that divides properties into units, such as front foot, square foot, dwelling unit, and number of beds. Once a value is estimated for a unit, the value of a property being appraised can be estimated by multiplying its number of units by the estimated unit value.

UNIT VALUE The value of a whole property divided into the value of a portion of the property known as a unit. *See* Units of Comparison.

UNIT WOOD BLOCK FLOORING A type of flooring made of wood blocks installed over an underlayment or directly to most subflooring.

UNITY, DOCTRINE OF A theory of appraising which states that all three approaches to value really reflect the market and therefore, if properly applied, should result in similar market value estimates.

UNITY OF INTEREST A requirement of the joint tenancy form of ownership that all interests must be acquired by the same conveyance.

UNMARKETABLE TITLE A title that has serious defects and is not saleable except at a discount to somebody who is willing to risk the potential problems of owning a property with a defective title.

UNRECORDED INSTRUMENT A deed, mortgage, etc., not recorded in a county recorder's office. It is valid between the parties involved but is not protected under recording statutes and is not valid against innocent third parties.

UNSEASONED LUMBER Lumber that has not been dried or not dried properly.

UNSUPPORTED HOOD A hood or covering that is not supported by columns.

"U" OVERALL COEFFICIENT OF HEAT TRANSMISSION The combined thermal value of all the materials in a building section, air spaces, and surface air films. U is expressed in Btu/(hr. × sq. ft. × °F)².

UPLAND **1.** A parcel abutting one with riparian rights, i.e., refers to an owner once removed from a water right. **2.** Land with high elevation relative to the surrounding area.

Commonly Used Units of Comparison

Land:
- Front feet
- Square feet
- Acres

Apartments:
- Square feet
- Room
- Individual units

Hotels and Motels:
- Square feet
- Rooms

Theaters:
- Square feet
- Seats

Hospitals and Nursing Homes:
- Square feet
- Beds

UNITS OF COMPARISON

UNSUPPORTED HOOD

UPLAND SOIL A type of soil developed through the disintegration and decomposition of rocks. It is found in hilly and mountainous terrain.

UPSET PRICE The minimum bid for which a property can be sold at an auction.

URBAN Pertaining to a city or town.

URBAN LAND ECONOMICS The study of the use of land with emphasis on its alternative uses and how they affect society as a whole.

URBAN NEIGHBORHOOD A neighborhood situated near or in a city or metropolitan area.

URBAN PROPERTY City property.

URBAN RENEWAL A controlled method of redeveloping and rehabilitating urban areas by demolishing, remodeling, or repairing existing structures, buildings, parks, and roadways through federal, local, and state financing or through private redevelopment efforts.

URBAN RENEWAL AREA A slum area that has been approved by the Department of Housing and Urban Development as eligible for an urban renewal project.

URBAN RENEWAL PLAN The plan that governs the proceedings in an urban renewal project area.

URBAN RENEWAL PROJECT Specific activities within an urban renewal area. Projects may involve razing slum buildings, rehabilitating existing buildings, and converting properties into new uses.

URBAN SPACE Urban real estate whose value stems directly from its location. Urban space is both land or space in buildings.

URBAN SPRAWL When an urban community spreads over a large geographical area.

USE A beneficial interest in land.

USE DENSITY The relationship of the number of buildings of a specific use to a given unit of area.

USE DISTRICTS City areas which have land uses that are different from adjacent land uses.

USE FACTOR (PALATABILITY) An index used by ranchers and those concerned with the conservation of forage plants and grasses. It is an indication of what percentage of the forage was eaten in relation to what percentage is the maximum use that will preserve the forage for future years.

USEFUL LIFE **1.** In appraising, the length of time a structure can be expected to perform the function for which it was intended. **2.** For tax purposes, the life set for depreciation.

USE MAP A map that shows important kinds of land use.

USE VALUE The special value a property has based on its current use by its current owners.

USE VALUE ASSESSMENT An estimate of the value of property in its present use rather than the value if it were used for its highest and best use.

USURY An illegal practice of lending money at a rate of interest above the legal rate.

UTILITIES Services provided by public utilities under the control of the Public Utilities Commission, such as gas, electricity, and telephone.

UTILITY The usefulness of a real property.

UTILITY ROOM A room designed to hold laundry or heating equipment or used for janitorial purposes. *See also* Laundry.

V

VACANCY A building or rental unit that is unrented.

VACANCY FACTOR A projection made of the future percentage of occupancy of a property.

VACANCY RATE *See* Allowance for Vacancy and Income Loss.

VACANT LAND Land without buildings. *See* Unimproved.

VACATE **1.** To move out of a property. **2.** To set aside, cancel, or annul.

VACUUM LINE Part of a vacuum cleaning system that is built into a building.

VA GUARANTEED MORTGAGE *See* VA Mortgage.

VALID Legally binding; authorized by law or incapable of being set aside.

VALLEY A depressed angle formed when the bottoms of two roof planes meet.

VALLEY FLASHING Pieces of lead, tin, or sheet metal applied to waterproof the valley of a roof.

VALUATION *See* Appraisal.

VALUATION PRINCIPLES A group of economic principles that apply to the valuation of real estate. They are the principle of anticipation, the principle of substitution, the principle of change, the principle of competition, the principle of balance, the principle of increasing and decreasing returns, the principle of contribution, the principle of surplus productivity, the principle of conformity, the principle of supply and demand, and the principle of highest and best use.

VALUATOR *See* Appraiser.

VALUE In real estate, the monetary worth of a property being appraised.

VALUE AFTER THE TAKING In condemnation, the value of that portion of a property that is not taken in the condemnation.

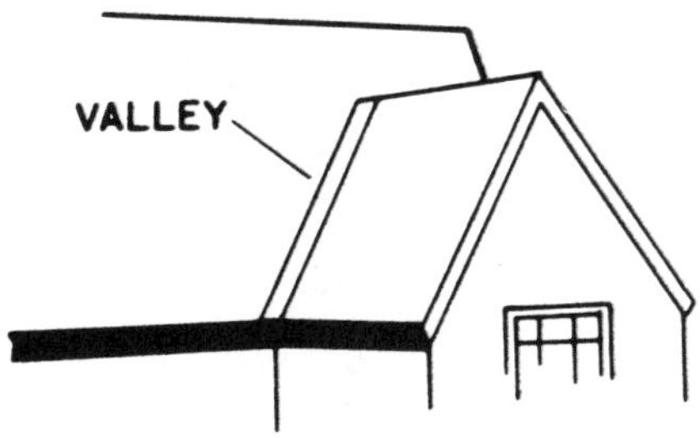

VALLEY

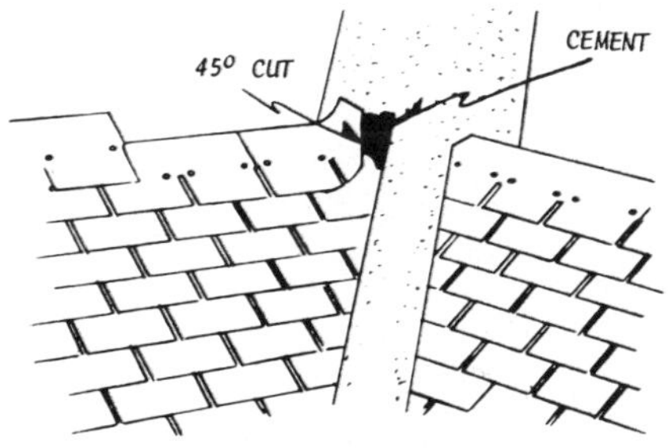

VALLEY FLASHING

VALUE BEFORE THE TAKING

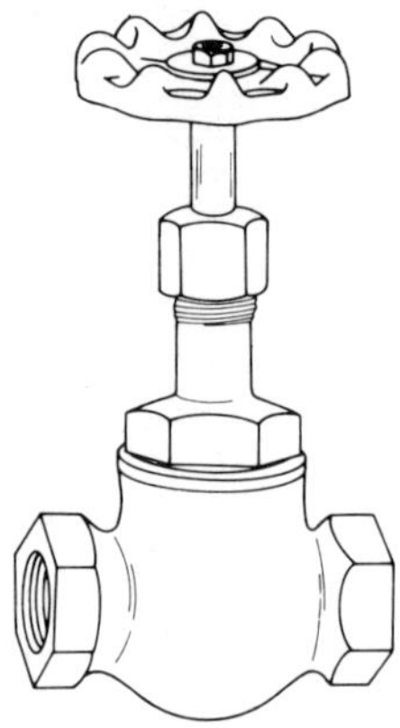

VALVE

Common Variable Expenses Incurred in the Operation of Real Estate

- Management
- Utilities
  - Electricity
  - Oil, Gas
  - Water, Sewerage
  - Air conditioning
- General payroll
- Maintenance and repair
- Service contracts
- Supplies
- Security
- Rubbish removal
- Grounds and Snow
- Exterminating

VARIABLE EXPENSES

VALUE BEFORE THE TAKING A property's market value before condemnation.

VALUE IN EXCHANGE The value of an investment or commodity relative to its power to purchase other goods.

VALUE IN USE *See* Use Value.

VALVE A device that is used to regulate the flow of a liquid or gas. A valve may be automatic or operated manually.

VA MORTGAGE A mortgage for which the Veteran's Administration guarantees part of the repayment.

VAPOR BARRIER Material or paint applied to a wall to prevent the passage of moisture into the wall.

VARGEBOARD *See* Frieze.

VARIABLE ANNUITY An annuity whose future periodic payments are not fixed but rather depend upon the value of the assets in the funding of the annuity, such as the value of its stock or bond portfolio.

VARIABLE EXPENSES Those expenses in an income and expense statement projected by an appraiser that tend to vary with the occupancy of the property, such as utilities, management fees, and waste removal.

VARIABLE INTEREST RATE An interest rate that changes with the prevailing rate. In mortgages, there is usually a limit to the frequency and amount of fluctuation.

VARIABLE RATE MORTGAGE (VRM) A mortgage with an interest rate that is not fixed but rather changes based on some other interest rate, such as bond interest rates, or prime interest rates. Often, the rate change is made at fixed, predetermined intervals, and it remains constant between the intervals.

VARIANCE An authorization, generally granted by a board of zoning appeals, that gives the right to improve or develop a specific property that is not authorized by the zoning ordinance. An exception is made, but the zoning itself does not change. Most zoning regulations require that a hardship be demonstrated in order for a variance to be granted.

VARNISH A finish for wood that dries and leaves a smooth, transparent, glossy protective film.

VAULT **1.** An arched masonry roof or ceiling. **2.** A small enclosure for the storage and protection of valuables.

VEGETATION Plants collectively; the group of plants in

an area, to be distinguished from the types of plants composing it.

VENDEE The buyer of property, particularly a real property.

VENDOR A person who sells a property.

VENEER A decorative layer of wood, brick, or other material that covers a structural material to improve its appearance. It is found on such things as wood panels and brick and block walls.

VENEERED CONSTRUCTION A type of construction where layers of facing material are applied to the external surfaces of steel and reinforced concrete.

VENT A pipe installed to provide the circulation of air or to furnish a flow of air to or from a drainage system.

VENTILATION A system of circulating fresh air through a structure.

VENT PIPE A small, vertical pipe connected to plumbing fixtures that carries sewer gases through the roof to the outside air.

VERANDA A covered porch extending along the outside of a building.

VERBAL By word of mouth.

VERGEBOARD *See* Bargeboard.

VERIFICATION In appraising, the process of confirming with either the buyer, seller, or broker the correctness of data about a comparable property.

VERIFICATION OF DATA *See* Verification.

VERMICULITE A type of insulation.

VERTICAL SIDING A type of exterior wall siding made of matched boards.

VESTED **1.** Placed in possession and control. **2.** Ownershiprights.

VESTIBULE A small foyer leading into a large room.

VETERAN'S ADMINISTRATION LOAN *See* VA Mortgage.

VETERAN'S TAX EXEMPTION In some states, an exemption from property taxes for qualified veterans or their widows.

VICTORIAN HOUSES A broad group of late nineteenth-century American house styles.

VIEW A drawing illustrating a particular viewpoint.

VENDEE, VENDOR

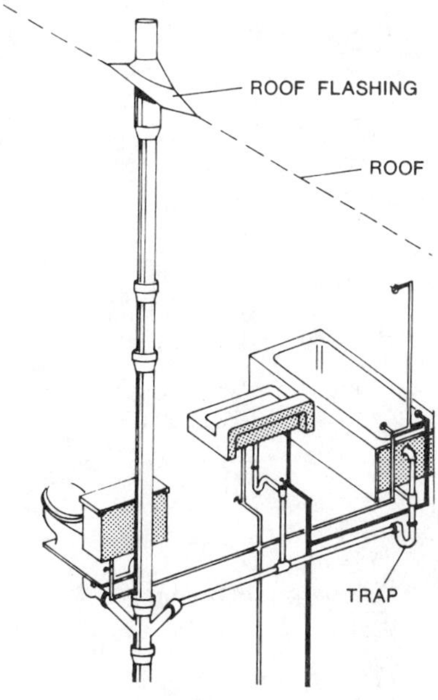

VENT PIPE

VIGA

VIGA

"V" SHAPED JOINTS

VIGA Ceiling or roof beams that stick out through the exterior walls in Adobe Style architecture.

VILLAGE A small community.

VINYL A type of kitchen countertop material that makes a smooth, quiet surface but can be easily cut, stained, or burned.

VINYL ASBESTOS TILE A type of tile that is durable and has good resistance to grease, alkalies, and burns. This tile, however, has poor stain and indentation resistance.

VINYL FLOORING A type of flooring that is made of solid vinyl tiles and comes in a variety of colors. Vinyl is durable, quiet, and has good resistance to stains, alkalies, and grease.

VIOLATION Breach of any law or contract.

VISUAL RIGHT The right to restrict structures and trees or shrubs at intersections, where, if visibility is limited, a dangerous situation could develop.

VITAL STATISTICS Information and statistics concerning deaths, births, marriages, health, or diseases. These records are usually held by a government bureau.

VITRIFIED TILES Clay pipes that have been baked hard and glazed to make them water resistant. They are used in disposal fields and other underground drainage.

VOID Not legally binding; entirely null.

VOIDABLE Provisions in a contract that may make the contract voidable should either party attempt to break it.

VOIDABLE CONTRACT A title that is valid until voided by the party who has a right to nullify it. *See also* Voidable.

VOID CONTRACT A contract that has no legal force.

VOID TITLE A title that has no legal force and is not binding so that it is actually no title at all.

VOLT A unit of measurement of the force of electricity. Most houses use 110 to 120 volts or 220 to 240 volts. It is like the measure of water pressure.

VOLUNTARY LIEN A lien placed on a property with the voluntary consent of the owner. It is usually a deed of trust or a mortgage.

"V" SHAPED JOINTS A "V" shaped mortar joint made with a steel jointing tool.

W

WAGES Payment for services performed by a hired person.

WAINSCOT *See* Wainscoting.

WAINSCOTING The wooden lining that covers an interior wall halfway to the ceiling. The remaining piece is wallpapered, covered, or painted differently than the lower half.

WAIVE To voluntarily surrender, abandon, or relinquish, a benefit, claim, or right.

WAIVER The intentional relinquishment of a known right.

WALL A vertical structure of plaster, wood, or masonry built to support, divide, or enclose a room or building.

WALL BEARING *See* Bearing Wall.

WALL-BEARING CONSTRUCTION A type of construction where the weight of the roof and floors is supported by the exterior bearing walls, and all the interior walls are non-load-bearing. Additional interior support is provided by posts and pillars where needed.

WALLBOARD A sheet (usually four feet by eight feet) attached to the frame of a wall to create a surface that can be wallpapered or painted.

WALL ELEVATIONS *See* Elevation.

WALL FURNACE A type of small furnace (often electric or gas) that is installed in a wall. The heat is distributed by a fan, usually without ducts. Often, it is called a wall heater.

WALL INSULATION Insulation in the wall of a building. It can be wallboard, batts between the studs, loose material, etc.

WAINSCOTING

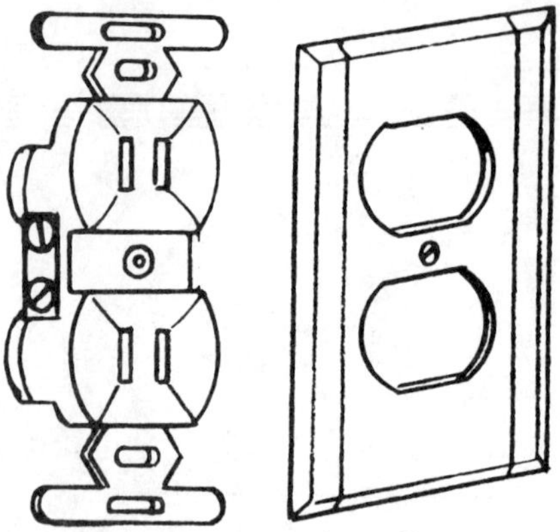

WALL OUTLETS

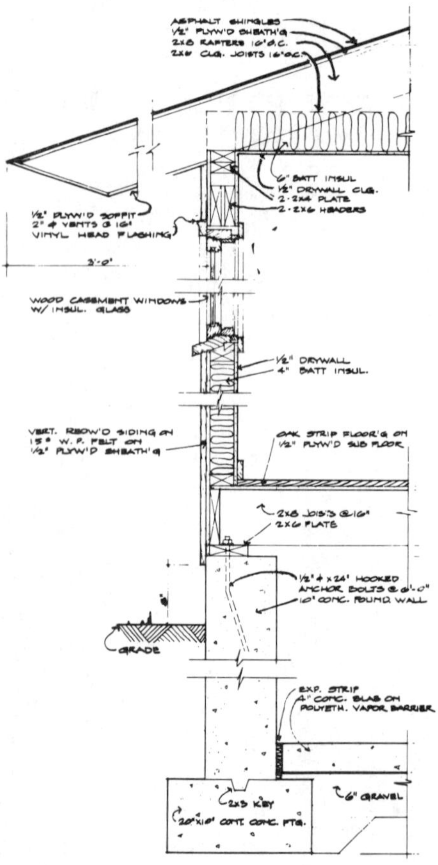

WALL SECTION

WALL OUTLETS Electrical outlets mounted on or in the walls of a building that provide a source of power for lighting fixtures, which are mounted on them, or plugs into which portable fixtures, lamps, appliances, and equipment can be connected.

WALL PANEL An exterior wall, usually in a high-rise office building, that carries no load. The load is borne by beams or girders in the framing skeleton.

WALL PLATE Horizontal pieces of timber placed on top of a masonry wall and under joists and other load-bearing members to distribute their weight evenly to the wall.

WALL SECTION One of the types of drawing that make up a set of building plans. It is views of vertical sections of the building's walls.

WALL-TO-WALL CARPETING Carpeting that touches all the walls in a room.

WALL VENT A device for ventilating the walls of a building or the crawl space, attic, or other areas where air does not freely flow.

WAREHOUSE A building used for the long- or short-term storage of goods.

WAREHOUSING OF MORTAGES A practice of mortgage bankers and other lenders which consists of depositing a group of mortgages or loans in a bank in contemplation of being sold at a future date. These mortgages and loans are used as collateral against which money is borrowed to make additional mortgages and loans. The purpose of this practice is to assemble a group of mortgages or loans to be sold together to a permanent lender, such as an insurance company or pension fund.

WARM AIR SYSTEM A heating system in which air is heated inside a furnace and distributed throughout the house either by the natural force of gravity or by fans.

WARRANT To attest that a title is good.

WARRANTY An assurance by the seller that the property is as represented or will be as promised.

WARRANTY DEED A type of deed used to convey the title of property that provides for the grantor to guarantee that the title be granted good and unencumbered. A warranty deed does not convey a better title than other types of deeds. It simply gives the grantee the right to sue the grantor if the title turns out to be defective.

WASHDOWN TOILET An inexpensive type of toilet that depends upon water flowing down the inside of the bowl to clean it.

WASTE Destruction or damage of a property by the person who is in rightful possession.

WASTELINE, WASTEPIPE A pipe that carries waste from a bathtub, shower, lavatory, or any fixture or appliance except a toilet.

WASTING ASSETS An asset, such as an oil field or a natural gas deposit, that is consumed or diminished in value due to use or lapse of time.

WATER *See* Groundwater, Irrigation, Surface water.

WATERFRONT PROPERTY Property that touches a body of water.

WATER-GAGE A sea wall to keep water from overflowing.

WATER HEATER A device for heating the domestic hot water in a building.

WATER-HOLDING CAPACITY The amount of water a certain quantity of soil will absorb under normal conditions.

WATER LEVEL The height of a body of water measured by a shore point. *See also* Water Mark.

WATER MARK Marks on the shore showing the highest point to which the tide rises under normal conditions.

WATER METER A device for measuring the amount of water consumed.

WATER POWER The energy and power created by the fall of a river or a stream over a person's property. The owner is entitled to its use.

WATERPOWER RIGHTS A property that contains the right to a water supply.

WATERPROOF Impenetrable by water; treating a material to withstand absorption of water.

WATERPROOFING Material used to coat surfaces, treat materials and plug up cracks and holes for the purpose of preventing the penetration of water.

WATERPROOF RECEPTACLES Electrical outlets, usually on the outside of a building, that have covers and are specially constructed to make them waterproof.

WATER REPELLANT A chemical that, when applied, helps prevent the absorption of water into materials it is applied to.

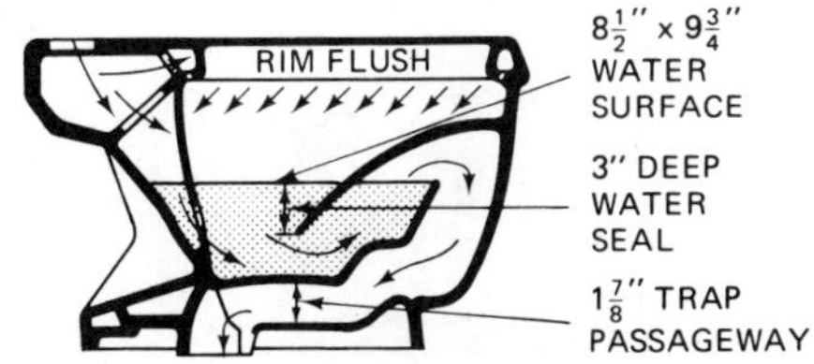

WASHDOWN TOILET

WATERPROOF RECEPTACLES

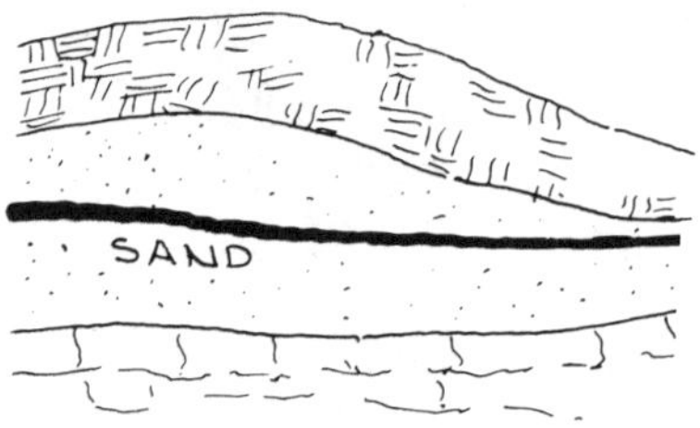

WATER TABLE

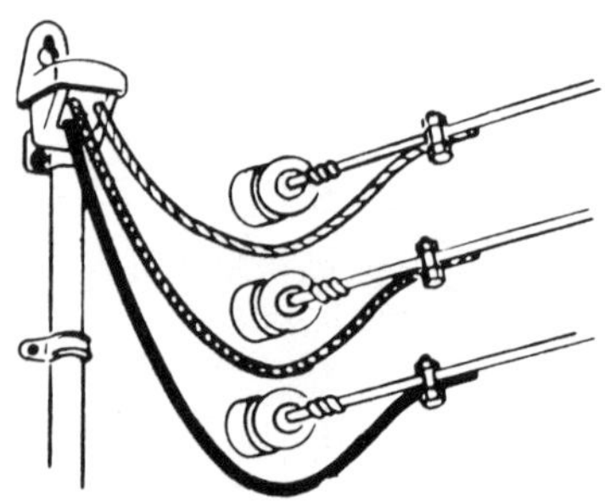

WEATHER CAP

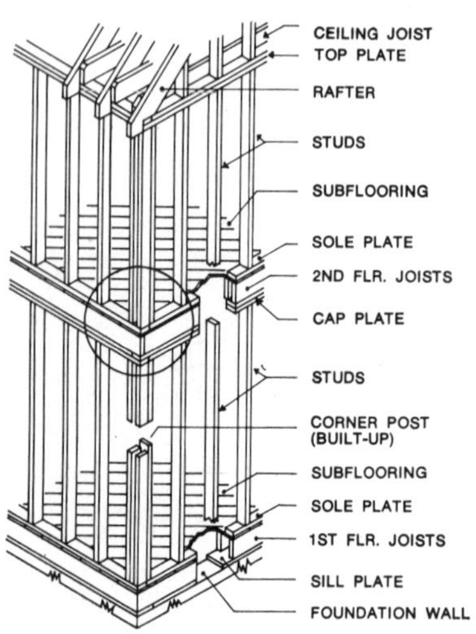

WESTERN FRAMING

WATER RIGHTS The rights of an owner whose property touches a body of water to use the water supply.

WATERSHED A ridge of land (such as a mountain) separating two river systems.

WATER SOFTENER A chemical process for treating hard water. A mineral called *zeolite* changes calcium and magnesium to salt, which is then removed.

WATER TABLE **1.** The depth from the surface to natural underground waters. **2.** A ledge along a building designed to aid the run-off of water.

WATT A measure of electricity. It is volts × amperes.

WATT-HOUR A unit of electrical energy used to determine electric bills.

"WEAR AND TEAR" The deterioration of property caused by age and use.

WEATHER CAP A part of an electrical service entrance designed to prevent water from entering into the system through the opening in the top of the conduit where the wires enter.

WEATHERED JOINT A type of mortar joint that sheds water.

WEATHERING Disintegration of a building's exterior due to exposure to weather.

WEATHERSTRIPPING A narrow piece of metal, felt, or other material installed between a window (or a door) and its casing to provide extra protection against moisture, dust, and wind.

WEEP HOLE A small hole in a wall that allows any trapped water to drain out to avoid a pressure build up.

WEIR **1.** A dam placed across a river or a pond to divert the water. **2.** A tool to measure water flow.

WEIR BOX A device to measure the flow of water across an irrigation ditch. An open wood or concrete box holds the weir.

WELL A deep shaft or hole dug or drilled into the ground to obtain gas, oil, or water.

WESTERN FRAMING One of the three major traditional types of framing systems widely used for building construction. It is characterized by short studs (usually two inches by four inches nominal size) that run from the floor of one level to the next level.

WESTERN PLATFORM FRAMING *See* Western Framing.

WESTERN ROW HOUSE A nineteenth-century American house style also known as a Western Townhouse. It is the western version of an Eastern Townhouse. It has party walls with the neighbors on both sides. Often, as a group, they cover an entire city block. They are distinguished by their pitched roofs, bay windows, and heavily decorated and painted exteriors. They differ from the Eastern Townhouse because each house has a unique design. They were built starting in the 1800s and are popular today.

CTS SYSTEM: Nineteenth Century American
Western Row House or
Western Townhouse
(West Row-714)

WESTERN ROW HOUSE

WESTERN STICK STYLE A nineteenth-century American house style, the Western Stick, is a large, rectangular house characterized by exposed structural framing, sliding glass doors, and shingles. The style originated in the 1800s and reflects Oriental and Swiss influence.

CTS SYSTEM: Nineteenth Century American
Western Stick
(W Stick-716)

WESTERN STICK STYLE

WESTERN TOWNHOUSE *See* Western Row House.

WET PLASTER Plaster spread wet over a metal, wire, or wood lath to form a wall or ceiling surface.

WHARF A landing place, like a dock or a pier, for loading and unloading ships.

WIDOWS WALK An open, railed platform over a peaked roof. It was first used on New England seacoast houses.

WILL-CUT CRUISE A forestry term for a technique for measuring the actual amount of lumber that can be sawed from the timber in a specified area. It takes into consideration an allowance for breakage and other waste.

WILLIAMSBURG GEORGIAN An English style also called Early Georgian. It is a kind of two- to three-story house style representative of the early Georgian homes built in the early 1700s and is characterized by simple exterior lines, few decorative devices, and two large chimneys. These houses were based on English styles during the reigns of the four King Georges and were restored by a Rockefeller grant.

CTS SYSTEM: English
Williamsburg Georgian or
Early Georgian
(Williams or E Georg-204)

WILLIAMSBURG GEORGIAN

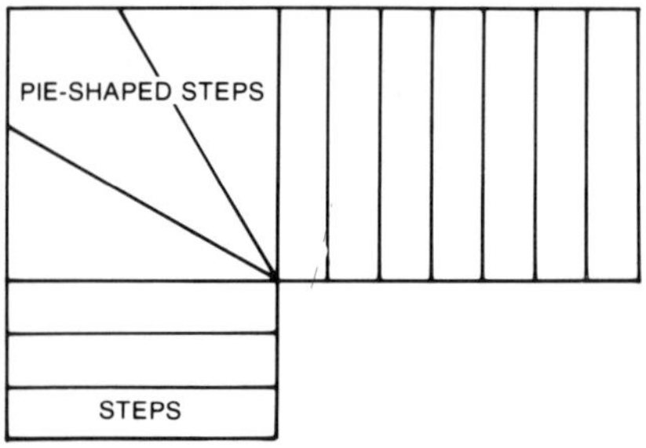

WINDER

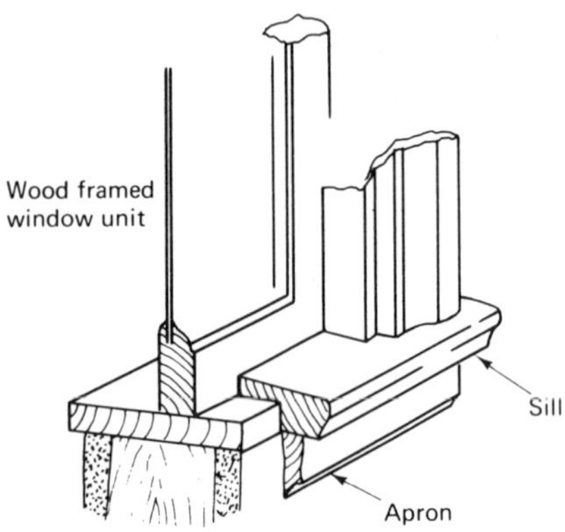

WINDOW SILL

"WILLING" Being ready to proceed. One of the standards applied to buyers produced by brokers to determine if the broker has earned a commission. In order for the broker to have earned the commission, the buyer must be "ready," "willing," and "able" to buy the property at the listing price.

WILL INTEREST The written declaration in which a person expresses his wishes as to the disposition of his property after his death.

WINDBREAK A fence, hedge, row of trees, or any other natural or artificial means used to break the force of the wind.

WINDER Treads of a curved staircase that are cut with one end wider than the other so they fit into place to make a curved form.

WINDOW An opening in a wall or roof framed with glass to admit light, a view, and air to a structure. It is usually capable of being opened and closed.

WINDOW SILL The horizontal framing of a window casing.

WINE CELLAR A storage area for wine. The cellar may range from a tiny closet to a small room and may not be in the cellar at all. The most important condition is steady temperature, which the connoisseur will provide with a cooling system. Proper lighting is essential to read the wine labels.

WING A part of a building which protrudes from the main structure as a bird's wing extends from its body.

WIRE A thin metal strand or rod, sometimes insulated, used to conduct electricity or for structural support.

WIRE GLASS A pane of glass reinforced with wire for strength and to prevent shattering.

WIRE LATH Metal mesh on which wet plaster is spread to make a wall or ceiling.

WITNESS **1.** To sign a note, deed, or other document to verify to its truth. **2.** The person who furnishes evidence.

WOMEN'S COUNCIL OF REALTORS (WCR) An affiliate of the NATIONAL ASSOCIATION OF REALTORS ® dedicated to the advancement and recognition of women in real estate.

WOOD The basic material out of which most houses are made. Wood is made from cut timber, and its popularity is due to its low price, availability, strength, durability, and beauty. There are two classes of wood: softwood, which comes from coniferous trees (trees that have cones and needles), and hardwood, which comes from deciduous (leaf shedding) trees.

WOOD FRAME CONSTRUCTION Structures in which wood frames the roof, walls, and floors despite the fact that other material may cover the framing.

WOOD SYMBOLS Symbols that represent the grain of wood.

WORKED LUMBER Wood that has been cut at the mill into a variety of different sizes of lumber, siding, and moldings.

WORKING CAPITAL Cash or easily liquidated assets that are required by a business to carry on regular operations without financial embarrassment.

WORKING DRAWING A sketch or drawing drawn to scale with enough detail of plumbing, etc., for workmen to use on a construction job.

WORKINGHOUSE Housing on top of a grain elevator for the mechanical operating equipment of that elevator.

WRAP-AROUND MORTGAGE *See* Mortgage.

WRIT OF EXECUTION A written order to carry out the judgment or decree of a court.

WROUGHT IRON An easily molded and forged form of iron used for the decoration of gates, railings, etc.

WYE The joining of railroad tracks in such a way as to form the shape of the letter "Y."

WYTHE (WITHE) A masonry wall that separates two flues in the same chimney stack.

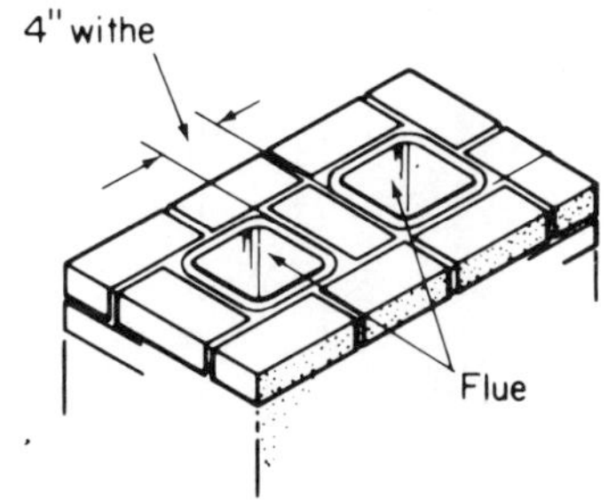

WYTHE

XYZ

X-BRACING X-shaped, cross bracing of a floor joist or a partition.

YACHT BASIN A group of channels and docks used for the keeping of yachts.

YARD **1.** A unit of 36 inches. **2.** The area between a building and its property, such as a backyard. **3.** A sometimes enclosed piece of property for a specific purpose (shipyard, lumberyard, etc.).

YARD LUMBER Lumber graded for building purposes. It is generally bought in a lumber yard.

YIELD **1.** Income from a property or other investment. It is often expressed as an annual percentage of the capital or investment. **2.** The amount of a crop or product produced on a specified amount of land.

YIELD TO MATURITY A term often used to express the true yield of a bond or other investment that is purchased at a discount. It is a combination of the annual interest earned plus the increase in value over the holding period until maturity.

YOKE *See* Head Jamb.

ZANJA A Spanish word for irrigation ditch.

ZEOLITE A chemical (hydrous aluminum silicate) used in water softeners that exchanges the minerals in the water for sodium chloride (common salt).

ZERO LOT LINE A provision in a zoning regulation or building code that permits construction of the improvements up to the edge of the lot.

ZONE **1.** An area where the use of land is restricted by a zoning ordinance for a specific use. **2.** A numbered area for the expedition of mail delivery.

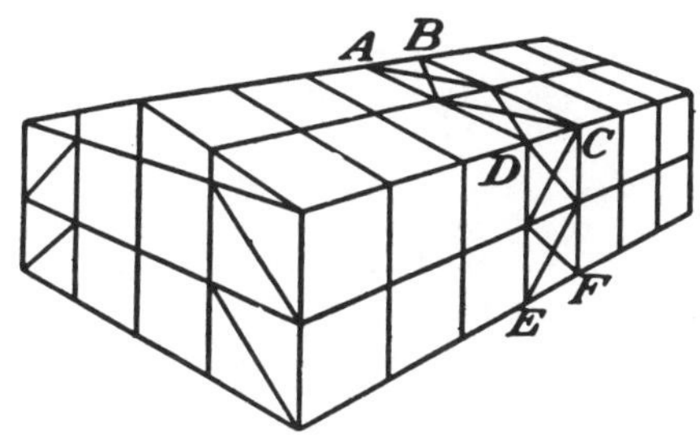

X-BRACING

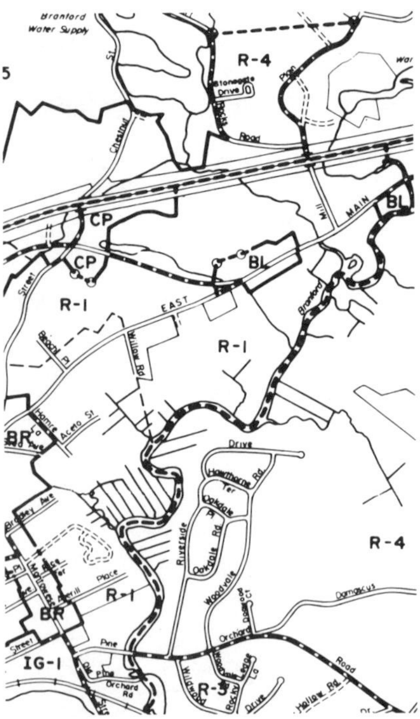

R-1 RESIDENCE R-1 DISTRICT
R-2 RESIDENCE R-2 DISTRICT
R-3 RESIDENCE R-3 DISTRICT
R-4 RESIDENCE R-4 DISTRICT
R-5 RESIDENCE R-5 DISTRICT
RM-1 RESIDENCE RM-1 DISTRICT

BC CENTER BUSINESS BC DISTRICT
BR RESTRICTED BUSINESS BR DISTRICT
BL LOCAL BUSINESS BL DISTRICT

IG-1 GENERAL INDUSTRIAL DISTRICT # 1
IG-2 GENERAL INDUSTRIAL DISTRICT # 2
CP COMMERCE PARK CP DISTRICT

ZONING MAP

ZONING The division and separation of a community into separate areas (zones). How the property in each zone may be developed and used is specified in the zoning regulations.

ZONING MAP A map illustrating how a community is divided into zones of permitted use under the zoning ordinance.

ZONING ORDINANCE Law restricting, regulating, and controlling the use of real estate for the general welfare.

ZONING VARIANCE *See* Variance.

ZYGOCEPHALUM In real estate, an inaccurate measure of land. Historically, it was the amount of land a yoke of oxen could plow in a day.

Bibliography

The American Heritage Dictionary of the English Language. American Heritage Publishing Co., Inc., and Houghton Mifflin Company, Boston, 1969.

The Appraisal of Real Estate, seventh edition. American Institute of Real Estate Appraisers, Chicago, 1978.

Arnold, Alvin L. and Jack Kusnet. *The Arnold Encyclopedia of Real Estate,* Warren, Gorham & Lamont, Boston, 1978, and 1980 supplement.

Black, Henry Campbell. *Black's Law Dictionary,* fifth edition. West Publishing Co., St. Paul, 1979.

Bloom, George F. and Henry S. Harrison. *Appraising the Single Family Residence,* American Institute of Real Estate Appraisers, Chicago, 1978.

Boyce, Byrl N. *Real Estate Appraisal Terminology,* revised edition. Ballinger Publishing Company, Cambridge, Mass., 1981.

Encyclopedic Dictionary of Real Estate Practice, revised edition. Prentice-Hall, Inc., Englewood Cliffs, N.J., 1962.

Feirer, John L. and Gilbert R. Hutchings. *Carpentry and Building Construction,* Chas. A. Bennett Co., Peoria, Ill., 1976.

French, William B.; Martin, Stephen J. and Thomas E. Battle. *Real Estate Review's Guide to Real Estate Licensing Examinations,* Warren, Gorham & Lamont, Boston, 1978.

Friedman, Edith J., ed. *Encyclopedia of Real Estate Appraising,* third edition. Prentice-Hall, Inc., Englewood Cliffs, N.J., 1978.

Gross, Jerome S. *Illustrated Encyclopedic Dictionary of Real Estate Terms,* Prentice-Hall, Inc., Englewood Cliffs, N.J., 1969.

Harris, Cyril M. *Dictionary of Architecture and Construction*. McGraw-Hill Book Company, New York, 1975.

Harrison, Henry S. *Houses—The Illustrated Guide to Construction, Design and Systems,* revised edition. Realtors National Marketing Institute, Chicago, 1976.

HUD Minimum Property Standards, revision 8. U.S. Department of Housing and Urban Development, Washington, D.C., 1980.

Levine, Mark Lee. *Real Estate Tax Shelter Desk Book,* second edition. Institute for Business Planning, New Jersey, 1978.

Ramsey, Charles G. and Harold R. Sleeper. *Architectural Graphic Standards,* sixth edition. John Wiley & Sons, Inc., 1970.

Real Estate Desk Book, fifth edition. Institute for Business Planning, Englewood Cliffs, N.J., 1978.

Real Estate Sales Handbook. National Association of Realtors® and Charles Scribner Sons, New York, 1980.

Reilly, John W. *The Language of Real Estate,* Real Estate Education Company, Chicago, 1977.

Ring, Alfred A. *Real Estate Principles and Practices,* seventh edition. Prentice-Hall, Inc., Englewood Cliffs, N.J., 1972.

Stipp, David R. *The Real Estate Reference Guide,* Jay Dee Publishing Co., Bloomington, Ind., 1974.

Weimer, Arthur M., Hoyt, Homer and George F. Bloom. *Real Estate,* seventh edition. John Wiley & Sons, New York, 1978.

Talamo, John. *The Real Estate Dictionary,* second edition. Financial Publishing Company, Boston, 1979.